DATE DUE

DEC 2 2 2000			

Demco No. 62-0549

AUBREY COHEN COLLEGE LIBRARY
75 Varick St. 12th Floor
New York, NY 10013

Classical Liberalism and Civil Society

THE LOCKE INSTITUTE

General Director
Charles K. Rowley, PhD

Financial Director
Robert S. Elgin, MA

Editorial Director
Arthur Seldon, BSc, CBE

Programme Director
Marjorie I. Rowley

Director of Legal Studies
Amanda J. Owens, LLB, JD

Founded in 1989, The Locke Institute is an independent, non-partisan, educational and research organization. The Institute is named for John Locke (1632–1704), philosopher and political theorist, who based his theory of society on natural law which required that the ultimate source of political sovereignty was with the individual. Individuals are possessed of inalienable rights variously defined by Locke as 'life, health, liberty and possession', or, more directly, 'life, liberty and property'. It is the function of the state to uphold these rights since individuals would not enter into a political society unless they believed that it would protect their lives, liberties and properties.

The Locke Institute seeks to engender a greater understanding of the concept of natural rights, its implications for constitutional democracy and for economic organization in modern society. The Institute encourages high-quality research utilizing in particular modern theories of property rights, public choice, law and economics, and the new institutional economics as a basis for a more profound understanding of important and controversial issues in political economy. To this end, it commissions books, monographs, and shorter studies involving substantive scholarship written for a wider audience, organizes major conferences on fundamental topics in political economy, and supports independent research. The Institute maintains a publishing relationship with Edward Elgar, the international publisher in the social sciences.

In order to maintain independence, The Locke Institute accepts no government funding. Funding for the Institute is solicited from private foundations, corporations, and individuals. In addition, the Institute raises funds from the sale of publications and from conference fees. The Institute is incorporated in the State of Virginia, USA. The Institution is a non-profit educational organization recognized under Section 510(c)(3) of the US Internal Revenue Code.

Officers of the Institute are listed above. Please direct all enquiries to the address given below.

4084 University Drive, Suite 103 • Fairfax, Virginia 22030, US
(703) 934-6960

Classical Liberalism and Civil Society

Edited by
Charles K. Rowley

General Director, The Locke Institute and Professor of Economics, George Mason University, USA

THE SHAFTESBURY PAPERS

Edward Elgar
Cheltenham, UK • Northampton, MA, USA

© Charles K. Rowley 1997

All rights reserved. No part of this publication may be reproduced, stored in a retrieval system or transmitted in any form or by any means, electronic, mechanical or photocopying, recording, or otherwise without the prior permission of the publisher.

Published by
Edward Elgar Publishing Limited
8 Lansdown Place
Cheltenham
Glos GL50 2HU
UK

Edward Elgar Publishing, Inc.
6 Market Street
Northampton
Massachusetts 01060
USA

A catalogue record for this book
is available from the British Library

Library of Congress Cataloguing in Publication Data
Classical liberalism and civil society / edited by Charles K. Rowley.
— (The Shaftesbury papers)
1. Liberalism. 2. Civil society. 3. Post-communism. I. Rowley, Charles Kershaw. II. Series.
JC574.C58   1998
320.51—dc21   97–41481
                                                              CIP

ISBN 1 85898 660 5

Typeset by Manton Typesetters, 5–7 Eastfield Road, Louth, Lincolnshire LN11 7AJ, UK.
Printed and bound in Great Britain by Biddles Ltd, Guildford and King's Lynn

Contents

List of contributors
Preface

On the Nature of Civil Society
Charles K. Rowley

9 Liberalism Defended: The Challenge of Post-Modernity
Douglas B. Rasmussen and Douglas J. Den Uyl

10 Lessons for Citizens of a New Democracy
Peter C. Ordeshook

11 Promises, Promises: Contracts in Russia and Other Post-Communist Economies
Paul H. Rubin

12 Ethnic Diversity, Liberty and the State: The African Dilemma
Mwangi S. Kimenyi

Contributors

Douglas J. Den Uyl, Professor of Philosophy, Bellarmine College, USA

Mwangi S. Kimenyi, Professor of Economics, University of Connecticut, USA and Senior Research Associate, African Research Centre for Public Policy and Market Process

Peter C. Ordeshook, Professor of Government, California Institute of Technology, USA

Douglas B. Rasmussen, Professor of Philosophy, St John's University, USA

Charles K. Rowley, General Director of the Locke Institute and Professor of Economics, George Mason University, USA

Paul H. Rubin, Professor of Economics, Emory University, USA

Preface

This book is the seventh volume published by The Locke Institute in *The John Locke Series in Classical Liberal Political Economy*. It brings together four monographs published simultaneously and separately in paperback form in *The Shaftesbury Paper Series* co-ordinated by Charles K. Rowley via a substantive introductory chapter. The book was made possible by a colloquium funded by Liberty Fund, Inc. on the theme of 'Ethics, Liberty and Markets' held under the direction of Charles K. Rowley in Boston, Massachusetts, June 24–27, 1993. The book would not have been completed without the financial support of the Lynde and Harry Bradley Foundation, the Sunmark Foundation, Robert S. Elgin and several anonymous donors. The congenial and scholarly working environment generously provided by Atlas Economic Research Foundation is a continuing source of strength for this growing programme of scholarship and publication. The administrative support of Marjorie I. Rowley and Amanda J. Owens is gratefully acknowledged.

For

Bryan Alexander and Peter Eliot Rowley

On the Nature of Civil Society

1. INTRODUCTION

The collapse of the Soviet Empire and the efforts made in Central and Eastern European countries to construct or to reconstruct civil society as the salvation of their nations have inspired Western intellectuals to reconsider the concept of civil society and to ask whether it may speak also to the condition of Western societies. In both cases, the crisis of socialism, as an ideology and as a practical experience, has proved to be the fulcrum for this search for alternative concepts. For the most part, the concept of civil society is viewed, by those active in its renaissance, as an attractive combination of domestic pluralism combined with a continuing role for extensive state regulation and guidance. As such, it offers a very broad tent capable of sheltering a multitude of diverse political systems. So broad indeed is this tent that it may be defined more appropriately as an 'empty shell' (Rowley 1996, 6).

In this chapter, I shall review briefly the history of the civil society concept and evaluate its relevance for classical liberal political economy. I shall suggest that the concept of civil society advanced by John Locke, the young John Stuart Mill and other like-minded classical liberal scholars best encapsulates the classical ideal and provides an intellectually rigorous basis for defining the appropriate role of government, for protecting individual liberties and for stimulating those private associations of individual citizens, all of which, in combination, comprise the fundamental basis for human flourishing and the wealth of nations.

2. THE CONCEPT OF CIVIL SOCIETY IN HISTORICAL PERSPECTIVE

Until the end of the 18th century, the term 'civil society' was synonymous with the state or political society. In this respect, the term reflected precisely its classical origins as a translation of Aristotle's

Koinonia politike or of Cicero's *societas civilis*. Civil society, in this conception, expresses the growth of civilization to the point where society is civilized, as classically expressed in the Athenian polis or the Roman republic. It represents a social order of citizenship in which men (more rarely women) regulated their relationships and settled their disputes according to a system of laws; where civility reigned; and where citizens took an active part in public life (Ferguson 1991; Kumar 1993, 377; Roepke 1996).

Following directly in this tradition, John Locke (1991) was able to write about civil government as a synonym for civil or political society, Kant was able to define *bürgerliche Gesellschaft* as that constitutional state towards which political evolution tends, and Rousseau felt able to define the *état civil* simply as the state. In all these uses, civil society is contrasted with the uncivilized condition of humanity, whether in a hypothetical state of nature or under an unnatural system of government that rules by despotic decree rather than by laws.

In *Democracy in America* (1969), Alexis de Tocqueville narrowed the concept of civil society along sociological lines by delineating three realms of society. First, there is the state, which comprises the system of formal political representation, with its parliamentary assemblies, courts, bureaucracies, police and army. Second, there is civil society, which essentially comprises the system of private and economic interests. Third, there is political society, with its political associations such as local government, juries and political parties, and with its civil associations such as churches, schools, scientific societies and commercial organizations.

The life of all these associations; the 'super-abundant force and energy' that they contribute to the body politic, constitutes political society. Political society supplies 'the independent eye of society' that exercises surveillance over the state. It is that which educates us for politics, tempers our passions and curbs the unmitigated pursuit of private self-interest.

In the post-communist order, it is Tocqueville's third category, political society, that has become the principal fulcrum for the reconstructed concept of civil society. The tendency has been for ex-Marxists and non-Marxists alike to stress the specifically non-economic and non-state dimensions of civil society and to focus attention on civic, cultural, educational, religious and other organizations operating at the periphery of the capitalist system, yet essentially autonomous from the state itself.

In a sense this preoccupation is entirely understandable, though misguided, among the intellectuals of Central and Eastern Europe, where the elevation of civil society, prior to 1989, was perceived not as constituting a new relationship between state and society but rather as an uncoupling of that relationship. Since the state could not effectively be challenged, it was to be ignored. Civil society aspired to be an alternative society, a parallel society coexisting, for the time being, with a delegitimized and weakened official state (Kumar 1993, 386). This parallel was nowhere better illustrated than by the role of 'Solidarity' in Poland from the late 1970s, cohesive until the collapse of communism, but thereafter fragmenting into sectorial squabbles and personal rivalries, incapable of evolving the institutions necessary for a safe transition to constitutional democracy.

In no small part because intellectuals had evaluated civil society above the state, viewing it as the solution to all problems accumulated by socialism, a serious lack of concern was evident, post-1989, with regard to the reconstitution of the state and the private economy from the broader perspective of civil society in its classical conception. This lack of concern was especially serious (Klaus 1996) because communism had collapsed and was not defeated, leaving weak and inefficient markets and weak and inefficient democracies, conditions that continue to plague the entire post-communist order, the Czech Republic included. Tocqueville, remember, noted that it was politics that spreads, 'the general habit and taste for association', not vice versa. In the absence of an appropriately formulated polity, civil society, both in its broad classical sense and its narrow late 20th century conception, simply will not exist.

Much less excusable, and at least equally misguided, has been the post-1989 reaction of too many Western intellectuals. By claiming 'the end of history' (Fukuyama 1992), and by assuming too easily that the collapse of communism implied the success of Western (that is, US-style) capitalism, the large majority of Western intellectuals forgot the maxim that 'vigilance is the eternal price of liberty' and focused attention excessively on the resurrection of civil society (in the narrow 'political association' sense of Tocqueville).

By inferring the final victory of democracy and capitalism over autocracy and socialism, these Western intellectuals proclaimed (at least implicitly) that any preoccupation with classical political economy was unnecessary and suggested instead that the results of majoritarian democracy represented the highest level of political economic achievement (Nozick 1989; Gray 1989, 1993). These judgements were (and are) insane.

There can be no doubt that the free society rests upon, and is intended to nurture, a solid foundation of competent, self-governing citizens, fully capable of, and personally responsible for, making the major political, economic and moral decisions that shape their own lives and those of their children. There can be no doubt that such personal qualities are nurtured and passed on to future generations by healthy families, churches, neighbourhoods, voluntary associations and schools, all of which provide training in, and room for, the exercise of genuine citizenship. There can be no doubt that this expansive understanding of citizenship is subject to challenge in the late 20th century United States, in a way that it was not 150 years earlier when Tocqueville wrote *Democracy in America*, by contemporary forces and ideas that regard individuals as passive and helpless victims of powerful external forces.

It is a fundamental error, however, to assume that these contemporary forces and ideas are exogenous elements of the state of nature to be counteracted by some narrow retreat into civil society, by some programme that seeks directly to reinvigorate and to re-empower the traditional local institutions that provide training in, and room for, the exercise of genuine citizenship. I shall attempt to establish in this paper that the forces and ideas that now erode good citizenship emanate from the consequences of a misguided 20th century political economy, not from any neglect of civil society in its narrow late 20th century form.

3. BEFORE RESORTING TO POLITICS

'Why does anyone want to resort to politics and why does anyone put one kind of political order above another?' Jasay (1996) suggests that 'those who are both very earthy and very frank approve (the political order) that they believe is doing the most good for them'. Such a 'grand criterion' of political hedonism has no prospect of generating basic agreement about the respective merits and consequences of political systems except for the low common denominator of democracy, namely the shared redistributive advantage of a winning over a losing coalition.

What is true in this crude and obvious way of the system of political hedonism that expects the state to cater for some interests to the relative neglect of others is true, if less conspicuously, of any other political order that fosters one value to the relative neglect of others. Not all values are compatible; most compete with one another. A political order reveals a hierarchy of values by what it promotes and demotes, by the marginal rates of substitution between them that it establishes through policy interventions.

Predictably, the value-oriented political order will be a less than perfect match for those who live within it, if the citizens are heterogeneous with respect to the values that they uphold. There is no discernible mechanism that would make global choice coincide with the best available choice of each individual consistent with the best available choice of every other – which is the equilibrium solution of ordered anarchy. Value-neutrality, where there is not too much of one thing and too little of another, can be achieved by the individual for himself, but not by a political order for many, let alone for everybody (Jasay 1996, 5).

Jasay (1996, 7) notes the pronounced danger for the equilibrium solution of ordered anarchy posed by the narrow consequentialism of utilitarian philosophy when promoted through the political process. Within the logic of consequentialist ethics it is all but incoherent to want to limit the scope of government. Limiting government on purpose would only be rational if the scope for doing good were in itself limited, which it no doubt is not.

Yet the utilitarian ethic as deployed in its late 20th century form ignores its own value judgement, namely the impossibility of comparing utilities across individuals. If alternatives are non-commensurate, no balance can be struck between the good and the bad consequence and consequential reasoning is simply out of place. This leads Jasay (1996, 10) to deploy his first warning to those who would resort to consequential politics: *first, avoid doing harm.*

In this view a political authority simply is not entitled to employ its power of coercion for imposing value-choices on society. Its sole guiding principle in all such cases can only be: when in doubt, abstain. This principle can be applied retrospectively to dismantle polities that have become suffused with consequential ethics as well as prospectively, in the state of nature, to prevent such a suffusion from ever occurring.

One implication of this guiding principle for political ethics is that applying coercion is legitimate only when it is positively invited by those who will be coerced. Assuming that property rights are given (see section 4) the only circumstances where rational individuals might choose coercion would be where transaction costs, default and free-rider temptations, and hold-out temptations obstruct the solution of bargaining problems. In such circumstances, Jasay (1996, 7) suggests that hypothetical invitations to be coerced have no better standing than hypothetical contracts. Those who will be coerced must actually invite coercion. Only then is it that certain tasks become duties that the state must assume.

Each individual is endowed by circumstances with a set of actions that are feasible from a material perspective. Some of these actions are inadmissible because they would harm others in a way that would constitute a tort by the conventional norms of the society. Other actions are inadmissible because individuals have contracted with others not to choose them. To choose such actions would constitute a default or a breach of an obligation. Every other feasible act is admissible (Jasay 1996, 29–30).

With torts and obligations taken care of, the set of admissible actions becomes a residual. Harm and obligations together exhaust the set of valid objections, establishing a strong presumption that the feasible residual subset of actions should be allowed.

Coercion by the state fits well into this categorization of feasible actions. Applied to the inadmissible subset, coercion functions to deter tortious harms and contract breaches. State coercion applied to the admissible subset of actions *prima facie* is illegitimate. It deforms the value of rights and liberties and does so by threatening or by committing a tort (in principle, if not by social convention). Only by the explicit invitation of those who are coerced can this presumption conceivably be over-ruled. Doubt about an issue creates a presumption to abstain and against resolving it by state coercion (Jasay 1996, 54).

4. OF PROPERTY

If this concept of the role of politics is accepted, the 20th century view that notions of fairness call upon the state to play a deliberately redistributive role is severely misplaced. Redistributive politics clearly creates gainers and losers. As such it necessitates a balancing between the good of some and the bad of others. If such a balancing is ruled inadmissible, redistribution cannot serve as a warrant for the use of coercion. If consequentialism is disallowed, there can be no legitimate role for politics with regard to redistribution.

Fundamental to this thesis is the presumption that property is partitioned before resorting to politics, that it is not some common pool resource, the use of which and the partitioning of which remain permanently under the control of the political process. This presumption runs counter to late 20th century practice, which emphasizes a redistributionist ideology. The only difference between this redistributionist ideology and socialism is that the former still pays lip-service to efficiency gains and accepts, on consequentialist grounds, some limited version of the exclusion principle implied by private property, whereas the latter does not. The tragedy of the commons overhangs all societies in which property is not strictly partitioned among private individuals, quite independently of whether such societies are redistributionist or socialist, autocratic or democratic in nature.

In the view of John Locke (1991), even prior to the social contract that establishes political or civil society, every individual has a property in his own person and a right to the product of his own labour. In addition, individuals create property rights out of the common pool of available resources by mixing their labour with such resources and thus by annexing them. These rights are natural rights, at least where the Lockeian proviso is satisfied:

> Whatsoever then he moves out of the State that Nature hath provided and left it in, he hath mixed his *labour* with, and joyned to it something that is his own, and thereby makes it his *Property*. It being by him removed from the common state Nature placed it in, it hath by this *labour* something annexed to it, that excludes the common right of other Men. For this *Labour* being the unquestionable Property of the labourer, no Man but he can have a right to what that is joyned to, at least where there is enough and as good left in common for others (Locke 1991, 288).

It is important to note that this natural right to property is not an inalienable right, at least in the sense that I shall outline. It is for that reason that the United States' founders, who were influenced greatly by John Locke's writings, failed to list property as one of the inalienable rights in the preamble to the constitution. If we define an inalienable right as a right that cannot be lost in any way, then such a right would incorporate both a disability and an immunity; the possessor of the right would not be able to dispose of it, voluntarily or involuntarily; nor would any other person, group or institution be able to dispossess him of it. Property clearly does not fall into this category of a right since it can be given away or exchanged voluntarily (*alienated*) and it can be lost involuntarily through negligence or wrongdoing (*forfeited*).

The natural right to property does imply, however, that it cannot be taken away by some other party, including a government (*prescribed*).

In this sense we may denote the natural right to property to be an *imprescriptible right*. What revolutionary authors such as Locke had in mind was not the notion that the right to property was a right that no government could take away, but rather that this is a right that no state legitimately could take away without the owner's consent. The force of this claim can only be appreciated when we remember that Locke's *Treatises* were written under the influence of contractarian accounts of government authority (Simmons 1993, 107):

> The Supreme Court cannot take from any Man any Part of his Property without his own consent. For the preservation of Property being the end of Government, and that for which Men enter into Society, it necessarily supposes and requires, that the People should *have property*, without which they must be suppos'd to lose that by entering into Society which was the end for which they entered into it, too gross an absurdity for any Man to own (Locke 1991, 360).

The Lockeian assertion that each individual is born free in the state of nature correctly recognizes that we are not born into political communities. We are not naturally citizens and we must do something to become citizens. Locke clearly depicts that the state of nature as a state of, '*perfect freedom* to order their Actions, and dispose of their Possessions, and Persons, as they think fit, within the bounds of the law of Nature, without asking leave, or depending on the Will of any other Man' (Bk II, para. 4). The state of nature has a law to govern it, which obliges every individual: no individual, 'ought to harm another in his Life, Health, Liberty or Possessions' (Locke II, para. 6).

The law of nature essentially reflects the moral claim of each individual to negative freedom and the duty and responsibility of each individual to uphold the negative freedoms of all others. To this end, each individual has an executive power to punish transgressors of the law of nature, 'to such a Degree as may hinder its Violation' (ibid, para. 7). Indeed those who transgress the law of nature to a sufficient degree may forfeit their own rights to life, liberty and property. Only the constant danger of the state of nature degenerating into a state of war leads individuals to commit to a social contract that creates civil society and a limited government entrusted with the executive authority to preserve and to protect their natural rights.

Civil societies and governments do not possess rights naturally; only individuals have that capacity. By agreeing to leave the state of nature and to enter into civil society, individuals necessarily sacrifice their right to judge and to punish breaches of their natural rights by others. This is no small sacrifice and will not be countenanced unless civil or political society is strictly limited with respect to the powers that it subsumes. With respect to their natural rights to life and liberty, Locke thus implies that individuals cannot make transfers to government even by consent, for these rights are inalienable. With respect to the natural right to property, individuals can make transfers to government by consent, for these rights are not inalienable. They cannot legitimately have these rights taken without consent (except perhaps by forfeiture), since these rights are imprescriptible.

Although Locke views natural rights essentially as a gift from God, he justifies the natural right to private property primarily on utilitarian grounds, rejecting Robert Filmer's argument that original communism could not give way to private property without the universal consent of mankind:

> God gave the World to Men in Common; but since he gave it them for their benefit, and the greatest Conveniences of Life they were capable to draw from it, it cannot be supposed he meant it should always remain common and uncultivated. He gave it to the use of the Industrious and Rational, –; not to the Fancy or Covetousness of the Quarrelsome and Contentious (Locke II, para. 34).

Locke's theory of first possession as the fundamental basis for property rights offers an essentially utilitarian justification for privatizing the initially common gift from God, on a basis that confirms a clear-cut route to the determination of title. Because his focus was naturally on land, he was overly concerned to condition privatization by the proviso that, 'there is enough, and as good left in common for others' (ibid, para. 27). In countries where available land has largely been privatized, this proviso may seem to threaten the natural right proposition, even to lend succour to socialism.

Such an interpretation, however, is incorrect. The modern theory of property rights concerns itself more with legitimate exploitation of opportunities than with the narrow concept of ownership focused upon by Locke. If 'the right to property is a right to action' (Rand 1961, 94), a theory of property rights relates much more to the intellectual and physical efforts of individuals than to a common stock of assets. Property rights concern allowable acts of transformation of the material world among which individuals possessing such rights are free to choose.

Since property is created largely through an act of transformation rather than a circumstance of possession, the Lockeian proviso seemingly is moot. For there can never be 'enough and as good' left for others if every action issues in a unique transformation (Rasmussen and Den Uyl 1991, 120). Acts of transformation under conditions of original acquisition are not rights-violating because no one has rights to the pre-transformed objects under consideration. We shall see (section 5) that this concept of property rights has powerful implications for the nature of civil society.

For those who do not subscribe to Locke's notion of a natural right, Jasay (1996) outlines an alternative notion that is fully compatible with Locke's first possession commitment. Jasay's defence of the first possession rule is general and unambiguous. If an individual is in a position to take first possession, then such a taking is a feasible act of his that is admissible if it does not constitute a tort (trespass) and if it violates no antecedent right (the case by definition). In such circumstances, taking exclusive possession is a liberty that can only be obstructed by a contrary right, which does not exist.

Two alternative acts constitute an appropriation which vests ownership in the performer, namely: (1) finding and keeping, and (2) enclosure. Since the right to property is the fulcrum of a civil society, it is worthwhile briefly reviewing each of these constitutive acts. Accepting the notion of finding and keeping as the basis for property rights involves respecting the moral arbitrariness of luck. Redress, then, cannot be called for on moral grounds. Any judgement that the resulting distribution of wealth is right or wrong involves a category mistake by reference to the finding and keeping rule. Finding and keeping poses no question of justice and creates no liability to compensation or redress.

Suppose alternatively that the potentially useful resource is there for all to see – neither chance nor finding cost is required to realize its existence – yet it has not been appropriated. Any squatter can establish first possession by enclosing it, thus excluding everyone else's access to it. However, in this case the analogy with finding is incomplete since those who used to enjoy access to the unenclosed resource are now denied such access.

The enclosure worsens their situation even though it does not violate their rights. If the unowned resource has been used regularly by an identifiable set of individuals, common pool ownership may be implied, in which case compensation in the case of enclosure should be paid in the form of reliance-based damages. Enclosure itself is not a tort. It constitutes a clash between two liberties, not between a liberty and a right. If exclusion is successful and just claims for compensation on grounds of reliance are satisfied, the resource passes legitimately into the ownership of the finder-encloser.

5. THE LAW OF NATURE AND HUMAN FLOURISHING

The state of nature, as earlier defined, is not a state of licence, even though man in that state has an uncontrollable liberty to dispose of his property. The state of nature has a law of nature to govern it, which obliges everyone (Locke II, para. 6). Since every individual is equal and independent under that law, no one ought to harm another in his life, liberty or possessions. In the state of nature, the law of nature provides that every man has a right to punish the transgressions of that law to such a degree as may hinder its violation. All who are damaged by the unlawful act have a particular right to seek reparation from the transgressor. In this sense every individual has executive power in the state of nature.

Since men are free, equal and independent, by nature, no one can be subjected to the political power of another without his own consent. Why will such consent be given? Locke's answer is that, although in the state of nature men have such rights, the enjoyment of them is very uncertain and constantly exposed to the invasion of others (Locke II, para. 123). The principal reason that men create civil society is for the mutual preservation of their lives, liberties and estates, which Locke calls by the general name, *property*.

Although man gives up the executive power to protect his own property when he enters into civil society, he does so only the better to preserve his property. The power of civil society thus is constrained to secure everyone's property by providing against the defects inherent in the state of nature. Even if, as Locke supposed, majority rule governs society, it does so subject to the severe provision that every man's life, liberty and estates must be protected at least as well as he could achieve in the state of nature. Evidently such an outcome can be achieved only by the minimal state which exists solely to determine and to defend property rights against potential internal and external aggression. Note that this definition of the minimal state leaves a state of flexible size, dependent on the nature and scale of the forces of aggression that it is obligated to confront.

I shall now argue that human flourishing occurs best in the environment provided by the minimal state; that political societies composed of individuals characterized by diverse interests predictably stifle human flourishing unless the state is obligated only to uphold the negative natural rights of all citizens and is prescribed from any other action. This argument falls into the lineage of classical liberal scholars perhaps best epitomized by John Locke (1991), Wilhelm von Humboldt (1969) and John Stuart Mill (1989).

It is instructive to initiate this analysis of human flourishing with Aristotle's concept of *eudaimonia*, which describes a state of individual well-being, induced by living rationally or intelligently, and characterized by self-actualization and by maturation. Use of the term *eudaimonia* in no sense implies an endorsement of Aristotle's ethics, which does not embrace the notions of natural rights and individual liberty central to this paper.

Although *eudaimonia* is usually translated as 'happiness', this is misleading if not qualified. Happiness should be understood not simply as the gratification of desire, but rather the satisfaction of right desire – those desires and wants which will lead to successful human living (Rasmussen and Den Uyl 1991, 36). Of course, man is not only a rational being but also an animal with the biological capacity and need for sensory experiences. Emotions play a significant role in achieving *eudaimonia*. Nevertheless, human flourishing requires that the emotions must be controlled by man's capacity to reason; that for a successful life, man must live in such a way that he achieves goals that are rational for him not only from an individual perspective, but also as a human being (Machan 1975, 75); and that in so doing he controls his animal passions.

In a society of diverse individuals, the outcomes of human flourishing predictably will reflect that diversity. Human flourishing is unlikely to lead to some consensus of the good, despite much modern consequentialist reasoning. The issue of value pluralism which so concerns conservatives and communitarians will be confronted in section 6 of this essay, where we shall argue that it constitutes a problem only within the context of the non-minimal state.

Human flourishing or *eudaimonia* must be attained through a person's own efforts. It cannot be achieved as the result of factors that are beyond his control. The cardinal virtue if a human is to flourish is rationality, and this can develop only when an individual is fully responsible for his own choices. The individual cannot flourish or grow when others make choices for him or when he is not held responsible for such choices as he makes; because the human faculties of perception, judgement, mental activity and even moral preference are exercised only in making a choice:

> He who lets the world, or his own portion of it, choose his plan of life for him, has no need of any other faculty than the ape-like one of imitation. He who chooses his plan for himself, employs all his faculties. He must use observation to see, reasoning and judgment to foresee, activity to gather materials for decision, discrimination to decide, and when he has decided, firmness and self-control to hold to his deliberate decision. And these qualities he requires and exercises exactly in proportion as the part of his conduct which he determines according to his own judgment and feelings is a large one. It is possible that he might be guided in some good path, and kept out of harm's way, without any of these things. But what will be his comparative worth as a human being? It really is of importance, not only what men do, but also what manner of men they are that do it (J.S. Mill 1989, 59).

Of course, the laws of nature do not guarantee that every human being will flourish. Not every one will seize the opportunity provided by liberty to fulfil their lives to the limit of their respective capacities. Many will evade the burdens and constraints of choice and make their way in life through imitation or servitude rather than creativity. Others will be overwhelmed by their passions, discarding rationality in favour of purely sensory pleasures. The laws of nature offer only opportunities, not a guarantee of utopia. They also protect individuals from those choices by others that otherwise would threaten their lives, liberties or property. The freedom to flourish is not a licence to behave in ways injurious (in this sense) to others. Fundamentally, the law property, of contract and of tort, effectively enforced, would control the injurious impulses incidental to human flourishing.

In the Lockeian tradition of negative natural rights, the natural right to private property arguably is its most controversial component. This controversy extends to the relationship between property rights and human flourishing (Rawls 1971). This relationship, therefore, requires particular attention. Individuals are material beings, not, as Rawls supposes, disembodied ghosts. Being self-directed or autonomous is not some psychic state but pertains to actions in the real world, often involving material resources. It is through the use and manipulation of material resources that autonomous individuals, in large part, develop and exercise their creativity under conditions of liberty.

For individuals to flourish, they need to maintain control of what they have produced (Rasmussen and Den Uyl 1991, 116: Buchanan 1993), and to retain or dispense with their accumulated resources according to their own judgement. In this respect, the imprescriptible right to property takes its full place with the inalienable right to life and liberty as the strongest foundation for human flourishing.

6. THE NON-PROBLEM OF VALUE PLURALISM

John Gray (1989, 1993) has argued the case for what he calls 'plural realism in ethics' which takes the view that, whereas there are definite limits on the varieties of human flourishing, there are many forms of life (often exhibiting divergent and uncombinable goods) in which human beings may flourish, and none of these is the one right way of life for man. Plural realism thus differs sharply from Aristotelian ethics which claims that there is one best form of life for the human species that is rationally discoverable. Plural realism, in contrast, argues that there are many, diverse and incompatible, forms of life in which human well-being may be realized. With this judgement, I have no quarrel, indeed it is the essence of the political philosophies both of Locke and Mill (Waltzer 1994).

Gray (1993) deploys plural realism, however, as a weapon to attack classical liberal ethics, most certainly the brand of such ethics that I have advanced in this essay. He claims that pluralism fells classical liberal meliorism – the position which ranks societies by the degree to which they approximate to a classical liberal order; that it overwhelms the notion that all human beings are endowed with rights since highly stratified societies may give rise to some form of human flourishing; and that it destroys the notion of Kant that only persons have intrinsic value since elements of a 'rich cultural environment' may enter into autonomous choice constitutively rather than instrumentally.

In passing this judgement, Gray lays claim to intellectual support from Isaiah Berlin, in his view the most compelling liberal political philosopher of the 20th century (Gray 1996). At the heart of Berlin's thought, he claims, is value pluralism, an idea of enormous subversive force. If there is no single master-value, if all values are not necessarily compatible or harmonious, no single moral theory will be able to guide our conduct when we are faced with moral dilemmas which force us to forsake one good for another. There is no metric which would enable us to make trade-offs. In such circumstances, classical liberal institutions have no universal authority.

Whether or not Gray is accurate in his reflections on Berlin (and there is a lot of evidence that Berlin is a fox who knows many things, rather than a hedgehog who knows one big thing) (Kukathos 1996), he deploys these reflections to attack classical liberal political orders, arguing that they have no general superiority. Value pluralism dictates, in Gray's view, pluralism in political regimes and undermines the claim that only classical liberal regimes are fully legitimate. As we shall see in section 7, Gray finds a wide range of past and present societies, that are far distant in nature from classical liberal orders, to be compatible with his concept of civil society.

In my view, the argument from value pluralism strengthens rather than weakens the case in favour of a political society grounded either on the law of nature or, equivalently, on Jasay's maxims set out in *Before Resorting to Politics* (1996). For only in such a society, where the negative rights of individuals are strictly enforced, will value pluralism withstand public choice pressures to conform either to the values of transient majorities or to the dictates of an autocrat. Gray falls into a categorical error, in his critique of classical liberal political orders, of assuming that the whole of society is politicized, that the supposed monism of classical liberal values will be imposed on all aspects of an individual's life.

This is not the case. By definition, a classical liberal order constrains politics to its minimal form, leaving individuals free to form their own associations and groups and to pursue their own goals subject only to the law property, of contract and of tort, uninhibited by political pressures. Ultimately it leaves individuals free, should they so choose, even to abandon the order itself. Classical liberals will not force individuals to be free (Rowley and Peacock 1975). Citizens who flourish within the framework of classical liberalism, however, will not easily choose to deny themselves the advantages that they enjoy

7. A FLAWED CONCEPT OF CIVIL SOCIETY

Gray (1993) claims that classical liberalism, as a doctrine with aspirations for universal prescriptive authority, is dead; its philosophical foundations are in a state of collapse. All that remains is, 'the historic inheritance of civil society that has now spread *to most parts of the world*' (Gray 1993, 314). Civil society, as defined by Gray, superficially conforms with the basic tenets of a classical liberal order, although, on a closer examination, this conformity is seen to be a mirage.

By civil society, Gray (1993) means a number of things. First, it is a society which is tolerant of the diversity of views, religious and political, that it contains, and in which the state does not seek to impose any comprehensive doctrine. In this sense, Calvin's Geneva was not a civil society, nor were any of the societies characterized by 20th century totalitarianism.

Second, it is a society in which both government and individual citizens (Gray significantly refers to these latter as 'its subjects') are restrained in their conduct by a rule of law. A state in which the will of the ruler is the law cannot contain a civil society. In consequence, such a society presupposes a government that is omnipotent, but limited.

Third, civil society is characterized by the institution of private or several property. Societies in which property is vested in tribes, or in which most assets are owned or controlled by governments, cannot be civil societies. Private property is defended as an enabling device whereby individuals with radically different goals can pursue such goals without recourse to a collective decision-procedure that must be highly conflictual. Private or several property, in Gray's view, is compatible with a wide range of political institutions.

These institutions need not conform to classical liberal predilections. Nor need they contain the culture of individualism. Nor need they embrace the institution of market capitalism, which, in Gray's judgement, is not the only market institution compatible with private or several property. Both in Russia and in Japan, for example, municipal, village and cooperative forms of ownership of property are likely to prove greatly superior to the capitalist form (Gray 1993, 316).

The criteria set out by Gray as the defining characteristics of civil society are capable of defining a narrow or a broad tent depending on the manner in which the words are interpreted. By his selection of societies that fall within the category of civil societies, Gray unequivocally chooses the broad tent definition. The societies of North America and Western Europe clearly qualify, although Gray is not uncritical of the growth of government in these countries, especially during the second half of the 20th century. One senses that something is seriously adrift, however, when Gray (1993) adds to this list of civil societies a range of past and present political orders of a radically different nature to the great democracies: Tsarist Russia, Meiji-period Japan, Bismarckian

Prussia, Duvalier's Haiti, Singapore, Hong Kong, South Korea and Taiwan. None of these latter orders has demonstrated great tolerance for diversity of opinions and lifestyles; none has provided great security for private or several property rights, recent indexes of economic freedom (Gwartney *et al.* 1996) notwithstanding; none has protected the lives and liberties of citizens by restricting government through any recognizable rule of law enforced by an independent judiciary.

It would be easy to take advantage of the poor judgement of John Gray to ridicule the concept of civil society advanced in his recent writings. It is more insightful, however, to review a stronger contestant for his lists in order to demonstrate the flawed nature of his broad concept. The government, certainly, and many of the citizens of the United States, claim pre-eminence for their political order as the leading example of civil society in the modern world. The concept of the new world order, advanced by Presidents Bush and Clinton, essentially involves a commitment to reshaping all nations in the American image. It is the essence of this paper, however, that the United States is not now a civil society in the true sense of that term, although it most probably was at its founding in 1787, the evil institution of slavery excepted.

In the late 20th century, the United States enjoys the highest murder rate of all advanced nations, clearly not protecting the lives of its citizens. It enjoys also the highest incarceration rate of all advanced nations, as a consequence of extremely interventionist legislation and administrative regulations, which further erode the liberties of its non-incarcerated citizens. Its taxes and regulations significantly erode the private property of its citizens and its takings of private property for public use in no sense honour the wording of the Fifth Amendment to the constitution. There is no imprescriptible right to property in the United States.

These characteristics are no accident of fate. They are the entirely predictable consequences of the expansion of government beyond the limits of the minimal state, of the abandonment either of natural rights or of Jasay's *maxims* before resorting to politics. In many ways Alexis de Tocqueville anticipated the likely regression of American democracy away from liberty and civil society in favour of equality and non-civil society in his *magnum opus*: *Democracy in America* (1969).

Tocqueville warned that, 'the type of oppression which threatens democracies is different from anything that has ever been in the world before' (Tocqueville 1969, 691). He envisaged, 'an innumerable multitude of men, alike and equal, consistently circling around in pursuit of the petty and banal pleasures with which they glut their souls' (1966, 692). Such a man, 'exists in and for himself, and though he may still have a family, one can at least say that he has not got a fatherland' (1966, 692). In a prophetic passage, Tocqueville sets out the implications for the political order of this state of affairs:

> Over this kind of men stands an immense, protective power which is alone responsible for securing their enjoyment and watching over their fate. That power is absolute, thoughtful of detail, orderly, provident, and gentle. It would resemble parental authority if, fatherlike, it tried to prepare its charges for a man's life, but on the contrary, it only tries to keep them in perpetual childhood... It provides for their security, foresees and supplies their necessities, facilitates their pleasures, manages their principal concerns, directs their industry, makes rules for their testaments, and divides their inheritances. Why should it not entirely relieve them from the trouble of thinking and all the cares of living? (Tocqueville 1966, 692).

The process of subjugation of such a population is subtle rather than brutal as in totalitarian orders:

> It does not break men's will, but softens, bends, and guides it; it seldom enjoins, but often inhibits action; it does not destroy anything, but prevents much being born; it is not at all tyrannical, but it hinders, restrains, enervates, stifles, and stultifies so much that in the end each nation is no more than a flock of timid and hardworking animals with the government as its shepherd' (Tocqueville 1966, 692).

Much of what Tocqueville feared in 1840 for democracy in America has come to pass with consequences for civil society that manifest themselves in high crime rates, in high rates of incarceration, in a cult of property theft by middle-income groups through the process of government, in a decline in thrift, in manliness and civility, in toleration, in duty and self-sacrifice, in service, in fidelity, in self-control, in fortitude, in honesty, honour and trust, in respect for each other, in diligence, discretion and self-improvement (Anderson 1992).

For the most part, these qualities of civil society may seem more psychological and sociological than economic. It is my central hypothesis that they depend not on the perfectibility of man but on sound political economy as enunciated by the great classical liberal scholars whose ideas form the basis of this essay. These lost values will return, if at all, only through a return to the minimal state obligated to preserve and protect the lives, liberties and properties of the citizens who create and effectively control it. Only in such a society will human beings flourish and assume for themselves duties and obligations that currently have been abandoned in an ever-escalating demand for rights and privileges.

8. THE RESTORATION OF CIVIL SOCIETY

In his *magnum opus*, *The History of the Decline and Fall of the Roman Empire*, Edward Gibbon (1974) describes the gradual emergence and consolidation, over a period of some 600 years, of classical civil society throughout the Roman Empire during the period of the Great Republic (SPQR). He chronicles the disastrous consequences of monarchy and the collapse of SPQR following the assassination of Julius Caesar, the subsequent civil war between Octavian Caesar and Mark Antony, the final victory of the former at the battle of Actium (31 BC) and the crowning of Octavian as the Emperor Augustus Caesar. He relates the slow but inexorable decline and fall of this once great Empire during the following several centuries, ravaged from within by internecine battles for the Imperial Crown always involving the Praetorian Guard and the Roman Legions, and from without by the barbarian hordes waiting at the boundaries for any perceived weakening of Imperial resolve.

Following the final collapse, 'the greatest, perhaps, and most awful scene in the history of mankind' (Gibbon Vol. VI, 2441), the institutions of civil society disappeared completely from the face of the earth for the better part of a millennium until Great Britain freed itself from the Stuart dynasty in 1688 and accelerated the slow process of evolution of the institutions of civil society which eventually were to extend beyond its own frontiers, like Rome before it, to encompass much, although by no means all, of its own extensive empire. The 20th century has witnessed the decline and fall of the British Empire and, with it, the erosion of classical liberal civil society ravaged alike by two world wars and by the subsequent follies of unlimited democracy. If this process of erosion is not checked, a new Dark Age beckons from which, given the destructive power of modern weaponry, mankind is unlikely to re-emerge.

Given that government has grown, both in absolute size and in the range of its functions, in all Western nations during the 20th century, as a response to the exigencies of war and the follies of democracy, the public choice constraints obstructing any rapid return to the minimal state are formidable. The advance of the welfare state has created a culture of dependency that manifests itself at the polls just as it corrodes human flourishing among individuals that become addicted to its offerings. The politicization of society which accompanies the growth of government essentially has destroyed the rule of law and, in so doing, has weakened the protection accorded to the lives, liberties and property of individual citizens. This weakening of protection, in turn, has curtailed human flourishing even among the more independent individuals in society, lowering the degree of vigilance on which the law of nature depends for its continued existence.

Public choice predictions for the restoration of the minimal state, in such circumstances, are less than propitious. Without the minimal state, the prospects for the restoration of civil society are as bleak as they were in the dying years of the Roman Empire.

It is instructive in this regard to switch attention from the fundamental characteristics of classical civil society as outlined in this essay to the complex of interlocking institutions and individual dispositions on which civil society may be expected to flourish in a 21st century environment. Insights are available concerning these latter interrelationships from the experience of Great Britain during the late 18th and early 19th centuries. The freedom available to British citizens at that time stemmed, as Oakeshott (1991) has noted, not from separate rights, laws or institutions, but from many mutually reinforcing liberties:

> It springs neither from the separation of church and state, nor from the rule of law, nor from private property, nor from parliamentary government, nor from the writ of *habeas corpus*, nor from the independence of the judiciary, nor from any one of the thousand other devices and arrangements and characteristics of our society, but from what each signifies and represents, namely, the absence from our society of overwhelming concentrations of power (Oakeshott 1991, 387).

In this perspective, individuals considered themselves free in classical liberal Britain because no one was allowed unlimited power – no leader, faction, party, no government, church, corporation, trade or professional association or trade union. Instead power was diffused through what Oakeshott refers to as a 'civil association' in which each individual acknowledges the authority in which he lives. Respect for the authority of law did not imply that every individual supported every law. The law itself was a slowly changing spontaneous order (Hayek

1973) which garnered respect not just for what it was but also for what it promised to become, always within the framework of the rule of law. In a civil association, the government, 'is an instrument of the people, charged with keeping in good order the institutions which allow people to pursue their self-chosen ideals' (Green 1993, 9).

The 20th century has witnessed major retreats by all such civil associations as nation states have thrown off the shackles of the minimal state and have reconstituted their citizens into what Oakeshott (1991) refers to as 'enterprise associations'. Nation states constituted as enterprise associations are composed of individuals related in pursuit of a common interest or objective. There is but one sovereign purpose. The task of leaders, 'is to manage the pursuit of this goal and to direct individuals as appropriate' (Green 1993, 8). Communism and national socialism were ultimate forms of the enterprise association. However, late 20th century social democracy has evolved as a less extreme form of this perversion of the civil association, unfortunately much better entrenched than either of its totalitarian close relations.

Hayek (1973) has demonstrated that the classical liberal experiment with democracy failed because the institutions chosen to preserve liberty proved to be inadequate. In particular, faith placed in the separation of powers – legislative, executive and judicial – was not justified even in the most sophisticated experiment of the United States constitution.

The United States Supreme Court, although only equal in status to the Congress and the president, had been designated as the crucial check against politicization of the law. It played this role effectively until, in 1937, a majority of its justices rendered themselves unlawful in the case of *West Coast Hotel v Parrish*, caving in to pressures from the White House to subvert the constitution in favour of illegal 'New Deal' legislation. Thereafter, periodic coalitions between Congress and presidents effectively destroyed the separation of powers and destroyed the rule of law.

In large part, classical liberal scholars underestimated the capacity of the state to subvert society from the civil to the enterprise association because they failed to anticipate the shift from the law of *Nomos* to the law of *Thesis* – from the common law to law-making by the state (Hayek 1973). The idea that the law was immune from interference by government, that it was discovered and not made, was fundamental to natural law or the law of God, was indeed the fundamental contribution of Judeo-Christian religion to the 17th and 18th century concept of civil society. That view was swept away by the extension of the franchise in the 19th and early 20th centuries and by the rise in the philistinisation of the majority vote in most advanced democracies.

That which was swept away had taken many generations to evolve. It cannot be re-established by constitutional decree, but only by another slow process of evolution. From a public choice perspective, such an evolutionary process faces formidable obstacles in the form of special interests that control the enterprise association. In a civil association, the law must not be the instrument of special interests, nor the tool of government. It must constitute a body of moral and prudential rules which is binding on everyone (Green 1993, 122). How can law-making be restored as an exercise in the making of the impartial rules of just conduct in an environment subverted by the forces of public choice? How can it be so established in environments that have never experienced the rule of law?

One route to such reform is the process of weakening central government through a process of devolving power (including the power to tax) to the states or provinces in a federalist system or to the local level in non-federalist systems. In and of itself, such a process of devolution does not guarantee a shift away from *Leviathan* in favour of the minimal state. In some instances, where the population is highly dependent on the state, devolution may shift the balance yet further in favour of *Leviathan*.

Nevertheless, decentralized communities then would be free to experiment (at their own cost) with differing forms of government. To the extent that such experimentation is not contaminated by the spending and taxing interventions of central government, those that are more successful in encouraging human flourishing signal to those that are less successful the existence of a better way. If civil associations once again are to replace enterprise associations, devolved competition may be the only feasible mechanism given the powerful forces ranged against such reforms at the level of the central or federal government.

The fine essays that follow in this volume explore in some depth the philosophical issues touched upon in this introductory paper and evaluate the prospects of establishing civil societies in countries of the former Soviet Empire and in Black Africa that have never fully experienced the joys of civil society but that now have a realistic prospect of evolving towards the minimal state if certain key obstacles can be overcome.

It would indeed be an ironic tragedy if the countries that have experienced the privilege of civil society, only to have lost it, were to fail to restore civil associations, while those countries that have endured the days of the devils (Johnson 1983) were to shake off the yoke of the enterprise association and to evolve into civil societies (Rau 1987, Gellner 1994). History tells us that such ironies should not be ruled out.

BIBLIOGRAPHY

Anderson, D. (1992), *The Loss of Virtue: Moral Confusion and Social Disorder in Britain and America*, London: The Social Affairs Unit (a National Review Book).
Buchanan, J.M. (1993), *Property as a Guarantor of Liberty*, The Shaftesbury Papers, I, Aldershot: Edward Elgar Publishing.
Ferguson, A. (1991), *An Essay on the History of Civil Society*, New Brunswick: Transaction Publishers.
Filmer, Sir Robert (1949), *Patriarcha and Other Political Works*, ed. Peter Laslett. Oxford: Basil Blackwell.
Fukuyama, F.C. (1992), *The End of History and the Last Man*, New York: The Free Press.
Gellner, E. (1994), *Conditions of Liberty: Civil Society and its Rivals*, London: Allen Lane, Penguin Press.
Gibbon, E. (1974), *The History of the Decline and Fall of the Roman Empire*, New York: The Easton Press.
Gray, J. (1989), *Liberalisms: Essays in Political Philosophy*, New York: Routledge.
Gray, J. (1993), *Post-Liberalism: Studies in Political Thought*, New York: Routledge.
Gray, J. (1996), *Isaiah Berlin*, Princeton, NJ: Princeton University Press.
Green, D.G. (1993), *Reinventing Civil Society*, London: IEA Health and Welfare Unit.
Gwartney, J., R. Lawson and W. Block (1996), *Economic Freedom of the World: 1975–1995*, Vancouver, Canada: The Fraser Institute.
Hayek, F.A. (1973), *Law, Legislation and Liberty. Vol. I. Rules and Order*, London: Routledge and Kegan Paul.
Humboldt, W. von (1969), *The Limits of State Action*, Cambridge: Cambridge University Press.
Hume, D. (1948), *Moral and Political Philosophy*, New York: Hafner Publishing Company.
Jasay, A. de (1996), *Before Resorting to Politics*, The Shaftesbury Papers, 5, Aldershot: Edward Elgar Publishing.
Johnson, P. (1983), *Modern Times: The World from the Twenties to the Eighties*, New York: Harper and Row.
Klaus, V. (1996), *Transforming Toward a Free Society*, Vienna: The Mont Pelerin Society Meeting.
Kukathos, C. (1996), 'What's the big idea?', *Reason*, November, 66–70.

Kumar, K. (1993), 'Civil society: an inquiry into the usefulness of an historical term', *British Journal of Sociology*, **44** (3), 375–401.
Locke, J. (1991), *Two Treatises of Government*, Cambridge: Cambridge University Press.
Machan, T. (1975), *Human Rights and Human Liberties*, Chicago: Nelson-Hall.
Mill, J.S. (1989), *On Liberty and Other Writings*, Cambridge: Cambridge University Press.
Nozick, R. (1989), *The Examined Life: Philosophical Meditations*, New York: Simon and Schuster.
Oakeshott, M. (1991), *Rationalism in Politics and Other Essays*, Indianapolis: Liberty Press.
Rand, A. (1961), *The Virtue of Selfishness*, New York: New American Library.
Rasmussen, D. and D. Den Uyl (1991), *Liberty and Nature: An Aristotelian Defense of Liberal Order*, La Salle: Open Court.
Rau, Z. (1987), 'Some thoughts on civil society in Eastern Europe and the Lockean contractarian approach', *Political Studies*, **35**, 573–92.
Rawls, J. (1971), *A Theory of Justice*, Cambridge: Belknap Press.
Roepke, W. (1996), *The Moral Foundations of Civil Society*, New York: Transaction Publishers.
Rowley, C.K. (1996), 'What is dead and what is living in classical liberalism', in C.K. Rowley (ed.), *The Political Economy of the Minimal State*, Aldershot: Edward Elgar Publishing, pp. 1–23.
Rowley, C.K. and A.T. Peacock (1975), *Welfare Economics: A Liberal Restatement*, London: Martin Robertson.
Simmons, A.J. (1993), *On the Edge of Anarchy*, Princeton, NJ: Princeton University Press.
Tocqueville, A. de (1969), *Democracy in America*, New York: Harper and Row.
Waltzer, M. (1994), 'Multiculturalism and individualism', *Dissent*, Spring, 185–91.

Liberalism Defended

Liberalism Defended

The Challenge of Post-Modernity

Douglas B. Rasmussen
Professor of Philosophy, St John's University, USA

Douglas J. Den Uyl
Professor of Philosophy, Bellarmine College, USA

THE SHAFTESBURY PAPERS, 9
SERIES EDITOR: CHARLES K. ROWLEY

Edward Elgar
Cheltenham, UK • Northampton, MA, USA

© Douglas B. Rasmussen and Douglas J. Den Uyl 1997

All rights reserved. No part of this publication may be reproduced, stored in a retrieval system or transmitted in any form or by any means, electronic, mechanical or photocopying, recording, or otherwise without the prior permission of the publisher.

Published by
Edward Elgar Publishing Limited
8 Lansdown Place
Cheltenham
Glos GL50 2HU
UK

Edward Elgar Publishing, Inc.
6 Market Street
Northampton
Massachusetts 01060
USA

A catalogue record for this book
is available from the British Library

Library of Congress Cataloguing in Publication Data
Rasmussen, Douglas B., 1948–
　　Liberalism defended : the challenge of post-modernity / Douglas B. Rasmussen, Douglas J. Den Uyl.
　　— (The Shaftesbury papers : 9)
　　Includes bibliographical references and index.
　　1. Liberalism.　I. Den Uyl, Douglas, J., 1950–　.　II. Title.
III. Series.
JC574.R38　1998
320.51—dc21　　　　　　　　　　　　　　　　　　　　　　　　97–38258
　　　　　　　　　　　　　　　　　　　　　　　　　　　　　　　　　　CIP

ISBN 1 85898 557 9

Typeset by Manton Typesetters, 5–7 Eastfield Road, Louth, Lincolnshire LN11 7AJ, UK.
Printed and bound in Great Britain by Biddles Ltd, Guildford and King's Lynn

Contents

Acknowledgements vi

1	Introduction	1
2	Liberalism and Ethics	5
3	The Foundations of Liberalism	23
4	Analyses and Objections	40
5	Conclusion	69

Notes	71
Bibliography	77
Index	83

Acknowledgements

This work is in many ways a continuation of our earlier defence of liberalism, *Liberty and Nature: An Aristotelian Defense of Liberal Order* (Open Court, 1991). Further, it is part of an ongoing project. It uses and expands upon some insights from more recent defences of liberalism by us. (See our essays in Tibor R. Machan and Douglas B. Rasmussen (eds), *Liberty for the Twenty-First Century*, Rowman & Littlefield, 1995.) This work is, however, also a response to the challenge to liberalism offered by John Gray and Alasdair MacIntyre. We owe much to them for the task they have given us. Their challenge has helped us to face questions that have caused our understanding of liberalism to deepen.

Besides what is listed in the notes and bibliography, we owe special thanks to the following people for inspiration and assistance: Roger Bissell, David Gordon, Chandran Kukathas, Leonard Liggio, Loren E. Lomasky, Tibor R. Machan, Fred D. Miller, Jr and Henry B. Veatch. Special thanks are also due to an anonymous reviewer, the editors at Edward Elgar, Lucille Hartmann and, most of all, Charles K. Rowley. Finally, the following foundations and educational institutions have helped this project in various ways: Liberty Fund, The Locke Institute, Institute for Humane Studies, Bellarmine College and St John's University.

That freedom is the matrix required for the growth of moral values – indeed not merely one value among many but the source of all values – is almost self-evident. It is only where the individual has choice, and its inherent responsibility, that he has occasion to affirm existing values, to contribute to their further growth, and earn moral merit.

> F.A. Hayek, *Studies In Philosophy, Politics and Economics*

1. Introduction

Why bother about liberalism? In recent times it has been pejoratively called the 'L' word. And even though the 60s generation now taking the reins of power may still see something idealistic in liberalism, the rest of us know that more government is not the answer to our problems. It may even cause many of them. The people of the United States have turned more conservative politically – especially when it comes to economic matters. Liberalism, then, seems out of step politically. That also appears to be the case intellectually. True, thinkers such as John Rawls have spawned whole intellectual industries that defend various versions of the welfare state; but one gets the sense that these efforts are more along the lines of propping up a crumbling edifice than of laying out a new direction. Why bother, then, with liberalism?

'Liberalism' in its ordinary usage is not something we would defend and, given the already existing defences, another apology would be superfluous. There is, however, one other sort of liberalism. In ordinary conversation it is often called 'conservatism', but that is a confusion. Its more precise formulation would be 'classical' liberalism. It differs from the ordinary sort of liberalism by being significantly less inclined towards programmes typical of a welfare state. We would be inclined to defend this sort of liberalism, except that within the framework of liberalism it too has been done sufficiently by others, from Adam Smith to F.A. Hayek. So, again, why bother with liberalism?

Suppose, however, that there was something that connected the two liberalisms together and which was itself under attack. Would that not indicate that a deeper and more fundamental issue was at stake? Would it not seem necessary to see what could be mustered in defence of liberalism *per se* and not just a version of it? For although we regard the ordinary or modern form of 'liberalism', as that term is used in the United States, to be a perversion of liberalism, it still holds to many of the fundamental tenets of liberalism, namely that political power is not something due anyone by natural right, that progress is possible, that the individual is the basic social unit, that people should have the freedom to pursue their own conceptions of the good life, and that the state should be limited to protecting people in the pursuit of their own conceptions of the good life. These and other principles are a part of the very nature of liberalism, and it is these very principles that are being questioned today.

Liberalism is associated with the Enlightenment which has come under serious attack in recent times. It is not just that the Enlightenment is thought to be open to some objections, but rather that it is a movement that has failed completely and has now reached its end. Liberalism is seen, therefore, as an outmoded political philosophy based upon principles that are at best naïve, but mostly just false and pernicious. Liberalism is said to undermine its own principles, to have lost any strong claims to universal validity, to subvert moral life, and to foster injustice and inhumanity. It is no longer possible, then, to defend a *type* of liberalism as if we were all agreed that liberalism is generally the correct political framework. That is no longer the case. To defend a type of liberalism, whether it be classical or modern welfare state liberalism, inevitably draws one to the deeper issues about the very foundations of liberalism. It is for these reasons that we have chosen to retain the word 'liberalism' rather than use 'classical liberalism' or 'libertarianism', even though these are the types of liberalisms closest to what we regard as defensible.

In examining the basic structure of liberalism we shall concentrate on normative issues. This makes sense because the legitimacy of the liberal order is precisely what is at issue. Moreover, people such as Alasdair MacIntyre have claimed that liberalism feeds on continual debate about its own principles to the effect that it ends up undermining its own legitimacy (MacIntyre 1988, 343–4). Liberalism must do so because it decides questions of public policy by tallying and weighing preferences about what is right or good. Yet since liberalism presents itself as being officially neutral among rival conceptions of what is right or good, the effect is to trivialize all matters of substance, since in practice all issues are reduced to preferences. Substantive moral values thereby have no more inherent worth than the most minor of policy issues. If this is a tendency in liberalism, it is certainly necessary for us to devote much of our attention to basic normative issues of how the legitimacy of liberalism is to be secured.

It may very well be that recent criticisms of liberalism have recognized a crack in which to insert a wedge. One assumption, however, goes unchallenged by defenders and critics alike: that liberalism is locked into its traditional ways of understanding itself. Liberalism has, in other words, no capacity to be linked to either pre- or post-modern thought; it is on the defensive because it is unable to incorporate anything not already found within its own Enlightenment frame of reference. It is precisely here that we believe one should bother about liberalism, for we intend to bring some 'outside' elements to bear on this debate.

Our contention is that liberalism is both defensible and capable of being enriched by other intellectual traditions. Our defence of liberalism is a defence in terms not usually associated with liberal teachings. We believe the politics of liberalism can be supported with an Aristotelian framework, at least one broadly conceived. We also argue that this framework is the *best* one for supporting liberalism. In this respect two questions are being addressed: can liberalism be supported by an alternative framework, and is that account defensible?

In addition, our discussion proceeds at a fundamental level. It is no longer enough to provide evidence that liberalism 'works' or that the alternatives to it are themselves somehow defective. Enough doubt about the justifiability of liberalism has been cast to demand some discussion of basic approaches and principles. 'Basic' here points primarily to how a moral philosophy can serve to support a political philosophy. Unlike much of liberalism, which defends its politics by resorting to either moral scepticism (the view that no one is likely to be in possession of a moral truth) or moral minimalism (the view that there are only a very few moral truths dealing exclusively with matters of social cooperation), we employ a distinction between normative and metanormative principles. The latter are most directly tied to politics and concern principles that establish the social/political conditions under which full moral conduct can take place. We do not need to minimize the moral universe to support liberalism, nor do we need to ground morality in sentiment or contracts, as much of traditional liberalism has done, to generate a liberal politics. Of course, our claim is not simply that we need not resort to traditional doctrines in defence of liberalism, but also that those doctrines create their own paradoxes, which we examine in chapter 2. Chapter 3 spells out in more detail how the metanormative approach supports liberalism, and chapter 4 responds to some contemporary critics of liberalism.

If nothing else, the crisis of liberalism is an occasion for a deepened understanding of its nature. Self-reflection usually comes at a point where what has been taken for granted has passed. Liberalism in some form has been the political philosophy of the free West for centuries. Its opponents, except the communists, were marginalized and it was taken for granted. All that has passed. The communists are now intellectually marginalized and other critics of liberalism have taken the forefront. If the period in which liberalism was unquestioned master is called 'modern', we are now in a post-modern age. To defend liberalism other than through its traditional sources must be, therefore, 'post-modern'. But if our approach is 'post-modern' it is one that does *not* succeed by rejecting the whole of modernity.

2. Liberalism and Ethics

> He who renders to each his own through fear of the gallows is constrained in his action by another's command and threat of punishment, and cannot be called a just man. But he who renders to each his own through awareness of the true principle of law and its necessity, is acting steadfastly and at his own will, not another's, and so he is rightly termed a just man.
> Spinoza, *Tractatus Theologico-Politicus,* Chapter 4.

There is an ambivalence in liberalism with respect to ethics. On the one hand, the traditional role of ethics as exhortation to appropriate conduct seems anathema to liberalism. Leo Strauss has noticed, for example, that:

> The soul of modern development, one may say, is a peculiar realism, consisting in the notion that moral principles and the appeal to moral principles – preaching, sermonizing – are ineffectual. And therefore that one has to seek a substitute for moral principles which would be more efficacious than ineffectual preaching (Strauss 1988, 242).

The point Strauss makes here is a feature of the broader effort by early modern political thinkers to treat 'men as they are' rather than 'as they ought to be.'[1] To have a social system that 'works' means that we must discover the basic forces that operate in society and utilize this information to effectuate the outcomes we desire. The distance, therefore, between the normative and the descriptive must not be too great, if we are to have *workable* principles. Schemes that run contrary to basic inclinations or rudimentary social forces will be doomed from the outset. Ethical prescriptions, especially demanding ones, are therefore of dubious social utility.

Indeed, as the history of liberalism unfolds, increasing attention is devoted not to ethics but to what we would today describe as 'social science', culminating perhaps in the science of economics.[2] From this science (and others) it seems evident that ethical exhortations are rather weak tools in comparison with such forces as monetary incentives when it comes to controlling behaviour on either an individual or social level. It is perhaps no accident, then, that the fathers of liberalism were also the fathers of economics.

We can, however, look now to the other side. Freedom of thought and speech, along with toleration, were central features of the doctrines of early liberals. Moreover, peace, social order, material well-being and the benefits that flow from any realization of these values (the alleviation of poverty, ignorance and disease) were certainly also a part of the value structure of early liberalism. In addition, the language of liberalism was, and still is, framed in terms of rights – hardly a concept devoid of moral connotations. It could be argued, consequently, that as interested as liberals were in social science, they were equally as adamant about the moral justification and propriety of the liberal order.

Nevertheless, in liberal theory the descriptive and prescriptive (social science and normative ethics) seem to have a peculiar relation to one another. It is never clear which one is to dominate, yet neither seems able to survive on its own and still function as part of liberalism. The descriptive needs the prescriptive to support the notion that the conclusions of social science should have a bearing on public policy. The prescriptive needs the descriptive to present itself as realistic and to indicate the limiting characteristics of traditional social orders. For it is clear that traditional (that is, non-liberal) orders command a certain conformity of conduct that must inevitably place limitations on someone's free pursuit of his own ends. This limitation goes beyond what is a necessary consequence of the mere adoption of any rules whatsoever; for the limitations imposed by non-liberal orders are the sort that demand an orientation of individual purposes in light of a particular conception of the good.

It might be said, then, that liberalism seems to differentiate itself from other social orders by not trying to direct individuals towards some particular and socially uniform conception of the good. Thus it would seem to have less need of moral exhortation, and only then *in addition* to the other more 'effective' techniques discovered by social science. By the same token, however, liberal orders want to be considered as having at least equal moral standing to that of any other regime, but how far can it do this in the absence of traditional exhortation or a conception of the good?

While liberalism may have a certain ambivalence towards traditional moral exhortation, its critics have none when it comes to exploiting that ambivalence to their advantage. On the one hand, liberals are criticized for not adhering closely enough to the descriptive side of their theory in their positing of universal rights independent of all social contexts. It is argued that such moral claims ignore the very reality of moral prescriptions which necessarily occur in specific social orders and practices (compare, for example, MacIntyre 1981, 65). On the other hand, liberals are accused of abandoning the prescriptive side by a narrow *homo economicus* or 'atomistic' conception of human beings which serves to undermine the very possibility of moral values.

That these criticisms have hit their mark seems to us indicated by the recent attempts by defenders of liberalism to characterize liberalism as plausible because disagreements over the nature of the good are essentially intractable (Guttman 1985). If the good is intractable, it is not clear what it would mean to claim that liberal regimes can, after all, be defended on ethical grounds. One can beg all the important questions by suggesting that intractable disagreements about 'the good' say nothing about disagreements concerning 'the right'. To make this sort of response is ultimately question-begging, because it presupposes a distinction that opponents of liberalism may say is at the heart of what they are rejecting. It seems worthwhile, therefore, to give this sort of distinction further examination.

THE GOOD AND THE RIGHT

In an effort to accommodate both personal freedom and the demands of justice, liberalism would appear to require a basic distinction such as the distinction between the good and the right.[3] The general tendency has been to consider the good as essentially privatized and the right universalized. The good, in other words, comes to be regarded as the object of one's own interest and stands in contrast to what one may do with any right. What one may do by right is what is allowed to, or demanded of, all agents (or derived from such). Early liberal thinkers could speak comfortably of the 'rights of man', but it would be unusual for them to speak of the 'good of man'. The 'goods of men', by contrast, would have been an acceptable locution (just as 'the right of man' would not). These locutions suggest that the good and the right need not have any necessary connection to one another. What one may do or possess by right has no necessary connection to what will advance one's good; and what will advance one's good may conflict with conduct allowed or demanded by right. This asynchronous character of the good and the right is due in the end to the good being partial, interested and hence amoral, while the right captures the moral by being disinterested or impartial.

Nevertheless, the distinction between the good and the right in no way diminishes the fact that one of the central problems of liberalism has traditionally been otherwise to align or harmonize the two.[4] Indeed the very nature of the distinction creates a tension in search of a resolution, and a number of resolutions have been tried. For example, social contract theory, whether classical or contemporary, could be said to be the endeavour to generate the right from the good. Those rules that shall govern the social order (the right) are to be the product of the interaction of individuals pursuing their own interests (the good). If it all works out, the governing rules are the ones we recognize to be in our own interest (for our own good).

This process may indeed reconcile the good and the right, but one is left wondering whether our satisfaction with the various descriptions of the good is simply a function of what we have predetermined to be right. In other words, are not the constraints placed upon the contractors (whether they be 'veils of ignorance' or 'unanimity') a reflection of some conception of the right, and is it not that conception of the right that tells us what is most significant about the version of liberalism being advanced?[5]

As a consequence of the nagging suspicion that social contract theories are, after all, driven more by the right than the good, some have argued (probably beginning with Kant) that the foundations of liberalism must be deontic – that is, grounded in an appeal to principle, rather than consequences (see Mack 1995). In most cases, the good (interest) is simply rejected as being relevant to any determination of the right. The irrelevance of the good can take one of two forms: either the good is irrelevant because it is beneath the right or it is irrelevant because it is above it.

In the first case, the good is defined in terms of interest and then taken to be irrelevant to the determination of one's basic duties or obligations. Instead certain generic features of personhood, for example, might serve as the basis for generating primary rights or obligations.

In the other case, the good becomes heroic because it is pitched beyond what duty requires. For example, it may be that one deserves moral credit for giving aid to another while at the same time being under no obligation to do so. The other person has no right, let's say, to the one's resources. But it seems odd to suppose that the act of charity in question has no moral value whatsoever. Consequently, the good gets recognized as a moral one but then relegated to the category of the heroic. It has little or nothing to do with the determination of the right.[6]

There is a remaining possibility under the deontic rubric. This is the situation where one's good gets defined as being *equivalent* to actions performed from a recognition of the right. Here we are usually confronted with a 'true' good – that is, one that may conflict directly with our personal interests but that nevertheless embodies a certain principle or serves a larger universal purpose. A person might, for example, be told that his personal utility ought to match the utility of society as a whole, or that his own true good consists in respecting the rights of others.[7]

In this deontic context, the 'true' good does not simply mark the classical (that is, pre-modern) distinction between the apparent and real good. The classical view still held to the notion that the 'real' good was a good for particular persons. The modern deontic view, by contrast, holds the true good to be applicable to no one in particular and everyone equally. The true good is true precisely because it purges all elements of particularity, and thus it is only *one's* good to the extent one is undifferentiated.

One final possibility of reconciling the good and the right seems to be reflected in the theories of some 18th century liberals, where the good and the right, though distinguished, were nevertheless in a kind of natural harmony or equilibrium. If, for example, people would only adhere to rights respecting conduct (for example, act without recourse to force or fraud), the diverse pursuit of their own particular good would eventually redound to everyone's benefit. This sort of Smithian invisible hand concept is, we believe, more powerful than it has been given credit for,[8] but it does little to solve the priority problems we have been addressing. For if the invisible hand does not so steadily lead to harmony, the priority question again emerges. Moreover, the very idea of harmony presupposes the possibility of separation and disharmony, so one cannot assume away the priority question.

Our brief survey suggests that there is an inevitable tendency in the distinction between the good and the right to depreciate the moral nature of the good to the enhancement of the right. In other words, what is impartial and universal comes to take precedence over goods which are, almost by definition now, partial and particular.[9] The problem, then, of separating the good from the right[10] is that particularized ethical content is increasingly sacrificed to abstract and universalized norms. Consequently the individual, thought to be so central to liberalism, becomes ethically ever more irrelevant.

If liberalism eschews moral exhortation as a technique of social management, it is not simply due to its ineffectiveness. In spite of any rhetoric to the contrary by critics and defenders alike, *liberalism is not traditionally an individualistic ethical theory.* Quite the contrary; it gives the individual good, little or no moral standing. And while liberalism may speak of individual autonomy or personhood, its universalistic tendencies render any substantive individualism almost meaningless. This is because, as we have been noting, the distinction between the good and right inevitably raises a priority question which, under the universalistic tendencies of liberalism, gets resolved in favour of the right. Individual autonomy would, for example, be good because it has initial permission to be such by the right, not right because it contributes to the good (*pace* Mill).[11]

It shall be our contention that liberalism is quite correct to ignore the individual and be universalistic in its outlook. It is, however, correct in doing so only if it relinquishes all pretences to being an ethics.[12] Liberalism is no more an ethics than it is a theology. Yet while liberalism has managed to shed any connections to theology, it has failed to distinguish itself from ethics. Liberal theorists have retained the idea that politics is ethics writ large and that therefore liberal political principles are straightforward ethical principles like any others.

For liberalism the cost of retaining this way of looking at things has been the separation of the right from the good, because it is difficult for ethical principles to be both universal and particular if there is any real diversity at the particular level. To avoid the inconveniences a diversity of particulars would pose for ethical principles, there is an inevitable tendency to generalize or universalize, that is, to count as ethical only that which can be asserted equally across persons. This, however, has the effect of undermining the moral propriety of the individualism that liberalism is supposed to cherish and foster.

The endeavour to maintain the idea that political principles are ordinary ethical prescriptions broadly extended actually has the effect of socializing ethics, that is, of giving the individual little or no ethical significance. This is exactly what one finds in the depths of liberal theory. By removing the ethical significance of individual pursuits the socialization of ethics played an important role in establishing the eventual priority of the right over the good. As a consequence, ethical norms in a liberal environment became increasingly identified with justice. Classical liberalism, in its effort to maintain the value of individual liberty, drifted inevitably towards a moral minimalism, since that best justified diversity.[13] The so-called 'new liberalism'[14] thought that moral minimalism permitted all sorts of social abuses and sought to give justice a more expanded conception, since as liberals they too were compelled to hold that the only legitimate function of the state was the enforcement of the rules of justice. Our focus below, however, will be on indicating the ways in which liberalism has socialized ethics and not upon the divergent implications of that phenomenon.

THE SOCIALIZATION OF ETHICS

Within the very seeds of liberalism[15] we find the phenomenon to which we have just referred. Consider the following from Thomas Hobbes:

> [T]hat moral virtue, that we can measure by civil laws, which is different in different states, is justice and equity; that moral virtue which we measure purely by the natural laws is only charity. Furthermore, all moral virtue is contained in these two. However, the other three virtues (except for justice) that are called cardinal – *courage, prudence,* and *temperance* – are not virtues of citizens as citizens, but as men, for these virtues are useful not so much to the state as they are to those individual men who have them. ... For just as every citizen hath his own private good, so hath the state its own public good. Nor, in truth, should one demand that the courage and prudence of the private man, if useful only to himself, be praised or held as a virtue by states or by any other men whatsoever to whom these same are not useful. So, condensing this whole teaching on manners and dispositions into the fewest words, I say that good dispositions are those which are suitable for entering into civil society; and good manners (that is, moral virtues) are those whereby what was entered upon can be best preserved. For all the virtues are contained in justice and charity (*De Homine* XIII, 9).

Notice how all the virtues are reduced to two, and the two virtues are themselves virtues because of what they contribute to social cooperation. The passage begins with Hobbes correctly identifying that the cardinal virtues, with the possible exception of justice, were historically centred around the perfection of the individual (one's 'private good'). And although he seems to allow for the distinction between the private and public good, the reduction of all virtues to two, and the interpretation of those two virtues exclusively in terms of their contribution to social cooperation, renders the good of individuals otiose as an ethical category. The 'private good' thus disappears as being of ethical significance, however important it may be in describing life in the state of nature or predicting the terms of the social contract.

Other liberals, or figures important to its development, make similar suggestions. Consider the following from Lord Shaftesbury:

> We may consider first, That PARTIAL AFFECTION, or social Love in part, without regard to a compleat Society or Whole, is in it-self an Inconsistency, and implies an absolute Contradiction. Whatever Affection we have towards any thing besides our-selves; if it be not of the natural sort towards the System, or Kind; it must be, of all other Affections, the most dissociable, and destructive of the Enjoyments of Society: If it be really of the natural sort, and apply'd only to some one Part of Society, or of a Species, but not to the Species or Society it-self; there can be no more account given of it, than of the most odd, capricious, or humoursom Passion which may arise. The Person, therefore, who is conscious of this Affection, can be conscious of no Merit or Worth on the account of it (Shaftesbury cited in Selby-Bigge 1897, 1:40).

David Hume makes a similar comment: 'But on the whole, it seems to me, that, though it is always allowed, that there are virtues of many different kinds, yet, when a man is called virtuous, or is denominated a man of virtue, we chiefly regard his social qualities, which are, indeed, the most valuable' (Hume, *Enquiry Concerning the Principles of Morals*, Appendix IV). Such remarks are not limited to British Empiricists. Kant claims, for example, that, 'we have reason to have but a low opinion of ourselves as individuals, but as representatives of mankind we ought to hold ourselves in high esteem' (Kant 1930, 126).

It might be objected, especially with authors such as Hume, Smith and Kant, that they were careful to separate the self-regarding from the social virtues or duties, both of which are necessary for a complete account of morality. This objection, however, simply reinforces the point. Whatever independence the self-regarding virtues or duties may possess, their value is determined almost completely in terms of their contribution to social cooperation. Consider, for example, these words from Smith:

> That wisdom which contrived the system of human affections, as well as that of every other part of nature, seems to have judged that the interest of the great society of mankind would be best promoted by directing the principal attention of each individual to that particular portion of it, which was most within the sphere both of his abilities and of his understanding (Smith, *The Theory of Moral Sentiments*, VI.ii.2.4).

Thus although liberalism may grant the individual freedom to act as he or she pleases, this in no way implies an *ethical* individualism. And while critics of liberalism[16] are eager to point to the 'atomistic' or 'possessive' character of individuals found within liberal theories, the fact is that liberal theory is historically driven by the need to socialize rather than atomize. It is little wonder, then, that by the time one gets to Smith and Kant impartiality is the central feature of ethical theorizing, the partiality of individuals being considered the main obstacle to social cooperation and peace. It is also, in this connection, quite telling that the attack on liberalism begins in earnest with one who actually does attach positive normative value to the truly atomized individual, namely Rousseau and his 'savage man'.

That ethics is socialized under liberal theory, and therefore that traditional liberal theory is not an ethics of individualism, is itself a function of the abandonment of another feature of classical ethics – the replacement of prudence by justice as the supreme cardinal virtue. That justice could come to replace prudence is undoubtedly at least partially due to the abandonment of 'self-perfection' in favour of social cooperation, harmony or peace. Apart from what is indicated in the Hobbes passage already cited, there is little doubt that other thinkers are equally insistent upon making the substitution. Consider, for example, these passages from Hume and Mill, respectively:

> The necessity of justice to the support of society is the SOLE foundation of that virtue; and since no moral excellence is more highly esteemed, we may conclude, that this circumstance of usefulness has, in general, the strongest energy, and most entire command over our sentiments. It must, therefore, be the source of a considerable part of the merit ascribed to humanity, benevolence, friendship, public spirit, and other social virtues of that stamp; as it is the SOLE source of the moral approbation paid to fidelity, justice, veracity, integrity, and those other estimable and useful qualities and principles (Hume, *Enquiry Concerning the Principles of Morals*, Sec. 3, Pt. 2).

> It appears from what has been said, that justice is a name for certain moral requirements, which, regarded collectively, stand higher in the scale of social utility, and are therefore of more paramount obligation, than any others. (Mill, *Utilitarianism*, Ch. 5, Paragraph 37).

The urge to equate justice with the whole of ethics is virtually irresistible to liberalism. From one perspective, if liberals take the proper province of state action to be limited only to matters of justice, then all matters of serious moral concern become relegated to issues of justice. For to leave a serious moral matter outside the sphere of justice would deprive it of sanction and render it a mere matter of individual choice. It is not clear, in such a case, how serious the moral matter could therefore be if, being now left up to the individual alone, it fails to be *necessarily* social in nature and without social sanction.

Looked at from another perspective, the socialization of ethics would indicate that what is necessarily and inherently social would come to have primacy of place over that which is not. Justice would seem to be the best candidate for being central to ethics because of its apparently inherent interpersonal structure. In addition, the interpersonal character of justice seems to legitimize the *management* of interpersonal relations, bringing us back again to politics.

Since the socialization of ethics through justice tends to focus ethics upon what *can* be managed, one effect of this is to secularize ethics. Personal salvation, for example, which might have historically made some claim to primacy, is pushed to the fringes of private conscience. If social cooperation is our end, our actions or dispositions towards others must be paramount. That leaves little room for the personal or 'private' to have much standing, and it provides an incentive to interpret whatever may have been private in a public way. It is no accident, therefore, that despite Hobbes's distinction between justice and charity, the latter concept has little independent value. Spinoza is even more explicit in this connection (Spinoza, *Tractatus Theologico Politicus*, Ch. XIV). Today, of course, we have virtually no conception of charity beyond what one does for others.[17]

A further indication of the reduction of ethics to justice comes with respect to the language of rights. Communitarians often lament the fact that ethics is conducted almost exclusively in the language of rights. At least as a descriptive matter, the communitarians are surely correct in identifying rights as the central concept of liberal ethics. Indeed, among contemporary political philosophers the problem of political philosophy seems to be exclusively one of justifying and specifying basic rights. It almost goes without saying that such concerns fall under the rubric of justice. And although the various theories and their conclusions differ with respect to what rights we do or do not have, they seldom deviate from the path of seeing ethics primarily in terms of issues of justice.

For the liberal, however, a certain significant problem arises when ethics is socialized through justice. The doctrine is called 'liberalism' because of its liberal character – that is, its love of liberty. But the combination of liberty with the socialization of ethics would tend towards moral minimization. If, in other words, one's central moral obligations tend to be defined in terms of what one owes others, and one should also be left free to pursue one's own interests as one sees fit to the maximum degree possible, then squaring these two would seem to require a minimal amount of restrictive interpersonal duty.

True, one might claim that while our interpersonal duties are kept to a minimum, we may have many other moral obligations we would need to attend to as individuals. These other obligations would suggest that moral minimalism is not necessarily accurate as a description of liberalism. But as we have seen all along, what does not enter the central fold is spun off to the edges and rendered insignificant. As a consequence, liberalism seems torn between maximizing liberty and minimizing obligation on the one hand, or increasing obligation at the expense of liberty on the other. This tension is created precisely because liberty itself gets filtered through justice.

If cooperation is possible with minimal constraints upon one's conduct, then it would seem that the demand of justice has been met. If, on the other hand, the sort of 'cooperation' that results from free association is considered to be in some way defective (for example, paying workers 'starvation' wages), then the push for the inclusion of other values besides liberty will inevitably restrict liberty. The tension seems to us irreconcilable so long as justice defines the structure of ethics and liberalism is itself regarded as an ethics.

For why and whether we should value liberty more or less than something else is a question whose answer will give content to the very meaning of social cooperation and thus to justice itself; that in turn can only be resolved either by an appeal to something beyond what is in dispute, namely beyond the meaning of social cooperation (and thus beyond liberalism), or by a practical solution which decides the meaning in terms of present sentiments or customs (but leaves the issue unresolved intellectually).

THE METANORMATIVE SOLUTION

We have seen that the relationship between liberalism and ethics is one of ambivalence and tension. This ambivalence and tension results from the failure of liberal thinkers to appreciate the true uniqueness of liberalism. These thinkers write as if they were simply continuing a long tradition in political philosophy of searching for the best social order, the good society or the ideal state. They regard their project as one of producing and justifying regulative norms for the best society which have the status of moral duties.

One recent author, for example, tells us that liberalism is a, 'normative political philosophy, a set of moral arguments about the justification of political action and institutions' (Kymlicka 1989, 9). From this description one could presume that there are moralities for personal conduct, membership of a club, and relations with one's spouse, business partner or friends, as well as for 'political action and institutions'. What exactly makes all these things 'moralities' is not made explicit, but apparently they are differentiated by their subject alone.

Another writer tells us that there is an 'opposition...between liberal individualism in some version or other and the Aristotelian tradition in some version or other (MacIntyre 1981, 241), as if liberalism were a philosophy of ethical individualism to be contrasted with other ethical philosophies.[18]

Herein lies much of the problem. Norms are not, in fact, all of one type, differentiated by subject or thinker alone. It may be that some norms regulate the conditions under which moral conduct may take place, while others are more directly prescriptive of moral conduct itself. In light of this possibility, we believe it is not appropriate to say that liberalism is a 'normative political philosophy' in the usual sense. It is, rather, a political philosophy of metanorms. *It seeks not to guide individual conduct in moral activity, but rather to regulate conduct so that conditions might be obtained where moral action can take place.* To contrast liberalism directly with alternative ethical systems or values is, therefore, something of a category mistake.

Liberalism is best understood if it is not treated as an equinormative system.[19] Equinormative systems are those which regard normative principles as differing only with respect to subject matter and not type. Another way of putting the matter is to say that in equinormative systems all justified norms regulative of the conduct of persons have status as moral rules. Some rules may be more important or more fundamental than others, more or less general, or more or less about one subject or another, but they all form a single class of moral rules differing only with respect to their degree of obligatoriness or point of applicability.

Political theory is seen, then, as an extension of a debate about the merits of various equinormative systems, for example, where one system requires that individuals are to be given basic abstract rights versus another where their duties are defined by a community to which they are subservient. Theorists invest their time in working out the implications of the various systems as well as how one might be superior to another. Common to all the approaches, however, is the idea that the end product is understanding what sort of moral orientation or outlook, whether it be 'liberal' or not, communities ought to have.

It is important to understand that the position we take against the usual views about liberalism – namely that it should be viewed in terms of metanorms rather than norms – is not another version of the priority of the right over the good. One is not necessarily outside an equinormative system when deontological principles trump 'teleological' (consequentialist) ones. All that may be established is the priority of the principles, not their kind. The same point would apply to systems (for example, utilitarianism) which give priority to the good over the right, for this too may be another priority matter. Indeed modern deontological and utilitarian ethical systems, being universalistic and inclusive in nature, have little sense of a typology of normative principles, although we are not claiming they necessarily preclude that typology.[20]

It is especially important, in addition, to note that theories sceptical of systematic ethics, such as one might find in Gray or Berlin, are also equinormative. To say that there are irreducible conflicts of value does nothing to suggest that the values or norms in conflict are of a different type. Indeed in some respects this sort of theory is the most equinormative of all, since conflicts are more apparent when values or norms hold the same status.

Our view, therefore, is simply that the malaise of liberalism is largely the result of treating it as an equinormative system. Liberalism is both more vulnerable to its critics and subject to its own 'tensions' when understood in this way. The point here is not merely of a theoretical nature, but of a practical one as well. It is quite possible, as some critics of liberalism have claimed, that the exclusive focus upon liberal values has led people to ignore other significant moral virtues and has thereby impoverished morality in the process.

If, however, liberalism is not an ethical philosophy, the promotion of 'liberal values' would hardly qualify as completing a process of ethical instruction and could not be faulted as such. Nor could one claim much by way of ethical accomplishment when one succeeds in *living* according to liberal values.[21] The traditional litany of liberal values says next to nothing about what it would take for an individual to exhibit moral excellence – a point critics of liberalism are quick to make (see, for example, MacIntyre 1981, Chapters 17 and 18). There is nothing particularly laudable, challenging or directive, in other words, about being, for example, a tolerant or an autonomous individual. That would depend in large part on what one is tolerant of or that with respect to which one is autonomous.

It is nonetheless tempting in this connection to see liberal principles as implying moral values. Charles Taylor, for example, tells us that:

> To talk of universal, natural, or human rights is to connect respect for human life and integrity with the notion of autonomy. It is to conceive people as active cooperators in establishing and ensuring the respect which is due them. And this expresses a central feature of the modern Western moral outlook (Taylor 1989, 12).

If liberal principles are metanorms, it is not at all permissible, contrary to Taylor, to derive or infer moral norms or values from them, however comfortable the fit may appear. Whether individuals actively cooperate in ensuring the respect that is due to them or passively languish in the hope of that respect is of no official interest to liberalism. Because liberalism is not an equinormative system, no particular set of moral values is dictated by it, although some values may be ruled out and various ranges and sets of values may be more workable than others, depending on circumstance. It is not, in other words, any more an implication of liberalism that one's life be justified according to the dictates of the Protestant work ethic than it is by working for causes in support of gay rights. Liberalism, then, is not designed either to promote, preserve or imply one form of flourishing over another. It is not thereby completely open-ended, however. Liberalism does prevent forms of flourishing which inherently preclude the possibility of the taking place alongside of other diverse forms of flourishing.

In this respect, it may be impossible for any equinormative system which must of necessity treat its norms, however abstract and general they may be, as implying a certain form of life finally to embrace diverse forms of flourishing.[22] This is why it seems more preferable to allow ethical norms to be substantive under the umbrella of metanorms, rather than increasingly to universalize and abstract the norms themselves.

When one does treat liberalism as an equinormative ethical theory one misses an important element of liberalism, that is, its claim about the ill-suitedness or inappropriateness of the state to regulate or promote moral conduct. It makes no difference whether the conduct accords with liberal or conservative, ancient or modern, commercial or pastoral values. Liberalism's true uniqueness as a social doctrine is its endeavour to distinguish ethics from politics in the same way everyone has recognized is the case with respect to theology.

When politics is used to promote particular ethical norms or modes of flourishing, the same mistake would be committed as if it were trying to instil a particular way of understanding God or religion. Liberalism is designed to transcend[23] the competition between equinormative frameworks. The metanormative solution thus calls a halt to the discussion of whether liberalism is an adequate ethical philosophy, by suggesting not only that it is not an ethical philosophy *per se*, but also that it is in the nature of politics to imply one form of flourishing over another, when politics is used as a vehicle for the regulation of ethical conduct. What liberalism presents instead is a doctrine that separates politics from ethics as far as possible without lapsing into either relativism, nihilism or historicism.[24]

In actual practice the debate about these matters today contains a mixture of the normative and metanormative; but the failure to sort out the levels of argument – or even to recognize that there are such levels – is virtually equivalent to denying them. The Taylor passage cited above, for example, clearly indicates how normative levels are simultaneously jumped. The formalistic and abstract requirement to give persons respect in order to establish human rights is structurally different from the respect one may claim because one wishes to secure one's autonomy or be appreciated for one's worth as a person, yet they are treated the same. In the former case (human rights), any norm exists independently of who or what one is in particular, one's narrative history, one's projects, and one's links to the narratives and projects of others. The other sort of norm would be critically dependent on such factors.

The classical (that is, Aristotelian) moral perspective we adopt makes it easy for us to distinguish the morally normative from the metanormative. From the classical perspective, moral conduct, and thus the norms that regulate and define it, has as its object the self-perfection of the individual. The line of demarcation between the normative and metanormative is thus relatively easy to draw, because norms not directly concerned with the self-perfection of particular acting agents would not be 'moral' in our sense of the term.

Therefore, to advance the notion that conditions of equal freedom should obtain among individuals in society might be an important normative social principle, but in itself it does little directly to further the self-perfection of any individual. It is therefore not a moral norm but a metanorm. In this respect it is important to realize that it is not the abstractness or generality that determine metanormativity. Nothing could be more abstract and general than 'do good and avoid evil', but this principle is clearly and directly regulative of personal conduct and is thus an ethical norm.

To some, however, all this may look like begging the question. After all, why should others look at morality this way, especially since morality is more commonly viewed otherwise? We do not think the metanormative distinction *requires* adopting our approach to ethics, although we shall argue further for its appropriateness in what follows. All that is required for the plausibility of the metanormative distinction is the possibility of recognizing a difference between norms which directly regulate moral conduct and those which regulate the conditions under which such conduct could take place.[25]

Two objections come immediately to mind from what we have said: (1) that there is no material difference between liberalism seen as a metanormative system and liberalism seen as a substantive ethical philosophy, because the metanorms will in fact engender the sorts of moral values liberals have traditionally admired; and (2) liberalism would appear to be committed to a strict neutrality due to its apparent amoralist transcendental commitments; and, if not, its deepest theoretical commitments would show after all that it is an equinormative theory like any other, as suggested by the first objection.

Taking the second objection first, the exact connection between liberalism and ethics must await the following sections. The purpose here must be first to remind ourselves that liberalism is not all-inclusive, and second that to say that 'liberalism is neutral' usually means that the right takes priority over the good and liberalism is neutral with respect to forms of the good. While it is mistaken to speak of liberalism as neutral in this sense, if one must talk this way, metanormativity would imply that liberalism is as 'neutral' with respect to the right as it is to the good. We believe, however, that the right and the good cannot be separated and that liberalism is quite compatible with a perspective which denies that separation.[26] It would therefore seem necessary to focus on the first objection.

To answer the first objection fully would take us far beyond what can be accomplished here. Part of our answer occurs in the sections which follow, particularly the one dealing with the conservative communitarian alternative. It must at the same time be recognized that part of the answer also lies in one's view of the relationship between theory and practice. If a traditional society, for example, were to liberalize and allow its members the liberty to pursue their own projects, which turned out to be primarily commercial in nature, would we say the commercial ethic is an implication of the newly adopted doctrine of liberalism, or that commercial pursuits are a natural human endeavour now given the freedom to be exercised?

Ever since Plato and Aristotle it has been believed that the constitutional structure of a regime at least influences, if not creates, the sort of persons one finds in the regime. Liberal regimes would, therefore, create a certain type of 'liberal' personality, while other regimes would do likewise (see, for example, Lerner (1979)). There is undoubtedly truth in this position, though less than would satisfy the vanity of political theorists and philosophers who seem to judge their every notion as fraught with clearly delineated real world applicability.

It is quite possible, by contrast, that the structure of a regime is a function of the people within it. Liberalism does not so much answer the priority question as it does point to an alternative conception. What liberalism implies, being grounded in metanorms rather than moral duties, is that the actual social and cultural implications of its principles remain to be worked out, indeed cannot be developed except in practice.

In this sense liberalism is radically incomplete. If there is such a thing as a 'liberal' personality, it is a severely underdetermined creature. While some would suggest that it is this very underdetermination that subverts the substantive components needed for both communal and personal flourishing, liberalism's retort is that flourishing is not in the end completely written into the structural principles of any regime.[27]

Liberalism's fundamental metanormative structure indicates that ethical conduct and ethical flourishing are to be found elsewhere from politics. The apparent *laissez-faire* posture towards ethics is not a sign of rejection but of recognition that ethics is grounded in practices that cannot be subsumed by the state, or law, or even the formally constituted community. The metanormative structure is simply the recognition of that fact.

We are still left, however, with the question of how we do see the role and nature of ethics in light of this metanormative framework. To deal effectively with that question, we must first understand something of the nature of the approach to ethics we adopt and then how that approach lends itself to a metanormative understanding of liberalism.

3. The Foundations of Liberalism

> For if our virtues did not go forth of us, 'twere all alike
> As if we had them not
> Shakespeare, *Measure for Measure*

NEO-ARISTOTELIAN ETHICS

There is available to liberalism an ethical view that holds the ultimate moral good to be self-perfection, or human flourishing, and that the central intellectual virtue of such a way of life is *phronēsis* (practical wisdom) or prudence. Self-perfection, or flourishing, is in this view: (1) objective, (2) inclusive, (3) individualized, (4) agent-relative, (5) achieved with, and among, others, and (6) self-directed. Despite its classical source, this view is in many respects a newcomer to contemporary ethical discussion. Its combination of interrelated features generates a conception of the human good that has seldom been considered in its own right and certainly not with respect to liberalism. The foregoing features can be outlined as follows.

(1) According to this neo-Aristotelian approach, the end, or *telos*, of human life is the self-perfection of the individual human being. The attainment of this end requires that one live intelligently – that is, with some reflection upon who one is and the circumstances under which one acts. An intelligent life is not primarily a matter of employing intelligence or reason to achieve whatever one happens to desire. Rather this way of life comprehends the ends one needs to desire and thus involves the satisfaction of *right* desire. The satisfaction of right desire in turn constitutes what Aristotle called *eudaimonia* or what many philosophers now call 'human flourishing'.

Self-perfection or human flourishing is thus an objective good or value. Its basic or 'generic' constituents – for example, goods such as knowledge, health, friendship, creative achievement, beauty and pleasure, and virtues such as temperance, courage and justice – are determined by a consideration of human nature. However, the exact character of these goods and role of these virtues are more complicated than generally supposed, because flourishing, as we will see, also depends on *who* as well as *what* we are and is not impersonal. As Aristotle states when criticizing the Platonists, 'of honor, wisdom and pleasure, the accounts are distinct and diverse. The good, therefore, is not some common element answering to one idea' (*Nicomachean Ethics* 1096b 23–25); and as J. L. Ackrill notes:

> [Aristotle] certainly does think that the nature of man – the powers and needs all men have – determines the character that any satisfying human life must have. But since his account of the nature of man is in general terms the corresponding specification of the best life for man is also general. So while his assumption puts some limits on the possible answers to the question 'how shall I live?' it leaves considerable scope for a discussion which takes account of my individual tastes, capacities, and circumstances (Ackrill 1973).

So this interpretation of *eudaimonia* does not entail 'genericism' – that is, the idea that all developmental processes are equivalent across individuals such that individuals come to be little more than repositories of generic endowments. It is also for this reason that the universalist propensities of modern ethical approaches such as utilitarianism and deontologism are avoided.

Furthermore, human flourishing does not consist in the mere possession of the foregoing goods and virtues. Flourishing or living well is not the same as having what it takes to live well. In fact, the basic or generic goods would not exist as *goods* for human beings (or the virtues as virtues) if they were not objects or manifestations of someone's effort. As Aristotle points out, flourishing is an activity (*Nicomachean Ethics*, X, 6). If people are to flourish, they must direct themselves to the attainment and coherent integration of these goods and virtues as best as circumstances will permit. Though self-perfection is an actuality, it is not a static state. *Omne ens perficitur in actu*: flourishing is to be found in action. The appropriateness of certain sorts of action is at least partly determined in light of human nature.

(2) The flourishing of an individual human being is an 'inclusive' (as opposed to 'dominant') end. Instead of there being one single dominant end, which is the only thing of inherent worth and which makes everything else valuable only as a means, flourishing is conceived as being constituted or defined by a number of virtues and goods, each of which is valuable in its own right. Such virtues as integrity, courage and

justice, and such goods as friendship, creative achievement, health and knowledge, for example, are not only productive of flourishing, but expressive, and thus constitutive of it, as well. Thus it is possible for flourishing to be something sought for its own sake (a final end) without it trumping other goods or virtues in the process.

Since human flourishing is not some end that competes with such basic or generic goods as health, creative achievement, friendship and knowledge, it does not dominate and reduce their value to that of mere instruments. It recognizes the inherent worth of each and does not require a pre-set weighting or evaluative pattern of these constitutive ends. Weighting is thus something that is left to the individual to work out for himself, making *phronēsis*, or prudence, central to the achievement and maintenance of human flourishing.

Finally, moral virtues, for example, pride, courage, temperance and integrity, are not merely external means. Desires move us to action: towards objects of apparent benefit and away from objects of apparent harm. Yet our desires can be mistaken. If prudence is to succeed at the task of achieving, maintaining, enjoying and coherently integrating the multiple basic human goods in a manner that will be appropriate for us as the individuals we are, then the use and control of desires – that is, the creation of rational dispositions – is pivotal to flourishing. As rational dispositions, the moral virtues are expressions of human flourishing and are thus valuable in themselves.

(3) Just as our humanity is not some amorphous, undifferentiated universal, so human flourishing is not something abstract and universal. There is no such thing as 'human flourishing'; there is only individual human flourishing (Rasmussen and Den Uyl 1991, 63–4, 89–93). Abstractly considered, we can speak of human flourishing and of basic or generic goods and virtues; but concretely speaking no two cases of human flourishing are the same, and they are not interchangeable. One person's self-perfection is not the same as another's, any more than A's actualization of his potentialities is the same as B's actualization of his. There are individuative as well as generic potentialities, and this makes human fulfilment always something unique.

Individuals are more than loci at which human flourishing becomes spatially individuated. Human flourishing becomes real, achieves determinacy, only when the individual's unique talents, potentialities and circumstances are jointly employed. The human good does not exist apart from the choices and actions of individual human beings, nor does it exist independently of the particular mix of goods that individual human beings need to determine as being appropriate for their circumstances. The human good is individualized and diverse.

Since the specifics of these individually distinctive features of human flourishing are neither implied by, nor included in, an abstract account of human flourishing, the problem of balancing and prioritizing virtues cannot be solved in an *a priori* manner. An abstract consideration of human nature does not tell one what the proper relation should be of one virtue to the other virtues and goods. The proper mixture of the necessary elements of human flourishing cannot be read off human nature like one reads the Recommended Daily Allowances for vitamins and minerals off the back of a cereal box (Den Uyl 1991, 187–223).

Rather this is a task for prudence, and prudence occurs only through individuals confronting the contingent and particular facts of their concrete situation and determining at the time of action what in that situation may be truly good for them. This does not, however, mean either that one can with moral impunity ignore any of the necessary virtues or goods of human flourishing, or that one course of action in the concrete situation is as good as the next. Neither conventionalism nor subjectivism is implied. It simply means that ethical rationalism is false and that pluralism is morally appropriate.

(4) Human flourishing is agent-relative. Flourishing involves an essential reference to the person for whom it is good as part of its description. Abstractly stated, the human flourishing, G_1, for a person, P_1, is agent-relative if and only if its distinctive presence in world W_1 is a basis for P_1 ranking W_1 over W_2, even though G_1 may not be the basis for *any other* person's ranking W_1 over W_2. The best way to understand what this means, however, is to contrast it with its contradictory view, a view that considers basic values and reasons to be agent-neutral and ethics to be impersonal.

An ethical theory is impersonal when all ultimately morally salient values, reasons and rankings are 'agent-neutral'; and they are agent-neutral when they do *not* involve as part of their description an essential reference to the person for whom the value or reason exists or the ranking is correct. 'For any value, reason or ranking V, if a person P_1 is justified in holding V, then so are P_2-P_n under appropriately similar conditions... On an agent-neutral conception it is impossible to weight more heavily or at all, V, simply because it is one's own value' (Den Uyl 1991, 27). Accordingly, when it comes to describing a value, reason or ranking, it does not ethically matter whose value, reason or ranking it is. One person can be substituted for any other.

Using impersonal moral theory to make judgements and guide conduct requires that one consider only values, rankings and reasons that could be held by a rational agent, considered apart from all individuating conditions – be they natural, social or cultural. By adopting the perspective of such a rational agent, a person could never use some value crucial to *who* he or she is as a reason to give extra weight or importance to that value when determining the proper course of action.

For example, in this view the fact that course of action A results in assistance to one's own personal projects, family, friends or country, where non-A does not, provides no ethical reason for preferring A over non-A. These factors could perhaps explain how a person might feel about the situation, but when a person is acting from a properly moral perspective, considerations of a personal nature are irrelevant and should not weigh more heavily. The individual *qua individual* is not important in an impersonal moral theory The individual only represents a locus at which good is achieved or right conduct performed.

An impersonal ethics and an agent-neutral conception of basic values and reasons are, according to the version of neo-Aristotelian virtue ethics advanced here, unsound from root to branch. Particular and contingent facts are ethically important, and though some of these facts may be more important than others in achieving human moral well-being, this cannot be determined from the armchair. There is no great divide in the nature of things between the facts that can and cannot be ethically relevant.

Certainly there is no basis for holding that individual, social and cultural differences among people are ethically irrelevant. To the contrary, they are highly significant. Furthermore, there is no foundation to moral impersonalism's claim that values central to one's very conception of oneself may not be valued more than less central values. The fact that a value is crucial to some person's deeply held personal project, but to no one else's, does not make it morally irrelevant. In fact just the opposite is true. Such value deserves even more careful consideration, precisely because of its relation to oneself.

Further, it is fundamentally erroneous to assume that abstract ethical principles alone can determine the proper course of conduct. Such ethical rationalism fails to grasp that ethics is practical and contingent, and particular facts – which abstract ethical principles cannot *explicitly* capture and thus cannot be discovered *a priori* – are crucial to determining what ought to be done. Thus contrary to much of modern and contemporary ethics, not all morally proper forms of conduct need be universalizable.

In addition, and what is even more important, the central intellectual virtue of ethics is *phronēsis*. This is not, as we have already suggested, merely means–end reasoning, however. Rather it is the ability of the individual at the time of action to discern in particular and contingent circumstances just what is morally required. Without such a virtue, morality can only deal with ethical abstractions and not real questions of personal conduct and human life.

Finally, it should be emphasized that agent-relativity of values does not preclude them from being objectively and inherently valuable. That something is only valuable relative to some person does not necessarily make its value merely a matter of that person's attitude towards it – that is, merely something desired, wanted or chosen. Instead it can be valued, wanted, chosen because of what it objectively is. Also something can be an objective value that is an end in itself and nonetheless agent-relative. The constituent goods and virtues of human flourishing are, for example, inherently valuable but essentially related to the lives of individual human beings. But even more to the point, something can be not only agent-relative and *an* end in itself, but also *the* ultimate end or value, human flourishing itself.

As such, human flourishing is not something that competes with the good of individual human beings, but is the very fulfilment or flourishing of their lives. The ultimate objective and inherent value, the human *telos*,[28] just is their self-perfection or human flourishing. There is no flourishing-at-large. Flourishing is always the good-for-some-person. Thus it is perfectly consistent for the flourishing of individual human beings to be an objective and inherent value *and* essentially related to individual persons.[29] A commitment to the objectivity and inherent value of human flourishing does not imply that its value is something that can be exchanged or promoted regardless of whose flourishing it is. Agent-neutrality is not necessary for upholding value-objectivity or choice-worthiness.

(5) Human beings cannot flourish in isolation. Our fulfilment demands a life with others. We are social beings, not in the Hobbesian sense of merely needing others to get what we want because we are powerless on our own, but in the sense that our very maturation as human beings requires others. Indeed a significant part of our potentialities is other-oriented. This need to live with others must be expressed in some form but, considered abstractly, it can be expressed in any.

The specific form in which human sociality is expressed can be termed an 'exclusive relationship'. Exclusive relationships cover a continuum of relations – everything from close friends and confidants to business and work relations to mere acquaintances – but they all involve a principle of selectivity on the part of the participants in the relationship. It is through exclusive relationships that various types of groups, communities and even cultures are formed.

Since human flourishing is individualized, however, the way or manner in which the need for sociality is expressed is not limited to some select pool or group of humans. Though nearly everyone starts life within a family, a community, a society and a culture, this does not mean that one must be confined to only those relationships that constitute one's family, community, society or culture. The forms of human sociality are not necessarily limited or closed to any human being. Human sociality can involve the exploration of relationships with new and different people and varied ways of living, working and thinking.

This open-ended character of human sociality leads us to describe relationships that might develop as being 'non-exclusive'. No principle of selectivity is involved, for we are noting that human sociality, prior to a person's choice and selection, imposes no limitation regarding with whom and under what circumstances one may have a relationship. Further, non-exclusive relationships often provide the wider context in which exclusive relationships are formed, because many, if not most, exclusive relationships come about only because there was first a non-exclusive relationship. Thus human beings are social animals in the sense that, though there must be some set of exclusive relations through which one expresses one's sociality, there is no *a priori* exclusion of anyone from participation in those relations.

(6) The view of human flourishing that has been presented so far could correctly be described as entailing a 'pluralistic realism' regarding human values. The human good is something real, *and* it is individualized and diverse. Further, it is agent-relative. But there is something at the concrete level that is common to all the various forms of flourishing and, indeed, must be. As noted earlier, human flourishing is not only an actuality, it is an activity. It is an activity according to virtue, and the central virtue of human flourishing is practical wisdom – that is, *phronēsis*.

Yet practical wisdom is not passive. It is fundamentally a self-directed activity. The functioning of one's reason or intelligence, regardless of one's level of learning or degree of ability, is not something that occurs automatically. It requires individual effort. Effort is needed to initiate and maintain thought. In fact, effort is needed for reason to discover the goods and virtues of human flourishing as well as to achieve and implement them.

It is crucial to grasp that human reason (or intelligence) and self-directedness (or what might be loosely called 'autonomy') are not two separate faculties but distinct aspects of the same act. The act of reason, of exercising one's intellectual capacity, is an exercise of self-direction, and the act of self-direction is an exercise of reason. Thus self-perfection suitably describes the nature of the human good, because not only is *the object of perfection* the individual human being, *the agent of perfection* is the individual human being as well. Together they characterize the very nature of human flourishing.

Self-directedness is, then, both a necessary condition for self-perfection and a feature of all self-perfecting acts at whatever level of achievement or specificity. Yet this is another way of saying that the phenomenon of a volitional consciousness[30] is both a necessary condition for, and an operating condition of, the pursuit and achievement of self-perfection. The relationship between self-directedness and self-perfection can be summarized as follows: the absence of self-directedness implies the absence of self-perfection, although the absence of self-perfection does not imply the absence of self-directedness; nor does the presence of self-directedness imply the presence of self-perfection (but the presence of self-perfection does imply the presence of self-directedness).

None of this, of course, is to say that any choice one makes is as good as the next, but simply that the choice must be one's own and must involve considerations that are unique to the individual. One person's moral well-being cannot be exchanged with another's. The good-for-me is not, and cannot be, the good-for-you. Human moral well-being, then, is something objective, self-directed and highly personal. It is not abstract, collectively determined or impersonal.

While the foregoing account may outline the type of ethical framework we employ in thinking about liberalism, the metanormative structure of liberalism is first defined by individual rights. It is, therefore, the connection between this sort of general ethical structure and liberalism that interests us here. This connection is made through the language and medium of rights. A two-fold problem thus presents itself: (1) how are rights connected to this neo-Aristotelian ethical framework, and (2) how can rights be so connected and still imply a liberal social order when the opposite is more commonly asserted? We take it as given that the presence of the concept of rights is not *ipso facto* a sign that one is speaking of a liberal order.[31]

RIGHTS, ETHICS AND LIBERALISM

> The most intractable struggles, political liberalism assumes, are confessedly for the sake of highest things.
>
> John Rawls, *Political Liberalism*

The individualized character of human flourishing creates a need for another type of ethical principle, once we realize that human moral well-being is only achieved with and among others. Sociality is an inherent feature of our flourishing. We can only flourish with and among others. This does not mean, however, that the particular social and cultural forms in which our sociality is currently manifested exhaust the forms that can and should be taken. Our interpersonal relationships are not limited to only those with whom we share values. They are open-ended. The interpersonal dimension of human flourishing allows for an openness to strangers and human beings in general. It needs to be possible for persons in pursuit of their self-perfection to have relationships with others with whom no common values are yet shared and where all that is known is that one is dealing with another human being.

If what has been said about our sociality is true, however, there is a difficulty. If one person's particular form of well-being is different from another's and may even conflict with it, and if persons can prevent others from being self-directed, then certain interpersonal standards need to be adopted if individuals are to flourish in their diverse ways among others. Ordinary prescriptive norms would seem to fly in the face of diversity by requiring conduct to be of a specific form or type. An ethical principle is therefore needed whose primary function is not guiding a person to well-being or right conduct, but providing a standard that favours no particular form of human flourishing, while at the same time providing a context for its diverse forms. Such a principle would seek to protect what is necessary to the possibility of each and every person's finding fulfilment, regardless of the determinate form virtues and human goods take in their lives. This sort of concept we describe as being a metanormative principle, and we would claim that basic rights, at least in liberal orders, are metanormative principles.

The problem of rights is a problem in liberalism itself, since rights are the language through which liberalism is spoken. In the simplest terms, the problem is how does one both recognize and provide for plurality in human flourishing and also simultaneously give a moral basis to one's civil order? Is not the choice one of abandoning morality for plurality or plurality for morality, or perhaps maximizing one against the other? Morality, in other words, would seem to call for a certain uniformity of conduct. Since people have diverse interests, values and conceptions of the good, uniformity would seem to come at the expense of diversity. Liberal political theory, then, must address the issue of pluralism, and this means more than acknowledging the existence of many views of the human good. It means grasping that the human good is plural and complex, not monistic and simple, and hence that pluralism is morally appropriate.

Traditionally, liberal rights theorists have tended to drift in the direction of solving the morality/plurality problem by upholding the primacy of the right over the good and viewing rights as totally independent of any consideration of human flourishing, consequences, circumstances, values, goals or interests. Rights so conceived have been generally construed as expressions of an impersonalist moral theory. We have, however, already seen some of the difficulties of such a theory and do not think that its ethical rationalism, particularly as illustrated in the use of the principle of universalizability, can be sustained. There are, however, two additional points to consider in this connection.

First, appealing to the principle of universalizability will not suffice as a solution to liberalism's problem of reconciling diverse forms of flourishing with moral uniformity, because the principle of universalizability does not: (a) solve value conflicts, or (b) prove that the human good is truly the same for each of us.

Just as the production of Fred's good is a reason for Fred to act, so is the production of Mary's good a reason for Mary to act. Fred cannot claim that his good provides him with a legitimate reason to act without acknowledging that Mary's good provides her with a legitimate reason to act. Agent-relative values thus can be universalized in this sense, but this form of universalization is obviously not sufficient to establish *common* values or a reason for other-regarding conduct among persons. The universalization of agent-relative goods does not show Fred's good to be Mary's good, or the production of Mary's good as providing Fred with a reason for action, or vice versa. Thus if Fred's good should conflict with Mary's, universalizability could not provide a way out of this conflict.

There is also a widespread tendency to confuse an objective value with universality. But this is an error. As Henry B. Veatch has observed:

If the good of X is indeed but the actuality of X's potentialities, then this is a fact that not just X needs to recognize, but anyone and everyone else as well. And yet given the mere fact that a certain good needs to be recognized, and recognized universally, to be the good of X, it by no means follows that X's good must be taken to be Y's good as well, any more than the actuality or perfection or fulfillment of X needs to be recognized as being the actuality or perfection of Y as well (Veatch 1990, 194).

It is not true that some thing or activity, call it G or G-ing, cannot be objectively good for anyone unless it is so for everyone.

Second, there is a fundamental difficulty that stands in the way of anyone who uses impersonal moral theory. The difficulty is simply that nothing can be said in reply to those who ask why they ought to be moral in an impersonal sense. Using 'ought' does not require the adoption of an agent-neutral view of values, reasons and rankings, because there is an agent-relative sense of 'ought' that can be used. There is, in other words, no self-contradiction in asking why one 'ought' to adopt an impersonal moral theory (and we mean here why it would be good, worthy or appropriate to do so). And since there is, *by definition*, no way that an impersonal moral theory can give a reason that is not an agent-neutral reason, it cannot provide an agent-relative reason why one should be moral in an impersonal sense. Any rights theory based on such an impersonal view of morality can provide neither reason nor motivation for moral conduct. This is a major, possibly insuperable, difficulty faced by anyone who bases the right to liberty on impersonal moral theory.

It is not necessary either to use impersonalist moral theory or adopt ethical rationalism in order to find a place for rights or a solution to liberalism's problem. The notion of human flourishing outlined above allows for the development of a conception of rights that is not reducible to other moral concepts, while at the same time being grounded in a personalist setting. We can best understand this by appreciating further the central role of self-directedness.

Self-direction is the exercise of practical reason, and this act of reason is present in every version of human flourishing, because it is that through which the individualization of human flourishing occurs. Without self-direction human flourishing would not be human flourishing. The protection of self-direction does not favour any form of human flourishing over any other, because it is the act of exercising practical reason that is being protected, not the achievement of its object. Further, self-direction is not amoral. Simply stated, one needs to exercise reason. It is good to do so; one ought to do so. Before ever addressing questions about what one should reason about or how one should conduct oneself, an analysis of the nature of human flourishing reveals that one should think and act for oneself, that is, be self-directed.

It is, of course, seldom the case that one ever confronts the issue of exercising one's reason or intelligence just as such. We reason about, pass judgement on and give priority to, some issue or object; and so this abstract point about the fundamental importance of self-direction to the nature of human flourishing is rarely faced in ethical conduct. Yet since neither speculative nor practical reason simply occurs 'naturally', the primary importance of self-direction becomes more apparent when abstracted from specific contexts and applied to politics.

The nature of political life forces us into the abstraction because we must look to that which applies to all. Since self-direction is not only common to, but required by, all forms of human flourishing (or their pursuit), regardless of the level of achievement or specificity, it is that unique feature of human flourishing that everyone must first have protected in the concrete instance if they are to flourish. A principle that provides for protection of self-directedness will not favour any particular form of flourishing, but will still allow the possibility that everyone can flourish.

We should not move too quickly here, however. Since the protection of self-directedness is central to the development of our theory of rights and thus crucial to our solution to liberalism's problem, the exact nature of the relation of self-directedness to practical wisdom, as well as to the other virtues and goods of human flourishing, bears repeating: practical wisdom cannot be practical wisdom without self-direction; and no constituent virtue or good of human flourishing can be such a virtue or good without practical wisdom. Thus self-directedness is both central and necessary to the very nature of human flourishing. It is the only feature of human flourishing common to all acts of self-perfection and peculiar to each. It expresses the fundamental core of human flourishing. Self-directedness is the only feature of human flourishing upon which to base a solution to liberalism's problem, because: (1) it is the only feature in which each and every person in the concrete situation has a necessary stake; and (2) it is the only feature of human flourishing whose protection is consistent with the diverse forms of human flourishing.

Rights are concerned with protecting the condition under which moral conduct – for us, self-perfection – can occur. Obviously, securing the basic condition for the possibility of self-perfection is logically prior to, and distinct from, the actual pursuit of self-perfection. But securing the condition must be understood as essentially 'negative'. This is because self-directedness does not imply or guarantee self-perfection and because one person's self-perfection is not exchangeable with another's. In other words, we are *not* trying with our theory of rights *directly* and *positively* to secure self-perfection, but rather to protect, and thus prevent encroachments upon, the condition under which self-perfection can exist. Our aim is thus to protect the possibility of self-perfection, but only through seeking to protect the possibility of self-directedness.

Because we are not directly concerned with the promotion of self-perfection itself, but only the condition for it, it is not the consequences *per se* that will determine encroachment. What is decisive is whether the action taken by one person towards another secures that other's consent or is otherwise in accord with that other's choices. One may violate another's rights and produce a chain of events that leads to consequences that could be said to be to that other's apparent or real benefit, or one may not violate another's rights and produce a chain of events that leads to one's apparent or real detriment.

Yet since the purpose here is to structure a political principle that protects the condition for self-perfection rather than the production of self-perfection itself, the consequences of actions are of little importance (except insofar as they threaten the condition that rights were designed to protect in the first place). Our concern here is not with how acts will turn out, but rather with setting the appropriate foundation for the taking of any action in the first place.

Thus though 'rights' are ethical principles, they are a special kind. Their function is *not* to provide persons with direct guidance in achieving good or conducting themselves properly. They are not normative principles, but are instead *metanormative* principles: that is to say, they concern the preconditions of moral conduct and arise because of the need to establish, interpret and evaluate political/legal contexts so that individuals can achieve their moral well-being in consort with others. Since the single most common and threatening encroachment upon self-directedness is the initiation of physical force by one person (or group) against another, rights – to borrow a phrase from Robert Nozick (Nozick 1974, 57) – allow 'moral space' to each person – a sphere of freedom whereby self-directed activities can be exercised without being trampled by others, or vice versa. Such is the right to liberty.

On the basis of what we have said so far, it should be clear that the only types of rights we possess that are consistent with protecting the condition necessary for the pursuit of any form of self-perfection are *rights of equal liberty*, where no one is allowed to take an action towards another that undermines the conditions required by that other's self-directedness. The basic rights we possess are thus principles of mutual non-interference. This translates socially into a principle of maximum compossible and equal freedom for all.[32]

The freedom must be equal, in the sense that it must allow for the possibility of diverse modes of flourishing and, therefore, must not be structurally biased in favour of some forms of flourishing over others. The freedom must be compossible, in the sense that the exercise of self-directed activity by one person must not encroach upon that of another. Thus a theory of rights that protects persons' self-directedness can be used to create a political/legal order that will not necessarily require that the flourishing of any person or group be sacrificed to any other.

If rights are metanormative principles that concern the basic structure of a civil order, how can they be said to provide any moral guidance to individuals? If one person murders another, for example, does not the one violate the other's rights, and is it not appropriate to say that one ought not to do such a thing? And if one is told not to do such a thing, is it not the case that an ordinary moral norm has been provided and that one is under an ordinary obligation to refrain from such actions? Further, would not one have this obligation irrespective of the presence of the state (as Locke suggested) in the sense of there being a *natural* right on the part of each of us against such actions?

At the risk of some repetition, it is important that we be clear about the status of rights in answering these questions. Rights are not normative principles in the sense of guiding us towards the achievement of our self-perfection. And contrary to appearances, they are not ordinary interpersonal normative principles either. Rights express the moral principle that must obtain if we are to reconcile our natural sociality with diverse forms of flourishing. We need, in other words, social life, but we also need to succeed as individuals approaching a particular form of flourishing. Norms which specify how to live among others and the obligations one is likely to incur in such a life are one thing; norms which define the setting for such interactions and obligations are quite another. The 'obligations' one has to another in the latter case are due to a shared need to act in an orderly social/political context.

The obligations one has in the former case are a function of what is needed to live well and cannot be generated apart from the particular actions, context, culture, traditions, intentions and practices in which one finds oneself acting. These actions and contexts call forth evaluative norms by which success, propriety and merit can be measured and judged in particular cases. Metanorms (rights) are not, however, *called* upon by the progress of a culture or individual, but rather *depended* upon. From our perspective, then, it is likely that something multifaceted is taking place in the example where one person 'murders' another.

At one level, the person's 'natural' rights are being violated. That is, by our nature as social and diverse creatures, the action in question is not suited to setting an appropriate context for human flourishing; nor does it seem likely that it will be conducive to actual progress towards flourishing itself. The latter aspect, however, is very much tied up with moral elements besides those needed to set a basic context (for example, considerations of country, family, friends, fellow citizens, the law, and so on). The moral norms at work here presuppose an environment where moral conduct is possible. In addition, these norms specify the sort of conduct that will be considered appropriate or worthy or justified. In the case of basic 'natural' rights, by contrast, the obligations are not so much to individuals *per se*, because such rights are fashioned independently of particular practices, circumstances and agents. The norms for basic rights apply to no one in particular and to everyone equally at all times.

In this respect, the standard sort of 'state of nature' analysis may actually confuse the issue, rather than help clarify it. We are tempted to abandon the social and ask what one would be obligated to do if there were no law, society, culture or political authority around one to define any duties. If one person does injury to another in such a state of nature, it looks as though only one level of obligation is present, since by definition there is no particular society or political context to offer any other. The normative and metanormative seem to collapse into the single duty of respecting another's natural rights. Securing the setting (non-interference), in other words, appears to be the same as undertaking appropriate conduct itself.

It may be, of course, that we are obliged to take some actions because of their necessary connection to achieving an appropriate context for ourselves and others. In this respect, metanormative obligations would be no less important and binding than any others. But injuring another in a state of nature recalls more than simply signifying conduct in violation of actions needed to secure and maintain the appropriate conditions for flourishing in a social context. Such an action calls forth a whole normative tradition about the proper treatment of persons. This is fine provided we distinguish the metanormative from the normative elements. But a state of nature analysis does not allow us to do this well. Murder, for example, is usually defined by particular social, political and cultural contexts. To abandon these for the state of nature gives us the illusion that society is only marginally relevant to a determination of what will count as murder and that *all* norms are context-setting norms (for example, rights).

Individuals must, therefore, respect the natural rights of others not because they will be better persons or be 'doing the right thing', but because their very ability to act *jointly* as persons depends upon securing the conditions necessary for such action. A state of nature approach may help us identify those metanormative principles, but it does next to nothing towards generating the normative rules or obligations that are equally necessary for a life of moral excellence. For that, one needs actors in concrete social settings. Consequently, if the metanormative conditions are threatened or destroyed (for example, by a Nazi takeover), the language of natural rights would not be inappropriate. It is both right by nature (that is, by appeal to human nature) that a certain context for human action be secured and a *right* (in the sense of a claim about a certain sort of treatment due one) that one not be treated in certain ways *in light of what is necessary to secure that context*.[33]

What one cannot do is pretend that when one refers to 'murder' in a state of nature the reference is devoid of any conception of social life. The full horror of a violation of someone's 'natural rights' comes precisely because one has an idea of how human beings should treat each other, both in civilized society and with respect to what it takes to establish such a society. Our point here, then, is that state of nature analysis is usually parasitical upon civilization.[34] No one could disseminate Hobbes's rules for peace (as found in Chapter XV of *Leviathan*) who was unfamiliar with civilized life.[35]

Part of the problem we are addressing arises because we are under the illusion that we can imagine ourselves as asocial beings. Asocial beings might worry about why they have any obligations at all towards others. One would then have to conjure up arguments as to why it might be in someone's interest to respect another's 'rights'. Social beings, by contrast, would never have a radical worry about why they should concern themselves with others because they come, as it were, already concerned.

A social being, in other words, is not likely to wonder why he or she should be concerned about setting the context for their own flourishing. We do not deny the heuristic value of state of nature thought experiments, but, with Aristotle, we do deny their value as a fundamental platform for moral analysis and understanding. In any case, liberalism *per se* does not require the radicalized version of such an approach (where morality itself is generated by a 'contract'); and it is arguable in most cases whether the fathers of liberalism (for example, Locke and even Hobbes) saw the moral as exclusively derived from the state of nature.

Liberalism's problem, in any case, can be put another way: how can liberalism retain any connection to a substantive moral philosophy and demand so little politically? We need not repeat the account given in chapter 2 in response to this question. All that needs to be noted here is that the preceding theory retains a strong connection with a substantive moral position (the Aristotelian) without lapsing into a moralistic politics. Liberalism can not afford to close off the path to a rich moral posture any more than it can still remain a liberalism while politically dictating a particular form of moral living. There are those, however, who claim that liberalism cannot succeed either in remaining uncommitted to particular forms of flourishing or to a substantive ethics. To such issues we now turn.

4. Analyses and Objections

THE CHALLENGE OF LIBERAL COMMUNITARIANISM

> Recognition of a pluralism of forms of human flourishing, each objective, of which only some can exist in a liberal regime, destroys the authority of liberalism as a universal, trans-historical and cross-cultural ideal.
> John Gray, *Post-Liberalism: Studies in Political Thought*

John Gray is a post-liberal, for he does not think that it is any longer plausible to claim that liberty is a universal human value. He is also a communitarian, because he thinks that the attempt to find a *theoretical* basis upon which to ground liberal political philosophy is doomed. According to Gray, the liberal form of civil society only survives and prospers because of our commitment to it. This commitment is manifested in the realm of practice and is not fully theorizable. Thus when it comes to determining the meaning, scope and validity of liberty, neither political nor jurisprudential theory is adequate. Such determinations are provided only by a form of political reasoning that is essentially circumstantial. Consequently, the political has primacy over the theoretical and legal. Further, though Gray is sympathetic to aspects of neo-Aristotelian virtue ethics, he is quite sure that such an ethics cannot employ a meaningful notion of perfection as an adequate foundation for liberalism's claim that liberty is a universal political value.

The basic reason for Gray's abandoning liberalism, adopting a communitarian perspective and rejecting the very idea of perfection can be summed up in two words: value pluralism. Or maybe it would be more accurate to say, Gray's *understanding* of value pluralism, for it will be with his understanding of it and with what he claims flows from it that we will take issue.

Gray makes it very clear that value pluralism is not ethical relativism, be it in either conventionalist or subjectivist form. Nor is it moral scepticism. Rather it is a species of moral realism that Gray calls 'objective pluralism'. Thus there is moral knowledge; there are real goods, values and excellences. However, they are diverse, irreducible and incommensurable – with nothing that necessarily unifies them. Indeed they are so radically plural that rational choice is limited. We often face moral dilemmas for which there is no way to avoid doing wrong or suffering an irreplaceable loss of value.

As a result of this pluralism, liberal rights are not uniquely legitimate for all human beings. There have been human beings who have flourished in regimes that are not liberal, and there are forms of human flourishing that are driven out by liberal regimes. Overall, there is no single, determinate way of life that is right or best for all human beings. Thus Gray concludes that liberalism cannot use the notion of perfection to justify its claim to offer liberty as a universal political value.

Gray's claims and charges are complex. We need to be very clear about exactly what he means by 'objective pluralism'. The following two statements by Gray, the first from 'What is dead and what is living in liberalism?' (Gray 1993, 291) and the second from 'Agonistic liberalism' (Gray 1995, 116) are worth quoting at length:

> *Objective pluralism* of this sort affirms that ultimate values are knowable; that they are many; that they often conflict and are uncombinable, and that there is no overarching standard whereby their claims are rationally arbitrable: there are conflicts among the incommensurables. The diversity of ultimate values, great as it is, is not infinite; it is bounded by the limits of human nature. 'Incompatible these ends may be; but their variety cannot be unlimited, for the nature of men, however various and subject to change, must possess some generic character if it is to be called human at all.' This pluralism, bounded as it is, may come in several varieties, and may operate at several levels. Within the moral code of a particular culture, there may be lacunae that generate dilemmas which neither the code itself, nor the practical reasonings of the individual, can resolve. Hence are generated the radical or tragic courses among competing evils or rival excellences, in which whatever is chosen entails some great loss or irreparable wrong ... Also, there is the variety of pluralism which illuminates value conflict, not within cultures or individuals, but between cultures or whole forms of life having incommensurable values as constitutive elements. These varieties of pluralism may interpenetrate one another, especially when (as in the late modern world) cultures and forms of life have come to interact deeply with one another, are no longer easily individuated, so that many individuals find themselves (in Fulke Greville's phrase) 'suckled on the milk of many nurses', formed by many distinct cultural traditions.

> [T]here is an irreducible diversity of ultimate values (goods, excellences, options, reasons for action, and so forth) and that when these values come

> into conflict or competition with one another there is no overarching standard or principle, no common currency or measure, whereby such conflicts can be arbitrated or resolved ... Value pluralism imposes limits on rational choice that are subversive of most standard moral theories, not merely utilitarianism, and it has deeply subversive implications for all the traditional varieties of liberal theory. In particular, it has the implications that we often face practical and moral dilemmas in which reason leaves us in the lurch and in which, whatever we do, there is a wrong or irreplaceable loss of value. Value pluralism implies that the fundamental rights or basic liberties of liberal thought cannot be insulated from conflicts among incommensurables.

We can note right away that objective pluralism carries with it a rejection of two classical ethical beliefs: (1) that the human good is a single, common form, a monistic whole, with no intrinsic constituents that are irreducible and valuable in themselves; and (2) that all the goods and virtues that constitute the human good are in principle harmonious, with only lack of sufficient knowledge or moral commitment preventing their unification. Instead the goods and virtues that constitute human flourishing are often incompatible, and there is no overarching standard whereby conflicts among these goods or combinations of them might be solved – that is, these goods (or combinations of them) are incomparable and incommensurable. They are incomparable because there is no relevant respect in which one may be judged in relation to another, and they are incommensurable because there is no scale of reference in which one may be judged higher or lower than the other. Thus there are many irreducible values, which are valuable in themselves, that are incompatible, incomparable and incommensurable.

Incommensurability is, however, even more extensive. Values are integrated within cultural and social wholes; they belong to the form of life which generates them. Thus incommensurability can occur not only within cultures and individuals, but also, 'when goods, virtues, and excellences are elements in whole ways of life that depend on uncombinable social structures as their matrices' (Gray 1995, 118). Incommensurability can thus be found between cultures or whole forms of life. This form of incomparability and lack of a common measure is possibly the fullest expression of the value-conflict generated by objective pluralism.

Gray holds that objective pluralism is destructive of the very idea of perfection. It:

> strikes a death-blow at the classical foundation of our culture, expressed not only in Plato and Aristotle, but in the Stoic idea of the *logos* and in

Aquinas's conception of a world order that was rational and moral in essence, even as it was the creation of the Deity, one of the central attributes of which was perfection (Gray 1993, 291).

It is not merely that human beings cannot achieve perfection; rather it is that the very idea of perfection makes no sense.

'Human flourishing' remains, however, valid for Gray, because it is reconceptualized. It still consists of more than mere subjective preferences or desires and encompasses the use of human capacities that are reflectively judged as worthwhile, but it is now non-hierarchical. Incommensurability precludes objective rankings or weightings of ultimate values. No one form of life – say, the life of rational inquiry, of contemplation, of wealth creation, of prayer or selfless devotion to others – is the best for the human species. The virtues are not necessarily unified; and the conflicts among goods or excellences, many of which are neither comparable nor commensurable, reveal that there is no uniquely rational combination of them. Indeed the variety of incommensurable forms of human flourishing is so radically underdetermined by the generic powers and capacities of human beings that it must be frankly acknowledged that human beings are partly self-creators over time and in history.

Gray takes this objective pluralism as having fatal implications for liberal political philosophy (Gray 1995, 119–120). Two of these we need to consider here. First, the structure of basic liberties or the content of fundamental rights is massively underdetermined by any general ethical theory. Gray agrees with Raz that rights are not foundational. Rather they are intermediaries between claims about human interests that are vital to human flourishing and claims about what obligations are reasonable to impose upon others in respect of those interests; and since there are different forms of human flourishing which spawn different judgements of human interest and, thereby, of the weights or values of rival liberties, there is no uniquely rational way to solve conflicts of liberties. Rights claims cannot be sealed off from the effects of objective pluralism.

Second, hard cases abound because of the conflicts among rights and liberties that express incompatible, incomparable and incommensurable values. These hard cases, which are undecidable by reasoning from any overarching theory, are the rule, not the exception. Accordingly no right answers to hard cases about what constitutes restraint of liberty can be provided at the theoretical or jurisprudential level. Rather answers can only be provided at the political level through a form of practical reasoning in which no step is necessitated.

Politics is, therefore, an autonomous sphere of practical life with primacy over the theoretical and legal:

> This way of treating questions about the restraint of liberty appeals to a conception of political life as a sphere of practical reasoning whose *telos* is a *modus vivendi*, to a conception of the political in which it is a domain devoted to the pursuit not of truth but of peace – an approach that has the authority of Hobbes (Gray 1995, 122).

However, the thinker whose conception of political life best conforms to Gray's position is not Hobbes, for Hobbes is too much of a rationalist. Rather, as Gray notes, it is Machiavelli. It is Machiavelli's cardinal achievement, according to Isaiah Berlin, to have recognized that ends, 'equally ultimate, equally sacred, may contradict each other; [and] that entire systems of value may come into collision without possibility of rational arbitration, and not merely in exceptional circumstances, as a result of abnormality or accident or error ... but as part of the normal human situation' (Berlin 1982, 74–5).

Though there is more that can be said about Gray's own version of liberalism, our first concern is with his account of objective pluralism and its implications for a self-perfectionist virtue ethics and the view of rights that we base upon it. Beginning with Gray's account of objective pluralism, we can see many features that coincide with our view of human flourishing.

These are as follows: that human flourishing is not a single dominant good or excellence – a monistic whole – but is, instead, composed of many goods and excellences that are valuable in themselves; that there is no one single combination or weighting of goods and excellences that can be 'read off' an abstract account of human flourishing and taken as the best for human beings (the first classical view mentioned above); that an ethical rationalism that tries to determine *a priori* for someone what is good and ought to be done in the concrete situation is inadequate; that the number and variety of the goods and excellences that constitute human flourishing are not infinite; that there is generic content to the notion of human flourishing which, though it must be fleshed out by individual and cultural considerations, is not merely a place-holder whose content is determined entirely by communal practices and traditions; and, accordingly, that ethical relativism – be it subjectivism or conventionalism – is not true.

The major difference between objective pluralism and our conception of human flourishing concerns the implications of agent-relativity. Gray believes that if one holds an agent-relative conception of basic or ultimate value, then such value can be neither inherent nor objective. Agent-relativity requires denying inherent value to various forms of human flourishing and endorsing ethical relativism (Gray 1993, 309). Thus, perfection cannot be, as it is for us, individualized, agent-relative, and self-directed. Rather, it has to be universal, agent-neutral, and cosmic. We hold, for reasons already presented, that agent-relativity does not require denying inherent value or objectivity to versions of human flourishing. Nor does it imply ethical relativism. This difference is crucial, because it goes to the very heart of Gray's claim that the idea of perfection is incoherent.

If perfection is agent-relative and individualized (the self-directed character of perfection will be discussed later), then Gray's claim that versions of human flourishing (that is, combinations, patterns or weightings of generic goods and virtues) are incomparable and incommensurable is either pointless or not the problem he supposes it to be for ethics – at least, that is, for the virtue ethics we have been advancing. Thus Gray's attack on the concept of perfection is undercut. We will examine this issue in some detail.

Versions of human flourishing are incommensurable when two conditions are fulfilled: when neither is better than the other, that is, they are incomparable, and when another version of human flourishing is better than one of the other two valuable forms of flourishing but not better than the other. This is a breakdown in transitivity in practical reasoning and the basis for Gray's claim that objective pluralism destroys the very idea of perfection: 'Incommensurability ... is the radical denial of the very meaning of perfection' (Gray 1995, 117). However, if we are to speak of versions of flourishing that are more or less valuable, we must consider the question: 'valuable to whom?' We cannot assess the significance of Gray's claims unless we first answer this question.

If we assume that human flourishing involves no essential reference to the person for whom it is valuable as part of its description, and that individuals are no more than loci for instantiations of human flourishing, then pointing out that there are versions of human flourishing that are incomparable and incommensurable has a point. It shows the error in believing that practical reasoning requires everyone in the same situation to hold the same valuation, reason and ranking regarding a certain version of human flourishing. It also shows the error of 'genericism' – that is, the error of assuming that all developmental processes are equivalent across individuals, such that individuals come to be little more than repositories of generic endowments.

Incomparability creates a problem, and incommensurability arises for versions of flourishing only if it is assumed that the individual is ethically irrelevant to determining the value and character of a given form of flourishing. There is a breakdown in transitivity in practical reasoning primarily because it is assumed that the aim of ethics is to provide a set of specific, impersonal, equally suited rules of conduct for everyone instead of providing individual guidance. Incomparability and incommensurability do, indeed, destroy the idea of perfection for those who see flourishing as a manifestation of a universal order or cosmic *logos*.

But if perfection is realized in an agent-relative, individualized, self-directed manner, then the destruction Gray sees as following in the wake of incomparable and incommensurable versions of human flourishing is not so evident. Indeed, if human flourishing involves an essential reference to the person for whom it is valuable as part of its description, and if the individual provides relevant content to the character of human flourishing, then pointing out that there are versions of human flourishing that are incomparable creates no problem. This is entailed by the claim that human flourishing is both agent-relative and individualized. There is no version of human flourishing that is better or more valuable than some other version *period*; versions of human flourishing are only valuable *relative* to some person. Thus if we are careful not to confuse abstractions with realities, we see that one person's version of human flourishing is not strictly comparable with another's. The pursuit and achievement of human flourishing is not a race in which everyone competes for the same prize; there is no unified race, with a single standard for swiftness. Instead each person must himself run according to a standard of swiftness that is linked to that person's successful completion of a race against *dysdaimonia* (unhappiness or lack of flourishing).

Could a person, after considering what we call his 'nexus' – that is, the set of circumstances, talents, endowments, interests, beliefs and histories that descriptively characterizes him and which he brings to any new situation – discover that there is more than one combination, pattern or weighting of generic goods and virtues that are equally valuable for him? This is possible. Yet it does not follow that there are no parameters or limits on choice. Practical reason is not destroyed. A consideration of generic goods and virtues imposes some limitations. For example, could anyone reasonably claim to flourish if they neither had nor sought friends; had no integrity, courage or justice; let their passions run wild or repressed all emotions; or cared nothing for knowledge, reason, consistency or truth? Is not Socrates dissatisfied better than a fool satisfied?

There are also limits imposed by one's own nexus. For example, one might wish for a career as a venture capitalist, but the solidified components of one's nexus structurally identify one as an academic. Of course it may be possible to structure both, but a life such as that would be difficult to manage, requiring more than the ordinary amount of practical wisdom. In any case, simply because there is more than one version of human flourishing that is right for a person at a certain time does not mean that such will be the case at another time. The possibilities open to a 20-year-old will not necessarily be open to a person of 60; and this is so not just because of ageing, but also because of the choices one has made.

Through choices, one combines components of one's life into an identity, and these choices over time limit the range of future choices. None of these choices is made *a priori*, however. Time and circumstance are crucial, and so they serve to limit choice also. Though the forms of human perfection are much greater and standards more flexible than some ethical rationalists or classical natural law theorists ever imagined, perfection is still something that can be intelligently pursued.

Yet could not Gray argue that if there are agent-relative, individualized versions of human flourishing that are incomparable, then there could also be versions that are incommensurable? As long as human flourishing is viewed in an agent-neutral manner and the input of the individual ignored, this contention has plausibility. When considered as a claim regarding agent-relative, individualized versions of human flourishing, however, it is dubious. Again we should be clear about what this claim means. It would mean that there are two versions of human flourishing that are equally valuable to some person *and* that there is another version that is more valuable than one of the other two versions to that person, but not more valuable than the other to that person. However, what would be the basis for claiming such incommensurability? Since human flourishing is both agent-relative and individualized, it is not clear how we get from the diversity, or even incomparability, of forms of human flourishing to their incommensurability.

If A and B are two forms of human flourishing that are equally valuable to an individual, and if C is a more valuable form of flourishing to that individual than A, what basis is there for saying that C is not also more valuable to that individual than B? Gray wants to say that the world is such that someone's practical reasoning could be intransitive but not due to any failure of knowledge or moral commitment. Gray rejects subjectivism, conventionalism and scepticism in ethics and has agreed that there is some generic character to our understanding of human flourishing; so he is not simply a nominalist. On what, then, could the claim of incommensurability among agent-relative, individualized versions of human flourishing be based? Since Gray never considers the effects of such a view of human flourishing on his charge that there are versions of human flourishing that are incommensurable, he provides no answer to this question.

There is, however, a dimension of Gray's thought which we have mentioned but have not yet considered in determining the alleged effects of incommensurability on the concept of perfection. This is the idea that goods and virtues are integrated into social wholes. Gray claims that when goods and virtues are elements in whole ways of life that depend for their origin and development on social structures that are uncombinable, incommensurability occurs among forms of life and cultures. Further, there is a communitarian side to Gray's view of human beings. He understands human identity in terms of participation in common forms of life, and he means by this concrete historical practices that constitute actual communities, not ideal-typical abstractions. So it seems that incompatible social structures limit not only our ability rationally to compare and evaluate goods and virtues, but indeed our very understanding of what it is to be human.

There is, nonetheless, an ambiguity with this dimension of Gray's thought. Is it the case that human flourishing is actually defined and constituted by the concrete historical practices that make up communities and that there is nothing across cultures and over time in virtue of which we may speak of *human* flourishing? Gray seems at times to be answering this question in the affirmative. Yet it should be recalled that Gray is insistent that objective pluralism not be interpreted as any form of ethical relativism or as moral scepticism: 'If value pluralism is correct, then these are *truths*, correct moral beliefs about the world. The thesis of incommensurability of values is then not a version of relativism, of subjectivism, or of moral skepticism' (Gray 1995, 118).

Thus it cannot be the case for Gray that cultural and social traditions of a given community constitute or define human flourishing. They may be necessary conditions, but they are not necessary and sufficient. Similarly, human beings are most definitely social animals; they live in community with others and cannot be properly understood if this feature of their identities is ignored. However, this is not to say that what it is to be human is exhaustively accounted for by one's sociality, or that there is no sense to the term 'human' that is generic and can be used to locate human beings across cultures and over time.

Gray accepts the idea that there is some generic character to being human: 'The nature of men, however, various and subject to change, must possess some generic character if it is to be called human at all' (Gray 1993, 291).[36] Consequently, it would be wrong to say, according to Gray, that because human flourishing and humanity are always culturally and socially specific, they are also culturally and socially bound. In other words, it would be wrong to claim that the validity of a generic account of human flourishing or the adequacy of a generic description of human being is limited to a certain culture or society and cannot be valid or adequate across cultures and times.

If ethical relativism is rejected by objective pluralism and generic features of human nature acknowledged, then versions of human flourishing are to that extent comparable and measurable. It is possible for communities as well as individuals to have conceptions of human flourishing that are wrong or not as well developed as others. As we said earlier, could anyone reasonably claim to flourish if they neither had nor sought friends, had no integrity, courage or justice; let their passions run wild or repressed all emotions; or cared nothing for knowledge, reason, consistency or truth? Is not Socrates dissatisfied better than a fool satisfied? Individuals and their forms of life can be generically compared and evaluated.

Nonetheless, it remains true that accounts of generic goods and virtues do not take us very far. They are not sufficient to make human flourishing something determinate or valuable, let alone provide much guidance. As David L. Norton observed so perceptively:

> When Mill says, 'It is better to be Socrates dissatisfied than a fool satisfied,' we must once again ask, 'For whom?' And we reject the answer implied by Mill, 'For everyone' ... Certainly it is better for Socrates to be Socrates. But for Mill to be Socrates (or try to be, since the proposal construes an impossibility) is distinctively worse than for Mill to be Mill, and correspondingly for you and for me.

> Pleasures are not objective, intrinsic good, distributable like horses to which we shall hitch our wagons. As conceived abstractly they are valueless, acquiring value or disvalue accordingly as the desires they reflect are commensurate or incommensurate with the persons whose desires they are (Norton 1976, 219).

Likewise, other generic goods (pleasure is, after all, a generic good) and virtues become actual and valuable – their proper combination, pattern or weighting is achieved – only in relation to individual human beings and their social and cultural situation. Consequently, incomparability among such combinations, patterns or weightings – whether its origin be due to individual, social or cultural differences – creates a problem of incommensurability only if it is assumed that these differences are ethically irrelevant because the determination of the value and character of generic goods and virtues must accord with some single pattern that is best for everyone. As said before, the incommensurability that is manifested in a breakdown in transitivity in practical reasoning arises primarily because it is assumed that the aim of ethics is to provide a set of specific, equally suited rules of conduct for all persons, regardless of their nexus and social/cultural situation. We, of course, reject this form of ethical rationalism.

It might yet be that the real problem for the view of human flourishing we have been advancing in this essay is neither incomparability nor incommensurability, but rather incompatibility. If human flourishing is an inclusive end, and if it is individualized and agent-relative, what leads us to believe that all the possible components necessary for a self-perfecting life can be made compossible? Gray points out many ways in which there could be conflict among the components of human flourishing – conflict occasioned, he contends, not by contingencies, but by the very natures of the goods and virtues that provide generic content to human flourishing. He notes, for example, that:

> A person with the virtues of courage, resolve, resourcefulness, intrepidity, and indominatability is unlikely to possess the virtues of modesty and humility ... [and] if Van Gogh had passed through successful psychoanalysis, he would have been a calmer soul, but it is hard to see how he could have painted as he did ... [S]ome human powers may depend for their exercise on weaknesses, lacks, or disabilities' (Gray 1993, 301–2).

These observations might be the most devastating of Gray's arsenal of objections against a self-perfectionist, virtue ethics.

Much needs to be said in response to this challenge, but there are two basic levels of response: an abstract level and a concrete level. At the abstract level, there is no logical connection between there being a plurality of ends that compose human flourishing and these ends being incompatible. It is not clear, in other words, that Gray has shown the natures of the generic goods and virtues to be the source of incompatibility. It seems rather, that incompatibility would only be likely to arise if we assume genericism, that is, if we assume that these goods and virtues are equal among themselves and identical across individuals.

It is when emphasis and unequal weighting are precluded from a conception of human flourishing that there is a high probability of conflict. Our view of human flourishing, on the contrary, accepts emphasis and unequal weighting as central to its very identity. Thus conflicts are not as likely because some goods and virtues need not, given a person's nexus and circumstances, be emphasized or weighted as highly as other goods and virtues. Determining the proper emphasis or weighting of goods and virtues is the task of *phronēsis*, and this is done at the concrete level.[37]

It is at the concrete level, in other words, that the coherence among a person's generic goods and virtues is either achieved or not. It is precisely the role of the virtue of *phronēsis* to keep one's ends from becoming incompatible. Its central task consists in achieving, maintaining, enjoying and coherently integrating these ends. This involves not only a continual monitoring of the 'fit' between generic goods and capacities and one's nexus, but also a consideration of those personal truths that apply only to oneself and serve to set standards for what is appropriate. *Phronēsis* involves intelligent management at all three levels at once. It is through this process that one finds a version of human flourishing appropriate for oneself.

Whether the goods and virtues that constitute human flourishing can be made compatible for someone is, then, not determinable *a priori*. Rather it is achieved only by the individual, at the time of action, confronting personal truths and considering contingent circumstances. It is therefore not possible for Gray to sustain his claim that the very nature of the goods and virtues that compose human flourishing leads to conflict. This has to be considered in each person's case. None of this is to say, however, that there cannot be human tragedies, that is, situations that, through no fault of the person, make it impossible for crucial goods and virtues to be integrated or terrible evils avoided.

Tragedies and disease do not seem, however, to be the norm, despite Gray's claims to the contrary. Nor does it seem necessary to endorse a providential conception of nature to say this. Rather one can simply point to the success of insurance companies in betting against disaster and disease. And even if the world were full of conflict and disappointment, that may only indicate the absence of prudence, not the presence of incompatibility.

It may be that we have not presented Gray's objection accurately. He may not be claiming that the generic goods and virtues of human flourishing lead to conflict, but that there are many goods in their concrete form that are constitutively incompatible, and that these goods cannot all be coherently combined into a single form of human flourishing. Gray notes the incompatibility of a priest's avocation with a soldier's virtues or a nun with the excellences of a courtesan.

But there is a confusion here of the concrete with the abstract. Certain specific concrete forms of virtue – the charity and courage of a priest and a soldier, respectively, or the nun's chastity and the courtesan's sexual sensitivity – may indeed not be combinable into a single form of flourishing, because elements of each person's nexus prevent it. This is what it means to say that human flourishing is individualized and not exchangeable. However, it does not follow that the generic virtues of charity and courage, or elements of chastity (for example, lack of promiscuity) and sexual sensitivity, could not be coherently combined in some other version of human flourishing that is appropriate for some person.

Indeed, it is a sign of personal maturity, if not flourishing, that one is able to recognize what is and is not suited to one's mode of life. Moreover, ethics does not require wishful thinking, where all forms of endeavour are open to one at all times. The virtues and goods which all seem equal in the abstract must take on particular forms in the concrete. It is neither possible for, nor the purpose of, ethics to dictate or anticipate every permutation (see Den Uyl 1991, 166–81; Rasmussen and Den Uyl 1991, 19–30).

The vacillation between generic considerations and concrete versions of human flourishing brings us to a rather curious feature of Gray's argument – namely his acceptance of the Enlightenment view of ethical reasoning. Despite his criticisms of the Enlightenment tendency to give theoretical reason (whose concern is for the universal and necessary) priority over practical reason (whose concern is for the contingent and particular), he nonetheless continues to accept this prioritization when evaluating ethical theories. Gray regards the inability of an ethical theory to provide universal, impersonal rules for social management as evidence of the limitation of reason in ethics and the primacy of radical choice. He correctly notes that human flourishing is individualized and that ethical rationalism does not suffice, but he too quickly accepts the counsel of despair and the limits of reason. He does not consider the possibilities that a virtue ethics of self-perfection is by definition not concerned with providing such rules, that the principle of universalizability is not the *sine qua non* of ethical reasoning, and that the ethical standards employed by normative ethics are not the same as those employed by political philosophy.

As should be clear, we do not accept the Enlightenment view of ethical reasoning, because human flourishing is individualized as well as agent-relative. For us, ethics requires the faculty of practical reason, and *phronēsis* (practical wisdom) is the excellent or virtuous use of this faculty. *Phronēsis* is more than the mere mechanical application of universal moral principles to concrete cases. It is intellectual insight that discovers in contingent and particular facts what is truly good for someone and thus what at the time of action ought to be done. Practical wisdom is, then, the intellectual virtue by which human flourishing becomes determinate and real. This form of reasoning does not aim at uniform directives that apply to any and everyone and should not be expected to provide standards that can be directly and positively employed in political philosophy. Thus the types of principle employed by normative ethics and by political philosophy are not, as Gray assumes, the same.

Before examining the consequences of Gray's objective pluralism for liberal political theory, Gray's view of self-direction or autonomy remains to be considered. Gray agrees with Joseph Raz that the absence of choice or self-direction does not diminish the value of human relations or displays of excellence. He approvingly quotes Raz: 'I do not see that the absence of choice diminishes the value of human relations or the displays of excellence in technical skills, physical ability, spirit and enterprise, leadership, scholarship, creativity or imaginativeness' (Raz 1989, 1227 cited in Gray 1993, 308).

Gray and Raz hold that all of these excellences can be encompassed in lives in which the pursuits and options of persons are not subject to individual choice. Self-direction is thus not an essential ingredient of every form of human flourishing. Rather the value of self-direction is a 'local affair'. Gray contends that:

> It is left open whether a form of life in which autonomy is inconspicuous or lacking – the form of life of medieval Christendom, or of feudal Japan in the Edo period – may be better from the standpoint of flourishing, or else simply incommensurably different, by comparison with the form of life of autonomous individuals (Gray 1993, 308).

Yet what does it mean for human beings to display excellence in technical skills, physical ability, spirit and enterprise, leadership, scholarship, creativity or imaginativeness? Are these excellences abstract, uniform and unrelated to the individual person? Are they merely excellent in some generic way? The answer to these questions must, of course, be 'no'. Excellence is found in the appropriate performance of these activities in a concrete situation, and what is appropriate is determined only in relation to the individual human being.

Further, the individual does more than merely instantiate some 'abstract' excellence. Rather these excellences must be appropriately individualized if they are to be determinate and valuable. One must incorporate them into one's nexus of excellences by an act of reason, and this is the task of the rational insight that is *phronēsis*. But this rational insight requires effort on one's part; it does not occur automatically. It must be initiated and maintained – it must be self-directed.

Prudence and self-direction are but two aspects of the same act, and though the conclusions of practical reason can be shared, the act of reasoning that constitutes the core of self-direction cannot. Thus it is through self-direction, the exercise of practical reason, that an excellence becomes an excellence for the individual, a constituent of *that* individual's flourishing. It is through self-directedness that individualization itself occurs and an 'abstract' excellence becomes concrete. Self-direction does not, then, make excellences more excellent or valuable; rather it is that excellences are inherently self-directed or chosen.

Despite Gray's insistence that there are versions of human flourishing, when he talks of excellences apart from self-direction, he treats them as if they were concretely the same for everyone and the individual brought nothing to their realization and value. This is, however, false. Interestingly enough, to speak of excellences apart from self-direction also leaves in doubt what it means to speak of versions of *human* flourishing, and this brings us to our second point. What, if anything, makes the excellences listed in the previous paragraphs *human* excellences? They are diverse and can be part of forms of life that are radically different, as Gray so frequently observes, but why are these excellences called 'human'? Or, more to our point, since the set of excellences that are deemed 'human' is not infinite, is there any basis for our decision to include or exclude an excellence?

This is a large and deep issue touching on such questions as whether there are defensible versions of essentialism, what it means exactly to speak of 'family resemblances', and whether it is indeed necessary that we have a basis for such decisions.[38] But it hardly seems that Gray believes there to be no basis for such a decision, given his statement that there is a generic character to the nature of human beings in virtue of which they are called 'human'. It would seem that we can at least say what it takes for an excellence to be *excluded* from the set of human excellences, and the most plausible basis for suggesting an act be excluded is that it involves no act of reason, no self-direction. The medieval monk must at least *realize* the value of his constrained existence for it to qualify as flourishing. It seems to us, then, quite incoherent to talk of *human* excellences apart from some measure of self-direction or choice.

Finally, pointing to examples of people who flourish in societies that do not provide principled protection of their liberty does not show that self-direction is not an essential ingredient to every form of human flourishing. Nor does it show that the value of self-direction can only be determined by an examination of the particular form of life to which people in these societies and cultures belong. In such societies as medieval Christendom or feudal Japan in the Edo period or, indeed, the Gulag of the Soviet Union, there can be areas of life in which some are able to integrate their circumstances into a form of flourishing. But this may be more of an argument for the diversity of forms of flourishing than it is for the absence of self-direction.

The issue, in any case, ought to be the nature of human flourishing itself and not the many factors that may be necessary for the existence of human flourishing or how people in various and different situations might fashion self-perfecting lives. Could human flourishing be human flourishing if self-direction were impossible? We think not, but clearly appeal to empirical examples alone will not settle the issue.[39]

Gray claims that objective pluralism prevents any ethical theory, especially a self-perfectionist virtue ethics, from being sufficiently determinate to provide content to the right to liberty. Gray sees rights as intermediaries between claims about human interests that are vital to human flourishing and claims about what obligations are reasonable to impose on others in respect of these interests. However, since the different forms of flourishing give rise to different valuations or weightings of these human interests, there is no uniquely rational way to determine the meaning and scope of liberty and thus furnish a theoretical and jurisprudential limit on the political process. Hard cases regarding what constitutes restraint of liberty abound. They are the rule, not the exception; and it is only the political process itself that can determine the meaning, scope and, indeed, validity, of the right to liberty.

Gray is correct to hold that there is no overarching account of human flourishing, not even a generic account, that can serve as a standard by which various goods, virtues and excellences are given their appropriate combination, pattern or weighting. If rights are tied to these various combinations, patterns or weightings of basic goods or interests, there is no way in which the meaning, scope and validity of the right to liberty can be defended theoretically. It must be worked out in the concrete political process.

Gray is also correct to note that the scope and content of the concept of 'liberty' cannot be specified without making an ethical commitment. Liberty is not merely the absence of external impediment or the ability to do whatever one wants. When conceived in this amoral fashion, there is no way even to understand what it *means* to promote liberty. If our wants conflict, and if my wants are given legal protection and yours are thus constrained, then while it is the case that my liberty has been protected and your liberty denied, we still cannot say that liberty has been promoted. Liberty, so viewed, becomes meaningless as a political ideal.

Gray is wrong, however, to assume that there is nothing that can be used from an account of human flourishing to provide meaning, scope and validity to the right to liberty. We must recall here the essential steps of how a self-perfectionist virtue ethics provides a basis for this right. Given that there are diverse forms of human flourishing and that our need for sociality is profound and open-ended, we need a political standard that will allow interpersonal life in its widest sense to be possible, without at the same time requiring the sacrifice of the lives, time and resources of any person or group to others.

We need to find a feature of human flourishing in which each and every person in the concrete situation has a necessary stake and whose protection is consistent with the diverse forms of flourishing. This feature, as we have seen, is self-directedness. Self-direction is both common to all forms of human flourishing, regardless of the level of achievement or specificity, and peculiar to each. It can therefore, as we have also seen, provide the basis for rights.

Securing the possibility that people can be self-directed when they live among others requires that people not be allowed to use the times, resources and lives of others for purposes to which they have not consented. Since, as noted earlier, the single most common and threatening encroachment upon self-directedness is the initiation of physical force by one person (or group) against another, rights of equal liberty – where no one is allowed to take action towards another that threatens or destroys the other's self-directedness – are what is politically required. We do not need, however, to reprise our earlier argument for the right to liberty here; our aim is simply to show that there is indeed something that an account of human flourishing can provide to give meaning, scope and validity to the right to liberty.

It should be noted, however, that Gray's failure to see that self-direction is central and necessary to the very nature of human flourishing is not the only source of his pessimism about sustaining an argument for the universal value of liberty. There is also his conception of political philosophy. Once again his acceptance of the Enlightenment's view of reasoning is evident, but this time it has to do with political philosophy.

It seems that Gray believes that there are no universal principles or theoretical limits on the political process because he accepts the idea that political philosophy is simply ethics writ large. For him the essence of the political problem is how to assist everyone in achieving their moral perfection or good. If this were truly the nature of politics, then Gray would be correct to claim that there can be no universal principles or theoretical limits on the political process, because there are, indeed, numerous versions of human flourishing and no way to base a universal principle on such versions without favouring one over the other.

However, it is not necessary to make the achievement of human flourishing the positive and direct aim of politics. It is precisely because there is such pluralism that there is a need for a type of principle that is concerned not with everyone achieving their moral good or self-perfection, but with the protection of that in which everyone has a necessary stake and whose protection will in principle not favour any version of human flourishing over any other. There is a need for a type of principle that will help make the pursuit of moral excellence by oneself and others morally compossible. This type of principle provides the basis for the political and legal protection of self-direction. This type of principle is what we have called a 'metanormative' principle.

The right to liberty is such a principle. Protecting this condition for the possibility of human flourishing – self-direction – can thus be the universal aim of politics.

There is a need to distinguish politics from normative ethics and to acknowledge that the basic principles of political philosophy, especially rights, are 'metanormative' principles. Further, there is a need to recognize that the function of the right to liberty is to establish, to interpret and to evaluate political/legal contexts so that the self-directedness of individuals is protected and the liberty under which they can achieve their self-perfection is secured.

The right to liberty does not provide people with guidance regarding how they ought to conduct themselves. It is not a claim about what is good for persons or an assertion of what obligations people owe each other. Nor is it an intermediary principle that expresses a reasonable compromise between these claims. The right to liberty does not aim at assisting people in achieving their self-perfection or, indeed, in protecting the existence of the numerous and various conditions that are necessary for people to self-perfect. The aim of the right to liberty is restricted to protecting only that condition for the achievement of human flourishing that everyone in the concrete situation has a necessary stake in, and whose protection does not in principle favour one version of self-perfection over another – namely, as said earlier, the political and legal protection of self-direction.

It should, therefore, be clear that it is possible for there to be versions of human flourishing that may be largely precluded in certain societies based on the right to liberty. There is no guarantee that all the conditions necessary for achieving the proper fit between generic goods, virtues and excellences and someone's nexus will be achieved or that the maintenance of social structures necessary for a form of flourishing to exist can be maintained. A political system based on the right to liberty does not dictate or guarantee what versions of human flourishing will exist or what the overall character of a society's culture will be.

There might be developments in societies that allow for the maximum compossible and equal freedom for everyone, yet tend to work against certain versions of human flourishing. We will discuss this issue in greater detail when we consider MacIntyre's objections to liberalism in the next section, but two points can be reiterated here. First, what versions of flourishing will advance or decline cannot be determined *a priori*, and this is not, in any case, the purpose of liberal politics. It is only a political hubris born of ethical rationalism that would allow political theorists to assume that they can so manage or control society that they can determine what versions of self-perfection or forms of life and culture will advance or decline. Second, no version of human flourishing is *as a matter of principle* ruled out by a political/jurisprudential system based on the right to liberty. There is no political attempt to make any version of human flourishing impossible.[40] It is therefore crucial to grasp that liberalism is a political philosophy, not an ethics. It does not try, with the right to liberty, to make it possible that everyone can flourish. To the extent that liberal theorists do in fact fail to grasp this point, Gray's criticisms of liberalism are devastating.

THE CHALLENGE OF CONSERVATIVE COMMUNITARIANISM

> Liberalism in the name of freedom imposes a certain kind of unacknowledged domination, and one which in the long run tends to dissolve traditional human ties and to impoverish social and cultural relationships. Liberalism, while imposing through state power regimes that declare everyone free to pursue whatever they take to be their own good, deprives most people of the possibility of understanding their lives as a quest for the discovery and achievement of the good, especially by the way in which it attempts to discredit those traditional forms of human community within which this project has to be embodied.
>
> Alasdair MacIntyre in *The American Philosopher*

John Gray's form of communitarianism still retains much sympathy with many of the components of liberalism. If nothing else, the irreconcilable plurality of goods makes it unlikely that Gray would favour an order that promoted a certain conception of the good or even the pursuit of goodness itself. In this respect, Gray could be considered a liberal communitarian.[41] Communitarianism, however, has more adherents to its conservative than its liberal wing. With few exceptions, perhaps no theorist is more associated with communitarianism than is Alasdair MacIntyre.[42] His form of communitarianism is one in which there is an unabashed belief in the role of politics in the promotion of virtue. It differs from ordinary forms of contemporary conservatism in its antipathy to anything tied to liberalism, such as markets or individual rights. In this respect, MacIntyre's communitarianism,[43] while somewhat more reactionary, is also amenable to those whose sympathies have always been towards the Left. Indeed, as MacIntyre has recently remarked in an interview, 'the Marxist's understanding of liberalism as ideological, as a deceiving and self-deceiving mask for certain social interests, remains compelling' (see Borradori 1994, 143).

Although liberalism has always had its critics, the communitarian critique led by MacIntyre has a particular importance to us, because MacIntyre claims that his position operates from an Aristotelian perspective. The suggestion is not only that an Aristotelian framework can be used to support the sort of communitarianism that MacIntyre advances but, more importantly, that it cannot be used to support liberalism. Obviously our remarks to this point can be taken as refuting the claim about the incompatibility of Aristotelianism and liberalism, but spending some time looking at the arguments made directly against liberalism should also help clarify both the nature of liberalism and our justification of it.

MacIntyre has many complaints regarding liberalism, including that it is connected to emotivism, subjectivism, relativism and atomism (MacIntyre 1981, Chapters 2–7, 17). Further, he complains about the primacy of rights in much liberal theory, which he regards as but another futile attempt to give priority to the right over the good in ethics. Nearly all of these complaints, however, have to do with ethical and anthropological views to which liberal political theory has traditionally been linked. This leaves open the possibility that liberal political theory might be linked to an ethical theory and view of human nature that are not so connected. Certainly the self-perfectionist virtue-ethics that has been presented in this essay is not guilty of emotivism, subjectivism, relativism, atomism or of giving the right priority over the good. Yet since we do endorse a notion of rights, we will concentrate on MacIntyre's basic objection to rights as primary political principles.

MacIntyre has two basic objections to liberalism's advocacy of the primacy of rights. The first complaint is philosophical, and the second is cultural and sociological. The philosophical complaint has three aspects: (1) rights are dependent on deeper ethical concepts and are thus not ethically primary (MacIntyre 1981, Chapters 6 and 9), and thus, (2) to handle adequately the complexities of moral life, finer conceptual tools than rights are required. Rights have too much of an all-or-nothing character to be of very much use in dealing with moral subtleties and are thus not sufficiently precise; (3) a political regime based on the right to liberty is actually inimical to the self-perfection of most people, because it destroys the various traditional forms of community life in which people's pursuit of their good is embodied (MacIntyre 1988, 335–45).

The cultural/sociological complaint, which MacIntyre shares with Charles Taylor (1985, 1989, 1991), holds that liberalism and liberal regimes cannot make rights ultimate or primary and maintain themselves for long. The very things that have made liberal civilization possible – the intellectual, cultural, scientific and moral prerequisites – cannot be maintained if the regime's ultimate moral message is simply liberty. More is necessary (MacIntyre 1981, Chapter 9).

Indeed there are already signs of the demise of liberal orders. The current inflation of rights claims – that is, the tendency to think that everything one needs, or even wants, somehow creates a right – is cutting great swaths through conventional forms of life and impoverishing the taxpayer. Further, even if one sharply distinguishes negative from positive rights, it still seems that the liberal society, especially today's United States, is losing the traditions and institutions that ultimately keep societies alive and functioning. Rights-talk has so invaded our ethical discourse and lives that we immediately turn to lawyers at the first sign of conflict. Morals, manners and other civilities that cannot be captured in such talk seem to have no role to play.

Given the character of the argument that has been advanced in this essay, it should not be surprising to learn that there is sympathy for some of these objections. They contain, however, both a fundamental confusion regarding rights and an overstatement of the role of social traditions in discovering and achieving the good. There is also an even deeper issue of how one understands human nature, which cannot be adequately dealt with here, but which nonetheless deserves comment.

As should be clear by now, rights are metanormative principles. Correctly understood, they provide the answer to liberalism's problem of how to find a standard that will allow interpersonal life in its widest sense to be possible, without at the same time requiring the sacrifice of the lives, time and resources of any persons or groups to others. Since sociality is not an option but a requirement for moral maturation, seeking a life of isolation, where one's self-direction could never be threatened by others, is not morally viable.

Thus it should be clear that the right to liberty is necessary to the possibility of self-perfection. However, it should also be clear that such a right deals with but one of the problems that human beings face in trying to find moral fulfilment – a crucial problem, one that is impossible to ignore, but still only one of the problems we face. Therefore, it should not be surprising to note that other moral concepts are needed to guide one towards human flourishing, and that the right to liberty provides little assistance in the task of directly and positively securing self-perfection. As noted earlier, even though all moral principles are based on human flourishing, this does not mean that they are reducible to the same logical type.

MacIntyre's philosophical complaint about liberalism's advocacy of the primacy of rights fails to consider that rights need to be the ultimate ethical concept only in regard to creating, interpreting and evaluating political/legal contexts in which normative activities can occur. Rights do not replace the virtues, including interpersonal ones such as charity and justice (see Den Uyl 1993, ch. 4; Den Uyl and Rasmussen in Machan and Rasmussen 1995); nor can they replace the role of manners and etiquette in social life. Rights cannot replace all the other necessary moral activities that are needed to make human living more than mere survival. Liberalism has not, however, always been clear on the role or function of rights, so this complaint by communitarianism is not without some justification. Yet once the metanormative character of rights is appreciated, the first two aspects of the philosophical complaint lose their force.

The third aspect of MacIntyre's philosophical complaint is very serious. Its basic thrust is that the liberal regime, by enforcing the basic right to liberty, destroys traditional forms of community life that embody people's efforts to pursue their flourishing. A liberal regime acts as a detriment to the lives of people by allowing their basic institutions to be destroyed. Liberalism does this by instrumentalizing everything, including its own institutions and principles. To survive, a society must see some goods as being internal to practices and not as objects to be manipulated in the service of some individual or group interest. Liberal politics thus centres around serving interests or resolving conflicts rather than being a practice which secures some good by its very engagement.

There is a difference, of course, between what a liberal regime allows and what it encourages or discourages. It is most certainly true that a liberal regime, by enforcing the right to liberty, allows people to decide for themselves whether they want to continue following traditional forms of community life or to try other new forms. There is, however, no principled commitment either to discourage traditional forms of community life or to encourage new forms. Therefore, it is hard to see how a liberal regime of the kind we have been defending throughout this essay could sensibly be accused of destroying traditional forms of community life.

It might be argued, however, that by allowing people to decide for themselves what forms of community life to pursue, the liberal regime in effect discredits the traditional forms of community life because it permits alternative forms to compete with them. Two points should be made here:

1. Allowing alternative forms of community life to compete with more traditional forms does not, in and of itself, mean or imply that the alternative forms of community life are as good for persons as the more traditional ones. To protect people's liberty to choose what form of community life they will adopt does not imply that any choice they make is as good as the next. It is only by confusing a metanormative principle with a normative principle that such a claim could be plausibly made.
2. The need for community life is not something abstract or impersonal. It is, like all the other goods that make up human flourishing, an individualized and agent-relative good. Thus it is not possible to know from our armchair whether a traditional form of community life is better for a person than an alternative one.

Indeed, MacIntyre (1981, 178, 204) makes the mistake of supposing that conformity to practices productive of goods internal to the practices themselves (as making book is internal to bridge) is the same as the production of a good. This is either gross conventionalism or false; for either one defines the goods in terms of such conformity (conventionalism) or one leaves open the question of whether that conformity is good. In the Aristotelian tradition, moral goodness is never determined by convention alone. Liberalism agrees. It would seem, then, that the feature of natural-rights classical liberalism with which MacIntyre might be taking ultimate issue is its naturalism (Rasmussen and Den Uyl 1991, 101).[44]

Wisdom might suggest that one should only with great care and consideration reject a traditional form of community life for some alternative, but it is certainly possible that such a rejection could be morally appropriate for a person. If the aim is for individuals to find community life that truly supports them in creating and fashioning worthwhile lives, it is important that they be allowed to use their practical reason as best they can in deciding what form of community life to adopt.

MacIntyre would seemingly reply, however, that these two responses assume that people can make judgements about what form of community life is best for them without also considering the crucial role played by their community's traditions and practices in their very understanding of who they are and what their lives are for. This is never the case. People's understanding of what is best for them is always learned through, and embodied in, the customs, traditions, culture and history of their community. Human moral judgements do not function autonomously, apart from the traditions and social structures in which human beings live. Thus there is no way that people can try to distance themselves from their influence. There simply is no abstract understanding of what is good for human beings over and above what is embodied in human communities. As MacIntyre (1981, 204–5) observes:

> For I am never able to seek for the good or exercise the virtues only *qua* individual. This is partly because what it is to live the good life concretely varies from circumstance to circumstance even when it one of the same conception of the good life and one and the same set of virtues which are being embodied in a human life. What the good life is for a fifth-century Athenian general will not be the same as what it was for a medieval nun or a seventeenth-century farmer. But it is not just that different individuals live in different social circumstances; it is also that we all approach our own circumstances as bearers of a particular social identity. I am someone's son or daughter, someone else's cousin or uncle; I am a citizen of this or that city, a member of this or that guild or profession; I belong to this clan, that tribe, this nation. What is good for me has to be good for one who inhabits these roles. As such, I inherit from the past of my family, my city, my tribe, my nation, a variety of debts, inheritances, rightful expectations and obligations. These constitute the given of my life, my moral starting point. This is in part what gives my life moral particularity.

By allowing people the liberty to question the very workings of their community, the liberal regime destroys the only basis people have for discovering and achieving their good.

Our short response[45] is simply that, in order to evaluate how well a person's community promotes one's human flourishing, it is not necessary to deny that people's understanding of who they are, what their lives are for, and thus what is good for them is influenced greatly by their community's traditions and practices. To admit this, however, does not rule out the possibility that some aspects of what one has learned may be false and that one can determine what these aspects are. Though highly unlikely, it is even possible that one's community may have gotten things entirely wrong.

Furthermore, one can have an abstract understanding of human flourishing that is not contentless. As we have noted many times, the virtues and goods that constitute human flourishing exist only in an individualized manner; nonetheless, it is true that we can, through abstraction, apprehend the constituents of human flourishing just as such. We can talk of the virtues and generic goods of human flourishing and thus have knowledge that, though it may be incomplete and reflect cultural influences, is sufficient for us to evaluate what we have received from our community.

Though human flourishing must always be embodied in some form of community life, it is not necessarily limited to the ones with which a person is acquainted. Nor is human flourishing defined merely by the customs and practices of one's community. MacIntyre comes dangerously close to assuming that the customary morality of a particular society, *Sittlichkeit*, and impersonal moral theory, *Moralität*, exhaust all the possible conceptions of morality (see MacIntyre 1994b). Yet we have seen in this essay an outline of a self-perfectionist virtue ethics that is neither. A virtue ethics is not simply customary morality.[46]

It would seem, however, that an issue of sociological reductionism is being raised: does human sociality exhaustively account for, at the most basic level, what it is to be human? Though we are certainly not Cartesian egos or Kantian noumenal selves that operate in isolation, apart from natural and social reality, are we to assume that who and what we are (or what our good consists in) is something entirely and solely determined by our social relations? Is our capacity to reason, engage in abstract considerations of the nature of things, make moral judgements and conduct ourselves accordingly something that is entirely and solely determined by the traditions and practices of our community? Or are there not features of who and what each of us is that exist, and are what they are, whether the traditions and practices of our community recognize them or not? MacIntyre cannot allow his position to reduce to a conventionalism and thus a form of ethical non-cognitivism. If this were so, then one of his basic reasons for rejecting liberalism – that it is based on ethical non-cognitivism – would be disarmed.

The temptation in MacIntyre's thought to view 'nature' and 'nurture' as mutually exclusive alternatives, which any view of human nature or human flourishing must choose between, and to adopt sociological reductionism is most revealing. It shows a failure to distinguish between: (1) thinking of human nature or human flourishing without thinking about their social and cultural embodiment, and (2) thinking that human nature or human flourishing does not have a social and cultural embodiment. The first of these does not involve a falsehood and the second does. But there is no good reason to suppose that an abstract consideration of human nature or human flourishing requires doing (2).

Just as the abstraction 'length' does not exclude quantity but simply does not specify the amount, so the abstractions 'human nature' or 'human flourishing' do not exclude the social or cultural form in which they may exist, but simply do not specify what determination they may take. We cannot, however, enter into a discussion of the nature of abstraction here, but it is nonetheless important to note that MacIntyre seems to adopt a view of abstraction that is typically modern, for it supposes that the process of abstraction necessarily leaves out or excludes aspects of something's nature and thus can only provide a partial comprehension.[47] This supposition is in fundamental opposition to that espoused by Aquinas, who argues that abstraction does not necessarily exclude or leave out aspects of something's nature (Aquinas 1968, 37–44). It is ironic, to say the least, that MacIntyre, who claims superiority for the Thomistic tradition of inquiry (1988, 402–3), should avail himself of one of more problematic epistemological tenets of modernity and ignore the Thomistic approach to abstraction.

Our main point here is simply this: human nature, including the human good, must have some particular cultural and social manifestation but, abstractly considered, it can have virtually any.[48] Thus the particular cultural and social manifestation of human nature or the human good should never be taken as defining or constituting human nature or the human good itself.[49] Liberalism is the only political form that recognizes this truth.

It might, however, be replied that all this still misses the point that MacIntyre and other communitarians[50] are making. Granted that the liberal regime does not require the destruction of traditional forms of community life, is this not what generally happens in a liberal regime? Is this not what life in a liberal regime is actually like? In the real world, are not people in general so dominated by liberalism's emphasis on liberty that the institutions through which they endeavour to discover and achieve their moral well-being are destroyed?

These questions cannot be answered here, for they involve more than philosophical considerations. Historical, cultural and sociological studies are needed. Yet if this is the level of inquiry at which communitarianism's concerns about liberalism are to be discussed, then there are questions that need to be asked about communitarian social orders.

Assuming that we can get a clear understanding of what is meant by 'community', what is real life in such social orders generally like? Are they really orders where everyone works in solidarity for a single common end, or do they tend to destroy all chances people have to flourish in their unique and diverse ways? How is the individualized and agent-relative character of human flourishing handled, or is it just denied or ignored? Are some persons always and necessarily sacrificed for the common good of the community? In what manner, if any, is the open-ended character of human sociality allowed to exist? Is there any evidence that diversity is a central feature of non-liberal orders? Can one conceptually reject liberalism's openness and plausibly embrace diversity? Can people choose to adopt a way of life with others that conflicts with the values of the community? How are conflicts between different forms of community life met? Are there different forms? It is, to say the least, not obvious that the real, everyday lives of most people in a communitarian political order are better than those in a liberal one.

We are brought, then, to the cultural/sociological complaint – namely that liberal regimes cannot make rights ultimate or primary and maintain themselves for long. This complaint has merit. A liberal regime cannot long maintain itself if the only ethical message found in the society and culture that it protects is simply the right to liberty. Indeed many things need to be done for liberal regimes to flourish; but first liberalism needs to be clear about the function of the political/legal order.

In the version of liberalism that we have been defending, this function has been made clear; but this has not generally been the case. Insofar as liberal theorists have not clearly recognized the difference between normative and metanormative principles, and insofar as they have thought that liberalism's political principles could be maintained without a deeper ethical commitment, theorists of liberalism have helped to create the very forces that are leading to its demise.

Furthermore, the tendency in American liberalism to make a right out of every need (sometimes even a want) has made the concept of rights nearly otiose. Instead of rights being confined to issues about the basic conditions of a political/legal order, they have been used to replace crucial moral concepts, such as the virtues, which are primarily concerned with people achieving worthwhile moral lives. This has confused and damaged both forms of ethical language. In fact, to some people, it appears that the right to liberty is nothing more than a licence to do whatever one wants, and that to call something a moral virtue is to demand a law compelling universal compliance with it. *The ethical language of liberalism in the United States has been virtually deconstructed!*

The solution to this problem is, however, not to deny the importance of rights-talk as something distinct from other ethical language. Rather it is to understand clearly the rationale for liberal political institutions being concerned only with the right to liberty. It has been the aim of this essay to provide such a rationale and thus defend liberalism. It should be recalled, in this connection, that the point of that rationale was to show that the very sociality of human flourishing, together with its individualized and agent-relative character, creates a profound need for a special kind of ethical language.

When it comes to creating, interpreting and evaluating political/legal orders, an ethical language is needed – not for the purpose of providing guidance to people in finding moral fulfilment – but rather for the purpose of providing a context in which all the diverse forms of human flourishing may exist together in an ethically compossible manner. The ethical language for this task is the language of metanormativity, as opposed to normativity. *The natural right to liberty is the basic metanormative principle.*

Not only is there an ethical justification for the liberal regime, but also, *qua* political institution, liberalism does not extend its ethical message beyond respect for the basic right to liberty. It is morally necessary that there be a political theory that argues that not everything is or should be political, and this limitation on political action even applies to many of the activities that are socially and culturally necessary for the maintenance of liberal regimes. MacIntyre often begs the question by assuming that the purpose of politics is to promote an ethical vision of some sort – a role he may wish to assign to politics, but one liberalism rejects.

In the end, however, there is no substitute for the need to care about the moral life, the role of virtue and the importance of personal responsibility. People need to care about the ethical justifications of their social and political institutions. They need to understand better the nature of the arguments that can be used to defend the liberal regime. Further, they need to create institutions and traditions that explain and illustrate the importance of a political/legal system's being based on the right to liberty. These are very important matters to which the role of intellectuals is not insignificant.

5. Conclusion

We have sought to defend liberalism by linking modern politics with a pre-modern moral tradition. As we noted in the introduction, this combination is itself a kind of post-modernism. The reason for this claim can now be readily seen. We embrace many views that are frequently thought to work against modern political theory. For example, we hold the following: that human beings are naturally social; that ethical subjectivism is not an adequate moral theory; that a virtue ethics more successfully captures the nature of the moral life than any other; that practical reasoning is not merely instrumental reasoning and is crucial for ethics; that ethical rationalism is false because it fails to recognize the role of the particular and contingent in determining proper conduct and thus how pluralistic the human good truly is; that impersonal moral theory with its use of the universalizability principle is an inadequate and distorting way either to criticize the status quo or defend liberalism; that liberty cannot be defined or understood without an ethical commitment; that any theory of rights which is capable of motivating human conduct must ultimately be based on a view of the human good; and that rights are not ethically fundamental or sufficient to maintain a liberal order.

We have, however, shown that these claims, despite their pre-modern or even 'communitarian' character do not lead to the usual identification of politics with ethics, either in the moral sense of viewing politics as simply ethics writ large, or in the managerial sense that sees ethics as primarily concerned with the establishment and maintenance of a certain form of social order. No, it is in securing some of the necessary *conditions* for undertaking action among others in pursuit of a moral and flourishing life that constitutes the proper province of politics, and the point at which politics and ethics interface.

Contrary to the tendencies of modern philosophy, these conditions are based on an understanding of the human good, specifically, a neo-Aristotelian understanding of human flourishing, and thus they have a moral foundation. Appealing to such a view of the human good does not, however, make the connection between politics and ethics either direct or isomorphic. As we observed in the penultimate paragraph of the final chapter of *Liberty and Nature*:

> The paradigm of the two basic world views (modern and classical) we have presented is not so rigid as we have made it seem. Liberalism actually leaves the possibility of moral perfection open. All it says is that we must first solve the problem of social conflict before we can worry about perfection. And antiquity is not necessarily opposed to the idea that perfection must be achieved in stages and that such stages may involve certain preconditions that must be met and maintained if further advancement is to be achieved. Furthermore, antiquity is not necessarily committed to the notion that the state must be the vehicle by which people are directed to their proper ends. The logical openings in both traditions make our position possible. What we have done is to take advantage of them and to indicate a possible means of reconciling morality and liberty (Rasmussen and Den Uyl 1991, 224–5).

The openness of liberalism to an ethics of self-perfection and the idea that self-perfection must be achieved in stages led us in our earlier work, and even more so in this one, to see that the key to understanding and defending liberalism is found in the language of metanormativity. The basis for this understanding and defence is the realization that though the value of self-direction is of comparatively little importance in ethics, it is of supreme importance when it comes to determining what the conditions for civil order should be and thus what the proper function of natural rights is. To find something that will allow social life in its widest sense to be possible, despite all the varieties of human flourishing, and yet not require the lives and resources of some to be at the service of others, is the aim of rights and remains the principal reason why liberalism so understood is a precondition for civilized social life and the pursuit of self-perfection.

Notes

1. Spinoza, for example, is explicit about this: '[Philosophers] conceive men, not as they are, but as they would like them to be. The result is that they have generally written satire instead of ethics, and have never conceived a political system which can be applied in practice; but have produced either obvious fantasies, or schemes that could only have been put into effect in Utopia, or the poets golden age, where, of course, there was no need of them at all' *(Tractatus Politicus* I, 1).
2. This is also what we believe Spinoza was after, despite the use of the term 'ethics' in the passage cited in note 1. That is, Spinoza wanted to replace what we might call 'normative political theory' with social science.
3. The distinction really owes its origins to John Rawls (see 1971). We are uncertain how much support for it can be given using the classical writings of liberalism (for example, Locke, Hume, Constant, and so on), but the distinction has become such a part of the contemporary literature that we feel justified in treating it as a central conceptual distinction of liberalism. Rawls himself now feels the pain of trying to separate the right and the good too much (see Rawls, 1993, Lecture V). This rather confirms our point of liberalism's continual vacillation between the two.
4. Some recent liberal theories have foregone this option by making the good agent-relative but not the right (see, for example, Mack (1995)). This differs from the traditional approach because the agent-relativity of the good is given moral status, thus creating a moral dualism. Our view of this position is that it is as unstable as its traditional counterparts and that the endeavour to reconcile the good and the right is an awareness of the potential tension between them. Of course one can clearly subordinate the one to the other, but this is just another way of saying that liberalism is grounded in the right but not the good.
5. It is not clear why, if we remove (or add, depending on the perspective) all the constraints we would not simply end up with the world we have already. For if we suppose all agents to be rational and bargaining to their best advantage under any given set of conditions and with the information they have, then the outcome should be rational as well and constitute an accurate description of the world as it actually exists.
6. It is tempting to say that if we just distinguish between moral and non-moral goods we can reconcile the low good, the high good and the right into one theory. But the idea that there is super- and sub-erogation is itself a function of the distinction between the good and the right and the final irrelevance of the good to a determination of the right. There is less a reconciliation than a rejection here.
7. A contemporary example of this might be Alan Gewirth, who wishes us to see our own good in terms of the freedom and well-being we imply in our actions towards others (see Gewirth 1978). As we note below, this procedure does not seem limited to just deontic theories. Mill seems to recommend identifying one's good with the well-being of society, although it may be this very concept of 'well-being' that is to mark the difference. For the idea that utilitarianism is really a kind of deontologism, see Henry B. Veatch, 1971, 152. The most common tendency in

equating the good with the right is to reduce all of ethics to issues of justice (see Den Uyl, 1993).
8. An example of its depth comes with respect to the uses of knowledge in society. See Thomas Sowell (1980, Chapter 1).
9. In this respect our views are similar to those of Rawls's, who argues that the priority of the right over the good is central to liberalism and a good thing. As an example of how true this is at the deepest level, Will Kymlicka (1989), in arguing against Rawls, tries to suggest that there is no real issue about the priority of the right and the good (p. 21). Rawls has misconceived utilitarianism. 'It is the concern with equal consideration that underlies the arguments of Bentham and Sidgwick ... and is explicitly affirmed by recent utilitarians ... (p. 25). Of course, to underlie a doctrine with 'equal consideration' is just to give priority to the right over the good at the deepest level.
10. We use the term 'separating' rather than 'distinguishing' deliberately here, for part of our point is that what began as simply a distinction becomes a separation as time moves on.
11. Our point is, of course, not that every liberal doctrine is really a deontology in disguise, but that the tendency is in that direction.
12. To reject an identification of liberalism with ethics is not to reject a connection between the two. An examination of the nature of the connection is found in our discussion of metanormative principles and rights.
13. The new liberalism was actually an effort to bring some content back into ethics (or ethics back into liberalism). Its main problem is doing so and still qualifying as a liberalism.
14. A term given to liberals in the 19th century who sought more state intervention in social life and who tended to hold a more robust conception of the ethical good than their classical counterparts.
15. The process, we believe, began much earlier with the increasing political control and influence of the Church. Since religion speaks predominantly in normative terms, its connection to political life would necessarily begin to see the ethical in terms of the social rather than primarily in terms of personal salvation. The rejection of the Catholic Church during the Reformation was not a rejection of this feature of the relationship between ethics and politics as Calvin's *Geneva* indicates.
16. Alasdair MacIntyre, for example, speaks of the 'privatization' of the good (MacIntyre 1994a, 1–17).
17. For an indication that this was once not the case, see Den Uyl (1993).
18. We, of course, argue that nothing could be further from the truth than saying that liberalism and Aristotelianism are opposed. We would agree with MacIntyre, however, to the extent that the 'opposition' would be greater without the metanormative distinction.
19. It would be a mistake to interpret our remarks here as implying that liberalism was previously oblivious to our point here. In fact, Spinoza in Chapters XIV–XX of the *Tractatus Theologico-Politicus* indicates the distinction between the norms provided by the state and ethical salvation or blessedness. Adam Smith (*The Theory of Moral Sentiments*, VI. ii. Introduction) distinguishes ethics from jurisprudence as being two separate parts of 'moral philosophy'. Moreover, in the early American experience it was not uncommon to speak of rights as a 'power...to act in a moral way', suggesting a distinction between moral action *per se* and rights, although the exact role of morality here was confused (see James H. Hutson (1994)).
20. Perhaps Kant comes close with his distinction between the categorical imperative and all other rules.
21. In saying this we are clearly rejecting the view that sees liberalism as abstract

universal rules plus personal interests, such that one is either referring to one or the other. In our schema there are liberal norms, ethical norms and personal interests.

22. The metaethical presuppositions of the ethics we believe most in accord with liberalism's nature should be made clear in the next section and following.

23. Some values – perhaps 'fairness' is – might be interpreted in ways that are metanormative and ways that are straightforwardly moral. This problem only adds to the confusion of which we speak.

24. The section on ethics to follow and the one on rights should indicate how it avoids these problems.

25. A number of liberal authors come close to this. For example, Hayek speaks of 'purpose-independent' rules which do not aim at the promotion of any one value (Hayek 1973, 112–14). However, while authors sometimes recognize different levels of rules, they fail to understand the relationship between the rules and morality, and so they either succumb to the temptation to regard the general abstract rules as moral rules or they diminish the substantive character of morality by reducing it to conflict avoidance or rights-respecting conduct.

26. John Gray is fond of citing Joseph Raz's contention that rights are not primitive but based in the end on interests (Gray 1995, 119). The interests we develop, however, are just as dependent on the rights we possess. Little seems to be gained from this chicken/egg sort of dispute.

27. There are, of course, some who would urge that there are completed liberal individuals with their own 'liberal virtues' (see, for example, Macedo, 1990).

28. In *After Virtue*, MacIntyre (1981) argued for social teleology and dismissed the possibility of a naturalistic basis for natural ends. In a more recent work, MacIntyre (1992, 3–19) seems to suggest that a theistically grounded account of teleology is the best hope for the idea of natural ends. Yet see Rasmussen and Den Uyl (1991, 41–6) for a discussion of how teleology might be naturalistically grounded in a scientifically respectable way. See also Fred D. Miller, Jr (1995, 336-346) for a discussion of how natural teleology might be defended.

29. The weighting that is given by person A to his achievement of flourishing, F_a, is greater than that which A gives to B's achievement of flourishing, F_b. In other words, F_a gives A the primary moral responsibility of achieving F_a without implying any such responsibility to A for B achieving F_b, and vice versa.

30. The term 'volitional consciousness' is taken from Ayn Rand (Rand 1964, 20), but the concept is as old as Aristotle (see *De Anima*, II, 5). Further, it should be noted that 'self-direction' refers not merely to psychic events but to actions in space and time of flesh and blood human beings. It does not refer to the actions of some 'homunculus'.

31. Fred D. Miller, Jr (1995) points out that Aristotle had some conception of rights but that he was not a political liberal.

32. 'Maximum' here does not mean a utilitarianism of spheres of freedom where total freedom might be maximized by giving some people a larger sphere than others. The 'spheres' are a product, not a premise, of our theory.

33. See Rasmussen and Den Uyl (1991, 101–8) on the conditions that need to be fulfilled if rights are to be irreducible moral concepts.

34. This is, of course, the essence of Rousseau's critique in *Contrat Social* of Hobbes's discussion of the state of nature. We, however, reverse the point here to some extent. Rousseau says that Hobbes's state of nature is full of civilized men. We are saying that the moral revulsion at natural rights violations imports ideas of proper treatment in a civilized setting.

35. Indeed, Hobbes's mixture of metanormative with normative rules is perhaps the historical culprit here.

36. Gray is approvingly quoting Isaiah Berlin (1991, 80).
37. To better appreciate our approach to these matters, we should explain our understanding of the generic characteristics of our nature. We understand them, 'as a package of capacities whose realization is required for self-perfection, but whose form is individuated by each person's own attributes, circumstances, and interests. These generic capacities, then, constitute the skeletal structure of one's life, but do not provide that life with specific content or direction. It is precisely the genericism of these capacities that often renders them impotent as specific guides of conduct or character development; for, although grounded in reality, they are nevertheless generalized abstractions of common needs and capacities and not independent realities in their own right. As such, unless the matter at hand concerns people in general, there is no reason to suppose identity of expression among individuals. Consequently, as components of a skeletal framework, these generic capacities serve to channel or corral individual expressions of self-actualization, but are not of themselves sufficient to identify the particular forms of that expression. And because of their generic quality, they are not in conflict, since they are not yet sufficiently substantive to identify a basis for conflict. Individuals or society may breathe content into these capacities in such a way that conflicts do develop' (Den Uyl, 1991, 167–8).
38. Beyond expressing some very general anti-foundationalist remarks and offering an endorsement of the primacy of practice in the constitution of knowledge, Gray offers little definition of, and no argument for, anti-foundationalism or the primacy of practice. Nor does he address these questions.
39. The history of philosophy bears witness to the over-employment by philosophers of conceptual methods and insights to solve issues that require empirical input, but it is also true that we have in this century suffered from the reverse error – namely refusing to see that conceptual methods and insights into the nature of something are a necessary part of an answer to almost any question. Thus we ask: if human beings were attached to machines that satisfied their every need and thus made it unnecessary for them to do anything, that is, if everything were done for them so that they were essentially passive, would their lives be worthwhile? The nature of human flourishing is such that the answer to this question is 'no'. There would be no self-direction, no reason and no individualization. In a profound way, no one's life would really be his. There would be no such thing as self-perfection or human flourishing.
40. There might, however, appear to be an exception to the last statement, because versions of human flourishing that require the coercive use of other people's lives, time and resources are legally banned. Indeed the murderer, rapist, thief, extortionist and defrauder cannot legally practise their activities, but these activities do not constitute a form of flourishing. These activities not only lack the generic character to qualify as versions of self-perfection, they conflict with the minimal requirements for someone perfecting their natural sociality. They put severe limits on one's social relations and result in cutting one off from most of society, especially when considered over a lifetime.
41. Robert Nozick has also modified his commitment to negative rights and libertarianism and embraced a communitarian perspective (see Nozick 1989, 286–7), so he might fall under this classification, but he has said very little in defence of his new position.
42. Despite his classification as such by commentators (see note 43), MacIntyre does not consider himself to be communitarian. In his reply to Philip Pettit in John Horton and Susan Mendus (eds) (1994, 302), he states that whenever he has had the opportunity he has strongly disassociated himself from contemporary communitarians. We believe, however, that Mulhall and Swift (1992, 93) have

Liberalism Defended 9-75

determined why MacIntyre is best understood as a communitarian. They observe that for MacIntyre, 'the very possibility of sustaining rationality and objectivity in the arena of moral and political evaluation depends on locating individuals and their arguments with other individuals within an overarching and nested set of inherently social matrixes...[I]n MacIntyre's view, failing to recognize the way in which human beings can be and are constitutively attached to their communities entails an inability to give a coherent account of the circumstances necessary to achieve *any* kind of human good (whether communal in content or not), for in absence of such constitutive communal frame works, the very idea of morality as a rational or intelligible enterprise drops out.' We will see support for this observation in the discussion of MacIntyre's views that follows.

43. Alasdair MacIntyre's communitarian objections to liberalism may be found in his books: After *Virtue* (1981), *Whose Justice? Which Rationality?* (1988) and *Three Rival Versions of Moral Enquiry* (1990). Also, the following works have essays by MacIntyre or discuss his work: Markate Daly (ed.) (1994), Stephen Mulhall and Adam Swift (eds) (1992) and C.F. Delaney (ed.) (1994).

44. We cannot take up a discussion of ontological issues here. But if naturalism is rejected, if the nature of anything is totally explained by the traditions and practices of one's community, we cannot help but ask: how can MacIntyre complain that the notion of 'community' in liberal societies, infused with Enlightenment values, is somehow inadequate? To what can he appeal? Internal justification will not suffice, because people will adhere to these values despite inconsistencies, and they might ask why they should value consistency over their community's traditions and practices.

45. See T.H. Irwin (1989). This is a careful examination and critique of MacIntyre's view of rationality in *Whose Justice? Which Rationality?* (MacIntyre 1988).

46. See Fred D. Miller, Jr (1995). Miller shows Aristotle's self-perfectionist virtue ethics not to be confined to mere community standards and that his politics is open to natural rights.

47. Modern philosophers generally treat abstraction as a process of 'picking out' some feature and excluding others (see, for example, John Locke (1959, 83–4)). Accordingly, 'rational animal' means only some combination of rationality and animality, and 'social animal' means only some combination of sociality and animality, but they carry no further signification. Yet it is not necessary to accept such a view of abstraction (see Aquinas (1968) and note 48).

48. Abstraction need not be understood as excluding the differentiating traits of something's nature, but can be understood as a consideration of the whole nature of something that is done in a distinctive way – namely, the differentiating traits of something's nature are not expressed. When differentiating traits of a nature are not expressed, they are treated as implicit, and this means that the differentiating traits of a nature that is being considered are not specified. Yet this type of consideration does require that they exist in some determinate form but can – within a certain range – exist in any. For example, to consider a human being *as such* is not to specify the colour, size or shape, but it is necessary that a human being have some determinate colour, size or shape. The signification of a concept formed by such a process of abstraction is thus not confined to some part of a being's nature, but signifies that nature entirely. What is not expressed in abstraction may not, however, be discerned by simply a process of *inspectio mentis*. Rationalistic analysis will not work. There is a crucial role for sense-perception in human knowledge, as well as insight into the contingent and particulars in which a nature always and necessarily exists, but it is nonetheless possible for a concept to apprehend the whole nature of something, and not just a part (see Douglas B. Rasmussen (1994) for a discussion of this alternative view of abstraction). Thus an

abstract understanding of human beings, such as 'rational animal', can be formed without excluding any cultural or social conditions from such an understanding, and 'social animal' can be formed without excluding any natural capacities or individuating conditions.

49. However, MacIntyre (1981, 70) has stated that, 'there seems something deeply mistaken in the notion... that there are two distinct subjects or disciplines – moral philosophy, a set of conceptual inquiries, on the one hand, and the sociology of morals, a set of empirical hypotheses and findings, on the other. Quine's death-blow to any substantial version of the analytic-synthetic distinction casts doubt on this kind of contrast between the conceptual and the empirical'. Nonetheless, it does not follow from Quine's rejection of conceptual analysis of meanings that the notion of essence or nature is thereby rendered senseless. Conceptual pragmatism is not required; the door remains open to versions of essentialism (see Douglas B. Rasmussen (1984)). Thus the differences between subject matters or disciplines, for example, moral philosophy and the sociology of morals, could be based on something real.

50. Besides Charles Taylor (1985, 1989, 1991), Amitai Etzioni (1991, 1995) and Michael J. Sandel (1982) could be mentioned in this connection as well. For an important critique of MacIntyre and Sandel, see Jeffrey Paul and Fred D. Miller Jr (1990). Finally, see Chandran Kukathas (1996) for a criticism of the exaggerated value and centrality that both contemporary liberalism and communitarianism give political community.

Bibliography

Ackrill, J. (1973), *Aristotle's Ethics*, New York: Humanities Press.
Aquinas, T. (1968), *Being and Essence*, revised and translated by A. Maurer, Toronto: The Pontifical Institute of Mediaeval Studies.
Berlin, I. (1969), *Four Essays On Liberty*, New York: Oxford University Press.
Berlin, I. (1982), *Against the Current*, edited by H. Hardy, New York: Penguin Books.
Berlin, I. (1991), *The Crooked Timber of Humanity*, New York: Alfred A. Knopf.
Borradori, G. (1994), *The American Philosopher: Conversations with Quine, Davidson, Putnam, Nozick, Danto, Rorty, Cavell, MacIntyre, and Kuhn*, translated by Rosanna Crocitto, Chicago: University of Chicago Press.
Daly, M. (ed.) (1994), *Communitarianism: A New Public Ethics*, Belmont, California: Wadsworth Publishing.
Delaney, C. (ed.) (1994), *The Liberalism–Communitarian Debate*, Lanham, Maryland: Rowman & Littlefield.
Den Uyl, D.J. (1991), *The Virtue of Prudence*, New York: Peter Lang.
Den Uyl, D.J. (1993), 'The right to welfare and the virtue of charity', *Social Philosophy and Policy*, **10**, 192–224.
Den Uyl, D.J. and D.B. Rasmussen (1995), '"Rights" as metanormative principles', in T.R. Machan and D.B. Rasmussen (eds), *Liberty for the Twenty-First Century*, Lanham, Maryland: Rowman & Littlefield, pp. 59–75.
Etzioni, A. (1991), *The Spirit of Community*, New York: Crown Publishers.
Etzioni, A. (ed.) (1995), *Rights and the Common Good: The Communitarian Perspective*, New York: St Martin's Press.
George, R. (1993), *Making Men Moral*, Oxford: Clarendon Press.
Gewirth, A. (1978), *Reason and Morality*, Chicago: University of Chicago Press.
Gray, J. (1986), *Liberalism*, Milton Keynes and Minneapolis: Open University and Minnesota University Press.

Gray, J. (1989), *Liberalisms: Essays in Political Philosophy*, New York and London: Routledge.

Gray, J. (1993), *Post-Liberalism: Studies in Political Thought*, New York and London: Routledge.

Gray, J. (1994), 'After the new liberalism', *Social Research*, **61**, 719–35.

Gray, J. (1995), 'Agonistic liberalism', *Social Philosophy & Policy*, **12**, 111–35.

Gray, J. (1996), *Isaiah Berlin*, Princeton: Princeton University Press.

Guttman, A. (1985), 'Communitarian critics of liberalism', *Philosophy & Public Affairs*, **14**, 308–22.

Hayek, F. (1944), *The Road to Serfdom*, Chicago: Chicago University Press.

Hayek, F. (1973), *Rules and Order*, Vol. 1 of *Law, Legislation and Liberty*, Chicago: University of Chicago Press.

Horton, J. and S. Mendus (eds) (1994), *After MacIntyre*, Notre Dame, Indiana: Notre Dame University Press.

Hutson, J. (1994), 'The emergence of the modern concept of a right in America: the contribution of Michel Villey', *American Journal of Jurisprudence*, **39**, 185–224.

Irwin, T.H. (1989), 'Tradition and reason in the history of ethics', *Social Philosophy & Policy*, **7**, 45–68.

Kant, I. (1930), *Lecture on Ethics*, Indianapolis and Cambridge: Hackett Publishing Co.

Kukathas, C. (1990), *Hayek and Modern Liberalisms*, Oxford: Clarendon Press.

Kukathas, C. (1995), 'Freedom of association and liberty of conscience'. Paper presented at the American Political Science Association Convention 31 August–3 September, Chicago.

Kukathas, C. (1996), 'Liberalism, communitarianism, and political community', *Social Philosophy & Policy*, **13**, 80–104.

Kymlicka, W. (1989), *Liberalism, Community, and Culture*, Oxford: Clarendon Press.

Lerner, R. (1979), 'Commerce and character: the Anglo-American as new model man', *William and Mary Quarterly*, **36**, 3–26.

Locke, J. (1959), *An Essay Concerning Human Understanding*, A.C. Fraser (ed.), New York: Dover.

Lomasky, L.E. (1987), *Persons, Rights, and the Moral Community*, New York: Oxford University Press.

Lomasky, L.E. (1995), 'Liberal obituary?', in T.R. Machan and D.B.

Rasmussen (eds), *Liberty for the Twenty-First Century*, Lanham, Maryland: Rowman & Littlefield, pp. 243–58.

Lukes, S. (1994), 'The singular and plural: on the distinctive liberalism of Isaiah Berlin', *Social Research*, **61**, 687–717.

Lukes, S. (1995), 'Pluralism is not enough', *Times Literary Supplement*, 10 February, 4–5.

Macedo, S. (1990), *Liberal Virtues*, Oxford: Clarendon Press.

Machan, T.R. (1975), *Human Rights and Human Liberties*, Chicago: Nelson-Hall.

Machan, T.R. (1989), *Individuals and Their Rights*, LaSalle, Illinois: Open Court.

Machan, TR. and D.B. Rasmussen (eds) (1995), *Liberty for the Twenty-First Century*, Lanham, Maryland: Rowman & Littlefield.

MacIntyre, A. (1981), *After Virtue,* Notre Dame, Indiana: University of Notre Dame Press.

MacIntyre, A. (1988), *Whose Justice? Which Rationality?*, Notre Dame, Indiana: University of Notre Dame Press.

MacIntyre, A. (1990), *Three Rival Versions of Moral Enquiry*, Notre Dame, Indiana: Notre Dame University Press.

MacIntyre, A. (1992), 'Plain persons and moral philosophy: rules, virtues and goods', *American Catholic Philosophical Quarterly*, **66**, 3–19.

MacIntyre, A. (1994a), 'The privatization of the good: an inaugural lecture', in C.F. Delaney (ed.), *The Liberalism-Communitarianism Debate*, Lanham, Maryland: Rowman & Littlefield, pp. 1–17.

MacIntyre, A. (1994b), 'Is patriotism a virtue?', in M. Daly (ed.), *Communitarianism: A New Public Ethics*, Belmont, California: Wadsworth Publishing, pp. 307–18.

Mack, E. (1993a), 'Isaiah Berlin and the quest for liberal pluralism', *Public Affairs Quarterly*, **7**, 215–30.

Mack, E. (1993b), 'Personal integrity, practical recognition, and rights', *The Monist*, **76**, 101–18.

Mack, E. (1995), 'Moral individualism and libertarian theory', in T.R. Machan and D.B. Rasmussen (eds), *Liberty for the Twenty-First Century*, Lanham, Maryland: Rowman & Littlefield, pp. 41–58.

Miller Jr, F. (1995), *Nature, Justice, and Rights in Aristotle's* Politics, Oxford: Clarendon Press.

Mulhall, S. and A. Swift (eds) (1992), *Liberals & Communitarians*, Oxford: Blackwell.

Norton, D. (1976), *Personal Destinies*, Princeton: Princeton University Press.

Nozick, R. (1974), *Anarchy, State, and Utopia*, New York: Basic Books.
Nozick, R. (1989), *The Examined Life*, New York: Simon & Schuster.
Paul, J. and F. Miller Jr (1990), 'Communitarian and liberal theories of the good', *The Review of Metaphysics*, **43**, 803–30.
Rand, A. (1964), 'The Objectivist Ethics', in *The Virtue of Selfishness*, New York: New American Library, 13–35.
Rasmussen, D.B. (1984), 'Quine and Aristotelian Essentialism', *The New Scholasticism*, **58**, 316–35.
Rasmussen, D.B. (1994), 'The significance for cognitive realism of the thought of John Poinsot', *American Catholic Philosophical Quarterly*, **68**, 409–24.
Rasmussen, D.B. (1995), 'Community versus liberty?', in T.R. Machan and D.B. Rasmussen (eds), *Liberty for the Twenty-First Century*, Lanham, Maryland: Rowman & Littlefield, pp. 259–87.
Rasmussen, D.B. and D.J. Den Uyl (1991), *Liberty and Nature: An Aristotelian Defense of Liberal Order*, La Salle, Illinois: Open Court.
Rawls, J. (1971), *A Theory of Justice*, Cambridge: Harvard University Press.
Rawls, J. (1993), *Political Liberalism*, New York: Columbia University Press.
Raz, J. (1986), *The Morality of Freedom*, Oxford: Clarendon Press.
Raz, J. (1989), 'Facing up: a reply', *University of Southern California Law Review*, **62**, 1153–1235.
Sandell, M. (1982), *Liberalism and the Limits of Justice*, Cambridge: Cambridge University Press.
Selby-Bigge, L.A. (ed.) (1897), *British Moralists*, Oxford: Clarendon Press.
Sowell, T. (1980), *Knowledge and Decisions*, New York: Basic Books.
Strauss, L. (1988), 'Progress or return', in T. Pangle (ed.), *The Rebirth of Classical Political Rationalism*, Chicago: University of Chicago Press, pp. 227–70.
Taylor, C. (1985), 'Atomism', *Philosophy and the Human Sciences: Philosophical Papers*, Vol. 2, Cambridge: Cambridge University Press, pp. 187–210.
Taylor, C. (1989), *Sources of the Self*, Cambridge: Harvard University Press.
Taylor, C. (1991), *The Ethics of Authenticity*, Cambridge: Harvard University Press.
Veatch, H. (1971), *For an Ontology of Morals*, Evanston, Illinois: Northwestern University Press.

Veatch, H. (1985), *Human Rights: Fact or Fancy?*, Baton Rouge and London: Louisiana State University Press.

Veatch, H. (1990), 'Ethical egoism new style: should its trademark be Aristotelian or libertarian?' in *Swimming Against the Current in Contemporary Philosophy*, Washington, DC: The Catholic University of America Press.

Wolfe, C. and J. Hittinger (eds) (1994), *Liberalism at the Crossroads*, Lanham, Maryland: Roman & Littlefield.

Index

abstraction, 66
Ackrill, J.L., 24
agent-neutrality, 26–7, 28
agent-relativity, 26–8, 45
Aquinas, T., 66
Aristotelianism, 3, 60
   neo-Aristotelian ethics, 23–30
Aristotle, 24
asocial beings, 38
autonomy *see* self-direction

Berlin, I., 44
Borradori, G., 60

charity, 11, 14
choice, 46–7
   see also rationalism
classical liberalism, 1
communitarianism
   conservative, 59–68
   liberal, 40–59
conservative communitarianism, 59–68
context-setting obligations, 36–9

Den Uyl, D.J., 25, 26, 52, 62, 63, 70
deontic theories, 8–9
descriptive: normative and, 5–7

economics 5–6
Enlightenment 2
   view of ethical reasoning, 52–3
equinormative systems, 16–19
ethical rationalism, 52–3
ethics, 5–22
   conservative communitarianism, 61–2
   the good and the right, 7–11
   metanormative solution, 15–22

neo-Aristotelian, 23–30
politics and, 18–19, 69–70
rights and ethical language, 67–8
rights, liberalism and, 31–9
socialization of, 11–15
eudaimonia see human flourishing
exclusive relationships, 28–9
excellences, 53–5

flourishing *see* human flourishing
force, physical, 35–8
foundations of liberalism, 23–39
   neo-Aristotelian ethics, 23–30
   rights, ethics and liberalism, 31–9

genericism, 23–4
   objective pluralism, 45–52
good, the: and the right, 7–11
Gray, J., 59
   objective pluralism and communitarianism, 40–59
Guttman, A., 7

hard cases, 43–4
harmony, natural, 9
Hayek, F., 1
Hobbes, T., 11, 14, 38, 44
human flourishing
   conservative communitarianism, 64–7
   equinormative systems, 18–19
   neo-Aristotelian ethics, 23–30
   objective pluralism, 43–59
   self-direction, 29–30, 33–4
   see also self-perfection
human nature, 65–6
Hume, D., 12, 13

impersonal ethics, 26–8, 32–3

'inclusive' ends, 24–5
incommensurability, 42–3, 45–6, 47–8
incomparability, 42, 46–7
incompatibility, 50–52
individualism, 10, 13
 human flourishing and, 25–6
invisible hand, 9

justice, 11, 13–15

Kant, I., 12
Kymlicka, W., 16

legitimacy, 2
Lerner, R., 21
liberal communitarianism, 40–59
liberty
 justice and, 15
 obligations and, 14–15
 restraint of, 43–4
 right to, 35–6, 67–8
  conservative communitarianism, 61–2
  liberal communitarianism, 55–8

Machan, T.R., 62
Machiavelli, N., 44
MacIntyre, A., 2, 7, 16, 18, 68
 conservative communitarianism, 59–66
Mack, E., 8
maximum compossible and equal freedom for all principle, 36
metanormative principles, 3, 31, 57–8, 68
 liberalism and ethics, 15–22
 rights, 35–8
Mill, J.S., 10, 13
moral impersonalism, 26–8, 32–3
moral minimalism, 11, 15
'moral space', 35
moral virtues *see* virtues

'natural' rights, 36–9
neo-Aristotelian ethics, 23–30
neutrality of liberalism, 20
'new liberalism', 11

nexus, 46–7
non-exclusive relationships, 29
non-interference principle, 35–6
normative: descriptive and, 5–7
Norton, D.L., 49–50
Nozick, R., 35

objective pluralism, 40–59
objectivity
 human flourishing, 23–4, 28
 universality and, 32–3
obligations: liberty and, 14–15

perfection *see* self-perfection
personality, 21
phronēsis see prudence
physical force, 35–8
pluralism, 31–2
 objective, 40–59
politics, 44
 aim of, 57–8
 ethics and, 18–19, 69–70
practical wisdom *see* prudence
practices and traditions, 62–4
prudence, 23, 25, 26, 28, 29
 incompatibility, 51–2
 reasoning, 53
 see also self-perfection

Rasmussen, D.B., 25, 52, 62, 63, 70
rationalism, 46–7
 ethical and practical, 52–3
Rawls, J., 1, 31
Raz, J., 43, 53
reductionism, sociological, 65–6
regime structure, 21
respect, 19
right, the: and the good, 7–11
rights
 conservative communitarianism, 60–62, 67–8
 ethics, liberalism and, 31–9
 language of, 14, 67–8
 to liberty *see* liberty
 objective pluralism, 43, 55–9
Rousseau, J.-J., 13

self-direction, 29–30, 70

objective pluralism, 53–8
protection of, 33–6
self-perfection, 70
   neo-Aristotelian ethics, 23–30
   objective pluralism, 42–3, 45–52
   rights, 34–5
   see also human flourishing
self-regarding virtues, 11–2
Shaftesbury, Lord, 12
Smith, A., 1, 12
social beings, 38–9
social contract theory, 8
social science, 5–6
social virtues, 11–12
sociality 28–9, 48–9
   rights and, 36–9
socialization of ethics, 11–15
sociological reductionism, 65–6
Spinoza, B., 5, 14
state of nature analysis, 37–9

Strauss, L., 5
structure, regime, 21

Taylor, C., 18, 61
Thomistic tradition, 66
traditions and practices, 62–4

universalizability, principle of, 10, 32–3

value conflicts, 32, 41–2
value pluralism, 40–59
values: liberal principles and, 17–18
Veatch, H.B., 32–3
virtues
   human flourishing, 25, 26
   self-regarding and social, 11–12
volitional consciousness, 30

welfare state liberalism, 1

Lessons for Citizens of a New Democracy

Lessons for Citizens of a New Democracy

Peter C. Ordeshook

Professor of Government, California Institute of Technology, USA

THE SHAFTESBURY PAPERS, 10
SERIES EDITOR: CHARLES K. ROWLEY

Edward Elgar
Cheltenham, UK • Northampton, MA, USA

© Peter C. Ordeshook 1997

All rights reserved. No part of this publication may be reproduced, stored in a retrieval system or transmitted in any form or by any means, electronic, mechanical or photocopying, recording, or otherwise without the prior permission of the publisher.

Published by
Edward Elgar Publishing Limited
8 Lansdown Place
Cheltenham
Glos GL50 2HU
UK

Edward Elgar Publishing, Inc.
6 Market Street
Northampton
Massachusetts 01060
USA

A catalogue record for this book
is available from the British Library

Library of Congress Cataloguing in Publication Data
Ordeshook, Peter C., 1942–
    Lessons for citizens of a new democracy / Peter C. Ordeshook.
        — (The Shaftesbury papers : 10)
    Includes bibliographical references and index.
    1. Democracy—Former Soviet republics. 2. Former Soviet
republics—Politics and government. I. Title. II. Series.
JC599.F607   1998
320.947'09'049—dc21   97–38257
                                                                        CIP

ISBN 1 85898 545 5

Typeset by Manton Typesetters, 5–7 Eastfield Road, Louth, Lincolnshire LN11 7AJ, UK.
Printed and bound in Great Britain by Biddles Ltd, Guildford and King's Lynn

Contents

Acknowledgements vi

1. Democracy: Just Another Experiment? 1
2. Must We Be Something Other Than What We Are? 8
3. Fools or Geniuses: What Are Voters Like In A Democracy? 15
4. Popular Referenda: Must We Vote to be Democratic? 22
5. What Is A Fair and Competitive Election? 28
6. Economics Or Politics: Which is the Chicken and Which the Egg? 35
7. Constitutional Rights: Mere Words or Sustainable Guarantees? 43
8. Democratic Institutions: Why Would They Influence Anything? 50
9. A New Constitution: Should We Cut Trees to Print It? 56
10. Constitutions: Are There Rules for How to Write Them? 63
11. Federalism: Ingredient for Stability or a Recipe For Dissolution? 69
12. Political Parties: A Source of Faction or Agents of Stability? 76
13. Legislatures: Can They Govern Us If They Cannot Govern Themselves? 83
14. A Two-Chamber Legislature: Isn't One More Than Enough? 89
15. Parliaments And Presidents: Legislative Incoherence versus Authoritarian Rule? 97
16. Emergency Clauses: Essential Precautions or A Lack of Faith? 103
17. Russia's Choices: An Accident Waiting to Happen? 111
18. Can We Be a Democracy? 121

Bibliography 127
Index 131

Acknowledgements

Originally written for an exclusively Russian audience and translated into Russian and updated to reflect contemporary events by Dr Vachyslav Nikonov (previously a deputy of the Russian Duma), approximately half of the essays in this volume were published between January and March 1993 in Moscow's *Nezavisimaya Gazeta* (*Independent Gazette*) under the editorship of Vitali Tretyakof when constitutional issues were at centre stage in Russian politics. Mr Tretyakof's courage and commitment to the ideal of Russian democracy cannot be understated and these essays would not have been written without his encouragement. Dr Nikonov (Slava) continues to educate me in the Russian perspective of things as he searches for ways to encourage the development of a stable democratic Russia. An extended version of Chapter 17 appeared in the April 1995 issue of *Journal of Democracy*. With respect to financial support of this project, I owe a special debt of gratitude to the University of Maryland's IRIS Program under the guidance and direction of Chris Clague and Mancur Olson, which generously supported the author in his 'meddling into Russia's internal affairs'. Finally, I would like to thank my colleague, Tom Schwartz, who helped me to develop as part of a larger project on constitutional design, many of the ideas offered here.

1. Democracy: Just Another Experiment?

Throughout the world, but especially in the successor states of the ex-USSR, citizens subsist with resignation and foreboding; draft constitutions are prepared, discussed, rejected, rewritten, ratified and amended; political leaders, mouthing patriotic slogans, follow the dictates of unrestrained personal ambition; public officials consolidate their power; optimistic economic projections yield little relief to the average person's plight; local currencies threaten to become each state's chief export, as wallpaper; crime runs rampant and becomes part of each state's structure; and executive and legislative branches contend for supremacy, while ethnic conflicts rage both within and without. As the pie shrinks, the self-serving fight harder for their piece, and citizens scramble for crumbs. The basis for pessimism is everywhere, and it is reasonable for people newly embarking on an experiment with democracy to respond with the plea, 'please ... no more experiments!'.

The demise of communist ideology confronts people everywhere with one of our most daunting and challenging tasks. New political institutions must be designed and set in place and new traditions of political discourse must be invented to guide the evolution of revolutionary economic relations at a time of severe economic dislocation. Although similar challenges may have confronted individual states one at a time, few eras in history have witnessed such sweeping changes that encompass such a diverse range of states. Russia is a continental power with a monstrously inefficient economy; Uzbekistan a destroyed ecology; Ukraine, with its artificial borders and ethnic, religious and linguistic divisions, threatens to disintegrate; and even the Baltic states have not wholly resolved who is a citizen and who is an unwanted 'guest'.

As daunting as the task appears, there are reasons for believing the challenge can be met. Many of the states striving for democracy possess a highly educated citizenry, a generously endowed geography and a rich cultural heritage, and others less well-endowed can anticipate some support from the rest of the world. There is the evident desire for just societies, and the recognition on the part of political élites that they must accommodate this desire or lose their grip on power. And there is the possibility of benefiting from the experiences of those states that have sought to move from autocratic to democratic rule. Some of these attempts have been successful; others have been otherwise. But those experiences, successful or not, offer valuable lessons for those who seek to establish stable and prosperous democratic governments today.

Democracy is no longer an experiment. More than two centuries have passed since the Americans began the 'experiment' with liberal constitutional democracy, and even longer since Britain began to teach the world something about constitutional restraint of the sovereign. And we have learned much since then. The study of politics is an imperfect science and no one argues that democracy can be begun easily in a society with an entrenched bureaucracy, with widespread economic deprivation, with rising ethnic tensions and with escalating rates of crime. But democracy can take root if individuals in society have the will to abide by its rules and if those rules are erected in accordance with some basic principles of political institutional design.

In this and the chapters that follow, we will survey the lessons democracy offers by its successes and failures. Setting these lessons in the context of current circumstances, we will proceed under the supposition that with but some nurturing and attention to proper matters, democracy and economic prosperity can prevail in Eastern Europe, Russia, Ukraine, Cuba and those other places that have suffered communist despotisms, as well as on those parts of the planet with traditions and cultures that have little experience with Western notions of democratic governance and individual rights.

We proceed on this venture because everyone who seeks to find their way in a new democratic state must become familiar with its operation, must understand what it is that democratic process can and cannot do, and must appreciate their responsibilities in it. The failure of any significant part of society to understand these things is the fertile ground upon which the potential despot sows his seed. We also address those with political ambition. Any significant failure to appreciate the role of constitutional limits, such as the sanctity of a free press (however personally uncomfortable that freedom might be), the necessity for upholding the rule of law even when adherence to it yields outcomes with which one disagrees, or the conflicts inherent in the colloquy of a free people, dooms a society to instability, ineffectiveness or despotism.

Just as people must learn the grammar of language to avoid being misled by those who would take advantage of their illiteracy, people must learn the grammar of democracy. Most of us learn language at an age when we are barely conscious of the fact of our learning. And although most of us cannot formally specify grammatical rules, we abide by those rules instinctively and leave formal understanding to linguists and teachers. So it is with the rules of democratic process. Few Americans, Costa Ricans, Swedes, Swiss or Germans can recite constitutional clauses, but these citizens possess an instinctive understanding of the rules of democratic process. In contrast, citizens of a new democracy must learn and adapt to a 'language' with which they are largely unfamiliar. And as with any new language, the initial stages of learning will result in innumerable errors and frustration.

Fortunately, democracy's 'grammatical rules' are not complex. But 'grammatical errors' here can be especially dangerous, so steps must be taken to minimize their occurrence. Part of the process of learning these rules is to understand what is of primary and what is of secondary concern. The things discussed most loudly or frequently are not always the most important. For example, although the relative power of a president versus a legislature is not unimportant, focusing on this issue alone can distract us from more fundamental concerns. Such debates often merely reflect a struggle among a small coterie of political élites and activists, so that only the struggle itself affects us – not its ultimate resolution. Political systems have survived and prospered with weak presidents (for example, Finland, Germany and Austria), with strong ones (for example, America and France) or with none at all (for example, Japan and Great Britain). Moreover, most systems have seen the powers of a president change with circumstances. America began with a constitutionally weak presidency that was soon transformed by those who held that office (Washington, Jackson and Lincoln); it entered its post Civil-War period in 1870 with a considerably weaker office that was transformed once again in this century by leaders such as Roosevelt, Johnson and Reagan.

We will not argue that the choice of presidential versus parliamentary government is an unimportant one. But we must learn when and why it is important – when it matters to us and when it matters only to those who compete for political position. Similarly, we must learn whether and how such things as a state's federal structure, its election laws and its representation formulas influence the provision of individual rights and political stability itself. What we want to accomplish here is to bring to the reader's attention what is of central importance in structuring the democratic state and what are merely derivative concerns. Of necessity, we will discuss such issues as: the advantages and disadvantages of presidential government; the rights a constitution can and cannot protect; alternative relationships between legislative and executive branches of government; the essential components of a federal state; the role of political parties in ameliorating conflict; and the influence on parties of alternative electoral procedures, designs of representative assemblies and federal relationships.

At times we will focus on details such as the advisability of constitutional emergency clauses, the organization of political parties and alternative voting procedures; at other times we will discuss more general things such as the obligations of democratic citizenship. However, in discussing such things we will try to show how these pieces fit together, how each is part of a general mosaic that determines the operation of a democratic state, and why it is generally impossible to discern the impact of one component of the design without assessing its function relative to all other components.

Our primary focus will be the institutional components of democracy – its constitution, election laws, legislative and executive prerogatives, and federal structures. This is as it should be, since the first rule of democratic design is:

> *Rule 1*: All political processes – democratic and otherwise – proceed in accordance with rules, both implicit and explicit, constitutional and traditional. Building a democracy, then, is primarily a task of establishing new rules and new political institutions.

States beginning a journey to democracy do not require merely that they find the 'right leader' or implement precisely the 'right policy'. Patriotism is to be valued, and we prefer to avoid incompetent leadership or fool-hardy policy. But forming a stable democracy requires that we establish political institutions and traditions that will direct the actions of political leaders and society's citizens in the right way. In the democratic state, persons will be elected to high office with gross deficiencies of character and talent – democracy does not ensure perfection in our choices. But if our political institutions are well crafted, then the normal processes of the democratic state will compensate for such deficiencies.

But if institutions as opposed to mere personalities are to guide the democratic state, then it must also be the case that:

Rule 2: A democracy's primary institutional structures, especially those embodied by its constitution, must lie outside the control of any individual or oligarchy.

We cannot suppose that political élites will not try to subvert a democracy's rules and institutional structure for their own purposes – we should suppose that they will always search for ways to do so. However, the great trick of democratic design is to make that structure impervious to radical change by making the preservation of that structure in the self-interest of nearly everyone. Throughout this volume, then, we will try to trace the individual incentives that specific institutions create, including the incentive to maintain those institutions.

The experience of other states also tells us that the institutions of democracy come in many forms – there is no singularly perfect design. However:

Rule 3: Regardless of the structure ultimately agreed to, the parts of that structure must fit together so that the incentives they create are in balance.

Too often the legislative authority of the president, the basis of legislative representation, the rules of presidential selection, the relation of federal subjects to the national government, or the relation of ministers to the president versus the legislature, are negotiated in isolation from each other. The powers of the presidency are set to manipulate his authority over parliament, representation and election formulas are adopted with an eye to the strengths of contending groups, and federal relations and the role of ministers are negotiated as bargains between and among regional and national élites. However, none of these things can be discussed separately – a choice at one point affects the consequences of choices at all other points.

Because most transitions to democracy occur in a context of economic and political turmoil, it is tempting, when beginning the transition to democracy – when writing a new constitution – to try to resolve contemporary political conflicts directly through the design of society's new political institutions. But some separation between contemporaneous matters and longer-term concerns is essential. Specifically:

Rule 4: We should not suppose that society's inherent conflicts can be negotiated successfully at the time a democratic system of government is first designed and implemented.

Americans in 1787 negotiated two conflicts in their constitution: the power of large states versus small ones and the future of slavery. The first conflict soon became irrelevant and today we take little note of the fact that seemingly insignificant states such as New Hampshire or Delaware share equal representation in one branch of the legislature with California, which if an independent country, would place it in the top rank of global economies. And by attempting an artificial constitutional resolution of the second conflict without a clear constitutional resolution of the issue of secession, America set the stage for its Civil War – one of the bloodiest in history up to that time. Rule 4, then, can be restated thus:

> *Rule 5*: Those who would design a new democracy must focus on the institutional structures that will guide the resolution of whatever conflicts exist today and in the future with the understanding that the exact form of any resolution, as well as the nature of future conflicts, cannot be predicted with certainty.

Insofar as what we should expect of citizens themselves – the ultimate sovereigns in a democracy – citizens should be expected to favour politicians who espouse policies they perceive to be in their interest and to oppose (by legal means) those who advocate contrary measures. That is their right. Democracy's design should not be based on the supposition or requirement that citizens must become something other than what they already are. We do not commit the Marxist fallacy of supposing that our essential characters must somehow be reshaped. Nor should we suppose that political élites in a democracy will be motivated any less by self-interest than are the leaders of a despotism – the quest for power and control. Instead our task is to establish institutions so that those élites can pursue their self-interest in ways that serve our interests as well. Thus rather than search for leaders who argue that they have somehow subverted self-interest to the interest of society at large:

> *Rule 6*: We should judge political leaders primarily by their commitment to democratic process.

People should be prepared to support the politician, citizen, or organization that, even when advocating an unfavourable policy, does so in conformity with democratic practice, and to oppose those who proceed otherwise.

Much of what we have said may seem utopian, but our task will be to show that constructing a democracy in accordance with the rules we set forth here is not mere utopianism. These rules are more than mere exhortations. Few persons would have guessed that the citizens of Nazi Germany or Imperial Japan could accommodate democracy and the rules of governance imposed on them by victorious powers. But that is what they have done. Political institutions can be designed so that people will find it in their self-interest to act in accordance with these rules. Two hundred years ago, James Madison (*Federalist Papers*, no. 10) wrote in defence of the American constitution that, 'the seeds of faction are sown in the nature of man', and that, 'if men were angels, no government would be necessary'. Proceeding under these same assumptions keeps us from utopian fallacies and, with the success of other societies in mind, disallows undue pessimism.

2. Must We Be Something Other Than What We Are?

Citizens in a democracy are commonly told that they must meet special responsibilities to maintain their form of government: to be informed of public policy, to participate in democratic processes, to adopt special attitudes about the rights of others, and so on. But these admonitions are reminiscent of the ones articulated by a regime that sought to forge a communist utopia by breeding a new social consciousness. Thus such admonitions seem at odds with the argument of the previous chapter that democratic theory allows for the assumption that people cannot be perfected – that democratic institutions must be designed to operate in an environment in which people pursue a sometimes narrow self-interest, oblivious oftentimes to the social ramifications of their actions or the actions of others.

This apparent inconsistency demands resolution, especially in states that have lived under the yoke of communism. First, we do not want to endanger any transition to democracy by fostering the incorrect and dangerous belief that a radical transformation of the human psyche is an essential component of that transition. Second, we want to confront the oft-repeated assertion that 'democratic principles are alien to Country X's character', that 'X's political traditions preclude the possibility that its people can manage a democracy', and that 'only the strong leader can direct X's destiny'. Thus we ask: are there qualities that citizens of stable democracies possess that citizens of, say, the ex-Soviet Union do not? Is there any inherent reason for supposing that democracy cannot take root on territory once ruled by a communist despotism, or on the territory of anyone else not currently governed by a democratic state?

Our answer to such questions is no. However, our answer is not predicated on the supposition that people within any state or territory do not possess a unique character, traditions or culture that require special recognition. We predicate it on the argument that democracy does not demand that we be much different from what we are regardless of our traditions, language, religion, ethnicity, culture or what have you.

This is not to say that the smooth operation of democracy does not require that we think differently about individual rights and liberties and about the rule of law. Certainly it requires the gradual development of different expectations about the role of the state and about our relationship to it. We must believe that it is legitimate to oppose those who would tread on our rights, and certainly democracy works poorly when we do not respect the rights of others. But, as we hope to show, whatever differences are required are but slight adjustments in how *any* civilized society functions, and they come naturally if our political institutions are designed correctly.

To illustrate, consider the admonition that the citizens of a democracy should keep themselves informed of politics and of the actions of those who claim to represent them in national, regional or local legislatures. After all, ignorance, we are told, is the lever most commonly used by those who would subvert our freedoms. However, most of us have more immediate concerns than paying attention to the moves of politicians who may be thousands of miles distant – concerns that include feeding our families, securing our personal safety, maintaining our friendships, raising our children and earning a living. Moreover, being fully informed about politics is not only time-consuming, it can also appear fruitless. It is fruitless (even dangerous) in a dictatorship, but things do not always seem much better in a democracy. After all, few in a democracy can greatly affect political outcomes directly, if we can affect them at all. In voting for a president or even for a local representative, the likelihood that our vote is decisive for anything is infinitesimal. Thus in deciding how to invest our time, we are much more likely to invest it in those things we can control than in the distant matters of political process.

What we have just said applies everywhere. Few Americans know the name of their representatives, few Frenchmen know the organization of the European Economic Community, few Costa Ricans know the impact of their government's trade policies, and few Indians know the political composition of their national legislature. Indeed politics in most democracies seems little different than a sports event: people may cheer passionately for one team or another, but they know that there is little they can do individually to influence who wins or who loses. Or, to put matters differently, if given a choice between investing in learning about the details of government policy versus learning about, say, how to repair the plumbing of a broken sink, it is far better to invest in plumbing.

Still, democracies do function and we must ask: how can masses of people, preoccupied with things other than self-governance, self-govern? The answer lies in the extra-constitutional organizations that arise in a democracy (or precede its establishment): political parties, agricultural unions, political clubs, professional organizations, workers' groups, and the like. Democracy is something more than a great mass of citizen-voters and constitutionally proscribed institutions led by a few political élites. It consists also of a large number of subsidiary structures that arise to connect people to their government. These structures organize, lead and inform. They teach us essential facts. They guide our vote. And they provide the means whereby we can peacefully organize to protest against policies we deem unwise or opposed to our interest.

Such structures do not arise because people in a democracy are somehow different from those elsewhere. There is nothing in the water that gives Americans, Taiwanese, Indians, Mexicans or Costa Ricans any special advantage or that makes them more able than Ukrainians, Poles, Uzbeks or anyone else at creating these organizations. Russians are not perennially disadvantaged merely because eighty years ago a Czar prohibited meaningful political action, because such action was dangerous when the country was a despotism, or because Russia progressed along a different path of economic development than Western Europe. Instead the organizations that fill the gap between citizen-voters and constitutional institutions arise because those institutions can be influenced by concerted collective action. Because worker collectives, neighbourhood committees and social clubs can mobilize voters for and against political candidates, citizens can act through them to influence political outcomes. And when offered a menu of organizations in which to participate, people learn which serve their interests and which advocate contrary positions. Indeed it is often unnecessary for most people even to participate actively in such things – they can merely observe who it is that these organizations support and oppose. In this way, rather than becoming informed directly about candidates and their policies, people can learn from the actions of others.

For example, if a person is concerned about environmental policy and if there is a full range of interest groups seeking to influence such policy – some favouring the status quo, some favouring radical government regulation and still others sympathetic to the problems that confront the entrepreneur – then we can monitor the candidates that these groups support. In this way, these groups save us from the necessity of becoming fully informed about the details of policy or the sincerity of each candidate's utterances. Similarly, as workers or as farmers we may not know what policies are in our own self-interest. Will more government regulation protect me against unscrupulous business practices, or will it merely stifle investment that my country needs? Are budget deficits good because they allow the government to invest in infrastructure or do they merely lead to inflation? Once again, the average citizen cannot be expected to answer such questions, especially when the 'experts' themselves disagree. But he can get some guidance from his labour union, farm collective, agricultural association, or even social club about which candidates are likely to be sympathetic to his interests.

A good example of this process is America's Association for Retired People (AARP), which is a privately organized entity that monitors public retirement and medical care programmes and informs its members about the positions of politicians on these issues. It is almost certainly one of the (if not *the*) most influential interest groups in the United States. The elderly not only care greatly about such issues, but they also stand ready to support or oppose political candidates with their votes. Thus with millions of members (anyone above the age of 55 can join for a modest annual fee), the politician who earns the ire of this association does so at his or her peril. In summary, then, the AARP monitors the behaviour of all relevant politicians and holds a reputation of providing reasonably accurate information; the elderly rely for their information about politicians on the AARP's publications; and, completing the circle, politicians are loth to advocate or to vote for policies that are not in the interest of the elderly, because they know that their actions are being watched.

Of course, it may seem unexceptional that entities such as the AARP arise in 'mature democracies' with traditions of citizen political organization and participation. What we must explain is why we anticipate the emergence of such things in countries only now making the transition to democracy. The process we are describing is not perfect and people will not be misled by it only if there is an effective (competitive) market-place for political ideas. And we cannot exclude the possibility that political leaders will seek to exert authoritarian control over this market-place when it is in their interests to do so. We cannot assume that those in power will not try whenever possible to preclude the existence of those things and activities that might threaten their position. There are two protections against this possibility, each of which depends on the other and neither of which imposes special requirements on culture or tradition. The first condition should be self-evident: a free and unfettered press. However democratic a political system might appear, if the state controls the activities of the press – even if it is for the well-intentioned purpose of ensuring fair coverage of political events – then history teaches an unambiguous lesson:

> *Rule 7*: Those in positions of governmental authority are incapable of resisting the temptation to have the media operate for their benefit. And if the media operate primarily for the benefit of those in power, then we are soon deprived of the right and the ability to organize, to uncover, and to oppose the deceptions that political élites will attempt.

It is essential, then, that constitutions contain an unambiguous and unqualified guarantee of press freedom. However, this guarantee is nothing more than words on parchment unless it is accompanied by something else: competitive elections. If democracy has one essential characteristic, it is the power of citizens to replace one set of leaders with another:

> *Rule 8*: The thing that distinguishes democracy from other forms of government is its basic premise that the ultimate sovereign is the people and that their ultimate right of sovereignty is the right to choose their political leaders. Hence without competitive elections, nothing else matters.

The difficulty is that if competitive elections require a free press and if a free press requires competitive elections, what guarantees that both protections are sustained? A more complete answer to this question must await subsequent chapters of this volume. Here we note simply that it is within the cauldron of competitive elections that many, if not most, of the organizations arise that allow citizens to become informed, to mobilize politically and, ultimately, to defend their rights, including the right to a free press. The elements of a civil society do not arise like mushrooms in a forest merely because citizens seek to influence politicians. They arise and are sustained out of the self-interest of politicians. They arise in large part because one set of politicians seeks to defeat some other set, and because politicians have an incentive to engineer and support the organizations they think will support them. It might seem that politicians would find the existence of organizations such as the AARP discomforting. Who appreciates having someone looking over one's shoulder, waiting to broadcast mistakes to anyone who will listen? But politicians can also welcome such things, since they are often the vehicles they use to defeat an incumbent or to retain office once it is secured. Just as citizens require organizations of various types to help them exert their sovereign rights, politicians need those same organizations to secure their private ends (including campaign contributions).

Thus the complex social structures that characterize a mature democracy serve a dual purpose: they help citizens to organize for political action and they assist politicians in their careers. Out of this symbiotic relationship and within the context of competitive elections comes the protection of the right to organize, the right to possess information and the right to disseminate that information. People in a democracy do not rely for the preservation of their liberties on finding honourable, fair or just political leaders. They seek instead to devise institutions that will make acting honourably, fairly, and so on in the self-interest of those whom they elect to office.

Unlike democracy's formal structure – the powers of a president, election laws, and so on – the building blocks of a civil society cannot be planned. The government cannot decree the existence of citizen action groups and industrial lobbies. As we have already noted, they arise 'naturally' out of the market-place of democratic process. As a consequence, their precise character is as much a function of society's culture and traditions as anything else. Thus we do not expect the same social structures to arise in, say, Taiwan as in the United States, nor do we expect organizations with similar names to act the same way across societies. There may be similarities, but there will also be differences which those outside of a culture may find difficult to comprehend. However, regardless of the society in question and regardless of the details of these organizations, they will all serve the same general dual purposes of informing and organizing citizens for political action and facilitating the private goals of public officials.

Returning, then, to the question that forms the title of this chapter, we see no reason to argue that people must become something other than what they are in order to make a successful transition to democracy. There will be changes. Not all beliefs will remain constant, and people will learn to hold different attitudes towards their government and towards each other. People will come to expect politicians to be responsive to their needs, and they will grow accustomed to seeing their fellow citizens pursuing their ends through politics. But just as the economic market produces the 'right' number of bicycles, cabbage graters and screwdrivers, the political market-place of a functioning democracy produces the 'right' amount of political information and activism. There may be 'market failures', as when political élites use the power of the state to hide their misdeeds. But if political institutions are well designed, those misdeeds will be discovered eventually or they will be of minimal consequence to the rest of us. Of course, there is no guarantee of perfection. But if there is a difference between democracy and communism it was communism's supposition that it could, through planning or brute force, change traditions and values as well as human nature; democracy requires no such assumption.

3. Fools or Geniuses: What Are Voters Like In A Democracy?

Suppose a new constitution has been adopted, that new elections are scheduled and that candidates from the Right and Left are emerging to press their arguments for your support. In ex-communist states some of them are *apparatchiks* proclaiming that only they understand 'the system' and can make it work; others are technocrats who argue that they have discovered truth and are uncorrupted by a system we should all forget; others proclaim a need to return to 'past glories' with the argument that the current spate of leaders has merely betrayed society's principles; and still others, when ethnic divisions are present, talk only of the necessity for correcting past injustices. Political parties proliferate like weeds, each with the word 'Democratic', 'People', 'Worker', 'Progressive' or 'Liberal' in its name and each with a formal membership small enough to fit in your kitchen. Candidates promise instant solutions, while proclaiming their honesty, and devotion to family and to country. And there you sit, trying to decide what to think, how to vote and whether to give a damn.

The fear is that voters, out of apathy or ignorance, will elect candidates who will promulgate ill-conceived economic policies, who will merely provide ineffective leadership or who will ride to victory on divisive ethnic or nationalistic appeals. How can voters make sense of this rhetoric and act reasonably? How can one be certain that others will not act unreasonably, so that the only protection is to abide by a counter-balancing extremism?

Such questions have no simple answer. Democracy, as we said earlier, comes without guarantees, including one against our own folly. However, despite the centuries of despotic rule experienced by most of the world, there is no reason to suppose that voters in one country will act much differently to those elsewhere. If there are differences, they lie in the political institutions that direct the self-interest of people and their leaders, in combination with the pre-existing interests of people as determined by economic and social structures. And so, to gauge how people in Russia, Ukraine, Cuba or China might respond to similar institutions, let us look at how voters act in established democracies, both new and old. We begin with three myths about voters. First:

> *Myth 1*: After carefully studying the issues and candidates, voters in a democracy cast their ballots for whoever best serves their interest.

Few people believe this myth, for the simple reason that it cannot be true. As we argued in the previous chapter, most voters have better things to do than study politics. Given that a single vote is unlikely to change anything, it is more reasonable for people to learn about things they can influence – how to earn some extra income or where to go in search of lower prices. Most people accept a myth of the opposite sort, namely:

> *Myth 2*: Voters in most democracies are easily baffled by meaningless campaign promises. Confused by politics, they vote for the candidate with the best smile, the most money or the most emotionally satisfying appeal. In this way democracies, especially new ones, become vulnerable to dangerous demagogues and vile extremists.

But this myth is no more true than the first. Some voters will search for extreme solutions if they think 'the system' has failed – voters everywhere can believe for a time that there are simple solutions to complex problems or that only the existence of 'evil forces' explains their plight. But just as voters are not genius policy analysts, they are not fools. People may be poor or incompletely educated, but they are not necessarily more stupid than anyone else. Voters everywhere make mistakes, but often on the basis of criteria that make it obvious that they have acted unwisely only after the fact.

Some commentators might argue that the rise of an extremist such as Vladimir Zhirinovsky in Russia is a counter-example to our argument. How else can we understand an electorate that supports his preposterous promises and inflammatory rhetoric? But Zhirinovsky did not materialize and win votes because Russian voters are stupid, ill-informed or more nationalistic than voters elsewhere. Instead we can trace his success to stupidity on the part of those 'democratic reformers' who thought that the correctness of their policies should be self-evident to all but unrepentant communists; of those who, like Boris Yeltsin, thought it possible to maintain a Czar-like distance from electoral processes; of those who were more concerned with advancing their own careers than anything else; or of those who believed that voters were sheep, easily led by a broadcast media controlled by the state.

A third myth is less a myth than a misunderstanding of the importance of things. That myth is:

Myth 3: Money is the only important thing and elections are won by whoever spends the most.

Money is anything but unimportant – for good reason it has been proclaimed the 'mother's milk of politics'. But while it is critical in determining a candidate's ability to attract voters, a candidate must first *have* a message and voters must be susceptible to receiving it. If voters are satisfied, even well-financed challengers face difficult prospects; if voters are dissatisfied, a challenger can be victorious even if outspent.

Voters in stable democracies do make reasonable decisions by relying on three relatively accessible sources of information. The first is their personal experience. If voters believe that their welfare has improved and will continue to do so, they tend to vote for incumbents; otherwise they search for alternatives. A voter's second source of information are the opinions of friends or of people and, as we outlined in the previous chapter, organizations he or she trusts. People operate with the reasonable assumption that by looking at the experiences of those in similar circumstances, they gain a better sense of a government's competence.

Naturally, what we have said refers only to tendencies. Candidates must still find ways to mobilize people who are largely disinterested in politics. That 'way' is the voter's third source of information – the political party. Political parties in a new democracy do not always form, of course, to mobilize voters and to elect candidates. Some are merely ways for specific individuals to secure public visibility. Others are mere protest groups formed around a single issue, and are organizationally unsuited to compete in an election. And still others are remnants of alliances that sought to overthrow an old regime. When such alliances disintegrate (which they commonly do since their members often have little in common other than opposition to a regime), the fragments, for lack of a better label, call themselves parties.

Regardless of their genesis, parties are universal fixtures of democracies for two reasons, one having to do with voters and the other with candidates. First, parties are the link between political activists and the great mass of people for whom politics is often little more than a spectator sport. They give voters their voice through the ballot box in a normally functioning democracy, or they spur them to more violent action in an abnormally functioning one. In stable democracies, however, parties do more. Voters need a way to give structure to their political information and experiences. Party labels, much like the sections of a filing cabinet, are such a device. Using these labels, voters learn which parties are responsible and which nominate candidates that serve their interests. Over time, they begin to identify with specific parties and vote for them or their candidates unless presented with a compelling reason to act otherwise – scandal, economic depression, the mishandling of an international crisis. In fact, party identifications can become so strong that, even when compelled to defect, a voter will do so only temporarily.

Party labels, then, are the device whereby voters organize the incoherent political information to which they are subjected before, during and after an election. Politicians soon learn that success requires being associated with something other than a social club or protest group. A stable democracy cannot remain in a situation in which countless parties manoeuvre for position, constantly divide, subdivide, recombine and change labels. If a democracy survives, the parties that survive with it are those that establish brand labels for themselves like the brand labels of consumer products. People eat at MacDonald's or purchase Japanese electronics because of their reputation for quality or efficiency; people support parties that succeed in associating desirable policies, philosophies and candidates with their labels.

But now the imperatives of electoral competition exert two pressures on parties. The first leads them to consolidate; the second dictates the form of this consolidation. Because parties must try to establish brand labels, they must show some initial successes and they must grow and compete for a broader range of public offices. This leads some parties with similar philosophies to combine under the same label in much the same way as companies with similar products competing in different markets combine to take advantage of their mutual strengths.

Here, though, the form of consolidation depends on whether the political system is parliamentary or presidential. In a parliamentary system, a party's first priority is to secure legislative representation and to participate in the formation of a government. Party leaders may be satisfied with controlling only a few seats, especially if compromising their positions in the quest for greater representation only causes them to lose the support they originally enjoyed. Whatever forces operate to cause consolidation among parties will be further attenuated to the extent that parliamentary deputies are elected by party-list proportional representation (PR), as opposed to the single-member district election schemes associated with the United States, Britain, Canada and Australia, since PR allows even small parties to participate in legislative deliberations. Thus parliamentary government – especially one with PR – will commonly be characterized by a number of parties scattered across the political spectrum.

In presidential systems – in systems with a relatively powerful and directly elected chief of state – parties must focus on the main prize, the presidency, and they must consolidate further to win. Voters, in fact, lose interest in those that have no chance of winning the presidency. Few persons want to waste their vote by casting it for someone who cannot be anything but a footnote in a history book. Thus the actions of voters alone tend to eliminate small parties in presidential systems. This consolidation, in turn, will draw the surviving parties towards the centre of opinion on most issues rather than leaving them, as in a parliamentary system, scattered across the landscape. If parties on either the Right or Left fail to coalesce, then their opposite number can win the presidency by doing so. And if they coalesce at the extremes, then the party closest to the centre of opinion wins. In the long run, then, neither side can resist failing to consolidate under only a few brand labels near the centre of public opinion on salient issues.

Of course, consolidation and convergence take time, and if anything can derail this process it is ethnicity and nationalism. Indeed if there is a fear that the citizens of a democracy can act emotionally or dangerously, it is when we talk of ethnicity or its correlates – language and religion. But in judging how a democracy can contend with such issues, we should begin with the fact that if politicians seek one thing it is issues that work to their advantage, that mobilize voters to their side. Some candidates appeal to class, others to urban–rural conflicts, some try to gain entry by championing environmental matters and some take up the cause of pensioners, workers, and so on. In stable democracies, this search accounts for nearly all domestic legislation and new governmental programmes. Unfortunately, ethnicity and its dual, nationalism, are too obvious for politicians to ignore. And if ethnicity correlates with territoriality and class, then the contours of political competition become steep and dangerous.

In assessing how a political system and the voters in it are likely to respond to such issues, we must learn how parties are likely to respond.

Will ethnicity cause parties to splinter or to become more radical, or can they absorb and blunt ethnic and nationalist agitation? We can answer this question by first noting another myth of democracy:

> *Myth 4*: Under majority rule, a majority will control the state to the detriment of any minority.

Of course, Myth 4 need not be a myth at all. But Myth 4 has proven itself to be otherwise not because people were somehow evil, ill-informed or undemocratic by nature, but because those systems were designed to ensure such control through manipulations that rendered their political system anything but democratic. In contrast, in a well-designed democracy, parties or governmental coalitions are compelled, through a variety of institutional devices, to compete at the margin for minority support. In their search for ways to form or maintain winning coalitions, parties and politicians in stable democracies have incentives to attract the support of all ethnic groups and thereby to facilitate internal resolutions of ethnic conflicts.

We cannot understate the importance of co-optation. Martin Luther King succeeded in the United States without creating instability: rather than militant opposition, he advocated the extension of constitutional rights to blacks while offering political support to both the Democratic and Republican parties. Both parties, as a product of the competition between them, responded by passing the civil rights legislation of the 1960s, which in turn blunted the appeal of militant leaders. King anticipated this response – he anticipated that, although both black and white extremists would oppose him, 'the white establishment', acting in its own self-interest, would support him. Peaceful non-violent resistance, then, was more than mere ideological conviction – it was part of a strategy that induced the major parties to give him what he wanted. In this way, King's strategy, as leader of a minority, was not to protest the basic majoritarian form of US politics; rather it was to make himself pivotal between the two political parties that competed within the majority.

One can object that this scenario applies only to established democracies. In states with weaker traditions of democratic governance, different groups will believe that past injustices ought to be corrected immediately, and that the only correction is secession, independence or even bloodshed. This will be especially true among groups that have never experienced democracy and that have little reason to believe that opponents will abide by democratic process. Ethnic conflicts, however, are rarely spontaneous events. They have causes that can be treated with such devices as a decentralized federal system that invests regional and local governments with real power, a national legislative chamber that gives coalitions of federal subjects a veto over legislation, and electoral laws that remove the incentives for political élites to appeal to baser human instincts when searching for political support. Just as few voters gather detailed information about normal politics, few will act to secede or instigate violence unilaterally. Secession and violence must be organized. Thus the great trick of political institutional design in an ethnically heterogeneous state is to establish institutions that give political parties an incentive to co-opt ethnic leaders so that they can pursue their objectives within established structures.

This incentive to co-opt will, as we have already noted, arise naturally among national parties seeking to form winning coalitions. But this incentive can be re-enforced by noting that just as a society's majority is rarely homogeneous, minorities are not either (unless, through overt isolation and discrimination, ethnicity correlates with all other issues). Heterogeneity, in turn, opens the door to political competition within ethnic groups. And since the different sides to that competition will seek allies at the national and local political levels, the door is open as well to national and local parties that will try to extend their coalitions to these different ethnic groups and nationalities. Local political competition, then, should be encouraged, which is best done by ensuring that governments control real and valued resources and by allowing the citizens of those governments to direct the distribution and use of the resources. So democratic reform that encourages competition must do so at all levels of government, not just at the national level. Stating an argument that we will repeat frequently throughout this volume, the danger of democratic transition is often not too much but too little democratic reform. Reform must give local political leaders an opportunity to compete, it must give them an avenue to participate in national organizations, and it must give national leaders incentives to encourage this participation. If 'reform' does otherwise, the connection between national parties and ethnic minorities is destroyed. And once this occurs, political extremists will be only too happy to fill the void and mobilize people to political action of a different sort.

4. Popular Referenda: Must We Vote to be Democratic?

As charges and counter-charges of dictatorship, irresponsibility and simple stupidity filled the air early in 1993 in Russia's People's Congress, the only solution to the apparent paralysis of politics seemed to be to 'go to the people'. Let the people speak – hold a referendum! But what question would voters be asked? Will it be 'Should Russia be ruled by a president or the parliament?' or 'Should the Congress have the right to fire members of the president's cabinet?' or 'Should the Congress be dissolved and forced to confront new elections?' or 'Should there be a new presidential election?' or 'Should there be new elections to choose *everybody*?' or 'Does Russia need a new constitution?' or 'Should the constitution provide for a strong or weak president?' Russia held its vote, and although the returns gave Yeltsin a reason to argue that he enjoyed a mandate to lead, opponents used those same returns to claim the opposite. The referendum resolved little and only prefaced the eventual dissolution of Russia's parliament later that year.

Despite such events (not to mention Gorbachev's ill-fated referendum on the survival of the Soviet Union itself), referenda are viewed as an important part of democracy. Complexity may require that we write law through representative intermediaries – parliaments, presidents, ministers and governmental bureaucrats. But, the argument continues, because elected officials can be insensitive to, or can misinterpret, public needs, it is best to consult the public directly on important matters. Once a seemingly clear expression of the popular will is revealed, who in a democracy dares resist that will – who prefers to be labelled 'anti-democratic' or 'authoritarian'? Who could oppose a referendum's conclusion (except in those instances in which the referendum itself is worded so as to preclude anything but a single outcome, as was the case with Gorbachev's referendum)?

It is important, however, to have a realistic understanding of the use and misuses of referenda and of voting generally. This is especially true since, when we look closely at the assumptions that underlie a referendum's presumed legitimacy, we find three assumptions that cannot be sustained generally – assumptions that, continuing with the list we began in the previous essay, we can label as myths. The first assumption is:

> *Myth 5*: Even if we exclude those who don't care or don't know, a popular will exists.

The next myth about referenda in a democracy is:

> *Myth 6*: A referendum is the most straightforward way to reveal the popular will.

From these two myths we can infer a third, namely:

> *Myth 7*: A referendum is 'more democratic' than other forms of voting in a democracy.

A healthy respect for public opinion is essential in a democracy. But none of these myths, which try to justify an exalted position for referenda, is universally valid. Consider the existence of a popular will, Myth 5. Certainly this will exists if preferences are unanimous. But in this instance there is rarely a need to learn it through referenda; no balloting is required to justify the supposition, for example, that a prosperous and stable society is a socially desirable outcome. So suppose we want to learn the popular will when preferences are not self-evident and unanimous. In this instance we need a rule with which to define that will, and the most generally accepted rule is majority rule. We appreciate that we might not always be willing to abide by this rule. Because we should not want to violate anyone's constitutional rights merely because a majority prefers to do so, most constitutions make the adoption of constitutional amendments a difficult undertaking even if a majority prefers change.

Suppose, however, that we confront an issue in which people agree that majority rule is appropriate. Thus if policy A is preferred by a majority to policy B, then A ought to be chosen over B. However, not all issues can be reduced to two alternatives. Those who would draft a new constitution, for example, do not confront a simple choice between a strong president versus a strong parliament – there are many ways to form the relationship between the different branches of government. Moreover, the issue confronting people when moving to democracy is not simply whether to hold elections today or sometime in the future. They must also decide the form of those elections, the form of the legislature and the relationship of the national government to the different components of local and regional governments.

What we want to show now is that whenever there are more than two alternatives, we encounter problems in reaching a definitive determination of the 'public will'. Suppose a majority prefers policy A to B, and a majority prefers B to some third policy, C. It appears that A ought to be selected. But notice that we have said nothing about the relationship between A and C. Since A is preferred to B and B to C, we might infer that A is preferred to C. But this need not be so. For example, suppose: (1) A calls for new legislative elections and postponement of a presidential election; (2) B calls for no elections whatsoever; and (3) C allows the current parliament to continue, and requires that a new president be elected by that parliament. Suppose the president's supporters prefer A to B to C; suppose those who are fearful of what new elections might bring but who are dissatisfied with the policies of the current president prefer B to C to A; and suppose that those who are disgusted with everyone, but especially with a parliament elected under the rules of a previous regime (a situation not uncommon to several of the successor states of the USSR), prefer C to A to B. Notice now that if each of these groups is equally numerous, then A is preferred to B by a majority, B is preferred to C by a majority, and yet C is preferred by a majority to A.

This example is important for several reasons, the most important being that, since A, B and C are each defeated in a majority vote by something, there is no popular will to be discovered. Nothing stands highest in society's preferences and nothing can lay unambiguous claim to being 'socially preferred'. Hence the first myth that justifies the legitimacy of referenda in terms of their ability to discover the popular will cannot be valid in all circumstances.

Our example also reveals Myth 6 as a myth: instead of revealing a popular will, referenda can manufacture that will and give politicians the opportunity to manipulate events. Since a referendum usually allows a choice between only two alternatives – most are framed in yes-or-no form – the final outcome in our example is determined wholly by which two alternatives are considered. If the referendum reads: 'Should a new presidential election be held?' (A versus C), the outcome is C. If the referendum reads: 'Should new parliamentary elections be held?' (B versus C), the outcome is B. And if the referendum reads: 'Should the president or the parliament be subject to new elections?' (A versus B), the outcome is A. Thus even if there is no popular will to be discovered, it can be 'manufactured' and manipulated by those politicians who can frame the questions the rest of us are expected to answer.

This critique of referenda does not employ any assumption about the inability of voters to hold informed opinions. People may be misinformed or misled, but our concern with referenda is that even with a fully informed electorate, they can give a false picture of things. They can lead us to think that there is a popular desire to move in one direction when there is no agreement whatsoever about things.

In fact, contrary to Myth 7, voting in a democracy plays a role other than allowing the public to determine policy directly, and it is an error to equate democracy with any such device. So to see voting's role and to discover democracy's essential character, let us consider representative democracy, the thing referenda are intended to supplant. Suppose our elected representatives (legislators, presidents, governors) are somehow sensitive to the preferences of those they represent. If there is no popular will, they should learn this fact. Indeed they will have incentives to do precisely that, out of fear that their election opponents will take advantage of their ignorance. Politicians also have an incentive to learn something referenda cannot reveal: the intensity of preferences. In this way, they will be in a better position to invent new alternatives, to weight differences in intensity, to evaluate the 'fairness' of different policies and to negotiate compromises. Of course, they will not necessarily do this out of good-will – they will do it to preserve their positions.

This is not to say that all legislatures can do these things. Members of a legislature that pre-dates full democracy are unlikely to have adjusted their thinking to the imperatives of competitive elections – they may have no idea what those imperatives are. We suspect, however, that parliamentary confusion in newly formed democracies reflects the absence of a well-defined public will as much as anything else. Although the early parliaments of most states formed out of the Soviet Union suffered from the malady of not being wholly democratically elected and from not being threatened with the prospect of competitive elections, they suffered also from the malady of trying to represent a population with incoherent preferences. Most persons agreed that the circumstances that prevailed after the fall of communism were unacceptable – everyone wanted a stable currency, a prosperous economy, a guarantee of individual rights and some certainty that the state would continue to provide a minimum of social welfare entitlements. But what was the 'popular will' with respect to the policies that must be implemented to achieve these ends? Because there did not exist (and still does not exist in some countries) any consensus on means, the conflicts within a legislature, as well as between the legislature and other political leaders, merely reflected society's divisions. A referendum alone could not resolve these matters.

With this argument we can now begin to see the role of voting in a democracy. Put simply, voting is the device the people use to choose their leaders, to choose those who they think represent their positions and preferences most effectively, and to replace those who they do not think have performed their jobs well:

> *Rule 9*: Political systems that allow the people to change their leaders through competitive elections are democracies – all other systems are something else. A system that allows people to decide things by referenda – even important things – but that relegates the design of those referenda and all other decisions to an unelected élite is not a democracy.

Thus the answer to the question that forms the title of this chapter is yes. But our answer does not require voting on referenda. In evaluating a constitution, we should not focus on the opportunities it provides for deciding issues directly or on the power it gives a president or a legislature to call plebiscites. These things may influence the relative power of different parts of a government, but they do not always impact the power of the voters themselves. Of greater importance in determining the responsiveness of public officials to the people are guarantees of meaningful and competitive elections. Will elections be held with sufficient frequency? Who controls the rules under which elections are held (we should be certain that they are not controlled by those who are directly governed by those rules, lest they manipulate them to their own advantage)? What direct and indirect measures does a constitution contain to ensure that elections will be competitive (does the constitution offer promises of campaign funds that a majority party can manipulate)?

None of this means that we see no role for referenda. Referenda are important devices for bringing issues to the attention of voters or for building a consensus among decision-makers over what direction to move policy, and, if used properly, they can offer voters a way to constrain the actions of politicians and other public officials. For example, voters in Switzerland can veto legislation that affects their taxes. In local elections in the United States, voter approval may be required before officials are allowed to increase public indebtedness. And referenda – initiatives – that can be instigated by voters themselves can spur otherwise recalcitrant legislators to action. Nevertheless, the key feature of these examples is that referenda are only a part of the political process. Because they are something more than a public opinion poll, voters might have an incentive to become better informed when voting in a referendum. Referenda, moreover, can direct politicians to exert greater efforts at resolving an issue, as when voters reveal that they are against secession or in favour of something else. However, referenda should not be interpreted as a substitute for the power of voters to decide who shall lead or represent them. Referenda are merely an auxiliary control and not the key element of a democracy.

5. What Is A Fair and Competitive Election?

Throughout its history, the Soviet Union required that its citizens march to the polls so it could announce that the victorious (and only) candidate had won with a turnout exceeding 99 per cent. A failure to vote resulted in a knock at the door and a demand that a ballot be filled in. In this way Andrei Vyshinsky could assert in 1937 that, 'never in a single country did the people manifest such activity in elections as did the Soviet people. Never has any capitalist country known nor can it know such a high percentage of those participating in voting as did the USSR'. The democratic world laughed derisively, and brushed aside the assertion of democratic legitimacy and superiority. However, although we may think we know an unfair or uncompetitive election when we see it, can we recognize its opposite? Must all candidates or parties have an equal chance of winning? Must all candidates have equal access to the media? Must the media be unbiased? Must all parties have equal financing? Must turnout exceed 50 per cent? Must political candidates refrain from criticizing each other with personal attacks? Must political parties represent a cross-section of society, mirroring its ethnic, linguistic and cultural diversity? And must there always be more candidates than there are offices to be filled?

The meaning of *fair and competitive* has changed much over time – so much so that there need not be general agreement about the content of this idea. 'Democracy' began in the 18th and 19th centuries with property requirements that kept most people from voting. Elections that excluded the participation of women were deemed fair in most of the world until World War I and until only recently in Switzerland, as were elections that did the same to blacks in America and Indians in Latin America. Elections in which incumbent politicians enjoy as much as 100:1 advantage in financing are commonplace today throughout the world's democracies. And elections that keep certain philosophies from being represented at the polls – separatist movements, religious movements, racist ones and ideological ones – are often regarded as otherwise fair and competitive (witness the German prohibition of Nazi agitation and the nearly equivalent American prohibition of anything that hints at the possibility that blacks are in any way inferior to whites).

Despite this history, we worry about perceptions of fairness, because if candidates believe that elections are unfair or uncompetitive, then they and their followers are less likely to operate under democratic rules and more likely to prefer unconstitutional actions. And if this view is widely held, then the legitimacy of the entire system is undermined and people become more acceptant of the demagogue. Unlike a regime that used elections to register solidarity with a Communist Party, elections are the means whereby the people exercise their sovereign right to replace one set of leaders with another – the right to 'throw the bums out'. Stripped of this right, democracy becomes a sham. Stripped of the belief that elections are fair, the stability of the political system becomes dependent wholly on its ability to coerce. Of course, since societies have prospered and been stable under a variety of definitions of fairness and competitiveness, the question we should ask is: what definition is appropriate today – what standards facilitate a stable democratic regime in the 20th and 21st centuries?

Naturally there are some criteria over which there is universal or near universal agreement:

Rule 10: No one above the age of responsibility should be denied the right to vote or should confront excessive obstacles to voting. It is tempting to want to exclude those 'judged incompetent by the court'. Who, after all, wants public policy decided by 'incompetents'? But the excesses to which this dangerous idea can be extended were only too clearly illustrated in the Soviet Union. And even if we assume that courts operate honestly, we need not prohibit incompetents from voting: if they are truly incompetent, they are unlikely to move an election from one candidate or party to another; and their number will be too small to matter in any electorate we can imagine.

Rule 11: Only voters should judge a candidate's qualifications. Let the antisemite, fascist and unrepentant communist campaign. Once we allow some élite to enforce its judgements about seditious, inflammatory or immoral candidacies, or to deem certain parties illegal, democracy is compromised. The people can dispense with extremists by not supporting them.

Rule 12: New parties and candidates should be allowed to enter an election relatively freely. Just as the threat of competition keeps a firm from charging a monopoly price, the threat of competition compels those in power to work for the interests of society. Of course, just as every manufacturer prefers to be a monopolist, every politician prefers that no one contests his right to govern. But once the right of free entry is compromised, all other rights are jeopardized.

Rule 13: Elections should not be judged invalid if a candidate is unchallenged. Although the absence of a challenger might imply coercion, if all other requirements for a fair and competitive election are satisfied, the absence of a challenger may imply nothing more than the existence of a singularly popular candidate.

Rule 14: The media must have the right to publish any opinion regarding a candidate's qualifications and a party's activities. Public officials will try to use the power of their office to protect themselves from opposition. Allowing incumbents to wrap themselves in the protective cloak of official position precludes the possibility of fair and competitive elections. A wholly free press, able to investigate and report on the failings and accomplishments of incumbents and challengers alike, is essential.

Rule 15: No area of policy should be set off-limits for debate. All manner of issues should be subject to scrutiny, and the only criteria for their selection should be the electorate's willingness to listen to those who campaign on them. With an official gatekeeper of legitimate debate – a role despots and those who cannot comprehend democracy think only they should fill – the election is not unlike one in which the government controls the media.

Rule 16: Voters should be free from coercion and the voting booth should be off-limits to candidates and their supporters. In the long run, we would hope to see the formation of organizations whose express purpose is to oversee the honesty of voting procedures and whose charter is explicitly non-partisan.

Rule 17: No one should be compelled to vote by force or fines. Even though a number of democracies compel participation, this practice reflects little more than the naive view that high turnout is 'good' and low turnout is 'bad'. People choose to vote or to abstain for a great many reasons, but compelling them to do so does not make an election fair or competitive. It merely gives the state another excuse to interfere in our personal lives, and another way for it to tax.

Rule 18: Elections should not be judged invalid merely because turnout falls below some arbitrary threshold. If few citizens wish to participate, it is their free choice to allow the final outcome to be determined by those who do. Establishing a minimum turnout requirement merely gives citizens the opportunity to protest without incurring even the minimal cost of walking to the voting booth.

Rule 19: Elections should be regularly scheduled and not thrust suddenly upon an electorate. Too often this rule is violated to give incumbents special advantage. Sometimes that strategy is effective and sometimes it is not (a classic failure is Yeltsin's attempt to manipulate events by calling for new parliamentary elections before the rubble from the old parliament had been cleared away – rubble that hardly interfered with Zhirinovsky's campaign), but in either case, the election cannot be deemed fair.

Ensuring that all of these requirements are satisfied can be difficult. In Russia today, for example, there are suspicions of widespread vote fraud, since the administration of elections belongs largely to those whose fates depend on the outcome of those elections. We can only hope that, as representation becomes more meaningful and important to citizens, citizens themselves will demand electoral reform to guard against fraud. However, rather than lament that some of our criteria may be difficult to satisfy, it is more useful to consider something that does not appear on our list; namely the requirement that all candidates share equal resources (money) in a campaign. This supposition arises naturally out of the fear that unrestricted democratic process gives too great an advantage to the rich, to monied interests within society or to those who are willing to sell themselves to those interests. These concerns arise especially in societies that are experiencing primitive forms of capitalism in their transition to a market economy, owing to the perception (and to the fact) of extensive corruption in government. There is the temptation to restrict the ability of candidates and parties to raise money, and there is the parallel temptation to require the public financing of campaigns so as to equalize matters.

This argument has merit, and these concerns exist in established democracies if only because they have developed well-defined channels whereby money can flow from 'special interests' to politicians. However, against these concerns we must balance the idea that people participate in politics in many ways. They contribute not only money, but also time, energy and ideas. Do these contributions, and people's different abilities to make them, also violate any principle of fairness? And if we try to equalize resources across candidates, do we do this for all candidates and parties – including crazy extremists or those who can secure only their own vote?

Clearly, any idea can be carried to extremes. We cannot eliminate the influence of money or wholly equalize its availability. But there is in any argument for public financing of campaigns an implicit assumption that, unless uncovered, allows a naive view of politics. That assumption is that money operates in only one direction – to the disadvantage of those who do not have it. We are reminded here of the words of James Madison, the principal architect of the American constitution: 'The most common and durable source of [political] faction has been the various and unequal distribution of property'. From this excerpt we might infer that Madison foresaw the same class struggle as did Marx. To the contrary, however, he went on to note that, 'a landed interest, a manufacturing interest, a mercantile interest, a monied interest, with many lesser interests, grow up of necessity in civilized nations, and divide them into different classes, actuated by different sentiments and views'. Thus rather than view money as operating in any simple way so as to divide society into separate and permanent classes, Madison foresaw that the clash of interests would be multi-faceted and would divide society in innumerable ways.

For the most part, this has in fact been the course of history in stable democracies. Workers, businessmen, bankers or the 'middle class' rarely, if ever, vote with anything approaching unanimity. The trade policies of one party aid some sectors of the economy and workers in them, but damage and are opposed by others. The state subsidies that a candidate advocates may aid one industry, but only at the expense of those other parts of society that must pay for those subsidies. Farm policy assists one part of the agricultural sector, but often does so at the expense of another sector. An administration's decision to regulate prices and entry in one sector of an economy so as to bar competition injures those other sectors that use the output of the first as their input.

Politics in a stable democracy, then, is not dominated by the clash of class interests. There are too many interests for any category to predominate over the rest, and most interests cut across society in so many ways that they make that society look less like a layer cake and more like scrambled eggs. Workers hold investments in firms directly or through pension funds and thus are concerned about stock prices. Bankers are as concerned as anyone else with the cost of financing a new home or automobile – few are presidents riding in limousines. Trade policies that hurt one industry and aid another encourage alliances that cut across divisions of management and labour. And regional interests bisect almost any interest that does not correlate with geography. Moreover, if a policy aids one clearly definable segment of society at the expense of the rest, then generally that segment is too small to sustain itself as a winning coalition. And in the event that this segment is large – pensioners, veterans or farmers – there are other issues that divide these segments into opposing interests.

Parties and candidates must try to form winning coalitions in this scramble of interests, and it is here that we find an important source of democratic stability. We begin with the fact that the complexity of modern society makes any coalition of voters or legislators inherently vulnerable to disruption. Regardless of what combination of interests a politician might use to craft a winning coalition, the opposition can chip away at this support by offering some new advantage to elements of that coalition by framing an issue that divides it. This 'chipping away', however, occurs in all directions and along all dimensions – no coalition is invulnerable to disruption from any direction. The inherent instability of winning coalitions, in turn, makes all interests potentially pivotal. Indeed once a winning coalition is formed, all of its components can claim to be as critical to its existence as any other, thereby giving all a claim to the fruits of victory.

This coalitional instability need not translate into regime instability. It can strengthen it. Winners today, uncertain that they will not become losers tomorrow, are confronted with two choices. First, once in control they can try to maintain power by undemocratic means. This choice is viable, however, only if a significant part of society allows such actions. The second choice is to treat one's adversaries as they would wish their adversaries to treat them. Indeed the inherent instability of coalitions tells everyone that even if one loses power, there is a reasonable chance of regaining it in the future. And to the extent that the prospect of regaining power moderates the actions of those out of power, it also moderates the actions of those in power. All victories and all defeats are temporary.

Coalitional instability facilitates political stability in another way. If society consists of a complex array of cross-cutting interests, then the salience of issues that are especially disruptive of stability – ethnic and racial matters – diminishes. If different ethnic, linguistic or racial groups share economic and social concerns, coalitions based on emotional appeals to these dangerous cleavages can, in principle, be disrupted, and voters who are on different sides of some ethnic cleavage can be courted by the same candidates and parties who will have an incentive to moderate the salience of ethnic issues.

Of course, nothing we have said applies if elections are not fair and competitive. Voters must be able to implement the threat of punishing those who violate the norms of democratic process. And politicians must allow themselves to become temporary losers in the hope of becoming winners in the future. For a state accustomed to authoritarian rule in which winners vanquished losers, all of these things require a restructuring of beliefs about the consequences of winning and losing. Winners must come to believe that they will be punished at the polls for acting undemocratically, and losers must believe that, by playing the game of democratic politics skilfully, they can become winners. This restructuring is generally difficult, because beliefs change slowly and only with experience. Thus it is often said that the most critical election in a new democracy is the second, or at least the second in which there is a transfer of power. Once this election occurs, society's self-confidence in its democratic institutions is increased to the point where these new beliefs begin to predominate over the old ones. The trick, then, is to 'hold on' through the first few elections, since thereafter, if all other institutions are appropriately designed, fair and competitive elections will become a self-enforcing reality.

6. Economics or Politics: Which is the Chicken and Which the Egg?

Freed from authoritarian rule and the heavy hand of state control, the government of some newly formed democracy proceeds on the path of economic reform, basking in the glow of successful revolution and enthusiasm over new-found political freedom. But change soon generates undesirable side effects – unemployment, inflation, disparities in the distribution of wealth, corruption, illegality and violence. Enthusiasm is replaced by dissatisfaction and impatience, especially when the anticipated foreign aid and investment fail to materialize. Seeking to dampen discontent, the government makes bold promises it cannot keep or increases subsidies to failing industries. But dissatisfaction grows and champions of alternative policies multiply. Fearing a loss of power, the government vacillates between new decrees (some undemocratic) and accommodation with its critics. In the first instance, reform is clear and decisive (though not necessarily correct); in the second it is blurred by confusion and indecision. But vacillation between dictatorial decrees and soothing compromise, between policies formed by technocrats and policies formed by political holdovers from an earlier regime, and between rapid reform and no reform at all, erodes the government's ability to generate public support for any new decisive economic action. Soon only criminals or entrenched bureaucrats have control, and democracy becomes a sham since neither criminals nor bureaucrats seem willing to allow voters to dictate their role. Frustrated with the incapacity of democrats, with the disintegration of the state and with the threat to national sovereignty implicit in a state ruled by drug lords and pimps, the military acts!

Although this scenario, or at least its early stages, can describe any of the successor states of the Soviet Union, it also describes any number of countries in Eastern Europe and Latin America that have attempted political and economic reform simultaneously. As a consequence, no small number of countries have seen their transition to democracy derailed by a military dictatorship or a 'palace coup' that seizes power with the argument that only it can stabilize events and pull the country out of chaos.

An especially salient question, then, is whether it is better to implement democratic reforms as quickly as possible along with market reforms, or whether we should postpone political reform so the move to a market economy can be directed by decisive action. Which comes first: political or economic change? Can a transition to democracy facilitate a prosperous economy or is a prosperous economy a necessary condition for stable democracy? Is democracy possible when inflation exceeds 1000 per cent and prices are quoted in foreign currencies that only some élite can earn? Should a new constitution be adopted after the economy is reformed or should it be considered along with economic changes?

These questions do not arise merely because political turmoil appears only to exacerbate economic difficulties. They arise also because at almost the same time as the Soviet Union and Eastern Europe began their political liberalization, China embarked on its economic reforms but rejected political ones. Today, even though we must appreciate that it began at a pitifully low starting point, we see China as a whole experiencing one of the highest economic growth rates in the world. The Soviet Union has passed into history, with each of its former republics subject to double-digit rates of economic decline. These questions arise also because opponents of political liberalization point to the economic 'miracles' of South Korea, Chile, Taiwan and Japan, all of which had their economies directed by an oligarchy that did not confront competitive elections until recently, if at all. Each of these countries (and there are others) illustrates successful economic development without recourse to the incoherence of the Soviet Union's erstwhile democratic politics.

In one sense, then, the answer to all of our questions about the direction and order of reform is simple: if economic reform is to proceed along a well-defined path, then it is not unreasonable to postpone the transition to democracy in favour of the enlightened despot who does 'democratic things' when such things are required and who transgresses on democratic rights only when there is no alternative.

Unfortunately, this answer poses practical difficulties. First, what if there is no consensus about reform? What if some want to proceed slowly and others quickly? What if some want to privatize everything – industries, collective farms and retail stores – while others want only to privatize particular things? What if some want to protect against the threat of massive unemployment while others are more concerned about the prospect of hyperinflation? And what if some see the necessity for deep sacrifice among urban and rural poor while others are willing to trade such sacrifice for a less severe but more uncertain package of economic reforms?

Second, what guarantee do we have that the postponement of political reform favours the selection of an enlightened despot who will relinquish power and implement democracy at the appropriate time? China's leaders protected their despotism by killing and jailing opponents without regret; authorities are still looking for the victims of repression in Chile and Argentina; Taiwan's Kuomingtang Party jailed its political adversaries and, in its early history on the island, acted much like its communist counterpart on the mainland; news reporters continue to cover student riots in South Korea and ruling élites must live in the shadow of an unsavory past; and in Japan official corruption at the highest levels, despite the damage inflicted on governmental stability, seems a way of life. It should also be kept in mind, moreover, that these 'economic miracles' owe as much to the role of the United States in their economies as they do to any inspired leadership. Even today, China's growth could not be sustained without investment from, and trade with, Taiwan, Japan and the United States and from wage rates and labour practices that would repulse citizens in any stable democracy.

All we have said thus far, however, establishes that there are dangers along any path to reform. So let us look at the fundamental problem that confronts economic reform in an ex-communist state and begin from there. Briefly, that problem is the almost complete absence of property rights. Without 'property rights' – without the enforceable right of ownership and the corresponding right to buy, sell and trade, as well as other economic freedoms – markets uncorrupted by guns and violence cannot develop. With 'property rights' the state can abrogate at its discretion, and with contracts that are unenforceable in any court, efficient markets cannot exist. Without these things, economic reform remains but another version of state ownership, central planning or war-lordism, with all of the economic inefficiencies and threats to individual liberties that these things imply.

This is not to say that citizens of Russia, Ukraine, Belarus, Kazakhstan and elsewhere do not feel a sense of ownership. Apartments can be traded, goods and services can be bought in open (if inefficient) markets, and workers and management can capture some of the profits (if any) from their employment. But legal systems for defining, monitoring and protecting these rights are primitive. A system of property rights is something more than a set of labels that say 'I own this' or 'You own that'. It also includes political and legal institutions whereby people and firms can defend these labels against expropriation, whereby they can resolve disputes over labels, and whereby new rights can be defined as technology, opinion and circumstances change.

Without these rights and ways to assign them, and without ways to protect them once assigned, markets cannot develop, investments will not be made and new technologies will not arise. The transition to a market economy, then, is something more than the privatization of state property and the issuing of vouchers. This transition requires political institutional development: legislatures to create the laws that will define and protect rights as well as coherent tax codes; courts to interpret and enforce those laws; elections to direct the legislature and political parties to mobilize the population to political action and give their preferences a voice; and a government that feels sufficiently responsive to political pressures that it will act against at least the most corrupt and violent practices of whatever criminal element seeks to take advantage of the economic and political disequilibrium.

But now we come to the core question of economic and political transition: are there policies that democratic systems are inherently incapable of implementing but that are necessary for successful economic reform? Is a democracy capable of creating the system of property rights that a market economy requires, or must those rights and the institutions associated with their evolution and enforcement be set in place by an autocratic regime?

The problem, of course, is that reform is never smooth. Reform is necessarily accompanied by unpleasant things: unemployment, sagging investment, a decline in living standards for all but a select few, the erosion of savings through inflation, increased crime and the deterioration of social services. And, as in the scenario that introduces this chapter, these dislocations create political demands to stall or reverse reforms that governments, especially democratic ones, find difficult to resist. In contrast, the authoritarian state – one that controls the military or internal security police – seems better equipped to resist these pressures, to pursue reform with single-minded determination, to jail nearly anyone, and to try to substitute state power for market incentives whenever necessary. Thus although we may have to sacrifice on the issue of human rights, it seems reasonable to suppose that the authoritarian state is better positioned to implement the bitter medicine of reform.

But before we accept the superiority of authoritarian rule, let us consider more carefully the presumed failings of democracy. We want to argue that the fault is not with democracy *per se*, but with an incompletely formed democracy. If economic and political reform proceed simultaneously, then the democratic transition is incomplete by definition at the time economic reforms are begun. Constitutions are not yet drafted, or if drafted are poorly understood; their provisions have not yet been implemented by legislative action; and if implemented, the courts are only beginning to develop ways to enforce the law. Thus political leaders and public officials have at best only a weak relationship to the different interests in society, and these interests are often poorly organized and can exert political pressure in only the crudest ways.

The best organized interests in a newly formed democracy are those whose only common interest was their opposition to the old regime or those who believe that they can proceed with 'business as usual' under any regime. These interests are dominated by those with weak or nonexistent preferences for successful reform: bureaucrats with little incentive to compromise on anything that requires fewer resources being committed to the public sector; managers of state-subsidized firms that prefer anything but competitive markets; and leaders of specialized unions that represent but a small percentage of the labour force. Thus of the two approaches that a government commonly takes in a newly formed democracy – accommodation and decrees – the second, after revealing the true costs of transition, exacerbates the problem of support by focusing all responsibility on a small subset of technocrats which lacks the power or will to force compliance to its actions. The first course, accommodation, cannot work simply because it seeks an alliance of contradictory forces.

The usual failure of simultaneous political and economic reform is not too much democracy but too little. With political institutions that do not yet accommodate the range of social interests, with property rights still undefined and the institutions for defining them ill-formed, and with electoral institutions that do not allow voters to sanction public officials so that they have a self-interest consonant with the interests of the rest of society, the policies that emerge from accommodation are equivalent to policy by decree, except that now no one holds responsibility for its failure. Although they may have the appearance of democratic compromise, these policies have not been formed in a democratic way. As the product of temporary alliances among élites with contradictory preferences, they have little long-term economic or political justification. They are not policies designed by leaders of political parties with long-term goals of re-election who need to develop a broad base of mass political support. If they are the correct policies, they are correct by accident. Those party to the accommodation do not confront the necessity of having to explain their decisions to anyone but other élites. Their arena of conflict is among themselves. Because they lack electoral responsibility, they lack democratic responsibility. Their primary objective is to position themselves for succession to power. The incompletely formed democracy, then, combines the worst of both worlds: authoritarian rule by a committee that answers only to itself.

But those who oppose a full move to democracy – a new constitution, regularly scheduled elections, a new legislature, new courts and new laws – will object that, 'the people are unprepared for democracy. They do not yet understand the give-and-take of such politics and they will be too easily led astray by demagogues'. Wouldn't a more concerted move to democracy during a period of economic turmoil merely result in a replay of Weimar Germany's experience?

Germany, though, illustrates our argument that incomplete democracy poses special dangers. Hitler's accession to power was not the result of simple mass unrest; rather it was also the product of a poorly designed political system that was incapable of accommodating social tensions and implementing coherent policy – a system that virtually guaranteed governmental instability and a confusion of roles between president and parliament. Hitler was selected as chancellor by precisely those élites who would have objected most strongly to complete democratic freedom.

In fact warnings of the unavoidable dangers of democracy are too often uttered by those who know little about it. Why should we suppose that *apparatchiks* and members of the nomenclatura can judge what is required for democratic process? How do they know that the 'masses' are too ignorant to act in their own self-interest? Where is it proved that acting democratically is more difficult than running a tractor or maintaining a household? Are we better prepared beforehand to raise children than to vote? Why are those 'ignorant and easily misled masses' who emigrate to democracies from countries with little or no democratic tradition able to grasp quickly the essentials of organizing in their self-interest – is there something in the waters of Israel, the United States, Canada or Australia that makes immigrants suddenly wiser?

The assertion of ignorance and lack of preparation, we should remind ourselves, too often serves the self-interest of those who make these arguments. It is perhaps better to ask: what preparations are being made to inform people about democracy? What institutions of self-rule at the local and regional levels are being provided to 'train' voters and new political élites?

Nothing we have said implies that democratic transition in periods of economic turmoil does not pose great risks. Too many democracies have been launched with disastrous consequences for us to argue that we can proceed with unrestrained optimism. But there are also great risks associated with abiding by the assumption that there is a self-evident correct economic policy and that an autocrat will know and choose that policy. Finally, none of the presumed dangers of democracy mean that we cannot begin the process of democratic transition at the local level without any threat to the security of the state. It is here that people can practise and learn the mechanics of democracy. Democratic transition need not be 'top-down'. Just as the framers of the US constitution practised democracy first at the state and local levels in the 18th century, the citizens of Taiwan did the same in their transition to democracy in the 20th. Rather than a wholesale rejection of democratic reform in favour of authoritarianism, this is the lesson transitions to democracy teach. De Tocqueville's observation (*Democracy in America*) about America in the 1830s, then, that, 'the constitution of the United States is an admirable work, nevertheless one may believe that its founders would not have succeeded, had not the previous 150 years given the different states of the Union a taste for, and practice of, provincial governments' holds true for any state.

Finally, if we return once again to the issue of property rights, we should remind the reader that, before the break-up of the Soviet Union, the world's largest experiment in privatization did not occur in Britain, France or China. It occurred in the United States in the 19th century, when the federal government 'owned' virtually all land west of the Mississippi river (and a good share of the land east of it as well). In less than 100 years most of the usable parts of that land were privatized so that, even with the 'distraction' of a civil war, America began the 20th century as the world's largest and most productive economy. Certainly corruption and avarice characterized the process of privatization and not a few great fortunes were made with means of questionable legality. But the chief mechanism whereby the land was turned to productive use was simple and straightforward: property rights secured by democratic institutions. Economic prosperity did not bring democracy to America's west; democracy came first, and was subsequently refined as prosperity appeared.

7. Constitutional Rights: Mere Words or Sustainable Guarantees?

Citizens and political élites in most countries moving from the shadows of communism are schizophrenic. On the one hand, they are sceptical about democracy as a route to a prosperous future, and they are suspicious of the value of a constitution as a meaningful guarantor of individual rights and civil liberties. On the other hand, those who would write constitutions for these countries offer drafts replete with promises, directives and rights in a form that suggests that they believe every word will be faithfully executed.

Finding the source of this schizophrenia requires that we move to first principles – to the ways in which individual rights are secured in a democracy. We begin by noting that establishing any state requires granting its various parts the right to coordinate us, through coercion if necessary, so we can accomplish things that will not be accomplished otherwise. Thus acting as our agent, we allow the state to tax and to spend, to draft, to legislate and, in the event of illegality, to imprison. In ages past this coercive and coordinative function was claimed and imposed by a small élite. Today democracies are constituted with the understanding that the state should serve only with the consent of the governed and that the governed hold the ultimate voice in how the state acts. The great trick of democratic design, however, lies in constructing the state so that public officials do not exceed their authority.

An important part of this 'trick' is an appropriately designed constitution, which, in addition to defining the components of the state and their relationship to each other and to the people, sets limits on the state's power. But in drafting such a document two questions arise:

1. How can a piece of paper control anything, let alone those who direct the state's coercive parts and who might aspire to despotism or whose ego might lead them to believe that only they know what is best?
2. What is it that properly belongs in such a document – what should

be made specific, what should be made ambiguous and what issues should it confront?

These two questions converge when drafting constitutional guarantees of fundamental rights – those individual rights that define a free and just society. Some of these rights are well-understood and appear in virtually every democratic constitution, such as a guarantee of religious freedom, of the freedom of the press, of the right to peaceful assembly, of the inviolability of personal property, of equality in the right to vote, and of the right to a speedy and fair trial. The inclusion of other 'rights' – welfare entitlements – is more controversial, such as a guarantee of housing, employment and just compensation for labour. Our two questions, then, combine to form a third, namely: why should the second category of 'rights' be controversial, but not those in the first category?

Before we address these questions, there is a related matter that requires attention: the advisability of including citizen obligations or duties in a constitution. Put simply, clauses requiring, for example, that, 'man's exercise of his rights and liberties must not...be detrimental to the public weal or surrounding environment', that, 'everyone...display concern for the preservation of the historical and cultural heritage', that, 'everyone ...pay taxes...in the amounts established by law' or that, 'parents have the obligation to raise and support their children' – are dangerous not merely because they can serve no useful democratic purpose, but also because they pervert the function of the constitution. First:

Rule 20: Lists of citizen obligations in a constitution pervert a constitution's bill of rights by diffusing its primary intent: keeping states from tyranny. A constitution defines and places limits on the state and not on the sovereign, the people.

Rule 21: Such clauses serve no useful purpose. If people choose to place limits on themselves, they can do so through their representative assemblies, via the laws they allow those assemblies to pass.

Rule 22: Lists of citizen obligations are dangerous. They establish the precedent that a constitution can control and limit rights rather than protect them.

We can attribute such clauses to the fear of ambiguity, especially when it appears that the full expression of a person's rights might conflict with someone else's, and to the fear that people will not know their responsibilities as citizens. But here it is best to rely on a legislative or judicial resolution, as well as on the ability of people to learn their roles and responsibilities. If the other parts of our constitution are designed well, we can rely on the structure a constitution establishes to reach a just accommodation whenever rights appear to conflict and to guide our learning; if they are designed poorly, it matters little what rights and duties we specify.

Turning to the issue of what rights belong in a constitution, we should note that the state's role with respect to 'aspirations' can be decided as part of normal politics, but only if other rights are secure. If citizens are free to engage in political discourse, informed by a viable press, and able to displace one set of leaders with another, then they can use the state, if they so choose, to secure fair compensation for labour, safe working conditions, adequate housing, environmental protection and pensions. But if they lose basic rights, attainment or retention of these things is at best problematical and at worst subject to the whim of an otherwise tyrannical state. Indeed a society unable to partake of its fundamental rights has no protection against the avaricious official who acts in his narrow self-interest, regardless of the aspirations otherwise provided for in a constitution. Tradition may dictate the inclusion of aspirations in a constitution. But such things should not be confused with basic rights. We can direct the state to be concerned with just compensation for labour and health care. But requiring that the state *ensure* just compensation or that it *guarantee* medical care opens the door to contentious judicial and political processes as people attempt to decide whether legislation moves us close enough to the required goal. Should we declare a medical care bill unconstitutional because it only takes us part way to a wholly comprehensive solution to public health or would we prefer to view such legislation as an essential first step? More problematical is the fact that the state may be unable to satisfy such requirements, in which case its failure to satisfy these 'rights' undermines confidence that it will act to ensure others. Thus:

> *Rule 23*: Constitutions should make aspirations irrelevant to a court's deliberations so that they can focus on whether legislation is in conformity with fundamental constitutional rights.

Turning to fundamental rights, the safest way to approach matters is with a healthy dose of cynicism about how public officials will interpret various provisions. The prudent assumption is that legislators, bureaucrats and the like will operate in their own self-interest and that even a viable electoral system can only imperfectly regulate this self-interest. Thus although the other parts of the constitution should ensure that these motives are the correct ones, history has taught us the value of additional precautions. Among these precautions is a succinct statement of each right:

> *Rule 24*: Long or convoluted clauses detailing individual rights cannot substitute for simple admonitions and unqualified restrictions on state action.

Compare, for example, the American provision that the legislature, 'shall pass no law abridging the freedom of the press' with the more ambiguously identified 'right' in an early Russian draft constitution that, 'the media are free...[but] the seizure and confiscation of information material and the hardware for its preparation and transmission are permitted only in accordance with a ruling by a court of law'. Although such qualification may be designed to ensure flexibility in the event of unforeseen contingencies, it opens the door to judicial confusion as to original intent, and gives the bureaucrat and politician room to circumvent that intent. Concise statements of rights provide the court, moreover, with a valuable weapon in their defence of rights and in their inevitable conflicts with executive and legislative branches. Society may choose to adhere to certain qualifications (like a prohibition against shouting 'fire' in a theatre). But as with those instances in which rights might conflict, the way in which qualifications are best arrived at is a social consensus reached through legitimate political process rather than through constitutional edict. If consensual – if such qualifications assume the role of a social norm about civil conduct – then they can be easily specified and enforced through normal legislation.

But before we can write a concise constitutional delineation of rights, we must answer the question: what rights are an essential part of any democratic constitution? What is the common characteristic of those rights we normally think of as 'basic': the right to free speech, to assemble peacefully, to a speedy and fair trial, to protection of our property, to the free choice of religious conviction, and so on? The answer to these questions is contained in the core characteristic of democracy: that the people, and only the people, are sovereign and that the state is merely the sovereign's agent. Thus:

Rule 25: A right is basic and essential if its abrogation undermines the authority of the sovereign to control the sovereign's agent, the state. And since control in a democracy is exercised primarily through elections, a right is basic and essential if its abrogation undermines our ability to displace one set of leaders with another through election.

We protect speech, then, because it is impossible to have free and fair elections without the ability to confront political leaders with accusations of incompetence or even criminality; we allow adjustments in this right (again, as with prohibitions against yelling 'fire' in a crowded theatre) because it does not limit our ability to control the state. We protect the right of free and peaceful assembly, since free and fair elections are impossible if the sovereign cannot organize opposition to the state outside of the state's formal structure. We protect the right to petition the state for redress of grievances, since the sovereign should be allowed to convey its wants to those who hold official position so that they can adjust their policies accordingly. We protect religious freedom since, if the state can control our religious institutions, it can control all manner of thought and thereby undermine the essence of free democratic choice. We guarantee due process of law since we cannot have free and fair elections if the state can use its judicial arm to coerce or jail opponents. We ensure against discrimination on the basis of race, religion, sex and ethnicity since we cannot allow the state to use the principle of majority rule to abrogate the ability of minorities to participate fully in democratic process. And we protect the right to property not merely to have efficient markets but also to preclude the state from coercing us with threats of expropriation and government-sanctioned theft.

We arrive finally at the most fundamental question, the one that forms the title to this chapter: how are these basic and essential rights enforced? Certainly we should not suppose that merely setting words to paper provides any iron-clad guarantee. Too much history tells us otherwise. Instead the answer lies in the incentives of public officials that other parts of the constitution establish.

Constitutions seek to do more than merely define the various branches of the state with the idea that a bill of rights will protect us against any usurpation of power by these branches. The institutions a constitution establishes control the aspirations of officials by 'setting ambition against ambition' (Madison, *Federalist Papers*). This is accomplished in three ways:

1. It creates a balance of power among the separate branches of government. In presidential systems, executive, legislative and judicial branches are explicitly separate. In parliamentary systems, the executive is fused with the legislative, but the executive (prime minister) is given the authority (in conjunction, perhaps, with a president or monarch) to dissolve the legislature and call for new elections.
2. It gives the different branches of the government a different relation to the people. Thus a president is elected directly by all citizens; legislators are elected by smaller constituencies; and the court is selected indirectly by the people through joint legislative–executive action. In this way political leaders confront each other with as great a variety of interests as possible, so that public policy must be passed with some minimal level of consensus.
3. In large or heterogeneous states such as Russia, the United States and Switzerland, a federal governmental structure allows citizens to control as much of their destiny as possible in a part of government closest to them, and ensures that local and regional concerns are given full weight at the national governmental level.

All of this structure influences the incentives of political leaders to protect rights. If the system is designed correctly – if political careers depend on protecting rights or ensuring against bureaucratic infringement of rights – then those rights are preserved. Otherwise those rights are mere words on paper. Individual rights frequently succumbed to political ambition in Latin America not because the lists of rights in the constitutions were incomplete, but because the political systems did not function to them. And they were sometimes ignored in the United States, especially on racial matters, not because they failed to be well articulated, but rather because there was no consensual will to pay full heed to them and, correspondingly, because politicians gained little political capital by acting otherwise.

What is evident from this abbreviated answer to our question, then, is that the mechanism whereby rights are protected and the public interest served depends on a complex interaction of all parts of the government, in combination with the people's consensual determination to keep those rights. Thus when evaluating some part of a constitution, we must calculate how that part fits into the larger scheme of things. A debate over the appropriate relationship of the executive to the legislature cannot be resolved without also considering, among other things, the federal construction of the state, the likely character of political parties and the relationship of each branch of government to voters Similarly, in ascertaining whether a constitution grants local or regional government sufficient autonomy requires that we evaluate the extent to which the parts of the national government have an incentive to maintain that autonomy. This depends on whether national politicians will be led to care sufficiently about local interests, which in turn depends on whether people prefer to defend regional interests and regional governmental prerogatives against incursions by the national government. Completing the circle, this in turn depends on whether the state as a whole is structured so as to encourage that interest among its citizens.

8. Democratic Institutions: Why Would They Influence Anything?

This volume's theme is that the design of democratic institutions – constitutions, electoral laws, forms of legislative representation, and so on – can greatly influence outcomes, including the stability of the state itself. But why should we believe that institutions will influence anything? Don't fundamental forces, historical inevitabilities and the intervention of powerful personalities determine the flow of events? Isn't it more important to ensure that society chooses the correct leaders? Why should we suppose that 'democratic' institutions will not merely provide legal cover for the few who act to the detriment of the many? And how can institutions that seem alien to a society's traditions and alien to the social theories that justified an earlier regime change politics meaningfully?

These are profoundly important questions because they take us to the source of democratic stability and to the basis for asserting that democracy is a preferred form of social organization. Thus they warrant answers before we proceed further in this series to discussions of alternative institutional forms. We begin, then, with the fact that every society operates by rules that define admissible and inadmissible, encouraged and discouraged, behaviour. In primitive societies, these rules often appear as tradition and religious prescription. More modern societies set some of their rules to paper as laws, but most rules remain implicit and are referred to as 'social norms'. A norm may be a simple thing such as allowing those on a bus to exit before those who wish to enter move; or it may be more complex, as when it prescribes whom to give one's seat to on a bus and when to do so. Simple or complex, these norms guide behaviour on a day-to-day basis and it is difficult to imagine society without them.

But why do people allow themselves to be bound by norms, especially if, as is often the case, there are no laws to ensure compliance? The short answer is that society, implicitly aware of the order they provide and the benefits that flow from order, achieves a consensus about acceptable patterns of behaviour and teaches them to successive generations so that they become 'automatic'. At the same time, society sanctions those who defect from its norms, and so it must also establish norms that govern the application of these sanctions. Shoving one's way on to a bus before all who wish to leave it have done so may ensure a seat, but most persons avoid such behaviour because they know what everyone thinks of such acts – and few persons want to be scolded publicly by someone's grandmother. Norms of conduct on public transportation are adhered to, then, because it is not in a person's self-interest to act otherwise. And the norm is enforced because those who enforce – the grandmother who scolds – know that their actions are effective and acceptable.

Social norms cease serving their purpose when people believe that others will not adhere to them, when people fail to impose the requisite sanctions, or when they become confused over which norms are legitimate and which are illegitimate. Society, then, can encounter 'a crisis of norms' when it tries to establish new social and economic relations. If we are told in one month that private profit is a crime and in the next that it is a social virtue or that the accumulation of private property has been transformed from an act of exploitation to a right, then it may take some time before a new system of norms emerges to render society coherent and efficient.

Most norms come to us 'automatically' and, unsure of their source, we relegate their study to sociology and anthropology. But the 'norms of democracy' are established differently. These norms, which include such things as honouring individual rights provided for in a constitution, arise at least initially through acts of conscious creation. In fact the most explicit and expansive act of norm-creation is drafting a political constitution that specifies the restrictions that define the legitimate actions of the state.

In times past the norms of legitimate political action were directed at citizens and enforced by monarchs or dictators. There was no confusion over their content and little reason for most of us to become concerned with their genesis. Our primary concern was to make certain that we did not violate them. In turn, the security of the ultimate enforcer of these norms – the monarch or dictator himself – derived from our common fear and belief that if any person or small group acted otherwise, sanctions would be applied. No matter how well or poorly the dictator or monarch governed, we knew the cost of deviation, including the cost of failing to participate in a sanction we believed unjust. Revolutions, then, occur when a large enough part of society comes to believe that they will not be punished or, out of ideological or patriotic conviction, that the benefits of defection exceed the likely personal costs.

The transition to democracy is also a conscious process, except that unlike when a dictator asserts his will, democratic transition entails the establishment of a set of norms that are based on the principles of self-governance, the rule of law and respect for individual rights. A constitution, in turn, is the central component of this norm-generating process because it defines the institutions of governance – courts, legislatures, electoral laws and executive offices – and it defines the relation of these institutions to each other and to the people. These institutions are like norms because they consist of bundles of rules. The description of a legislature, for example, includes the rules whereby its members are elected, the rules that define legitimate and illegitimate political opposition, the rules under which voters vote and political parties operate to fill legislative seats, the rules that dictate legislative deliberations, and the rules that specify how the products of those deliberations (laws) are to be ultimately enforced.

That the construction of a democratic society focuses on the creation of institutions is one of the things that distinguishes it from an earlier, failed experiment. That experiment, the communist one, was predicated on the assumption that fundamental values would change and that people would come to equate private and social values. The assumption was that people could be 'perfected' to pursue purely social values. Those who could not be 'perfected' were simply eliminated, and little attention was given to guiding self-interest through the creation of new institutional structures. Although the leadership of the party or the dictate of an autocrat would substitute during any transitional period, eventually the state would 'wither away' so temporary repression could substitute for institutional design. That idea is now bankrupt: values and beliefs cannot be divorced from individual self-interest and, as we have learned all too painfully, the autocrat can too easily pervert the institutions he controls.

Democracy operates with a different assumption: to reiterate James Madison's famous premise, 'the seeds of faction are sown in the nature of man'. Hence rather than try to perfect people, democracy seeks instead to redirect self-interest and to develop a consensus about norms of an entirely different type. It seeks to develop norms about the legitimacy of procedures, rules and institutional structures that channel self-interest in socially acceptable ways and in ways that re-enforce people's incentives to maintain those institutions. Thus when we speak of a country as having a democratic tradition or democratic consciousness, we do not mean that its citizens are somehow more perfect or pursue different ends than people elsewhere. We mean that they share a consensus over the legitimacy of particular institutions and individual rights, that they expect their fellow citizens to act in accordance with the rules that describe those institutions, that they have incentives to sanction those who act contrary to these expectations, and that those who do act contrary to these expectations in fact expect to be sanctioned.

If the act of democratic norm-creation is performed well, these norms direct people's actions as intended; if designed poorly, they either fail to influence actions or they influence them in unintended and undesirable ways. But now we come to the critical question: what determines whether these norms, these bundles of rules, are designed well or poorly? How do we know that a constitution is complete or incomplete, well or poorly crafted, appropriate for a society or inappropriate?

Our other chapters try to give substance to different parts of the answers to these questions by focusing on specific institutions and processes. But in providing details, we should not lose sight of the mechanism whereby constitutional rules are enforced. Democratic institutions and rules that work well are followed and enforced in much the same way as are social norms. The politician who contemplates an action that dishonours his position, the legislator who subverts parliamentary procedure and potential tyrants will be constrained from these actions if they believe that existing political institutions give society the incentive to sanction such actions, if those institutions coordinate society to resist this subversion so that their self-interest is to act otherwise. The great trick to constructing stable democratic institutions, then, is this: rules (or the bundles of rules we call institutions) that are consistent with the normative values we associate with democratic practice – the values specified in a bill of rights – must be constructed so that it is in everyone's interest to abide by them, so that it is in society's interest to punish defectors (as when voters act to defeat an incumbent politician), so that we do not create incentives for subsequent detrimental changes in institutional structure, and so that the outcomes that eventually emerge are deemed as beneficial as those that any other feasible configuration of institutions can generate. Satisfying this requirement imposes at least the following general restrictions on feasible institutions and workable rules:

Rule 26: Democratic rules must be unambiguous. A rule such as 'the legislature will pass no law infringing on the freedom of the press' may seem in want of qualification (to avoid, say, the publication of pornography). But if there is a consensus over acceptable qualifications and if society's other political institutions are well crafted (if, for example, the legislature that appoints judges is responsive to society), the exceptions the courts allow will be acceptable. Similarly, we cannot leave electoral procedures ambiguous, lest those who fill public office manipulate those procedures to their own advantage.

Rule 27: Rules must be consistent. The rules of democratic process contradict each other, as when, for example, we give both a legislature and a president the constitutional authority to promulgate laws or when we give two government agencies jurisdiction over the same policy. Constitutions, then, should be examined as an exercise in logic, just as a mathematician checks the proof of a new theorem – by examining the proof for completeness and logical consistency.

Rule 28: Democratic institutions and rules should be promulgated under the assumption that public office holders will try to subvert those rules and procedures whenever it is in their interest to do so. Internal checks on the abuse of power – a presidential veto, judicial review of legislation, legislative oversight of the courts – are an essential component of democratic rules.

Rule 29: Democratic rules, especially constitutional ones, need to 'fit together' lest the law of unintended consequences operate with special force. Constitutions, then, cannot be written merely by taking different parts of the constitutional documents of other states as a child might choose candy in a candy store – 'I'll take one of those, one of those', and so on.

To this list we need to add one more item, namely that democratic rules must be manifestly fair. Rules cannot confer permanent advantage on one identifiable group at the expense of some other group. This is an especially difficult requirement to satisfy, since we do not mean by it that we merely give everyone an explicit guarantee of some minimal share of the spoils of politics. By themselves, such words are worthless guarantees. Instead we must constitute our rules and institutions so that the losers in any dispute can reasonably believe that they have a chance to become winners and that they are relevant to the resolution of future disputes. The particular difficulty here, however, is that although we can contribute to manifest fairness by the proper design of institutions, beliefs themselves are self-fulfilling prophecies. If people believe that the system is manifestly fair, then it will be; but if they believe otherwise, then it will be otherwise. If people believe that losing confers permanent disadvantage, they will act as if each battle is war. And if winners believe the same, then they must ensure that their victory is complete by vanquishing their opponents lest their opponents subsequently vanquish them. Thus how we satisfy the preceding requirements while at the same time constituting our rules so that they engender the correct beliefs is one of the things we address in the remaining chapters of this essay.

9. A New Constitution: Should We Cut Trees to Print It?

Most states – democratic or otherwise – possess constitutions, but it is generally assumed that the transition to democracy requires new political institutions, new political traditions and thus a new constitution. However, the people in such societies can reasonably ask why they should expect anything better from a new document than from their old one. After all, Soviet constitutions promised freedom of speech, of assembly, the right to vote, a free press, the right to express one's grievances, guaranteed pensions, health care, housing, vacations, and so on...and look what happened there! What can possibly be written on paper that will change anything? Why should we regard the promises contained in a new piece of paper as anything more than part of a fraud perpetrated on society by a handful of political élites concerned primarily with maintaining their position? Wouldn't it be better and less deceitful to dispense with experiments in democracy, return to political structures more in keeping with tradition (monarchy, autocracy, dictatorship?), and get the economy functioning so that people needn't be hungry and cold?

Regardless of whether such questions are framed seriously or cynically, they require answers. Otherwise there is no reason to suppose that anyone will pay much attention to any new constitutional document, however well crafted it might be or however noble the intentions of its authors. And in that event, the prediction that the constitution is meaningless can only become a self-fulfilling prophecy.

What we want to argue here, however, is that the Soviet bloc experience with 'constitutionalism' should not result in pessimism or cynicism. Specifically, we want to explore the argument that that experience should either be deemed as merely irrelevant to any debate over a constitution's role in facilitating the transformation to democracy or that it should be interpreted to give us confidence that democratic constitutionalism will in fact work in ex-communist states. We realize, of course, that in offering the hypothesis that the past is as much a source of confidence as it is of pessimism, readers might believe that we have smoked or drunk too much of some foreign substance. Nevertheless, let us consider for the moment the Soviet Union's '77 constitution, adopted with great fanfare throughout the USSR in a process in which innumerable people wrote letters offering input to which political élites pretended to pay some heed.

The fault of that document was not that it somehow failed, but rather that it worked precisely as designed. Those who believe it failed owing to the gap between promise and reality are correct to assert that merely setting words to paper about rights and social welfare entitlements did not, and in general cannot, accomplish much. But this presumption of failure is based on a preoccupation with only one of three questions we can ask about a constitution when evaluating its performance. In this instance the question being asked is: did the constitution lead to the realization of stated individual rights and social guarantees? The answer, evident to everyone but the most diehard apologist of an old regime, is no, and therein lies the source of pessimism about the prospects for a democratic society guided by constitutional principles in the successor states of the Soviet Union today.

That question, however, is not the only one with which to evaluate the prospects for democracy, because it focuses on but one of the things we want from a constitution. Before we can reach any conclusions, we must also answer two additional questions: did the constitution legitimize or contribute to the stability of the political institutions it prescribed for society; and were those institutions appropriate for the realization of the rights and social guarantees identified as goals within the constitution? Only if our answers to these questions are no and yes can we deem a constitution a failure. In fact our answers are exactly the opposite.

The problem with Soviet constitutions was that they were based on a social theory that assumed that people are perfectible and that beliefs and values can be changed fundamentally so that social goals become private ones. Thus they enshrined a political system that could not realize those goals. However, although they failed to do what no constitution can do directly – guarantee the realization of lofty principles by mere proclamation – Soviet constitutions succeeded to the extent that the system and institutions they legitimized did in fact function as described. Setting Marxist–Leninist principles at the core of Soviet social organization, both the '36 and, even more forthrightly, the '77 constitutions did one thing: they legitimized the dictatorship of the

Communist Party. And having done that, all the rest became mere window-dressing.

This is not to say that those constitutions played a role in forming political structures: those structures existed before the writing of either document. But they did give legal sanction to what existed. Thus with respect to our second question about their influence on political structures, these facts should cause us to regard Soviet constitutions as either irrelevant to events or they should lead us to believe that they contributed to the strength of existing institutions. In either case, the answer to our second question ought to be yes.

Turning to our third question – the adequacy of that structure for realizing stated goals – the social theory on which Soviet constitutions were based failed to appreciate that a top-down command–control economy cannot function in a world where prosperity and security depend on a vibrant consumer economy, high technology and efficiently operating financial markets rather than on simple directives concerning the manufacture of steel, cement, tractors and tanks. More importantly, that theory also failed to anticipate the inevitable consequences of the unchecked political power of the Communist Party – inefficiency and corruption – which appear regardless of whether that power is entrusted to some committee or to an individual. Nevertheless, this was the structure that Soviet constitutions sought to legitimize, and this was the one that prevailed. And herein lies the reason why those constitutions failed to deliver on their promises: they legitimized a political system that may have tried initially to fulfil its promises, but they succumbed eventually to the fact that they did not legitimize institutions that would ensure that the pursuit of self-interest would serve the public interest. Thus, the answer to our third question is no.

So if there is a lesson to be learned from the USSR's constitutional experience, it is not that constitutions cannot work. Rather the lesson is either that the experience is an irrelevant experiment or that even bad constitutions can, for a time at least, be stable. Of course, this argument does not challenge the view that history would have been unchanged if any of these constitutions was a wholly democratic document or even a blank piece of paper. It need not convince anyone that a new constitution can lead to something other than what exists. It does not contradict the assertion that the Soviet Union or any of its successor states must proceed along historical paths that can only be interrupted but not negated by attempts at developing a constitutional democracy. To counter these arguments requires consideration of the more general matter of how constitutions in fact influence political processes, how they ensure rights and how they facilitate the establishment of stable political systems.

We cannot address all of these issues here, but we can indicate how to avoid the excesses that occurred previously. Briefly, the core of any constitution, aside from rights, is a specification of a governmental structure that defines the relations of its different parts (the executive, legislature and judiciary) to each other and to the sovereign, the people. Their varied relations to the people determine the extent to which each part will find it in its interest to reflect a different feature of society and to facilitate the realization of constitutional rights. A president, for example, is elected directly or indirectly by everyone and thereby summarizes society's general aspirations; each member of a parliament represents the interests of his or her constituents (geographic or otherwise); members of a federal chamber if the state is a federation represent the interests of the government's constituent parts – states, lands, republics, oblasts – and members of high courts, freed from excessive political control, search for those general principles we must follow if society is to be something more than a discordant mob.

It goes without saying that the ultimate constraint on the state derives from these different relations with society's ultimate sovereign, the people. However, this fact has been a source of great confusion and has resulted in the erroneous belief, discussed in an earlier chapter, that merely to vote is to be democratic. Because it is necessary to grant government the power to coerce us into doing things we might not otherwise do (for example, pay taxes), and because public officials can sometimes act before we can successfully challenge those actions, even a popularly elected state can threaten our liberties. Hence being democratic also requires that we construct a government whose parts will each check the excessive accumulation of power by its other parts and the illiberal actions that accompany such an accumulation. Thus:

> *Rule 30*: It is the combination of relationships between citizen and state and among the parts of the state and not just one of them that determines whether a political system can adjust ineffective policy, policy that undermines the rights posited in a constitution, and policy that might ultimately undermine the state's very stability.

The relation of different parts to the people gives those parts a different interest and thus ensures that they will not collude against the people; the relation of those parts to each other ensures that no one part and no single interest within society can dominate all the rest. Of course, Soviet constitutions provided for a variety of representative assemblies and courts. But, operating under the assumption that the Communist Party would know and would necessarily act in the interests of society, those constitutions set this fourth part of government above all others, without also giving the people any direct or meaningful control over its actions. Hence the label 'democratic socialism' was little more than a sham – the more appropriate label was simply 'authoritarianism'.

Democratic systems contrast sharply with this picture, since they place no part of the government in a superior position. Parliamentary systems make all parts initially subservient to the legislature by giving it strong powers of appointment and dismissal. But a check on these powers is provided by allowing a chief of state or prime minister to dissolve the legislature and to call for new elections, and by giving the courts independent authority to judge the constitutionality of the government's and parliament's actions. Presidential systems sometimes tolerate a less direct relation between voters and public officials (members of one legislative branch may be appointed by regional governments, and presidents may be elected indirectly through such devices as an electoral college), but they compensate by requiring a 'balance of power' among the different parts of government while giving each part a different relation to the people.

Since many of the successor states of the USSR will most likely implement some form of presidential government and since the undecided issue here is the relative powers of that office, it is useful to consider the construction of this balance. Briefly, balance is achieved by implementing a *separation of powers* among the three primary branches of government, where this separation is intended to ensure that the excesses of one branch can be checked by the other two. Thus if the president fails to execute the law, the court can direct the executive to act otherwise and the legislature can use its control of state revenues to do the same. If the court fails its responsibilities, the executive and the legislature, together, can influence (albeit slowly) the court's direction by their joint power of appointment. Finally, if the legislature itself performs poorly, the courts can refuse to enforce unconstitutional laws, whereas the president, in addition to vetoing legislative acts, can use the prestige of his office to bring public pressure to bear on the legislature.

These checks, however, point to a practical difficulty. A complete separation of powers is impossible – each branch must have an interest in, and some authority over, the other two. We cannot have legislatures treating issues that do not concern the courts or the executive; and, by definition, the courts and the executive must implement the laws legislatures pass. So a stable constitution must allow some overlap in the jurisdictions of each branch. But in designing this overlap, we create chaos if we allow too much, as when we give legislative power to the president or the courts, or executive power to the legislature (the current Russian constitution does this by proclaiming the president the protector of the constitution, by allowing him to issue decrees whenever the law is silent, and by empowering him to abrogate regional executive actions he deems unconstitutional). Much of the conflict we observe in states in which chief executives regularly battle their parliaments derives not merely from political ambition but from the fact that the powers of these two branches impact each other too greatly. Thus:

> *Rule 31*: Too much overlap, then, creates confusion; too little threatens autocracy. A stable constitution requires a balance between too much and too little joint authority and reciprocal power.

So what precisely is the optimal balance? Should the legislature, for example, have the power to influence or even dictate the selection of the heads of ministries? Should the president be empowered to dissolve the legislature rather than merely being empowered to veto legislation? Should members of a Supreme or Constitutional Court be subject to periodic review and reappointment? These questions are not easily answered, but our prejudice is for overlap to be minimized and kept just great enough to ensure against the dominance of any one branch of government. In this event, each branch must act more responsibly, because it is less able to blame its failings on the actions of others. And with focused responsibilities, each branch becomes more amenable to control by the primary relationship a constitution establishes: the relationship between government and the people.

Presidential government aside, the point we want to emphasize is that all politics proceeds in accordance with rules, and by careful constitutional draftsmanship, we can coordinate political élites, as well as the rest of us, to the rules of democracy. The task of draftsmanship, however, is to devise rules to which we can all adhere – rules that no set of individuals has the means and the incentive to upset and that are themselves in balance. In the words of James Madison (*Federalist Papers*):

> In framing a government that is to be administered by men over men, the great difficulty lies in this: you must first enable the government to control

the governed; and in the next place oblige it to control itself. A dependence of the people is, no doubt, the primary control on the government; but experience has taught mankind the necessity of auxiliary precautions.

It is the absence of these precautions – the absence of a power that could offset that of the party or of the autocrat – that led to the conclusion that Soviet constitutions had 'failed'; it is the presence of these precautions that gives stable democracies their character.

10. Constitutions: Are There Rules for How to Write Them?

Because both the '36 and '77 Soviet constitutions embodied a concept of government that was inherently flawed and incapable of securing proclaimed rights and social guarantees, the unsatisfactory performance of these documents does not indicate the infeasibility of constitutional democracy in an ex-communist state. Nevertheless, few readers are likely to be convinced by that argument alone or led to the view that they ought to pay any attention to any constitution's content. Rather than concern themselves with political issues that occur at some rarefied level of power in Moscow, Kiev, Tashkent or Minsk, most people are understandably preoccupied with personal matters. A few may find ways to prosper, but the majority of the population in an economy undergoing wrenching transformation must be concerned with simple survival. Such circumstances are hardly ones that place arguments about new constitutions at centre stage.

But even if worrying about politics cannot put food on tables or shoes on feet, the design of a new constitution and the manoeuvres of political élites over its content warrant attention if only because of a constitution's role in a democracy. A constitution is not a piece of paper that, once written, can be filed away in some drawer, to be used by public officials as a justification for their actions and as a basis for securing political advantage over opponents. It ought to be a statement of society's highest political values and preferred forms of political organization. Constitutions are not prepared to give legitimacy to some predetermined governmental structure or to justify the actions of any particular faction in the government. They are written so people can organize and coordinate themselves to political purpose. Many of the things we want out of life – good schools, a prosperous economy, public safety – cannot be realized without coordinated social action. A written constitution is one of the things we must have if we are to rule ourselves and decide the government's role, if any, in the realization of those ends.

Primitive villages and tribes organized themselves through custom and tradition by accepting the leadership of elders and hereditary chieftains. Later, people gave their sanction (not always voluntarily) to kings and monarchs who may have ruled in their personal interest but who were expected to coordinate their subjects for some common purpose: even kings need a reasonably prosperous realm if there are to be things to tax. Communist ideology rejected the idea of the divine right of kings but, following earlier tradition, substituted the dictatorship of the party for that of the autocrat. People in a democracy reject the idea that any single individual or part of society has the right to rule. We seek to rule ourselves. However, self-rule does not materialize automatically merely by asserting a desire for it. It requires that we carefully construct some aids that were unnecessary when the power of the state was in the hands of an autocrat or a self-appointed oligarchy.

The nature of those aids is determined, first, by the fact that we must accept the idea that there will always be disagreements and honest differences of opinion as to how best to achieve social ends. There will also be honest disagreements over the ends themselves. We make no assumption of unanimity over anything except for the idea that people prefer to proceed peacefully as long as doing so promises them, their family and their friends a reasonably rewarding life. The character of those aids is determined also by the fact that we cannot try to reinvent procedures for resolving conflict every time we are called upon to make a decision. This approach – not too dissimilar from what currently characterizes politics in many states – leads to endless debate over the methods for making decisions, over the method for making decisions about methods of making decisions, and so on.

Of all the aids we might construct, none is more important than a constitution. This is the principal device whereby we coordinate our actions so as to select some set of rules and procedures for making social decisions. A constitution accomplishes these tasks in three ways:

1. It lists those basic values (rights) that are to remain unquestioned throughout our political debates.
2. It defines the domain of government and the relations of different levels of government to each other.
3. It prescribes the rules of political process, the rules whereby we select our leaders, and the ways in which those leaders are to organize themselves to serve us.

Thus the writing and adoption of a constitution is the ultimate act of democratic social self-organization and coordination.

Of course, it is not unreasonable for people to remain sceptical about a piece of paper and to ask: 'how can we ever hope to enforce its provisions when abiding by a written democratic constitution is not part of our tradition or culture?'. If there is a tradition, this argument continues, it is that of having constitutions enforced by an autocrat or, as in the Soviet case, by a tyrant.

Admittedly, trying to understand how a democratic constitution is enforced seems difficult. Such a document cannot be enforced by a legislature, a chief executive or the courts, since it is the constitution itself that defines the rules under which these parts of the government operate. If they have the ultimate power of enforcement, then they also have the power to change a constitution to suit their purposes. This is not to say that we do not hope to create institutions that make it in the self-interest of politicians to act to honour the provisions of a constitution. But seeing this as the ultimate source of constitutional stability merely pushes the problem back a step so that we must then ask: 'who enforces the provisions of a constitution that establish and define the self-interest of politicians?'.

In fact if there is a higher authority in a democracy and an ultimate source of enforcement, it can only be the people themselves. If constitutions are to guide our political deliberations and if they are to restrict our political leaders to act in our interest, then the people must consensually agree to abide by a constitution's terms. If the people are unwilling to act in accordance with it and to sanction those who fail to do so, then no special words, clauses, edicts, decrees or governmental forms will do the job for them. There is no precise relationship between a president and the legislature or between national government and regional governments that will guarantee constitutional stability. A constitution serves its purpose and endures only if the people – voters, soldiers, civil servants and public officials – are willing to abide by it and if they believe that others will do the same.

A constitution can accomplish this task in only one way: it must become a part of society's moral and spiritual fabric. As we argued earlier, acting 'constitutionally' must become equivalent to acting in accordance with other social norms, such as respecting and honouring one's parents, abiding by one's sense of patriotism or aiding strangers in peril. The 'trick' of democratic transition, then, is finding a way through public debate and through trial and error to render constitutional principles a part of our thinking about legitimate political process. Once this is done, a constitution's enforcement becomes a self-fulfilling prophecy.

We understand that this argument may seem utopian. Shouldn't we first get the economy functioning in some minimal way, even if that requires temporary autocratic rule, since only then can we begin to see what forms of political organization are best suited to our purposes? And even if we are forced to begin thinking about a constitution, shouldn't we leave the determination of things to specialists since we have had so little experience with democracy?

The answer to both questions should be no. We can take up again our earlier argument that democratic rules, especially those set forth in a constitution, are like the social norms that regulate and coordinate our day-to-day relations with people, in order to offer some general guidelines for writing and evaluating written constitutions. Because these suggestions apply regardless of whether the country in question adopts a presidential or a parliamentary system, regardless of whether the state is unitary or federal, and regardless of what choices are made with respect to the myriad of other decisions that go into the construction of a constitution, people can use these rules to evaluate any draft proposal set before them:

> *Rule 32*: Social norms do not arise from a single source – they are 'there' as part of custom and tradition. Similarly, just as no part of the government can be the exclusive guardian of a constitution's content, none can be the master of changes to it.

Allowing any part of the government the exclusive right to amend a constitution threatens instability. So when designing the procedures under which such a document can be amended, even if we choose to require the involvement of our legislature (since it is an important repository of relevant expertise and a valuable forum for debating the wisdom of any change), we should also involve the people directly (through referenda) or indirectly (via the acceptance of change by regional and republic governments). Social norms work because they are 'generally accepted' – constitutions and constitutional changes work the same way. Next:

> *Rule 33*: Social norms sustain themselves only if people expect others to abide by them and if they anticipate sanctions when they fail to do so, but doing so is impossible if they are confusing or poorly understood. Hence a

constitution should not be drafted with the idea that it will be a tool of lawyers. Long, convoluted clauses of uncertain meaning undermine constitutional stability; brevity is essential.

Plain language of common meaning provides a surer protection for society and a more effective device for coordinating opposition to those who would violate the spirit of a constitution than any number of clauses replete with concerns for extraordinary contingencies. Third:

> *Rule 34*: Social norms are simply stated. Similarly, we should resist elaborate statements of rights that give the appearance of making those rights immediately enforceable, since doing so merely compounds the problem of enforcement by adding additional layers to the document that require interpretation and legislation.

The temptation, regrettably common, is to view constitutions as contracts that seek to leave nothing to chance. But just as contracts can only be enforced by a higher authority, writing a constitution in this form tempts us to begin a futile search for the philosopher-king or to the dangerous creation of the dictator. People must instead begin placing their faith in the representative institutions and courts that a constitution establishes. Next:

> *Rule 35*: Norms are practical, and do not require that people do impossible things. A constitution should not be obscured by utopian requirements that the state accomplish things that may or may not be feasible.

There are policies we may want the state to pursue – protecting retired or disabled persons from poverty, providing for a viable system of education, ensuring an ample and affordable supply of housing. But a constitution should focus on the institutions and rights that are sufficient to ensure society's ability to coordinate for the realization of policy goals as expressed through democratically elected legislatures, governors and presidents. Fifth:

> *Rule 36*: Social norms guide our lives because we can all recognize the actions that violate them. Thus, it serves little purpose to assert in a constitution, for example, that 'the highest value is man and his life, liberty, honour and dignity', because such provisions do not direct the state to anything in particular.

Next:

Rule 37: A social norm is limited in scope. Similarly, constitutions add to society's social organization only in the limited domain of politics.

Including requirements that children care for their parents, that parents care for their children or that people care for the environment and for their cultural heritage are out of place in such a document. Other norms of social behaviour will attend to such matters – a constitution is not the place to attempt to structure all of society. Seventh:

Rule 38: Social norms are adaptable and timeless. A constitution should have the same character.

It may be difficult to avoid paying special attention to immediate problems – housing, ethnic conflict, inflation, and so on. But if we focus too strongly on the resolution of contemporary problems, we are unlikely to generate a document of lasting value. Instead a constitution seeks to create a set of institutions that will direct the resolution of all problems, both in the present and those that cannot be anticipated.

This last rule is especially difficult to follow, because nearly everyone will try to assess the immediate implications of a new constitution for their own welfare. This occasions a problem illustrated by card players who must choose the game they will play. If they choose before the cards are dealt, different players may hold different preferences, depending on which game best matches their beliefs about their comparative advantages in skill. But agreement should be possible, especially if each values the mere pleasure of playing. On the other hand, if they must choose after the cards are dealt, each person will prefer a game that makes his hand a likely winner Agreement will be reached only if the players allow their long-term interests to overcome their short-term ones. The situation is not much different in the transition to democracy. Although we may prefer to redeal the cards, this alternative is not wholly practical; and for most of us the cards have already been dealt. So each of us must somehow overcome our short-term concerns and try, as best we can, to look to the future. Unfortunately, there is no guarantee that people can or will do this. But we can offer one practical suggestion: write a minimal document that focuses only on the bare essentials of institutional design and that as much as possible leaves the ultimate resolution of specific policy issues up to, if not chance, at least to the skill of the players who play. In this way, players of the game of democracy will have an incentive to become skilled, which, in the long run, can only increase their commitment to the game.

11. Federalism: Ingredient for Stability or a Recipe for Dissolution?

Included in the list of pressing needs for ostensibly federal states such as Russia and Ukraine is a solution to internal ethnic and linguistic conflicts that at the same time create incentives for each state's separate parts to remain within their federations. There are three commonly discussed paths to this end. The first is force applied by a resurrected authoritarian state. We realize that a deteriorating economy has led more than a few people to believe that democracy exacerbates problems and that an increasing number of people point to China as an example of successful economic reform directed by a centralized, authoritarian state. But people, in addition to wanting to live in stable and prosperous states, also demand their individual rights and liberties. Hence before any coercive route is chosen and before any element of the ex-USSR once again travels the path favoured by extremists of both the Right and the Left, we need to explore the democratic institutions that might help resolve regional conflicts.

Quite understandably, a good number of leaders in the political capitals of the world argue that a stable democracy requires placing most power in the hands of a central government. Although regional and local governments might be afforded some degree of autonomy, their position relative to the national government should be negotiated on a case-by-case basis in such a way that the national government maintains the upper hand in these negotiations. In this view, a federation that accedes to regional demands for political and economic autonomy is little more than a recipe for the eventual dissolution of the country. Yugoslavia, for example, dissolved with decentralization and federalism seems incapable of providing any solution to Nigeria's ethnic–tribal problems.

However, aside from the possibility that there are engineering problems without solutions, a centralized democratic state is itself sometimes an unrealizable goal. National governments are often too weak to enforce central control even in ordinary matters such as tax collection.

Attempts to impose control can lead to further resistance on the part of regional authorities and to increased pressures for authoritarian methods. Here, then, we want to see how to construct a federalism that avoids these problems and that results in a stable democracy. After all, we cannot yet reject the hypothesis that Yugoslavia dissolved not merely because of decentralization, but because it implemented this idea in the wrong way. First, however, we need to divide our discussion into two parts: the formal, constitutional structure of a federal state and those 'informal' structures (for example, political parties) that arise to organize and direct political action. This chapter focuses on constitutional structures; later ones examine parties and the special role they play in ensuring a political system's stability.

We begin by first dispensing with the idea that the fragility of, say, Russia or Ukraine, derives mostly from economic problems. It is true that with an economy in free-fall, each region and district seeks to control the resources in its territory. Such is the explanation for the USSR's dissolution and for the problems of the Commonwealth of Independent States (CIS). But economics provides only a partial explanation of the centrifugal forces operating today. The depression of the 1930s impacted on everyone, yet only a few countries experienced revolutionary political change. The forces working today against the stability of Canada cannot be described as the consequences of severe economic dislocation – any of the successor states of the USSR would love to have Canada's economic 'problems'. Nigeria's economic problems are more the consequence of political instability than a cause of it. And few could argue that the USSR's dissolution was collectively economically rational – the motives of national leaders who sought to consolidate their power overcame any notion of collective economic rationality.

The fact is that disputes and competition between regional and national governments, as well as among regional governments, are ubiquitous and eternal. No one prefers to be taxed by a distant government; everyone prefers to control whatever they have or hope to have; national governments always prefer to increase their power; and regional authorities always resist the supremacy of national officials while at the same time seeking advantage whenever possible over other regions. The American Civil War did not end the dispute between state and national governments; Switzerland's cantons continue to compete against the national government for supremacy; and members of the European Community continue to struggle against the interests of the Community as a whole and against each other. Economic turmoil may exacerbate conflicts, but our task is to see if a well-designed federalism can moderate the effects of that turmoil.

So if we cannot eliminate national–regional competition, how do we control its effects? To answer this question we begin by viewing the national government as a referee that coordinates regions to do those things they cannot do separately in any reasonably efficient way – provide for the national defence, coin money, ensure the obligation of contracts, ensure free trade within the federation, and so on. But in constructing a federal state we must guard against two things: (1) competition among regions that would upset the federal balance; and (2) a national government that usurps power at the expense of the regions so as to drag things back in the direction of a unitary centralized state in which it is no longer possible to realize the benefits of decentralization. The first of these, illustrated by Yugoslavia, Nigeria and possibly Canada, can in a self-evident way result in political instability and the dismemberment of a state; the second can do the same to the extent that any increase in the power of the national government only increases the incentives of regional governments to go their own way, even to secede.

An important, even necessary, protection against the first possibility is the construction of a federation that avoids giving to some regions a different relation to the national government than is given to other parts of the federation. A federal system that is not symmetric – one in which degrees of autonomy vary from one region to another and in which a confusing array of bilateral and multilateral treaties characterize the state's organization – is untenable. One region's greater autonomy legitimizes demands for greater autonomy by other regions. In the asymmetric federalism, regions compete for special favours, for particular dispensations from central control and for recognition of their 'unique circumstances'. And it is the escalation of these demands, brought about by the general inequality of condition, that is the chief threat to the stability of any federal state.

This competition among political subunits requires that the national government be involved continuously in the allocation of differential benefits, with the inevitable result that some sub-parts will seek to win control of the national government and use its power for their own ends. Thus one key rule for creating a durable federation is this:

Rule 39: No federal subject should have any more or less autonomy than any other part. No region should be singled out as having characteristics that justify making its residents any less or more democratically free than people elsewhere.

Indeed, if there is reason to grant special autonomous rights to one region, that reason should apply to all regions equally.

Symmetric or otherwise, a national government will find it difficult to maintain the autonomy of federal subjects. All politicians seek power, and those who would lead a national government are no different than the rest. Thus another rule of federal state construction is:

> *Rule 40*: Maximize the autonomy of federal subjects by reserving for the national government only those functions it alone can perform (for example, maintenance of a national defence, maintenance of a stable currency, guaranteeing the free flow of goods, services and people across the different parts of the republic, and the establishment of a court system that provides for equal treatment before the law for all citizens).

This rule is supported by two facts. First, people learn to be democratic, to value rights, and to organize to press their demands on the state by learning how to organize and participate in local and regional politics. People will pay only slight attention to things they cannot influence and that influence them only indirectly. And they will be most cynical about processes that seem beyond their control. Local and regional matters should be otherwise; indeed local and regional politics should be the great classroom of democratic ideas and values. Democratic values are not learned by the exhortations of political and intellectual élites. They are learned by the practical experience that participation in local and regional politics provides. But this classroom cannot exist if local and regional governments have little control over those things that affect them and that do not affect other regions. It cannot exist if political élites in a national capital insist on appointing regional governors; it cannot exist if they insist on directing the design of local and regional governments (aside from ensuring that they are democratic); it cannot exist if they insist on deciding everything from local speed limits and school textbooks to the methods whereby local and regional officials are elected. These are the things that must be decided by people who are perfectly capable of making their own judgements about the things that most concern them.

The other fact that supports this last rule is that conflicts within a political subunit are less likely to disrupt national politics in a decentralized system than in a centralized one. All conflicts in the centralized state must be resolved by central authorities because only they, by definition, have the power to act. A decentralized federalism, in contrast, allows people to search first for local solutions, because doing so maintains their autonomy. Only when internal compromises cannot be achieved should the national government be called into the conflict to umpire a resolution. And the fewer conflicts we move up to the national level, the fewer conflicts we allow to threaten the state's ultimate stability. This fact as much as any other justifies Thomas Jefferson's assertion that, 'the government that governs best is the government that governs least'. This assertion is not a call for anarchy; it merely recognizes the fact that the dead hand of bureaucratic centralization leads to bureaucratic insensitivities to local and regional needs. This dead hand stifles innovation and experimentation with policy and it eliminates any incentives for local and regional authorities to take responsibility for their actions.

Rule 40, however, does not provide much practical guidance in the construction of a stable democratic federation, and thus we should ask: what are a national government's essential functions? We cannot, of course, list everything here, but again taking up the view of a national government as referee among, and coordinator of, regional governments, minimally it should be empowered to:

- prohibit restraint of trade across regions, since otherwise regional governments will seek to advantage industries within their border by taxing or regulating the free flow of goods and services;
- ensure that contracts agreed to in one region are enforceable in all regions, since we cannot allow people to escape their obligations by moving from one region to another;
- regulate the money supply, since it is best positioned to oversee macro-economic policy;
- provide for a national defence, since regional governments may not respond appropriately to external threats; indeed they will be tempted to provide only for their own defence and internal security;
- regulate environmental matters that impact several regions simultaneously whenever these regions act to pass environmental costs off to neighbours.

Even this abbreviated list requires one additional constitutional provision. Specifically, a national government cannot perform its coordinative function unless the constitution:

- establishes the supremacy of federal law over regional and local laws and defines the issue domains for the application of this principle.

Although the idea of supremacy is likely to be strongly resisted by regional governments, without such a constitutional clause the national government cannot establish a common economic market within its borders, cannot ensure the obligation of contracts, and cannot compel the different parts of society to contribute to the national defence. In short, without the supremacy of federal law, the national government cannot perform its essential functions.

The final issue that concerns us with respect to constitutional matters is the legitimate concern in Moscow and Kiev, as well as capitals elsewhere, that if left to their own devices, regional élites will take advantage of their isolation to subvert democratic process in their regions, either by engaging in wholesale fraud or by otherwise infringing on the constitutional rights of minorities in their regions. If democracy in a large republic functions because no interest or faction can form a permanent majority, then we need also to recognize the statistical fact that permanent (for example, ethnic) majorities are more likely in small political units than large ones. To protect against the abrogation of rights within regions, then, a democratic federal constitution should:

- guarantee to the citizens of each region a democratic form of government.

Although regions should be allowed to design governments that best suit their needs and traditions, including procedures for electing representatives to the national legislature, federal courts should have the authority to oversee matters so as to ensure that no one's constitutional rights are violated.

What we have said thus far may seem like a good deal of wishful thinking. On the one hand we have argued that those who would direct the destiny of any ex-communist state must unlearn the instinct to centralize; on the other hand it would appear that, especially with respect to a constitutional supremacy clause, we have given the central government a great deal of authority. Thus to the extent that there is no reason to suppose that mere words on paper can enforce anything, we have not yet responded fully to the question: what keeps a decentralized federalism decentralized and yet whole? What keeps the national government in a decentralized federalism from eventually usurping power? What keeps regional governments from coalescing against each other? And what ensures that we are not merely encouraging the ultimate dissolution of the state by deliberate decentralization? The responses to these questions require that we consider things other than mere constitutional guarantees and structures. We must also look at the form and operation of those organizations that people establish to influence political outcomes – political parties. The role of parties in a federal state, then, is the subject of our next chapter.

12. Political Parties: A Source of Faction or Agents of Stability?

In the previous chapter we argued that any state choosing to be a federation should grant as much autonomy as possible to its sub-parts and should treat those parts equally. However, we concluded with some unanswered questions concerning the overall stability of a federation and the maintenance of the federal bargain between the centre and federal subjects.

Political stability and the maintenance of that bargain are intimately connected. If federal subjects lose autonomy so that the political system moves in the direction of simple majority rule, minorities – especially territorial ethnic ones – are more likely to feel, and to be, disadvantaged. However, constitutional restrictions on a national government are, as much as anything else, subject to reinterpretation and manipulation. Giving regional governments control over some resource does not stop the national government from adjusting its taxation and regulation policies so as to circumvent the restrictions placed on it. Giving an ethnic group the right to educate its children in the language of its choice does not stop a government from imposing contrary requirements by nationalizing the funding of education and by creating onerous restrictions on what is required for a share of those funds.

Guarding against such possibilities with additional constitutional guarantees merely makes that document less enforceable. We cannot keep elaborating guarantees of autonomy. Doing so merely avoids the problem of determining how the last added clause, prohibition or requirement is to be enforced. More problematical is the fact that negotiating the precise terms of autonomy – deciding within the context of a constitution which matters fall under the jurisdiction of the national government and which belong to regional or district governments – is generally a protracted and contentious process that exacerbates conflict. As the dispute between Quebec and the rest of Canada illustrates, such negotiations can set region against region as each claims special privilege or fears that such privilege will be given to others.

These concerns are not arguments against constructing a decentralized federalism. After all, this approach is credited with being Switzerland's source of stability despite its linguistic cleavages, as well as an important component of America's stability despite its ethnic and geographic heterogeneity. But neither Switzerland nor the United States confronts economic problems of a type that pervade the territory of the Soviet Union. So even if we accept the idea that meaningful grants of regional autonomy are an essential part of a stable democratic state, we should ask whether there are ways to establish these grants without threatening dissolution, whether we can put in place a process whereby autonomous rights can be renegotiated without exacerbating conflicts, and whether this process can be designed to resist the forces that act to undermine any plan of decentralization and fairness.

Because the terms of federation set forth in a constitution must be self-enforcing, we must look to those extra-constitutional processes and the incentives of political élites that, although influenced by a constitution, act to undermine or to re-enforce its provisions. And of all the extra-constitutional things that emerge in a democracy that both shape and are shaped by the motives of political élites, nothing is more important than the political party. Until we describe and understand the role of parties, we cannot predict how any system will function and whether it will in fact be stable.

Political parties in a liberal democracy are not personal factions or social clubs designed to express one ideological position or another as loudly as possible. Parties are the things politicians use to get elected: to mobilize voters, to communicate their issue positions, to raise campaign funds and to organize legislative coalitions. But just as politicians and political structure influence the form and role of parties in a democracy, parties influence the actions of politicians. Directly or indirectly, they influence the incentives of candidates to negotiate compromises, and they determine which issues become salient in national elections and which ones are relevant only at local level.

To see, then, how parties contribute to federal stability, let us consider what lessons America provides. We realize that some people might object that, given its different traditions and economic circumstances, and given its absence of territorial ethnic groups, America is irrelevant to places such as Russia, Ukraine, and so on. However, America is not only a stable federalism, it is also one that experienced civil war in the last century. The sources of its stability and instability, then, may illustrate some general possibilities. In particular, America offers some important lessons about how some constitutional provisions in addition to those discussed earlier, facilitate stability, but that, until we examine the structure of political parties, might go unappreciated.

Since threats to regional autonomy are a precursor to instability, our focus is on discovering how federal subjects maintain their autonomy despite the authority we give to a national government, including the requirement that its laws be supreme. Turning, then, to the American experience, we can trace the ability of states there to oppose successfully the encroachments of the national government on to the structure of America's two major parties, which derives from the influence of four elements of the national constitution:

1. The requirement that national legislators – members of the House of Representatives and the Senate – be residents of their constituencies.
2. The flexibility it gives state governments (which have the right to design republican governments to their own liking) to prescribe the manner of election of national representatives (subject to the condition that those procedures be 'democratic').
3. The absence of any device (such as the authority to dissolve the legislature) that allows the president to control legislative parties or even the party he nominally heads.
4. The method of presidential election, which requires national support that transcends regional appeals.

These four points take us a long way in explaining the most evident feature of America's national parties: they are highly decentralized organizations that compete with seemingly obscure non-ideological platforms. In fact America does not have two *national* parties – it has 50 Republican and 50 Democratic *state* parties (more, since state parties are themselves coalitions of local organizations) that act every four years to compete for the presidency, but that otherwise function to compete for state and local offices. Hence national legislators are elected according to rules set by their states (including the geographic definition of their districts) and as part of campaigns run by local organizations. Consequently, these legislators, even if they seek national office or otherwise aspire to national and international visibility, cannot ignore local needs. And with a president who can influence their electoral destinies only slightly, that office provides only the weakest incentive to form strong national party organizations.

These facts mean that national legislators remain protective of local and regional concerns. But these facts do not explain why coalitions do not form on the basis of purely regional concerns. Part of the explanation is the absence of marked territorial differences – ethnicity that correlates with geography, for example. But in addition to this fortuitous circumstance, the danger of legislative and party coalitions organized on a purely regional basis is avoided because of the importance of the presidency and the way that office is filled. Parties outside the legislature and factions in it cannot ignore the importance of winning this office, and it is the quest for the presidency rather than purely geographic interests that is the primary basis for party structures in and out of the legislature.

That only two parties form and that the legislature organizes around two primary blocks labelled 'Democrat' and 'Republican' follows from the rules of presidential elections. Without examining details or the history of why it is so, the 'winner-takes-all' character of those rules and the limited opportunities they provide for minor parties to block the election of a winner compels politicians to coalesce into two blocks: Democrat and Republican. And insofar as regional coalitions are concerned, those laws give parties an incentive to make geographically broad appeals. Once a party wins a majority of votes in a state, it wins all of that state's electoral votes and increasing its vote there further serves no purpose. Thus rather than increase its vote in any state to the greatest extent possible, if it is reasonably certain of winning there, a party directs its remaining resources at states that are more competitive. Thus although local concerns and characteristics may give one party or another an advantage in specific states, Democrats and Republicans will compete across most geographic regions, thereby making those parties national.

Because they must compete nationally for the presidency, both parties must attempt to form coalitions that encompass a broad range of interests by negotiating a wide variety of issues internally. Thus even though local concerns remain dominant within parties, the quest for the presidency compels them to resolve innumerable conflicts internally before those conflicts bubble up to disrupt national politics. The one instance in which geographic conflict was negotiated outside of party structures led ultimately to civil war, which occurred when politicians short-circuited the natural process of intra-party compromise and upset a delicate constitutional balance by artificially maintaining a Senatorial representation of southern slave states equal to that of the north. Because this arrangement could not be sustained on moral and practical grounds (the practical matter being the predominance of northern industrial development), and because it was set in the context of a debate (since resolved) over the supremacy of federal law, it led to a split of one of the national parties and, subsequently, to a war between north and south.

So the primary guarantor of the autonomy of state governments and the primary obstacle to inter-regional conflict is not prosperity (which may be more the consequence of stability as its cause) or any explicit constitutional protection of autonomy. Rather it is a consequence of a delicate constitutional balance formed by a complex combination of provisions that lead to a decentralization of party structures but that compel parties to negotiate their internal contradictions as they search for ways to form winning national coalitions.

These devices may have been arrived at as much by accident as by planning (the framers of the American constitution failed to appreciate fully the role parties would play in their future). And we certainly have not argued that the internal conflicts of today's ethnically heterogeneous states are less divisive than those that confronted America in the 1850s. But the operation of these devices provides important lessons for those who would design a new federalism for, say, Russia or Ukraine. Political parties can unify as well as divide, and constitutional structures need to accommodate this fact. We should not look to any single clause or provision to accomplish our goal of stability – party structures and roles are determined by the interplay of many things. Looking at a single relationship, such as the relative powers of a president versus the legislature, will lead to unanticipated consequences.

Many things do distinguish America from any other state. Most important is the fundamental difference in the composition of ethnic group demands in America and states such as Russia or Ukraine. Owing to the structure of their economies, there is considerably less geographic mobility within these states and a good deal more territorial conflict. Combined with an economic deterioration that precludes an explicit or implicit process of 'buying off' these demands, compromise seems unrealizable. We cannot argue, then, that a properly designed federal system, with compatible election laws, will solve all the problems associated with ethnicity, language and religion. We can only argue that things should not be made worse by an inappropriate choice of institutional structure.

A second difference concerns the possibility that a state will choose to have a parliamentary rather than a presidential system. Much of what we have said about America requires that its regional parties have a strong incentive to coalesce to win the presidency. Without this incentive, inter-regional compromises would be more difficult (even impossible) to negotiate outside of the legislature. Thus the issue of a strong versus a weak president cannot be divorced from plans to ensure that a federal structure remain in place and that inter-ethnic compromises be encouraged. Until and unless proponents of a governmental form that emphasizes the power of parliament over that of a president can tell us how their federal structure will survive, we should remain prejudiced towards the establishment of a strong president – at least one capable of vetoing legislation and directing the operation of the executive branch of government. This is not to say that parliamentary government and meaningful federalism are incompatible, only that federalism is more difficult to sustain without the focus that presidential elections provide.

Returning now to the structure of parties in a federation, we have thus far focused on the features of the national constitution that engender decentralized parties. There are, however, some requirements that must be met by regional and local governments themselves. Specifically:

> *Rule 41*: The governments of federal subjects should make broad use of direct election not only for local and regional legislatures, mayors and governors, but for other public offices as well.

It might seem unproductive to follow this rule. After all, we cannot assume that many voters will have good information about a great many, if any, of the candidates for these offices. Thus we might ask: doesn't direct election open the door to the election of people who are merely adept at manipulating public opinion? Indeed a positive answer to this question is not unreasonable, and was not an uncommon opinion in the formative years of the United States. Whatever the benefits of widespread application of elections, they were not universally appreciated in the first quarter of the 19th century. But what are those benefits and, in particular, what is the relevance of the pervasive use of elections at the regional and local level to the character of federalism? Briefly, the benefits take three interdependent forms. First, pervasive use of elections at the state and local level facilitates the formation of state and local party organizations that become the building blocks for federal, national parties. In this way, then, local and regional elections begin the process of party formation that is essential to a stable democracy.

Second, application of Rule 41 strengthens national parties and integrates them with local and regional ones. It might seem that regional elections would only encourage the rise of regional parties and political élites which would act in competition with the national government and which, for their own purposes, would raise issues that would threaten political stability. This is sometimes true, but primarily in countries in which regional competition focuses on a single salient office such as governor. Consider, though, the candidate for local judge in New York City who, during one of Franklin Roosevelt's presidential campaigns, gave his campaign funds to the local Democratic Party in anticipation of professional assistance (as reported by Samuel Lubell in *The Future of American Politics*, 1954). Weeks went by, but he saw nothing – no posters or radio broadcasts that mentioned his name! Agitated and uneasy, he returned to party headquarters to complain. The head of the party took him to the southern tip of Manhattan where the ferry from Staten Island landed and, as a ferry pulled in, he pointed to the floating debris and garbage that swirled at the ferry's stern, towed by its wake, and said, 'the name of your ferry is Franklin Delano Roosevelt'. Thus in an election in which voters confront scores of candidates about whom they know little or nothing, the essential commodity possessed by candidates is their partisan labels and the fact that these labels are shared by viable candidates for national office. Extensive application of direct election at the local and state level, then, gives party leaders a valuable commodity with which to deal – the party's nomination and official sanction – which in turn gives those leaders an incentive to integrate their party with the national one. Moreover, the connection works in the other direction as well. While the name Roosevelt and the label 'Democrat' doubtlessly helped the local candidate for judge and countless other Democratic candidates for office, the organizations erected to nominate and facilitate local and state elections become an essential part of any national candidate's campaign. Thus in a symbiotic relationship, local and national parties rely on each other for their survival and success.

Finally, extensive application of direct elections gives those with political ambition a ready means of moving up the ladder of political position and a home to those who would compete for the next rung. Moreover, because it is only natural to recruit candidates for national office from among those who have demonstrated effectiveness at campaigning and governing at the local or regional level, it ensures that those who achieve national office have a strong genetic connection to local and regional parties and governments.

13. Legislatures: Can They Govern Us If They Cannot Govern Themselves?

Legislators scream epithets, someone pushes someone else, and soon a group charges the lectern, reaching, grabbing and punching. Does this sound like the old People's Congress of Russia before its dissolution or the legislature of any of the newly formed successor states of the Soviet Union? Perhaps. But this scene could just as easily describe Japan's Diet or Taiwan's Yuan (where not only punches but also chairs, microphones and desks occasionally fly through the air). Such events are not uncommon; indeed in the early years of the US Congress many legislators attended sessions armed with pistols, and as late as 1856 one of them, Charles Sumner, was beaten senseless on the floor of the Senate by the nephew of an irate political opponent.

Of course, the dangers of incompetence and conflict seem greatest when legislative 'misbehaviour' occurs in a country with nuclear weapons that must make a painful transition from an authoritarian, centrally planned state to a liberal democratic, free enterprise one. Legislative incoherence threatens that transition because it threatens the things society needs most: a well-functioning judicial system, a clear body of contract and property law, and attention to the macro-economic policies of the state.

Insofar as the causes of this incoherence or misbehaviour are concerned, there are those who believe that legislatures in Russia and elsewhere behave as they do because so many legislators are merely 'warmed over' communists or *apparatchiks*, unable to comprehend the failure of their ideology and unwilling to give up any of the benefits they enjoyed under the previous regime. And there are those who see misbehaviour among even democratic reformers and who attribute it to naïveté and inexperience with their new-found ideology of liberal democracy and capitalism.

These arguments may be correct. But they circumvent the root of the problem and they generate inappropriate, even dangerous, responses. One response, based on the idea that the legislature 'has the wrong people in it', is the one Yeltsin pursued when he forcefully dissolved the People's Congress and decreed new elections. However, as subsequent events revealed, there is no guarantee that this response produces a legislature that is much different than the old one. There is, in fact, little evidence that legislators in a new democracy – even ex-communist ones – act any more in accordance with some narrow definition of self-interest than do legislators in an established, stable democracy. Scandals of all types occur with some frequency everywhere.

A second response is to give more power to a single authority – a president or prime minister – by allowing that person to legislate by decree or to suspend constitutional rights. This approach assumes that legislative incoherence is a greater danger than dictatorship, and it thereby tolerates postponement or even termination of democratic reform. But while it is true that strong arguments can be made for the view that states experiencing radical economic transformation cannot function as 'normal' democracies and that a greater degree of central control is required to keep politics from becoming incoherent or violent, this argument fails to attack the root cause of the problem of legislative incoherence.

As with many other things that we have tried to understand in this monograph, the cause of legislative inefficiency, misbehaviour, or incoherence lies with incentives. Legislators fail to generate coherent law not because they lack ability, but because they do not yet have the incentives to do so, including the incentive to develop the internal organizational structures that facilitate coordination and compromise. This absence of appropriate incentives in turn derives from the fact that legislators in a newly formed democracy are unlikely to have yet felt the full force of the imperatives of running for *re-election*. Indeed some may have never even observed such an election, whereas others may have done so, but in an incoherent setting in which dozens of candidates competed for the same office and in which the relationship between voters' actions and campaign strategies and tactics were obscure.

Experience tells us that if there is anything that draws a politician's attention to his or her responsibilities, it is the prospect of competing in an election against someone who will publicly broadcast every personal flaw and every incorrect decision to anyone who will listen. Although the prospect of competitive elections may be frightening to most politicians, it brings order to legislative deliberations since legislators must now try to communicate to voters that they are acting in their interest. The absence of the electoral threat and inexperience with competitive elections, on the other hand, yields a fragmented legislative 'party' structure and a less coherent legislative process. Things labelled 'parties' typically are not parties at all, that is, organizations designed to present the electorate with alternative policies and programmes and to secure votes for those who compete under their labels. Instead they are largely protest groups, ideological cabals, special interest lobbies and personal factions designed to advance the careers of specific individuals. In the absence of the threat of competitive elections, there is little need for these 'parties' to coalesce, to negotiate seriously their differences or to act so that an electorate views them as offering responsible policy alternatives. In fact doing so is taken as a sign of weakness or a failure of leadership.

Political parties in 'mature' democracies are organized to win elections. They are the devices politicians use to organize support within their constituencies and to communicate to the electorate their policy predispositions and their commitment to a rule of law. Parties organize in this way because voters, concerned about more personal matters, have little reason to devote much time to learning which candidate best represents their interests. If forced to listen to every promise and every prescription for change, they are easily overwhelmed and confused. Ordinary citizens, then, look for cues as to how to vote, and one important cue is a candidate's party label. If a party label can be made to convey anything, including the integrity of those who run under it, voters will use these labels in deciding who to support. Parties that succeed in associating themselves with attractive policies and attractive candidates survive; all others eventually disappear or are relegated to the sidelines of political events. The imperatives of electoral competition, then, compel legislators to cultivate the labels under which they seek election and re-election, so that members of a party within parliament have an incentive to ensure that their actions are responsible and serve a clear purpose.

The absence of, or inexperience with, the immediate threat of competitive elections also impacts a legislature's internal structure and, correspondingly, the efficiency of its operation. Without such a threat there is little need to organize oneself to proceed efficiently in the public's interest. Instead committee structures and debates arise on an *ad hoc* basis, since the only compelling force is one's definition of patriotism, unguided personal ambition or whim.

This is not to say that such motivations cannot lead legislators to support correct policies. But democracies do not place their faith in the fortuitous or accidental selection of well-intentioned representatives. They place their faith instead in ensuring that legislators will be directed to organize themselves in our interest because to do otherwise would lead us to replace them in the next election. We should not suppose, then, that legislatures are organized to do 'good'. Instead they will organize themselves to serve their own self-interest – they will reveal their votes when it is in their interest to do so; they will vote by secret ballot when they fear that doing otherwise will be personally costly; they will use committees and subcommittees if doing so aids their re-election; they will service constituent complaints when failing to do so costs them electoral support; and they will consult experts when they might be sanctioned by voters for making ill-advised decisions. What we must do through constitutional design, then, is ensure that their self-interest parallels ours.

Competitive elections are the primary route to this end. They compel legislators, even those who seek merely to get re-elected without convictions about policy, to organize and act in ways that maximize their chances of survival. If we have designed our electoral and representative mechanisms well, legislators will, in developing a structure that best suits their purposes, organize to serve our purposes.

Several practical suggestions follow from this somewhat cynical but not ill-founded perspective. First:

> *Rule 42*: Rather than try to specify the 'correct' organization of a legislature, constitutions should focus on clear specifications of modes of representation and electoral processes.

If a constitution tells legislators to organize in ways that do not serve their interests, they will find ways to operate differently. Constitutional provisions that require specific committees, ways of resolving disputes between legislative assemblies, and rules of procedure (except those that specify a quorum – the minimum number of legislators required to be present in order to conduct business – and those that specify special rules for considering constitutional amendments and impeachment) are generally unenforceable and are the first things to succumb to reinterpretation and amendment. In contrast:

> *Rule 43*: A clear specification of the timing of elections, term limits, when legislative sessions begin and end, and the basis of representation (by federal subject, by party-list proportional representation, by single-mandate district) lies at the heart of constitutional design.

Not everything dealing with representation or the details of election rules can be specified in a constitution. Issues such as campaign finance, the creation of authorities to administer elections, ballot forms, access to the media, the drawing of district boundaries, and so on can only be addressed by complex legislation. Discussing such issues in a constitution merely makes that document unwieldy and unenforceable. Thus the question arises as to who will oversee the creation and enforcement of electoral laws. Will local or regional governments have the opportunity to determine the rules under which they elect representatives or will these matters be dictated by some central authority, or even the legislature itself? Again, to strengthen federal relationships, our preference is for local determination of such matters. Indeed we prefer moving as much as possible out of the hands of those whose immediate fates are to be determined by such laws, since they will try to manipulate them to their own advantage.

That legislators will attempt to manipulate the rules of election so as to make their own positions more secure might make us ask how the things a constitution says about elections and representation can ever be enforced and remain stable. Why should electoral institutions dictate legislative structure and action rather than the other way around? What keeps those with power from manipulating election laws so that those laws exclusively serves only their interests?

In fact at least the broad outlines of election laws are enforceable for a simple reason: maintaining them will soon be in the self-interest of legislators themselves. Here another American example is instructive. It is generally accepted that America's method of electing a president has certain disadvantages, including the possibility that a popular vote winner will not be elected (as happened in 1824, 1876, 1888, arguably in 1960 and nearly in 1968). Hence the US Senate periodically considers various 'reforms'. But to date nothing much has changed, because no one is certain that any change will provide as sure a guarantee of a two-party system as does the current arrangement. However, one thing is certain: legislators who must decide any constitutional matter are winners at the game of two-party politics and they prefer to maintain that aspect of the game. Winners in any game rarely want to change its rules, since such changes threaten them with the prospect of becoming losers rather than winners. Rarely does the person winning at some card game suggest playing a different game; arguments for change come from the losers. And rarely does anyone winning at roulette move elsewhere in a casino. The same is true in politics. Thus to the extent that the courts and public opinion allow it, the American Republican and Democratic Parties collude to ensure that third-party candidates have as small a chance as possible at disturbing their competition. And since they are confident that current arrangements disadvantage third parties, those arrangements are largely unchallenged.

This discussion of how electoral laws become self-enforcing suggests a final rule, namely:

> *Rule 44*: The things a constitution says about representation and elections should be crafted carefully and in full appreciation of their long-term consequences.

It is too easy to write those parts of a constitution or even to draft initial legislation with an eye to securing immediate political advantage. However, it is in the long term that acts of statecraft are judged, not in the short term. And the long term is likely to be stable and prosperous only if those parts create the proper incentives among legislators.

14. A Two-Chamber Legislature: Isn't One More Than Enough?

Although some democratic states exist with only one legislative chamber, most have two. We should not be surprised, then, by the fact that despite their many differences, all draft constitutions prepared for the Russian Federation between 1991 and 1993 proposed to create both a lower chamber (now the State Duma) and an upper one (now the Federation Council). And following conventional democratic practice (as opposed to the idea of a Supreme Soviet elected by a larger assembly), all serious drafts proposed that each chamber be selected or elected independently of the other. However, in light of the disarray exhibited by legislators not only in Russia, but in even more established democracies, we are entitled to ask why two legislative chambers are needed when one provides all the entertainment we can tolerate. Wouldn't two chambers, each vying for power, only add to the confusion and to the possibility of executive–legislative or presidential–legislative stalemate? Why create more public officials than we already have? After all, public officials demand salaries, but they do not seem to yield a large return on this investment.

But before we use the alleged failings of any specific legislative body as a basis for predicting the consequences of new arrangements, we should first restate some arguments as to why the future need not be like the past. Recall our argument from the previous chapter that the character of legislative bodies such as the old People's Congress of Russia should not be attributed to the supposition that they are dominated by large numbers of unrepentant communists, entrenched *apparatchiks*, and faceless mediocrities. Legislators inherited from a dead regime may be of less than sterling character, but a legislature is not some simple arithmetic sum of the people in it. Instead the various Congresses and Soviets of the successor states of the USSR acted as they did (or act today as they do) because they came into being before anyone knew they were to be national rather than republic legislatures and because their members did not feel or otherwise fully appreciate the need to organize themselves into professional law-making institutions.

We understand that it might be difficult to imagine some members of any old Congress or Supreme Soviet becoming professional at much of anything (aside, perhaps, from how best to stymie reforms that might threaten the security of their positions). However, the differences between old and new legislatures will not come from some magical process that fills public office holders with wiser and more deliberative people. This difference will come, if it comes at all, from the ways in which legislators are compelled to represent national or local constituencies in their respective countries and to compete for public office in meaningful elections. With the prospect of regularly scheduled, competitive elections – an especially frightening idea for those who have never confronted such things – legislators will have to do more than scurry about whispering rumours of cabals, dividing and redividing into innumerable factions, or hatching plots against a government or a president. They will instead be forced to take *positive* action, to formulate policy, to draft legislation that confronts directly the innumerable problems their countries confront, to learn what it is their constituents want, and to anticipate what policies an election opponent might propose in attempting to unseat them. They will find it necessary to maintain permanent staffs, and to deliberate, hold committee meetings, gather data and vote. The mouthing of ideological generalities and personal insults will not wholly disappear, but they should subside, if only because legislators will fear an electorate that views them as unprofessional and unable to express and represent their views effectively.

Of course, what we have just said does not address the issue of a two-chamber legislature and does not answer two questions, both of which may be relevant to any state redesigning its governmental structure:

1. If a state already possesses a single legislative chamber (a Supreme Soviet or a Congress of People's Deputies), wouldn't it be simpler to 'improve' on what already exists by merely holding new elections and, if necessary, by clarifying the relationship of the legislature to the other parts of the state?
2. If a parliamentary system is chosen in which the authority to form and dismiss a government is to be held primarily by the 'lower' legislative branch, isn't an upper branch redundant?

So turning to the issue of legislative design, we note that there are two basic arguments for a two- rather than a single-chamber legislature:

1. Legislators *represent*, and there are different things that require representation.
2. Division of the legislature makes it more difficult for this branch to do stupid or dangerous things.

The first justification takes us to an important issue that will concern anyone who drafts a constitution. That issue is what it means to have 'fair' representation, and who it is that is to be represented – individual citizens, specific ethnic groups or the different geographic regions of a country.

How we address this issue depends on the nature of the country under consideration. If it is a small homogeneous state – Finland, Iceland or even Hungary – without salient regional or ethnic differences, then the issue of geographic or ethnic representation may not arise and the concept of 'fair' representation may be a simple thing: divide the country into any number of equally populous districts and let each district elect the same number of representatives to the relevant legislative chamber. This rule can admit a representation scheme in which the country is divided into as many districts as there are legislators and in which each deputy represents a specific district. Or, at the other extreme, it can admit a system in which the country consists of a single district and deputies are elected by party lists, where each party is awarded a proportion of seats in the legislature equal to its proportion of the popular vote. Some countries, such as Hungary, combine these two systems and elect approximately half of the legislature one way and half the other.

But suppose, for the moment, that we are dealing with a state such as Russia or Ukraine in which there is considerable variation in the economic interests of different parts of the country, or in which one ethnic group is predominant in one part of the country and another ethnic group predominant in some other part. Imagine that we implement the same formula for representation as we do in Finland, Iceland or Hungary. The difficulty now is that different geographic regions, although represented in proportion to their population, may argue and in fact believe that 'fair' representation requires that all specific interests or ethnicities be equally represented in the legislature regardless of their numbers in the population.

We accomplish little by trying to counter these views with debates about the meaning of fairness, since purely philosophical arguments are unlikely to dissuade people that the only practical protection against majority tyranny is representation based on something other than simple head counts. It is for this reason, then, that a second legislative chamber may be a practical necessity. By first dividing a country into specific constituencies defined by their geographic or ethnic character (or, in the case of, say, Russia or Ukraine, by taking pre-existing political subunits such as oblasts and republics), by requiring that all regions have identical representation in an upper legislative chamber and by making that chamber an integral part of the legislative process (for example, giving it a veto over any legislation), we have a system in which every region has an equal chance of blocking legislation it opposes: no region is any more or less pivotal than any other.

For federations, we compromise the principle of equal representation of people because forging a federation is like forming an alliance, and a two-chamber legislature is one of the compromises we make to achieve that end. It is important to note, however, that the meaning of this compromise should change over time. In societies with little geographic mobility and sharp, territorial ethnic divisions, this compromise may be one of the most important ones that we can make. But in a society with an advanced market economy and, correspondingly, with a mobile labour force, the meaning of geography (as well as of ethnicity) should diminish with time. Thus although the issue of big versus small states or urban versus rural played a significant role in the early years of the United States, mobility and the general homogenization of America leaves people there unconcerned about the fact that, as of 1994, the majority leader of the Senate came from a state (Maine) that ranked 38th in population among the 50 states, the minority leader came from a state (Kansas) that ranked 32nd, the Speaker of the House of Representatives came from a state (Washington) that ranked 18th, and the president had been governor of a state (Arkansas) that ranked 33rd.

What is a momentous compromise in one era can become irrelevant in another. However, making that compromise raises a number of subsidiary questions. Why, as is usually the case, do we make the upper chamber smaller than the lower one? Should the term lengths of deputies to the two chambers be the same or different? Should the powers of the two chambers be symmetric or asymmetric? Who will determine the rules under which elections to each chamber are conducted?

These questions cannot be addressed separately. We cannot choose, say, a five year term merely because this number has been used in the past or because it is the average of some sample of legislatures from other countries. Our choice must be consistent with some overall idea about what it is we are trying to accomplish with legislative representation. To see what we mean, notice that if the only consideration in the creation of a two-chamber legislature is the desire to reach some geographic compromise, then we would be unable to explain why so many states, even small non-federal ones, abide by the same format. Britain's House of Lords may exist out of tradition, but what accounts for the upper chambers of Austria, France or Iceland?

In fact there are other considerations. First, imagine a country divided into some number of equally populous districts, each of which elects one representative to the legislature. If only one candidate is elected from each district, then a majority of voters in a majority of districts can control all legislation. Since 50 per cent of 50 per cent equals 25 per cent, as few as one-quarter of the population can, theoretically, control the legislature. Normally we would not expect such extreme events to occur. But the bias a one-chamber legislature allows can create significant tensions when, for example, agricultural interests predominate over industrial concerns despite an opposite population balance.

There are several ways to avoid such problems. One is to draw legislative districts that are homogeneous in terms of the character of the people within them. But this alternative is impractical when populations are mixed. More importantly, it is divisive because, in drawing district boundaries, it explicitly pits different parts of society against each other in the struggle for initial advantage in the political process. Another alternative is to elect legislators using nation-wide proportional representation (PR). But PR entails its own types of cost. First, it increases the incentives for a fractured party system, which is something that states such as Russia and Ukraine ought to avoid. Second, it opens the door to the formation of purely ethnic or regional parties that may be unable to compromise their positions for fear of losing electoral support.

The third possibility is the two-chamber legislature, which accomplishes our purpose by requiring that legislation secure two majorities, one in each chamber. Indeed it is at this point that we encounter the logic of several other alternative constitutional provisions. Notice that two chambers has the intended effect of making it more difficult for a minority to control the legislature only to the extent that their bases of representation differ: otherwise the same voters can control both chambers. Thus effective implementation of the two-chamber legislative design requires that we avoid electing members of one chamber from precisely the same districts that we elect the members of the other.

This guideline can be met in any number of ways. In the United States, representatives from the lower chamber are elected from narrowly drawn constituencies and members of the Senate are elected by states. Members of the Senate in Canada are elected by province, whereas members of the lower chamber are elected by party-list PR. Germany and Russia mix these systems: members of the lower chamber are elected in both single-member districts and by national party-list PR, whereas members of the upper chamber represent federal subjects as in Canada and the USA.

To illustrate the protection a two-chamber legislature can provide minorities, consider the following example with nine voters. Suppose each voter is either of type X or of type Y (for example, ethnic group X or ethnic group Y), and suppose they live as shown in the representation below:

$$X \quad X \quad Y$$

$$Y \quad X \quad Y$$

$$X \quad Y \quad Y$$

Thus there are four X-type voters and five Y types, so that if each of these voters is allowed to be represented by a deputy in one chamber of the legislature, that chamber will contain a majority of Y types. Now suppose we create a second chamber by creating three horizontal election districts, each with three voters (that is, each line in the example is a district). Hence X-types are a majority in the first district, and Y types are a majority in the second and third districts. We can therefore reasonably suppose that Y-type deputies will be elected in the second and third districts. Thus not only will Y types dominate the first chamber, they will dominate the second as well, which may cause X-type voters to believe that their rights will not be respected by such a legislature. However, suppose instead that we create a second legislative chamber with three voters in each district as before, but with districts drawn vertically. In this variant the first two districts will most likely elect an X-type deputy since X types are a majority there, whereas only the third will elect a Y type. Thus while we can easily create a chamber in which Y types are a majority, we can also create a legislative chamber in which X types are in control. If we now require that legislation receive majority approval in both chambers, it must be the case that laws appeal to both X and Y types, or at least that sufficient compromises be made so that some X- and Y-type legislators can vote alike. Thus by the simple expedient of creating two chambers and drawing district boundaries carefully, we can promote compromise and minimize the chances that a majority can injure some minority.

But while this precaution may protect some minorities against majority tyranny, it should be evident that our example only illustrates a very sweeping type of control – one that is unlikely to operate effectively if public passions are aroused against very small minorities – those which cannot be a majority in either part of the legislature. As an additional precaution, then, we can elect members of the lower and upper houses to terms of different lengths. Although it may seem reasonable to want to make the government more responsive to public opinion by electing everyone at the same time, doing so leaves the state vulnerable to transitory public passions. Distinct terms of office in which we elect members of the lower house, say, every three years and one half of the members of the upper house every three years for six year terms provides some insurance against this possibility and lends greater stability and continuity to the government. A longer term for the upper chamber also induces its members to look at policy differently than members of the lower chamber: because they confront less immediate electoral imperatives, deputies to the upper chamber can take a longer-term view of things, which once again changes the hurdles any bill must jump over before it becomes law.

There are a great many other issues that must be addressed in designing a legislature. For example, we must decide:

- who should ratify treaties (usually the upper chamber, which generally represents regions of a federation or which may be elected to a longer term than the lower chamber);
- who should approve ministerial and court appointments (usually the upper chamber in presidential systems, the lower chamber in parliamentary ones);
- who should declare war (usually both chambers);
- who should authorize or void a declaration of emergency (usually both chambers);

- who must approve of constitutional amendments (usually both chambers plus citizens, directly or through their regional representatives, since they are of central importance to everyone and need to be given especially careful consideration);
- who, if anyone, can dismiss ministers (usually the lower chamber in parliamentary systems since it is that chamber which, being larger, is thought to be 'closer to the people').

A two-chamber legislature creates a good deal of flexibility in the ultimate design of a government. But regardless of the specifics of that design, it is important to understand that two chambers need not be viewed merely as a way to slow the processes of government or as a source of confusion and stalemate. A two-chamber design allows us to choose different electoral methods and different bases of representation so that the different parts of society each feel adequately represented and protected, thereby giving the government legitimacy and stability.

15. Parliaments and Presidents: Legislative Incoherence versus Authoritarian Rule?

Although the successor states of the USSR each provides for the office of the presidency in some form, there are those in every country who want to move things more in the direction of parliamentary government and others who want to strengthen the powers of the president. A parliamentary form, championed usually by leaders of a sitting legislature, has the advantage, it is argued, of avoiding the legislative–executive stalemate that characterized the conflict between Boris Yeltsin and the old People's Congress. A presidential system, on the other hand, is credited with being more in keeping with traditions of strong leadership that, armed with the power to issue decrees and to dismiss a recalcitrant legislature, seems essential in a period of massive economic dislocation.

The debate over alternatives usually is little more than a power struggle among political élites and it is anything but obvious that average citizens should care much about who wins and loses this debate. The issues, however, are important, if only because understanding the difference between parliamentary and presidential government helps people to understand how their government, regardless of form and regardless of whether the debate is an active one, works.

Looking first at parliamentary systems, their key feature is that the government serves at the legislature's discretion – or, more precisely, at the discretion of a majority in the legislature. As long as the government can command a majority of votes in parliament, it survives. But if a majority cannot be sustained, the government resigns or the president or prime minister calls for new legislative elections. Although we can imagine a number of variations, a president plays a minor role and, by making the executive a part of the legislature, executive–legislative conflict is minimized. By thus avoiding conflict between the government and the legislature, the argument goes, countries can better pursue a rational policy of economic reform. The national government speaks with a single voice – the voice of the parliamentary majority – through the person of the prime minister. However, parliamentary systems have two potential drawbacks. First:

- if parties in a parliamentary system are highly fractionalized, then legislative coalitions, and thus governments, are likely to be unstable.

This instability, common in systems without established party structures, can be as threatening to rational economic planning as executive–legislative deadlock. The second drawback is:

- because a government is elected by parliament, and because citizens only vote for members of the parliament, citizens have only indirect control over state policy in a parliamentary system.

Although indirect control is, by itself, not a bad thing, in parliamentary systems there is nothing to preclude parties that suffer losses at the polls from participating nevertheless in a government. Thus parliamentary government can, at least for a time, act contrary to public preferences and the vote.

Thus the performance of a parliamentary system depends on the character of its political parties. That character, in turn, depends on whether and how we satisfy another demand that arises frequently: the demand for proportional legislative representation (PR). Fearing that they will be under-represented if legislators are elected in single-member constituencies and realizing that legislative representation is the primary way to influence a government, ethnic minorities, occupational interests and religious groups will each demand some guarantee of representation. PR is the usual route to that end.

A common way to implement PR is for parties to submit candidate lists, for voters to vote for a preferred party, and for parties to win parliamentary seats in proportion to their support. A country can be divided into any number of multi-member districts or, as in Russia, Hungary, Germany and Israel, it can elect some or all deputies in one national constituency. Since any party that secures enough votes to overcome some explicit or implicit threshold (say, 5 per cent) wins seats, parties will seek to represent specific ideological, ethnic, social or religious cleavages, where the actual number of parties depends on the number and salience of those cleavages and the details of electoral procedures (such as the actual size of districts and minimum vote requirements).

PR seems an attractive addition to any government, parliamentary or otherwise, since it promises groups explicit representation. Even if representation is merely symbolic, symbolism can go a long way towards generating a sense that the state is legitimate. But PR has disadvantages. First:

- PR increases the incentives for politicians to engineer cleavages or to increase the salience of pre-existing ones, as when someone wants to advance their position by forming and leading a new party.

Thus PR gives extremists an audience and a potential role in the formation of a government. Second:

- although the process of forming a government offers some incentive for compromise, this incentive is attenuated by PR to the extent that parties must differentiate themselves to maintain electoral support. Moreover, society's conflicting demands are unlikely to be negotiated within party structures since a party must maintain a clear focus lest it find itself prey to those parties that provide such a focus.

These problems need not be consequential in a homogeneous society, but they can undermine the stability of countries such as Romania or Ukraine, which require less, not more, fragmented parties and less, not more, reasons for increasing the salience of ethnic–geographic disputes. PR alone, however, does not determine the nature of parties. We must also look at whether the presidency is a meaningful office. We turn, then, to the opposite of parliamentary government, presidential government, which is characterized by a chief of state who is directly elected for a fixed term and who heads a government he appoints (with the 'consent of the legislature') and that only he can dismiss. The presumed advantages of this model are:

- a directly elected president provides a focus for its aspirations and sense of nationhood, and offers a clear point of leadership in emergencies;

- governments are likely to be stable since they serve at the president's discretion, whose term is fixed;
- an independently elected and meaningful office of the presidency allows for the full implementation of the idea of a separation of powers.

A separation of powers was one of the touchstones of the Framers of the US constitution: 'The accumulation of all powers, legislative, executive, and judiciary, in the same hands, whether of one, a few, or many, and whether hereditary, self-appointed, or elected, may justly be pronounced the very definition of tyranny' (Madison, *Federalist Papers*, no. 47). Nevertheless, this last 'advantage' of presidentialism is seen by some as a disadvantage. Separate election and powers open the door, so the argument goes, to legislative–executive conflict, which may be especially severe if the president's party is not the one that controls the legislature. Later we argue that this problem has less to do with the general character of presidential systems and more with methods of election, but we cannot deny that the choice of parliamentary versus presidential system is often a choice between an efficient unitary state with the potential for instability versus rancorous bargaining between the legislature and the president.

Presidential systems are said also to have the drawback of presenting voters with an all-or-nothing choice – one side wins, all others lose. Parliamentary systems, the argument goes, allow all sides to 'win' something: legislative representation. But even if a party wins representation in parliament, it needn't participate in the government, and even if some groups are not explicitly represented in a president's administration, their interests may still be attended to by candidates who seek to form a majority in order to win the presidency.

Another drawback is that there may not be a 'best' way to elect presidents. A direct vote seems the simplest and most 'democratic' alternative, but there are many ways to implement this idea. One way is to require that a victorious candidate receive a majority of votes and to allow a run-off between the strongest candidates if no one receives a majority on the first ballot. This method seeks to ensure against the election of a candidate who receives, say, 30 per cent of the vote and who cannot claim a mandate to lead. But like PR, this scheme allows minor parties to block a first-ballot victory so they can negotiate their support between ballots, and thereby eliminates one of the advantages of presidentialism: the incentive of parties to coalesce and to negotiate conflict internally. A direct vote's problems are compounded by the requirement, common in the successor states of the Soviet Union, that turnout exceeds 50 per cent. However, it is a fallacy to believe that low turnout is 'bad' and high turnout is 'good'. Voters may abstain because they are dissatisfied and repulsed by all alternatives; but they may also abstain because all viable candidates are acceptable. Regardless of its source, a formal turnout requirement can only allow extremists to call for election boycotts without requiring that they formulate explicit policy alternatives. Some defects of a direct vote can be corrected if the minimum turnout requirement is deleted and if, instead of a majority, we require that the winning candidate receive some lesser percentage of the vote (say 40 per cent) before requiring a run-off. But now consider the problem of ensuring against a 'regional president' who secures most of his support from one geographic region and whose election is strongly opposed by voters in all other regions. One alternative is to eschew a single president and, as in Switzerland, to select a president on a rotating basis from representatives of its larger cantons. But as Simon Bolivar argued over a century and a half ago (*The Angostura Address*), such a system lacks, 'unity, continuity, and individual responsibility' and undermines most of the advantages of presidentialism. Nigeria earlier took a different approach by requiring that presidents secure at least 25 per cent of the votes in each of its federal subjects. Czechoslovakia, prior to its dissolution, required a majority in both its Czech and Slovak halves. Such devices, however, can yield contentious bargaining whenever no one meets these requirements, and they too allow regional parties to block anyone's election.

As with parliamentary government, then, the problems of presidentialism have less to do with any one characteristic of the system and more to do with the combination of factors. This fact is perhaps best illustrated by noting an especially dangerous combination: a directly elected president and a parliament elected by PR. Here we need to note simply that the powers of effective presidents derive less from their formal constitutional authority than they do from the fact that, as a nationally elected figure, a president is in a position to draw people's attention to critical issues, to mobilize support for specific policies and to propose compromises among contentious groups. The mere device of direct election gives a president a mandate to lead, and it is this mandate, more than any formal power, that presidents must learn to use in order to be effective. Indeed:

> *Rule 45*: If we make the office of president constitutionally powerful, we only create incentives for the other parts of government to resist those powers.

Moreover, if parliament is elected by PR, the leaders of the larger parties there can also claim the same national mandate, which exacerbates conflict between president and parliament. In contrast, electing deputies by single-mandate districts leads them to focus on local issues and gives the president greater flexibility to negotiate compromises. Thus:

> *Rule 46*: With a presidential system, we should avoid structures that permit legislators or legislative parties to claim the same national mandate that we would rightfully reserve for the president.

In general, then, there is no singularly and obviously 'best' way to implement democracy, and debates over the system most appropriate for a country need to appreciate the fact that the character of a political system is determined not by any single factor, such as the relative power of the president versus the legislature. It is a function also of electoral procedures and the types of party that emerge to compete for public office. Moreover, no system is perfect and no system offers a guarantee of stability. PR promises minorities a formal voice; but it can result in a highly fractionalized party structure incapable of achieving compromise on divisive issues. A direct vote for president allows voters to pass direct judgement on a government's performance, but it need not preclude the possibility of parties that form merely to block one or another candidate from securing a mandate to lead. None of these difficulties, however, is an argument for not making any choice. People and political systems will adapt to different constitutions, and it is more important to choose *some* system and *some* constitution rather than search for a non-existent perfection.

16. Emergency Clauses: Essential Precautions or A Lack of Faith?

Few people question that most of the successor states of the Soviet Union are in crisis. Unsurprisingly, many point to mainland China or to Taiwan as models usefully combining authoritarian control and the development of a market economy. Others say to hell with markets or transitions to democracy; dictatorship and central planning wasn't so bad after all. Our sympathies obviously lie with democracy. But rather than merely expressing sympathies, our intent in this chapter is to examine the advisability of constitutional emergency clauses designed to deal with crises of different types. One reason for this focus is that such clauses seem a reasonable compromise between the desire to be democratic and the pragmatic requirement of strong leadership during a period of unsettling transition. Thus some constitutions direct the legislature to pass laws that grant special powers to a chief of state in an emergency; others offer elaborate provisions that identify who can declare an emergency, who must ratify such a declaration, the circumstances that qualify as emergencies, the duration of a state of emergency, and the procedures whereby an emergency regime is ended. Regardless of the details of how this compromise is attempted, we argue here that not only is no such compromise possible, but also that it is unnecessary.

The most evident problem with emergency clauses is their potential for abuse. Indeed it takes a good many fingers and a good many hands to count those 'democracies' that have been transformed into something else under the cover of a declared emergency. Our purpose here, however, is to make a different argument. In broad outline, the logical parts of this argument are as follows:

1. Avoiding any abuse of power in the event that an emergency regime is imposed requires that government function with some internal checks and balances.

2. The power of those authorized to declare a state of emergency must be controlled by the other parts of government, lest power be usurped.
3. If we can restrain the abuse of power in an emergency, then no such clauses are required.

Thus to state our argument as an additional rule of democratic institutional design:

> *Rule 47*: If a normally functioning state cannot accommodate emergencies, then the aggregation of power in a few hands will threaten democracy regardless of the controls a constitution tries to establish.

The opportunities for an abuse of power arise, of course, from the fact that a declaration of emergency allows the state or specific office holders in it to do unusual things, such as delay or otherwise cancel elections, incarcerate persons indefinitely or abrogate specified (and even some unspecified) rights. Each such action threatens a dangerous precedent, and any reasonable proposal for a constitutional emergency clause tries to ensure the existence of checks on emergency powers that can be applied by the legislature, regional governments or the courts. But such checks on abuse operate only if, aside from the special circumstances of the emergency, the state otherwise functions normally. This fact, which we discuss in more detail shortly, should be kept in mind as we examine the situations that an emergency clause seeks to treat.

Briefly, the situations commonly identified by different constitutions as an emergency include attempts to overthrow the constitutional system, large-scale economic dislocation, mass unrest, inter-ethnic conflict, natural disasters, epidemics and epizootic diseases, external aggression, threats to the people's safety and a general incapacity of the state to meet its obligations. This list yields four general categories of emergency: natural disasters, economic disintegration, external threats and internal threats. Of these four categories, only the second and fourth seem to require any special attention. The first, natural disasters, unless of unprecedented magnitude, are likely to be localized events and of no threat to the normal operation of the state. What special or unusual powers does the state require to treat floods or epidemics? If such events cannot be anticipated and provided for by normal legislation and treated with some measure of consensus, then no constitution, regardless of form, is viable. The third possibility, invasion, threatens not only the state but the nation and, as with natural disasters, it is difficult to imagine a society that cannot act to meet such calamities or that cannot reach a consensus on appropriate procedures, even 'extra-constitutional' ones. This type of emergency is perhaps the least ambiguous and is the one most easily treated in that part of the constitution that enumerates the powers of the legislature – for example, by including the clause, '[the legislature] shall make provision for the functioning of the state in the event that a state of war exists between _____ and any other foreign power'.

Looking more closely at the reasons for supposing that a normally functioning state can be expected to handle invasions and floods, we should of course recognize that states may be required from time to time to do unusual things with respect to, say, civil liberties. People may have to be quarantined, barred from entering territory, moved without immediate compensation or prohibited from revealing military preparations. But our willingness to turn such matters over to 'the authorities' – to the military, the police and the courts – and to allow them some freedom of action, requires the existence of internal checks. If the legislature and the courts can oversee and regulate these authorities, if a chief of state and the legislature can ensure that the courts are impartial, and if the courts and the president can focus public attention on the legislature to ensure that its actions are timely and constitutional, then a consensus on appropriate responses to an emergency is likely to emerge.

Democracies, then, allow various parts of the government temporarily to assume special powers to the extent that people are certain that they can be restrained from overstepping the bounds of reasonable action. And, most importantly, the thing that acts as the constraint on action is the *normal* system of internal checks and balances that a well-designed constitution establishes. In this way:

> *Rule 48*: A constitutional democracy is something other than a system of inflexible rules that require special provisions to handle every unusual circumstance and to treat every crisis. No one has yet discovered the trick to writing such rules, and indeed there are probably theorems in mathematics that tell us that such rules cannot exist. Instead we rely on a 'balance of powers' within the state, where the interests of the state's component parts are formed by each part's different connection to those the state is supposed to serve, the people.

Of course, if there is a test of this 'theory of democratic government', it lies in the area of the second and fourth categories of emergency:

economic turmoil and domestic insurrection. These circumstances appear to be a different species of animal, requiring separate treatment in a constitution. So let us consider them, beginning with insurrection.

Presumably, this type of emergency concerns an attempted secession by, say, one of Russia's republics, by the Crimea from Ukraine, or simply armed ethnic conflict and any of the parts of the ex-Soviet Union. Such emergencies may initially be confined to a small region but, as Britain's experience with Northern Ireland illustrates, they can be exported to endanger everyone. And whether localized or exported, such conflicts are often accompanied by the wholesale breakdown of law and order and, in the most extreme cases, by the takeover of a region by undemocratic forces. In this event, we cannot rely on regional authorities to resolve matters or to call for timely intervention by the national government.

Because unilateral action by a national government, without the constitutional authority that an emergency provision might offer, appears to violate federal principles, a true 'constitutional emergency' seems inescapable. Nevertheless, the granting of special authority to a chief of state or prime minister through the normal actions of the legislature should be adequate to treat this type of emergency. If a constitution guarantees a democratic government to all parts of a country, then the national government can justify intervention on the basis of an appeal to a part of the constitution that does not explicitly refer to emergencies. Moreover, the protection afforded a federation's constituent parts against unwarranted actions and unreasonable interpretations of 'democratic government' is the normally functioning national government itself, as a consequence of the fact that the legislature, in addition to representing people, also represents the federation's parts.

Turning, then, to our last category of emergencies – economic ones that are today most closely associated with the transition from a planned to a market economy – this is, of course, the arena that affords us an almost daily view of the inability of the state to formulate policies that are coherent, consistent and timely. With so much effort devoted to political manoeuvre and conflict, and with an unregulated self-interest appearing to drive economies to ruin, 'strong leadership' seems the only course: 'Give _____ [you fill in the blank] the authority to reshape the economy, our political and judicial system, and our system (or non-system) of property rights'. What choice do we have, some people can ask, but to take a temporary step back from the incoherence of democratic process when all that process can yield is chaos in the short term?

But what reasons do people have for supposing that such chaos is endemic to Russia, Ukraine, Armenia or wherever? Do we have some large sample of democratic experiments in these countries that all resulted in the same thing? Should we plan the transition to democracy on the assumption that chaos will persist into the indefinite future? Indeed are we certain that any apparent chaos is not without beneficial consequences, including the gradual accumulation of capital in the hands of those most likely to reinvest it productively in the future? Despite assertions to the contrary, no one knows with certainty what policies will move a country to prosperity with the least pain. There are no economic messiahs, no 'quick fixes' and no paths to progress that only a few can see. If no one knows what's best or if they know it only accidentally, what is the advantage of authoritarian rule, however temporary? How can we be certain that our choice of 'temporary dictator' *is* the person who knows best? The best we can hope for is that people will press their arguments upon each other, and that out of this debate, however incoherent, will come compromises, experiments (both successful and unsuccessful) and, hopefully, a few new ideas.

It appears, then, that we must reject any possibility of a constitutional accommodation of emergencies. We have rejected authoritarian rule, however authorized, and we have also argued that contentious debate, which implementation of emergency provisions can foreclose, can yield a clearer view of alternatives. Is there, then, any proper role for some form of constitutional emergency clause?

In fact there is a role: the *coordination* of the state. The problem with economic emergencies is that there are numerous competing alternative policies, each vying for the title 'best'. And because each of them gives special advantage to someone, it is difficult to use the ordinary processes of government to select one of them. Owing to disagreements within it, the legislature may be unable to organize itself appropriately, or the legislature and president, although appreciating the need for timely action, may be unable to agree on, or otherwise choose, some course of action aside from doing nothing. And although no one policy may be best, the selection of any one of them may be better than incoherence and no policy at all. In fact we suspect that it is here that we find the argument against what we have said thus far. Specifically, emergency clauses are not designed to choose 'the best' policy; they are designed instead to ensure that *some* policy, however imperfect, is adopted.

However, rather than conclude that advocates of constitutional emergency provisions are correct, viewing crises this way tells us how to fashion provisions that avoid excessive concentrations of power, but that give some part of government the ability to coordinate or to initiate those actions that will lead the different parts of the state to concerted action. For example, instead of granting a president the power of decrees, suppose we give him the right to call the legislature into special session and to require that it consider only the temporary emergency legislation he proposes. The special power of the president in this instance is the authority to focus public debate and to set the legislative agenda: to require that his proposals take precedence in legislative deliberations. There cannot be any usurpation of power since the legislature can continue to negotiate with the president over details. And since the state continues to function normally, there is no need to abrogate rights or at least to abrogate them in a way that sets dangerous precedents.

It may be hard to convince readers that so weak a provision can accomplish much of anything, especially in light of the economic distress that some states confront. Indeed what we propose leads to a process that is not much different from what occurred throughout most of 1992 in Russia. Although sometimes chaotic, and despite the events that unfolded in September and October of 1993, we should also keep in mind that throughout most of this period compromises were reached and no one was suddenly given a free but unwanted tour of Siberia. The eventual dissolution of the People's Congress had more to do with Yeltsin's failure to understand the mechanics of democracy – with the need to consult and cajole members of the Congress to bring them over to his side – than anything else. The new legislature does not function better today because it contains fresh faces, because deputies live in fear of tanks or because special emergency provisions direct events. It works instead because normal democratic process – the fear of elections and the promise of winning higher office – is now more salient to those who hold the reigns of power. Those who fear that normal democratic process can only lead to further chaos and eventual dictatorship should keep in mind that stronger emergency provisions in the constitutions of other countries are more often than not the source of emergencies and not their solution. Put simply:

> *Rule 49*: The most effective 'emergency clause' is a well-written constitution that establishes a viable balance of power among the different parts of the state, that gives those parts a clear connection to the people, and that gives political leaders an incentive to prepare beforehand for emergencies and to resolve them in an effective and timely manner when they arise.

Before we conclude this discussion of emergencies, there is one last issue that needs to be addressed: the widespread crime and corruption that seems an inescapable part of the transition from communism to democracy and free enterprise. News reports from Moscow, for example, amply reveal the extent of the problem, which is particularly damaging to democracy whenever it permeates official institutions – a circumstance that appears to describe Russian politics today as well as the politics of the other successor states of the Soviet Union. The temptation, then, is to combat the problem by suspending constitutional rights – especially those pertaining to due process of law – and to give special authority to various internal security agencies. This is the route presently being taken by Moscow authorities under the sanction of President Yeltsin.

We can appreciate the concern that crime occasions, especially violent crime (as when legislators and judges themselves are threatened or even killed), and the sympathy for special measures that is likely to be felt by the population generally. But even if corruption and crime permeate official institutions, there is little reason to disallow the judicial system from exercising oversight over whatever special measures are taken and whatever special authority is granted to internal security agencies. The dangers are especially great in presidential systems, since moving such authority to the office of the president or to some ministry under his control merely allows a dangerous concentration of power within one branch of the state, and forecloses the opportunity for the remaining branches – especially the judiciary – to act as a safeguard against abuse. And we can be certain that abuses will occur. The suspension of constitutional rights in the name of public safety is a dangerous act not merely because of the abuses it allows, but also because wresting back such authority is more often than not an impossible undertaking. Those with such authority normally have every incentive to resist a diminution of their power – a power that cannot be checked by any other branch of the government.

None of this is to say, of course, that the judicial branch is immune to corruption any more than any other part of the state. Nevertheless, every effort should be made to combat crime and corruption using 'normal' procedures until there is compelling evidence that one part of the state or another is incapable of functioning owing to the corruption that permeates it. Indeed even in states in which corruption seems a part of political tradition (Italy, Columbia?), members of the judiciary, often at great personal risk and sacrifice, have performed their duty.

Until and unless there is some consensus that this branch of government cannot function to provide oversight against abuses of constitutional rights, citizens in a democracy are well advised to resist the excuses offered by one part of government or the other to short-circuit constitutional limitations on their authority.

17. Russia's Choices: An Accident Waiting to Happen?

Reform has two dimensions – an economic one and a political one – and although lip-service is paid generally to the proposition that these two dimensions are fused and that one cannot be attacked without attacking the other, they are too frequently approached, especially on the territory of the former Soviet Union, as though different principles guide each. In fact the same basic principle ought to direct our confrontation of both.

The economic reformer's strategies are stated in terms of laws on private property, banking and contracts, and take the form of government policies on tariffs, taxes, privatization, borrowing and subsidies. Regardless of the school of thought to which a reformer adheres, it is understood that these laws and policies need to be manipulated in accordance with a common principle: socially desirable outcomes cannot be willed or wished into existence; they derive, if at all, from the ways in which government action and economic institutions channel individual self-interest. People cannot be made to work, save, invest or invent through mere oratory: people must be given the incentives to do these things in natural and self-sustaining ways. Thus by manipulating government policies and by nurturing the development of appropriate economic institutions, reform must make working, saving, investing and inventing in people's immediate self-interest.

Although how best to apply the principle of self-interest in economics is imperfectly understood, its applicability with respect to the second dimension of reform, the political one, is even less well appreciated. But appreciated or not:

Rule 50: The transition to democracy consists of the design and manipulation of institutions – of schemes of legislative representation, election laws and constitutional allocations of power – that render certain actions and the pursuit of certain outcomes in people's self-interest.

Circumstances differed greatly from those that characterize any ex-communist state, but the parallelism of economic and political reform was well understood by the framers of the US constitution. For example, when debating the method whereby judges ought to be selected, Benjamin Franklin sought to inspire a fuller consideration of the alternatives among delegates to the Philadelphia Convention by relating a Scottish method 'in which the nomination proceeded from the lawyers, who always selected the ablest of the profession in order to get rid of him and share his practice among themselves' (James Madison, *Notes on The Constitutional Convention*). Applied to the protections democracy provides against tyranny, James Madison generalized Franklin's example when he wrote: 'The great security against the gradual concentration of the several powers in the same department consists in giving to those who administer each department the necessary constitutional means and *the personal motives* to resist encroachments of the others...Ambition must be made to counter ambition' (*Federalist*, no. 51, emphasis added).

It is this principle that decision-makers elsewhere have not yet applied with consistency in their approach to political reform. Political reform is too often viewed through the old lens of command and control. Rather than pay heed to the complex and often imperfectly understood ways in which democratic institutions shape incentives and sustain themselves, it is only the outer shells of institutions that are manipulated. And with people's perceptions of the future obscured by the uncertainties of transition, and with those in power sharing an understandable reluctance to relinquish their authority, those manipulations are motivated less by a search for a stable democratic order than they are by the quest for immediate political advantage.

Even though it is arguably further along the road to reform than any other successor state of the USSR (except possibly the Baltic states), the problems here are best illustrated by Russia. The lament that politics there is merely a war of personalities may be an apt summary of the current situation. But describing the situation thus and searching for a cadre of new, more enlightened leaders can only yield disappointment. If the principle of self-interest is valid, then the actions of any new cadre will be dictated by the same incentives that guide the actions of the current ones.

Meaningful political reform requires that we look to those things that shape incentives, especially of those who control the coercive reins of government, and it is the failure to do these things carefully that now bedevils Russia's transition to democracy. Three things in particular confound the development of a stable democracy there:

1. The way in which the new Russian constitution shapes presidential–legislative relations.
2. The general approach to federalism and the way in which Moscow tries to meet the demands for regional autonomy.
3. The failure to understand the determinants of political parties, the role of parties in resolving conflict, and the relationship between parties and the variegated interests that characterize a market economy.

It might seem that each of these things can be treated separately: amend the constitution to reduce the powers of the presidency; negotiate new relationships between federal subjects and Moscow; and reform campaign finance laws. But such a view ignores how the incentives of *all* political élites are determined by their relationship to the ultimate sovereign in a democracy, and how these incentives interact to influence each other and all other things simultaneously. Our argument, then, is that piecemeal reform or the signing of Civic Accords will not resolve the problems of Russian democracy. Instead we need to look at the fundamental institutional determinants of incentives. Otherwise we can predict that:

- the president and factions within parliament will continue to claim a national mandate to lead, and all constitutional points of conflict between president and parliament will be active ones;
- the struggle between decision-makers in Moscow and regional élites will continue unabated;
- parties will remain highly fragmented, parliamentary elections will serve largely as primaries in the quest for the main prize of the presidency, and successful parties will be those that best frame nationalistic and authoritarian appeals.

PRESIDENTIAL–PARLIAMENTARY RELATIONS

Looking first at the relationship of the president to parliament, the new Russian constitution, ratified by popular referendum in 1993, gives every indication of extending the conflict between these two branches of government that precipitated Yeltsin's coup against the old parliament. Parliament legislates but the president can make law (by decree insofar as the law is silent). The president can veto acts of parliament, but the parliament can veto decrees (by passing contrary laws and by overriding presidential vetoes of those laws). Furthermore, the president can hire and fire ministers, but parliament can vote no confidence and compel the president to choose between replacing his ministers and scheduling new parliamentary elections. The constitution, then, adheres only to a superficial notion of a separation of powers and, aside from those special powers that give the president the upper hand in disputes (to dismiss parliament, to call referenda, to suspend local acts and laws, and to interpret the constitution as the 'protector of the constitution'), it places the president and parliament in direct opposition to each other.

In a state with strong democratic traditions, such institutional entanglements might compel compromise. But the likelihood of compromise depends not only on necessity, but also on incentives. The likelihood that Russia will choose the compromises that characterize stable democracies versus the conflicts that characterize an unstable one depends on whether political élites find it in their self-interest to engage in compromise rather than conflict.

In tracing the incentives of a president and parliamentary deputies, it is reasonable to begin with the assumption that, patriotic or venal, political élites seek power. But how power is secured and applied depends on the relationship between élites and those who directly or indirectly confirm their position: the people. It is this relationship that determines the fates of those who fill public office in a democracy, and it is this relationship that determines the private consequences of compromise or of the failure to compromise. Unfortunately, the details of the relationship in Russia between public officeholders and the people, as established by law, decree or constitutional provision, undermine the prospects for compromise and democratic stability.

Although the rules for presidential selection are not yet firmly established, it is almost certain that the next Russian president will be directly elected using the simple 'majority with run-off' procedure described earlier. We have no quarrel with direct elections. However, if Yeltsin could successfully claim a national mandate on the basis of the questionable 1993 referendum, then a new president, directly elected and guaranteed a majority vote on the first or second ballot, will claim the same mandate on an even firmer footing.

Mandates are valuable things for anyone choosing to exert leadership and it is imperative that, given his constitutional powers, a president possess a mandate to lead. But the problem here is the combination of direct election of the president with the electoral system used for the Duma elections. The current procedure for electing deputies there – half in single-member constituencies and half by national party-list proportional representation (PR) – was implemented to facilitate the formation of national parties and to ensure against the election of those opponents of reform that could marshall strong local electoral support. What was less well appreciated, however, was the fact that with candidates for the Duma competing through national party lists and with parliamentary elections occurring before, and independently of, the presidential contest, any majority coalition in the Duma can assert the same mandate claimed by the president – a mandate that Zhirinovsky claimed with only 23 per cent of the vote in 1993 and which someone with any larger percentage is certain to assert is his. Thus with both the president and parliament claiming the same thing – a mandate to lead – and with the new constitution confusing the issue of 'who is in charge', the stage is set for conflict and crisis of precisely the same sort that characterized the early stages of Russian democracy.

FEDERAL RELATIONS

A second manifestation of the failure to understand the role of incentives in political reform is the way Moscow tried to form its relations with subjects of the Federation. Aside from the conflict between the president and the Congress that characterized the first years of Russian democracy, no issue was more salient than that of federalism, especially the position of Russia's ethnic republics. Who was to control Russia's vast resources and who was to oversee privatization of state property? Were the republics sovereign? Could they conduct their own foreign policy and could they secede from the Federation? What power did Moscow have over regional Soviets? Whose laws were supreme? Should Russia's federalism be symmetric or should the ethnic republics, which historically enjoyed greater autonomy than the other regions, be treated differently than those other parts?

Rather than discuss the federal form a state should choose, here we want only to make three observations about the constitutional bargain that was ultimately established in Russia and the negotiations that preceded it. The first observation is that formal negotiations over this relationship focused on a Federal Treaty that enumerated the jurisdictions belonging exclusively to Moscow and jurisdictions shared by Moscow and the republic. Second, republics demanded that they be identified as 'sovereign states', with the presumption that this label, combined with the terms of the Federal Treaty, would protect their autonomy. Third, republics demanded the authority to renegotiate bilaterally the details of their relationships with Moscow, so that separate deals could be struck.

These facts give rise to several questions about whether an understanding of incentives played any role in the design of Russia's federal form. Was any mechanism envisioned for enforcing an agreement? Was any process identified for resolving the ambiguities inherent in a treaty that encompassed all activities and responsibilities of the state? What consequences were envisioned for the creation of a federation that treated republics differently than the predominantly Russian regions? Unfortunately, little attention was paid to the institutional determinants of incentives. With eyes focused on political expediency, Yeltsin's April 1993 draft constitution, offered when the resolution of his conflict with the Congress was in doubt, identified republics as sovereign entities, gave them the authority to negotiate their relationship with Moscow on a bilateral basis and, in a provision that could hardly be taken seriously, required that the republics' representation in the upper legislative chamber, the Federation Council, be increased to whatever extent necessary in order to ensure their control of it. All of these special provisions were dropped in the final version once Yeltsin no longer needed the republics in his struggle against the Congress.

The final version of the constitution adhered to the idea of enumerated powers, and incorporated the long lists of exclusive and joint jurisdictions that were the core of the Federal Treaty. Whatever protection the constitution provides for federal subjects is contained in the powers of the Federation Council. With two deputies selected from each of Russia's 89 regions, the Council approves any internal changes in borders, regulates the president's emergency powers, approves the use of troops and declarations of war, convicts the president following impeachment by the Duma, and approves presidential nominations to the Constitutional Court. Two constitutional provisions, however, weaken the Council's powers. First, the Duma can override (with a two-thirds vote) the Council's rejection of any law. The second provision is a vaguely worded requirement that the Council be 'formed' from the executive and legislative branches of federal subjects. Although compatible with the idea that the governor and chief legislative officer of each region should be deputies to the Federation Council, the president can use his decree authority to establish any method of selection he prefers.

The undifferentiated treatment of republics and other regions suggests that Russia has opted for a symmetric federalism in which the autonomy of federal subjects is protected by the upper legislative chamber. But because of the failure to consider incentives, we find no such guarantee. Recall our earlier discussion of federalism and the indirect mechanisms whereby states in the USA ensure their autonomy against the powers of the national government. Recall in particular that the source of that protection lies in the requirement that individual states control the election of the members of both branches of Congress that represent them and their residents, which ensures that political parties in the USA are primarily state and local organizations. Although competition for the presidency dictates an equilibrium of two national coalitions, it is a decentralized party system that oversees the re-election of individual members of the legislature. With their political fortunes tied to local constituencies and party organizations, national legislators have an incentive, insofar as it matches the incentives of their constituencies, to resist the encroachments of national governmental power.

Insofar as what it is that maintains this arrangement as an equilibrium we need look no further than legislative self-interest – legislators have no incentive to change the rules of a game in which they are the winners. Thus protection of state and local autonomy is provided by the connection between legislators and constituents and the incentives this creates among legislators to represent their constituencies; this connection, in turn, is maintained by the unwillingness of legislators to change a game they are especially skilled to play. Unfortunately, no such equilibrium is promised for Russia. First, although the first session of the Federation Council was filled by direct plurality voting, that procedure was a temporary measure dictated by Yeltsin's dissolution of regional Supreme Soviets. It remains an open question as to whether popular election will again be used or whether some type of appointment process, directed by Moscow or regional governments, will be used. Second, Russia's election law establishes a Central Election Commission with broad authority to regulate election rules and procedures. Thus once this Commission begins to exert its authority, there is no guarantee that Russia's regions will play any significant role in determining the election process. Finally, electing half the Duma by party-list PR undermines any incentive for Duma deputies elected by a party list to represent, and be protective of, local and regional autonomy.

POLITICAL PARTIES

Turning finally to the character of political parties, a common lament, summarized by Yegor Gaidar's adviser, Vladimir Mau ('The "Ascent of the Inflationists', *Journal of Democracy*, April 1994), is that: 'Economic interest groups are now the key players in Russian politics; political parties, by contrast, have been and remain weak and unstable'. Similarly, displaying a complete failure to understand how and why parties form, Vladimir Shumieko, Speaker of the Federation Council, proposed postponement of parliamentary elections until a strong party system emerged. But if, as we have argued throughout this volume, parties exist to win elections and if their character is determined by the rules under which elections are held, then three characteristics of Russia's electoral institutions inhibit the formation of parties of the type Mau, Shumeko and others profess to want. These features are: (1) non-simultaneous presidential and parliamentary elections; (2) implementation of the majority run-off election procedure for presidential elections; and (3) the election of half the Duma by party-list PR.

These three features operate individually and together. The failure to require simultaneous elections not only denies a president the opportunity to carry a workable legislative majority with him into office, but discourages having a president play the key role in organizing a party. The majority run-off procedure discourages the withdrawal of otherwise uncompetitive parties who might block a first-ballot victor so they can negotiate their support in the run-off. And electing half the Duma by national party-list PR contributes to party fragmentation and undermines the incentive for parties to consolidate around non-radical candidates and platforms. And together these features produce a system whereby the parliamentary election stage acts much like America's presidential primary elections. It is here that presidential aspirants can try to demonstrate their attractiveness prior to the presidential election. However, unlike the American process, there is no stage (except the very last ballot) whereby presidential aspirants *qua* parties are eliminated. Instead parties are encouraged to 'hang in there', both by the prospect of parliamentary representation and by the possibility of success or influence in the presidential balloting.

REFORM

Nothing we have said implies the possibility of a quick fix for Russia's political ailments. But we can offer three suggestions that can move things in a proper direction. The first change is to abandon the use of a 'majority with run-off' in presidential elections. Following Costa Rica (whose stability stands out among Latin American states), a run-off should occur only if no one receives more than 40 per cent of the vote. Indeed:

> *Rule 51*: By lowering the threshold to 40 per cent in a direct-vote run-off system, we give weak candidates and parties a stronger incentive to refrain from running or even forming, and we in fact make it more likely that some candidate will secure a majority on the first ballot.

Put simply, we can make a majority winner more likely by simply not requiring it.

The second suggestion concerns the method of electing deputies to the Duma. One possible reform is to allow each federal subject to determine the method of election of its own parliamentary representatives. Abandoning prescription and regulation by Moscow in favour of decentralization strengthens Russia's federal structure, decreases incentives for party factionalism, and decreases the ability of parties within the legislature to claim a mandate that contravenes the president's. Alternatively, following the German model, deputies to the Duma can be elected by PR within each of, say, 10 or 15 election districts, which would decrease party factionalism and would facilitate the growth of regional party organizations, but which would nevertheless give parties a national focus. However, regardless of the specifics of reform here, nearly anything is better than the current arrangement, which is simply the world's largest experiment with national party-list PR, which dooms Russia to a muddled party system, with all of the incoherence of parliamentary process such a system implies, and which allows one or more parties in parliament to claim a mandate in opposition to the president.

Our third suggestion is to hold presidential and parliamentary elections simultaneously. When combined with our other suggestions, simultaneous election affords the president a better opportunity to do what is uncommon in ex-communist states: to exert leadership. Leadership, however vague and ill-defined, needs to be distinguished from simple political control. Throughout Russian history, those directing the state have relied on the most evident and extraordinary instruments of political power rather than on the democratic arts of persuasion, compromise and the power that originates from being seen as the spokesman of the people. The lament that Russia is at the mercy of powerful personalities contesting for the reins of power may be accurate. But simultaneity allows an escape from this dangerous equilibrium. Coupled with direct election is:

> *Rule 52*: Simultaneous presidential and parliamentary elections allow presidents to bargain away some of their formal constitutional authority and to look instead to an even more secure basis of power – the people's mandate.

Our suggestions cannot resolve all of what ails Russia. Those ailments are too complex and pervasive to yield to any simple, short-term corrective. However, unlike mere exhortations to 'behave better' or unfeasible demands that this or that provision of the constitution be changed or abolished, our suggestions can be implemented without running afoul of any pre-existing self-interest. But regardless of the steps that are ultimately taken, it is imperative that political reform proceeds in accordance with the principle of self-interest and with the understanding that the implications of reform cannot be ascertained without first tracing the incentives it creates or fails to create. This is the lesson that Russia's transition to democracy – successful or otherwise – ought to teach other states. Others will choose constitutional electoral arrangements that differ from Russia's. But different or otherwise, those arrangements must be chosen only after a careful examination is undertaken of the incentives they establish both individually and in combination with each other.

18. Can We Be a Democracy?

The answer to the question that forms this chapter's title among people who must count their money daily to see if they have enough for a meal must be 'who cares – bring back the old days when we could at least afford whatever was available!'. And for others, especially if they follow politics closely, the only answer seems to be no. Other questions certainly look more relevant: will there be a coup? When will our anarchic politics require the intervention of a new authoritarian ruler? So accuse us of excessive optimism or unrealistic idealism, but *our* answer to this chapter's question, regardless of which part of the former Soviet Union we refer to, is yes! Our argument is that the politics of the Baltic states and of Central Europe will soon not look much different to those of Western Europe. Russia, Belarus and Ukraine are close to being democracies – messy ones, incomplete ones, unstable ones, ones in which fraud and corruption are the rule rather than the exception, and ones to which a goodly number of persons are only weakly committed – but they are very nearly democracies nevertheless. Pessimism rather than optimism seems warranted only for the states of the Caucasus and the remaining republics of the ex-USSR.

The assumption that few of these states are democratic or are about to become so rests in part on the belief that incoherent and inefficient political systems cannot be liberal democracies. Democracies – at least stable ones – are thought to be orderly things in which courts protect civil liberties, people vote on a regular basis, legislators deliberate, politicians abide by constitutional limits on their power, corruption is rare and policy-making proceeds according to well-defined procedures. Arguments over fundamental political structures, proposals to cancel the next election, shoving and pushing on the floor of the legislature, and ministers who contradict each other daily are things, it is assumed, that cannot be the elements of a stable democracy or of a democracy that promises to be stable in the future.

But the creation of a democratic state is rarely a simple process. The relationship between national and state governments in America is under continuous revision; Canada's future today hangs in the balance with the threat of secession by Quebec; Belgian unity strains under linguistic conflicts; and Italy in 40 years has had as many governments as America has had presidents in 200. It is true that most of the pieces of the ex-USSR do not possess many of the components of a normal democratic state: political parties with national organizations and comprehensive policy agendas, smoothly functioning courts, a well-defined system of property rights, an economic infrastructure that allows for rational economic planning, democratic local self-government, a professional legislature with a clear internal structure, a universal commitment to regularly scheduled elections, and the complex array of citizen interest groups that mobilize people in an orderly way to influence state policy. That these things do not exist in full measure, however, is no reason to predict that they cannot exist, albeit in primitive form. Governments may still rely too much on decrees to promulgate policy, they may continue to control the media and the press more than we prefer, and bribery and corruption may have become too pervasive and too readily accepted as a way to do business. But most citizens have made the commitment to constitutional democracy, and most public officials would prefer to advance their careers in accordance with constitutional principles, if only because that is the way to secure the approbation of other states.

It is true, of course, that the commitment to democratic process is not always made for reasons we might prefer. Yeltsin's strongest opponents, for example, may have moderated their criticism of his constitution not because they believe in democracy but rather because they see it as providing a route to securing the reins of power. Nor can we deny that government policies or pronouncements still vacillate between contradictions. But vacillation and contradiction only reflect the fact that no one knows the best course of economic reform. It is hard to believe that the same confusion and contentiousness would not characterize any democracy undergoing similar upheaval. And although we can detect the emergence of a commitment to individual rights, we would hardly argue that every public official shares this commitment or that everyone understands rights in the same way. We are certainly alarmed by decrees in Russia that violate constitutional rights in the name of social stability and the war against crime, just as we are concerned about the definitions of citizenship that have emerged in Estonia or Latvia. Nevertheless, people are increasingly free to express their views and judicial processes are gradually emerging whereby these rights and others can be protected. There is, in fact, as close an acceptance of these rights as we might expect to see in most democracies: a xenophobic Japan discriminates against its minorities; Western Europe struggles against fascist and Nazi nostalgia; and incidents of police violence directed at blacks in America have hardly disappeared from the news.

This is not to say that the job of political reconstruction in Central or Eastern Europe is done. No one believes that all that remains is to lead economies to recovery and to wait for democracy to develop on its own. Democracy's survival is not guaranteed. First, most of the states in question require new constitutions that give unambiguous guidance to the state's function, and even those states with new constitutions – Russia and Belarus, for example – merely possess transitional documents. Second, the sub-parts of the state – regional and local governments – require democratic constitutions or charters since, without them, democracy cannot flourish at any level. Third, ethnically heterogeneous states must develop federal forms and local governmental institutions that allow for a coherent pattern of regional autonomy. Fourth, states must construct election laws and procedures that make the competition for office coherent and responsive to citizen interests, and that at the same time minimize the possibilities of fraud. Finally, the people themselves must learn to stop looking for the 'right' leader; they must instead begin to place their faith in the political institutions they themselves create.

We need also to appreciate that being a new democracy is not the same thing as being a mature one. A new democracy should not be expected to produce the same things as one that has existed for 10 or 20 years. A baby has little control over what emerges from either of its ends, it cannot dress or feed itself, it operates largely by instinct, it relies on the paternalism of those around it for survival, and it can hardly explain or comprehend why all of this is so. It cannot move furniture, solve maths problems or raise a family. But these facts do not mean that a baby is not a person. We merely understand that to raise this person from childhood to adulthood requires having the right expectations about its capabilities at each stage of its development. So it is with democracies.

A two- or three-year-old democracy cannot produce instant guarantees of rights, well-ordered and smoothly functioning political institutions, coherent policy or even leaders who understand why things work as they do. It may seem difficult to answer questions such as, 'who needs this thing called democracy?' or, 'why don't we dispense with all this nonsense, and merely adopt a political system compatible with our traditions – autocracy or, minimally, a strong leader who can rule by decree?' in ways that accord with the recommendations of this volume. Nevertheless, we should be able to see now that the answers to these questions are contained in part in democracy's definition. People must have leaders because society must be coordinated to act, and democracy is merely a method whereby the people are empowered to choose their leaders and the directions of public policy in an orderly way that protects individual rights. All the rest – bicameral versus unicameral legislatures, presidential versus parliamentary systems, federal versus unitary states, direct versus indirect elections – is intended to allow the smooth functioning of the state and to guarantee that democracy's first principle, that the people alone are sovereign, is sustained.

The principle of citizen sovereignty is primary because we know of no other way to ensure that government remains accountable to society's interests rather than purely its own. This does not mean that a monarchy, autocracy or even a dictatorship cannot for a time produce the same policies as a democracy or that it cannot produce those policies more efficiently. History is replete with examples of benevolent dictators who have advanced their societies in useful ways. But no one has developed a way to ensure benevolence or even the competence of the autocrat. Democracy is but a modest human invention, albeit one replete with human frailties, that seeks to resolve this dilemma of leadership.

The resolution of this dilemma, however, places a strain on newly formed democratic institutions that frequently makes it appear as though democratic process is the least useful one to achieve specific results such as economic transformation and the realization of political stability. But efficiency and stability are not our only goals. We also seek a government that abides by several important normative principles, including the ideas that 'all men are created equal' and that 'each person is endowed with the right to life, liberty and justice'. These principles place constraints on the state that rarely apply even to the benevolent despot and which cause democracy itself to function in ways that sometimes seem less than perfect.

The dilemma of democracy is not the sacrifice of efficiency and stability, but that of combining the principles of citizen sovereignty and equality so as to ensure the protection of everyone's rights, including those of minorities against majorities. The dilemma of democracy, then, is finding ways to give both the majority and minority their rights simultaneously. In what might otherwise appear to be an unresolvable contradiction, we must decide when the majority ought to rule and when the minority should prevail, and then we must design institutions that guarantee outcomes that meet these constraints. So in asking whether we can be a democracy, we should not look simply at economic issues or at the prospects for peaceful transitions of power. We must ask whether we can envision political institutions that allow for the gradual realization of rights on everyone's part, because:

> *Rule 53*: A 'democratic' state cannot be stable for long if some minority cannot realize its rights; and if such a state is stable, then it cannot be a democracy.

Minimally, then, we must accept the idea that minorities ought to be protected when their interests are intense and when those of the majority are weak. The difficulty, however, is that we have no simple way to measure intensity. Thus we cannot ask how much a person is willing to pay for, say, freedom of speech – we simply grant that right to everyone. But mere words cannot ensure anything – rights are ensured only through the operation of institutions. Unfortunately, the principle of citizen sovereignty seems to dictate the application in one form or another of majority rule, which only returns us once again to the problem of protecting minority rights against majority tyranny. But there is a solution: eschew simplistic conceptualizations of democratic process – policy chosen by referenda, laws passed by a single legislative body, decrees issued by an otherwise unrestrained popularly elected president. Instead we require that to change a policy or to initiate a new one, a majority must sustain itself through a complex array of institutional hurdles. It must first elect a majority of representatives (usually to each of two legislative chambers); it must form a majority in each legislative chamber, if not in various subcommittees of the legislature; it must elect a president who will sustain this legislation without a veto; and that legislation must be deemed constitutional by a majority of members of some court that oversees the constitutionality of legislation. Each of these stages gives minorities the opportunity to block changes in the status quo that threaten their interests or violate their rights.

Creating a democracy, then, requires the design and implementation of institutions – legislative ones, electoral ones, judicial ones and even bureaucratic ones – where those institutions 'fit together' not only to protect individual rights but also to form a coherent state. It follows, then, that states making a transition to democracy cannot be content with some incomplete or simplified version of this form of governance. If democracy is to fulfil its full promise, it must be developed in its entirety. We cannot have merely a directly elected president or a newly elected legislature or newly appointed court. We must have all things simultaneously.

Admittedly, because it imposes a requirement on itself that despots and autocrats need not meet – that policies opposed by minorities progress through numerous hurdles before they are accepted – democracy often seems incapable of making definitive and timely choices. The temptation will be great to short-circuit democratic process in favour of expediency. But we have at least two facts to support the argument that people should sustain the course of democratic transition, however uncomfortable that might seem on occasion. First, democracies have survived, and even prospered, through eras no less trying than the one confronting the successor states of the Soviet empire. Second, when called upon to make the right moral choice, democracies have done so even though majorities initially opposed such decisions. Democratic process has not always worked perfectly and its record is not unassailable. But on average, it has worked better than the alternatives.

Bibliography

Aranson, Peter H. (1990), 'Federalism', *Cato Journal*, **10** (1), 1–15.
Bogdanor, Vernon and David Butler (eds) (1983), *Democracy and Elections*, Cambridge: Cambridge University Press.
Chandler, William M. (1987), 'Federalism and political parties', in H. Bakvis and W.M. Chandler (eds), *Federalism and the Role of the State*, Toronto: University of Toronto Press.
Dahl, Robert A. (1956), *A Preface to Democratic Theory*, New Haven: Yale University Press.
Dahl, Robert A. (1989), *Democracy and its Critics*, New Haven: Yale University Press.
Di Palma, Giuseppe (1990), *To Craft Democracies: An Essay on Democratic Transitions*, Berkeley: University of California Press.
Diamond, Larry and Marc F. Plattner (eds) (1993), *The Global Resurgence of Democracy*, Baltimore: Johns Hopkins University Press.
Diamond, Larry and Marc F. Plattner (eds) (1994), *Nationalism, Ethnic Conflict, and Democracy*, Baltimore: Johns Hopkins University Press.
Duverger, Maurice (1954), *Political Parties: Their Organization and Activity in the Modern State*, New York: Wiley.
Elster, Jon (1989), *The Cement of Society*, Cambridge: Cambridge University Press.
Elster, Jon and Rune Slagstad (eds) (1988), *Constitutionalism and Democracy*, Cambridge: Cambridge University Press.
Foley, Michael (1990), *The Silence of Constitutions*, New York: Routledge.
Grofman, Bernard (ed.) (1993), *Information, Participation, and Choice*, Ann Arbor: University of Michigan Press.
Grofman, Bernard and Arend Lijphart (eds) (1986), *Electoral Laws and their Political Consequences*, New York: Agathon Press.
Hardin, Russell (1989), 'Why a constitution', in B. Grofman and D. Wittman (eds), *The Federalist Papers and the New Institutionalism*, New York: Agathon Press.

Hermens, F.A. (1972), *Democracy or Anarchy: A Study of Proportional Representation*, 2nd edition, New York: Johnson Reprint Corp.

Hoag, C.G. and G.C. Hallett, Jr (1926), *Proportional Representation*, New York: Macmillan.

Horowitz, Donald (1985), *Ethnic Groups in Conflict*, Berkeley: University of California Press.

Horowitz, Donald (1991), *A Democratic South Africa: Constitutional Engineering in a Divided Society*, Berkeley: University of California Press.

Jones, Mark P. (1993), 'The political consequences of electoral laws in Latin America and the Caribbean', *Electoral Studies,* **12** (1), 59–75.

Lemco, Jonathan (1991), *Political Stability in Federal Governments*, New York: Praeger.

Lewis, David (1969), *Convention*, Cambridge: Harvard University Press.

Lijphart, Arend (1984), *Democracies*, New Haven: Yale University Press.

Lijphart, Arend (ed.) (1992), *Parliamentary versus Presidential Government*, Oxford: Oxford University Press.

Lijphart, Arend and Bernard Grofman (eds) (1984), *Choosing an Electoral System*, New York: Praeger.

Linz, Juan J. (1990), 'The perils of presidentialism', *Journal of Democracy*, **1**, Winter, 51–69.

Linz, Juan J. and Arturo Valenzuela (1994), *The Failure of Presidential Democracy*, Baltimore: Johns Hopkins University Press.

Mainwaring, Scott (1990), 'Presidentialism in Latin America', *Latin American Review*, **25**, 157–79.

Mainwaring, Scott (1993), 'Presidentialism, multipartism and democracy', *Comparative Political Studies*, **26** (2), 28–50.

Olson, Mancur (1965), *The Logic of Collective Action*, Cambridge: Harvard University Press.

Olson, Mancur (1982), *The Rise and Decline of Nations*, New Haven: Yale University Press.

Ordeshook, Peter C. (1993), 'Some rules of constitutional design', in E.F. Paul, F.D. Miller and J. Paul (eds), *Liberalism and the Economic Order*, Cambridge: Cambridge University Press.

Ordeshook, Peter C. (1995), 'Institutions and incentive: the prospects for Russian democracy', *Journal of Democracy*, **6**, April, 46–60.

Ordeshook, Peter C. and Olga Shvetsova (1995), 'If Madison and Hamilton were merely lucky, what hope is there for Russian Federalism', *Constitutional Political Economy*, **6** (2), 107–27.

Ostrom, Vincent (1991), *The Meaning of American Federalism*, San Francisco: ICS Press.
Popkin, Samuel (1991), *The Reasoning Voter: Communication and Persuasion in Presidential Campaigns*, Chicago: University of Chicago Press.
Rabushka, Alvin and Kenneth Shepsle (1972), *Politics in Plural Societies*, Columbus, Ohio: Merrill Publishing.
Rae, Douglas (1967), *The Political Consequences of Electoral Laws*, New Haven: Yale University Press.
Riker, William H. (1964), *Federalism: Origin, Operation, Significance*, Boston: Little Brown.
Riker, William H. (1982), *Liberalism and the Democratic Order*, Prospect Heights, Illinois: Waveland Press.
Riker, William H. (ed.) (1987), *The Development of American Federalism*, Boston: Kluwer Academic Publishers.
Rossiter, Clinton (ed.) (1961), *The Federalist Papers*, New York: Bantam Books.
Rowe, Nicholas (1989), *Rules and Institutions*, Ann Arbor: University of Michigan Press.
Sartori, Giovanni (1994), *Comparative Constitutional Engineering*, New York: New York University Press.
Schattschneider, E.E. (1960), *A Realist's View of Democracy in America*, Hinsdale, Illinois: Dryden.
Schmitt, Carl (1985), *The Crisis of Parliamentary Democracy*, translated by Ellen Kennedy, Cambridge: MIT Press.
Schwartz, Thomas (1989), 'Publius and public choice', in B. Grofman and D. Wittman (eds), *The Federalist Papers and the New Institutionalism*, New York: Agathon Press.
Scully, Gerald W. (1992), *Constitutional Environment and Economic Growth*, Princeton: Princeton University Press.
Shugart, Matthew S. and John M. Carey (1992), *Presidents and Assemblies: Constitutional Design and Electoral Dynamics*, New York: Cambridge University Press.
Sundquist, James L. (1992), *Constitutional Reform and Effective Government*, Washington, DC: The Brookings Institute.
Sunstein, Cass M. (1990), 'Constitutionalism, prosperity, democracy', *Constitutional Political Economy*, **2** (3), 371–94.
Taagepera, Rein and Matthew S. Shugart (1989), *Seats and Votes: The Effects and Determinants of Electoral Systems*, New Haven: Yale University Press.

Wagner, Richard E. (1993), *Parchment, Guns and Constitutional Order*, Brookfield, VT: Elgar Publishing.

Wallich, Christine I. (ed) (1994), *Russia and the Challenges of Fiscal Federalism*, Washington, DC: World Bank.

Index

abstention from voting, 30
abuse of power, 54, 103–4
accommodation, 39–40
activism, 10–13
ambiguity, 54
America's Association for Retired People (AARP), 11
Argentina, 37
aspirations, 45
assembly: right of, 46–7
asymmetric federalism, 71
authoritarian state, 38
autonomy, regional, 71–2, 76–7, 116, 117, 123

balance of power, 60–62, 105
Baltic states, 1
Belarus, 123
Belgium, 122
beliefs, 54–5
bilateral negotiation, 116
Bolivar, S., 101
Britain, 2, 93

campaign financing, 17, 31–2
Canada, 70, 76, 94, 122
Central Election Commission, 117
central government *see* national government
centralization, 72–3
challenger, need for a, 30
Chile, 36
China, 36, 37, 69, 103
citizens
  enforcement of constitution, 65
  lists of obligations, 44–5
  qualities needed for democracy, 8–14
  relationship of state to, 59–60
  sovereignty, 12–13, 46–7, 124–5
civil war, 79–80
cleavages, 32–3, 98–9
coalitions, 79–80
  instability, 33–4, 98
coercion, 30
collective action, 10–13
communism, 14, 52
Communist Party, 57–8, 60
competition
  local political, 21
  national-regional, 70–71
competitive elections *see* elections
conflict
  regional conflicts, 72–3
  society's inherent conflicts, 5–6
consensus, 52–3
consistency, 54
constitution, 78, 123
  emergency clauses, 103–10
  enforcement, 65–6
  expectations and importance of new, 56–62
  and legislature, 86–8
  and legitimization, 57–8
  norm-creation, 51–2
  resolving society's inherent conflicts, 5–6
  rules for writing, 63–8
  Russia, 61, 89, 113–14, 123
  supremacy of federal law, 73–4
constitutional rights, 43–9, 67–8
contracts, 73
co-optation, 20–21
coordination of the state, 107–8
corruption, 109–10
Costa Rica, 119
crime, 109–10
'crisis of norms', 51

cross-cutting interests, 32–3
Czechoslovakia, 101

decree, 39, 84
defence, 73
democracy, 1–7
  communism and, 14
  failings of incomplete, 39–41
  feasibility in Central and Eastern Europe, 121–6
  role of voting, 25–6
  rules of design, 4–6
Democratic Party (US), 20, 78–9, 82, 88
despotism, enlightened, 36–7
disasters, natural, 104–5
discrimination, 47
Duma, 89, 116
  elections, 115, 117–18, 119
duties, citizens', 44–5

economic problems, 70–71, 104, 106–7
economic reform: and political reform, 35–42, 111–12
election rules, 86–8, 118–20, 123
  parliamentary, 101–2, 115, 117–20
  presidential, 87–8, 100–102, 114–15, 118–20
  two-chamber legislature, 93–5
elections
  citizen sovereignty, 12
  constitutional rights and, 47
  fair and competitive, 28–34
  incentive for legislature, 84–8
  local and regional, 81–2
  political parties, 79–82, 85, 87–8
  scheduling, 31
  turnout, 30–31, 101
  see also voters; voting
emergency clauses, 103–10
enforcement of constitution, 65–6
enlightened despotism, 36–7
entry, 29–30
environment, 73
Estonia, 122
ethnicity, 19–21, 33, 80, 91–2

European Community, 70
executive
  conflict with legislature, 97, 100, 101–2
  legislature, judiciary and, 48–9, 59–61
extra-constitutional organizations, 10–13
extremists, 16–17, 29

fairness, 91–2
  competitive elections, 28–34
  institutions, 54–5
fascism, 123
federal law: supremacy of, 74
Federal Treaty, 116
federalism, 48, 69–75
  political parties and, 76–82
  Russia's choices, 113, 115–18
Federation Council, 89, 116–17
Finland, 91
Franklin, B., 112
fraud, vote, 31
free press, 12, 30
fundamental rights *see* constitutional rights

Germany, 7, 40, 94, 98
Gorbachev, M.S., 22
governmental structure, 47–9, 59–62
  see also state
grievances, redress of, 47

Hitler, A., 40
Hungary, 91, 98

Iceland, 91
ignorance, 40–41
incentives, 5, 112–13, 114, 120
  legislators, 84, 117–18
'incompetents', 29
information, political, 9–11, 16
  sources for voters, 17
institutions, 4–5, 123, 125–6
  constitution and, 47–8, 67–8
    appropriateness, 57–8
  influence of democratic, 50–55
  participatory organizations, 10–13

political institutional development, 37–8
insurrection, 104, 106
interests
    cross-cutting, 32–3
    in newly-formed democracies, 39
internal checks and balances, 54, 103–4, 105
internal security agencies, 109
invasion, 104–5
Israel, 98
issues, policy, 30, 67–8
Italy, 122

Japan, 7, 36, 37, 123
Jefferson, T., 73
judiciary
    and corruption, 109–10
    relationship to executive and legislature, 48–9, 59–61

King, M. Luther, 20
Korea, South, 36, 37
Kuomingtang Party (Korea), 37

language
    in constitution, 45–6, 66–7
    of democracy, 3
Latin America, 48
Latvia, 122
law
    due process of, 46–7
    supremacy of federal, 74
leaders, political, 6, 124
    citizen sovereignty, 12–13
    incentives and constitutional rights, 47–9
    legislative efficiency, 83–8
    referenda and, 26–7
    role of voting in a democracy, 25–6
learning, political *see* information
legislative districts, 93–5
legislature, 83–8
    conflict with executive, 97, 100, 101–2
    relationship to judiciary and executive, 48–9, 59–61
    two-chamber, 89–96
legitimization: constitution and, 57–8
local elections, 81–2
local government, 41, 123
local political competition, 21
losing and winning, 33–4
Lubell, S., 82

Madison, J., 7, 47, 52, 61–2, 112
    clash of interests, 32
    separation of powers, 100
majority rule, 20, 125
    popular will and, 23–4
    two-chamber legislature, 93–5
majority with run-off election procedure, 100–101, 118, 119
mandate, 101–2, 114–15
Mau, V., 118
media, 12, 30
military dictatorship, 35–6
minorities, 20–21
    protecting rights of, 93–5, 124–5
money
    election campaigns, 17, 31–2
    supply, 73

national government
    conflict with regional governments, 70–71
    functions in federalism, 72, 73–4
nationalism, 19–21
    see also ethnicity
natural disasters, 104–5
Nigeria, 69, 70, 101
norms, social 50–51, 66–8
    see also rules

obligations, citizens', 44–5

parliament: president's relations with, 113–15
parliamentary elections, 101–2, 115, 117–20
parliamentary systems, 18–19, 60, 80–81
    and presidential systems, 97–102
participatory organizations, 10–13
party labels, 18, 82, 85

see also political parties
People's Congress, 22, 84, 97, 108, 114, 116
personal experiences, 17
pessimism, 56–7
policy issues, 30, 67–8
political information *see* information
political leaders *see* leaders, political
political parties, 85
   and election rules, 86–8
   in a federation, 76–82
   and PR, 98–9
   Russia's choices, 113, 118
   USA, 77–82, 117
   voters and, 17–21
political reform, 111–13, 119–20
   and economic reform, 35–42, 111–12
popular referenda, 22–7
popular will, 23–6
power
   abuse of, 54, 103–4
   balance of, 60–62, 105
preferences, 25–6
preparation, 40–41
president/presidency
   emergencies, 108
   relations with parliament, 113, 113–15
   strength of, 3
presidential elections, 79–80, 100–102
   rules in Russia, 114–15, 118–20
   rules in USA, 87–8
presidential systems, 18–19, 60
   crime and corruption, 109
   and parliamentary systems, 97–102
   USA, 78–81
press freedom, 12, 30
privatization, 41
property rights, 37–8, 41–2, 46–7
proportional representation (PR), 19, 93
   election to Duma, 115, 118, 119
   parliamentary systems and presidential systems, 98–9, 101–2

qualifications, constitutional, 46, 54

redress of grievances, 47
referenda, 22–7
regional autonomy, 71–2, 76–7, 116, 117, 123
regional conflicts, 72–3
regional elections, 81–2
regional government, 74, 123
   see also federalism
regional-national conflict, 70–71
regions: representation and, 91–2
religious freedom, 46–7
representation
   legislature and, 86–8, 91–2
   voting in a democracy, 25–6
Republican Party (US), 20, 78–9, 88
responsibilities, citizens', 44–5
revolutions, 51–2
rights, 122–3
   constitutional, 43–9, 67–8
   dilemma of democracy, 124–5
   emergencies and, 105
   property rights, 37–8, 41–2, 46–7
   protecting minority rights, 93–5, 124–5
Romania, 99
Roosevelt, F.D., 82
rules, 3, 4, 61–2
   influence of democratic institutions, 50–55
   for writing constitutions, 63–8
Russia, 1, 31, 80, 91, 98
   choices, 111–20
      federal relations, 115–18
      political parties, 118
      presidential-parliamentary relations, 113–15
      reform, 119–20
   constitution, 61, 89, 113–14, 123
   emergency, 108, 109
   extremism, 16–17
   legislature, 83, 84
      two-chamber, 89, 94
   referendum, 22

scheduling of elections, 31
secession, 20–21

security agencies, internal, 109
self-interest, 52–3
　legislature, 85–6, 117
　political reform and, 111–12, 120
self-rule, 63–4
separation of powers, 48, 60, 100
Shumieko, V., 118
social norms, 50–51, 66–8
　see also rules
sovereign states, 116
sovereignty, citizen, 12–13, 46–7, 124–5
Soviet Union
　constitutions, 56–8, 63
　dissolution, 70
　voting, 28
speech, free, 46–7
state, 43
　authoritarian, 38
　coordination of, 107–8
　sovereign's agent, 46–7
　structure, 47–9, 59–62
Sumner, C., 83
supremacy of federal law, 74
Switzerland, 26, 70, 77, 101
symmetrical federalism, 71–2

Taiwan, 36, 37, 41, 83, 103
temporary dictator, 84, 106–7
terms of office, 95
Tocqueville, A. de, 41
trade, 73
turnout, election, 30–31, 101
two-chamber legislature, 89–96
two-party system, 87–8

Ukraine, 1, 80, 91, 99
United States (USA), 2, 77, 123

AARP, 11
civil rights movement, 20
Civil War, 70
constitutional rights ignored, 48
federalism, 77–82, 117, 121–2
inherent conflicts and constitution, 6
local elections, 27
political parties, 77–82, 117
presidential election rules, 87–8
privatization, 41–2
self-interest, 112
separation of powers, 100
strength of the presidency, 3
two-chamber legislature, 92, 94
violence in Congress, 83
Uzbeckistan, 1

values, 52
violence, 20–21
vote fraud, 31
voters, 15–21
voting, 30
　popular referenda, 22–7
　see also elections
Vyshinsky, A., 28

will, popular, 23–6
winning and losing, 33–4

Yeltsin, B., 16, 22, 31, 109, 117, 122
　1993 draft constitution, 116
　and People's Congress, 84, 97, 108, 114, 116
Yugoslavia, 69, 70

Zhirinovsky, V., 16, 31, 115

Promises, Promises

Promises, Promises

Contracts in Russia and other
Post-Communist Economies

Paul H. Rubin

Professor of Economics, Emory University, USA

THE SHAFTESBURY PAPERS, 11
SERIES EDITOR: CHARLES K. ROWLEY

Edward Elgar
Cheltenham, UK • Northampton, MA, USA

© Paul H. Rubin 1997

All rights reserved. No part of this publication may be reproduced, stored in a retrieval system or transmitted in any form or by any means, electronic, mechanical or photocopying, recording, or otherwise without the prior permission of the publisher.

Published by
Edward Elgar Publishing Limited
8 Lansdown Place
Cheltenham
Glos GL50 2HU
UK

Edward Elgar Publishing, Inc.
6 Market Street
Northampton
Massachusetts 01060
USA

A catalogue record for this book
is available from the British Library

Library of Congress Cataloguing in Publication Data
Rubin, Paul H.
    Promies, promises : contracts in Russia and other post-communist
economies / Paul H. Rubin.
      — (The Shaftesbury papers : 11)
    Includes bibliographical references and index.
    1. Contracts—Russia (Federation)   2. Contracts—Europe, Eastern.
I. Title. II. Series.
KLB858.R83   1998
346.4702—dc21   97–38256
                                                                                  CIP

ISBN 1 85898 558 7

Typeset by Manton Typesetters, 5–7 Eastfield Road, Louth, Lincolnshire LN11 7AJ, UK.
Printed and bound in Great Britain by Biddles Ltd, Guildford and King's Lynn

Contents

Acknowledgements		vi
1	Introduction	1
2	Alternative Methods of Legal Change	7
3	Contracts and Opportunism	14
4	Private Mechanisms	18
5	The Czech Republic, Hungary and Poland	27
6	Russia	31
7	Government Policy	54
8	Creation of Efficient Rules	59
9	Implications	63
Notes		68
Bibliography		70
Index		81

Acknowledgements

IRIS (Institutional Reform and the Informal Sector), at the University of Maryland initially contributed to this research.

I presented earlier versions of parts of this work at Emory, George Mason, Harvard and Lund Universities, at a World Bank seminar in the Czech Republic, at the Winter 1994 American Economics Association Meetings, and at a seminar at the Political Economy Research Center in Montana.

I would like to thank Peter Aranson, Martin Bailey, George Benston, Harold Berman, Jurgen Backhaus, Michael Block, Chris Clague, John Lott, Todd Merolla, Fred McChesney and Fred Pryor and especially Jean Tesche for helpful comments. In addition, assistance in various forms, including discussions of Eastern Europe and information about sources of information, was received from Dan Drachtman, Cheryl Gray, Heidi Kroll, Russell Pittman, Nancy Roth Remington and Jan Svenjar. In Europe I had useful discussions with Ronald Dwight, Allan Farber, Peter Fath, Randall Filer, Attila Harmathy, Zoltan Jakab, Laszlo Keckes, Vladimir Laptev, Katherine Martin, Ryszard Markiewicz, Carol Patterson, Andrew Pike, Vladimir Prokop, Roman Rewald, William Sievers, Tomasz Stawecki, Lubos Tichy, Boris Topornin, Tibor Varady, Karl Viehe, Alena Zemplinerova and John Zimmerman. None of these people necessarily agrees with the implications of this work, and of course none is responsible for any errors.

Related papers have previously been published: 'Private Mechanisms for the Creation of Efficient Institutions for Market Economies', in Laszlo Somogyi, (ed.), *The Political Economy of the Transition Process in Eastern Europe*, Edward Elgar, 1993; 'Growing a Legal System in the Post-Communist Economies', *Cornell International Law Journal*, Winter, 1994, 1–47; 'Growing a Post-Communist Legal System', in Terry Anderson and P.J. Hill (eds), *The Privatization Process: A Worldwide Perspective*, Rowman & Littlefield, 1996, 57–80.

I would also like to thank Charles Rowley and the Locke Institute for editorial suggestions.

1. Introduction

An integral part of 'Civil Society' is the 'Rule of Law', by which I mean an objective, impersonal method of establishing and protecting property rights and enforcing agreements. Creation of a rule of law, like the creation of any other part of the infrastructure needed for economic growth, is an investment. As with any other investment, agents will create a rule of law only if discount rates are low enough for the investment to pay. If agents discount the future at too high a rate, investment will not be profitable. Uncertainty about the future can increase the discount rate to the point where otherwise profitable investments will not be worthwhile.

While Poland, the Czech Republic and perhaps Hungary and other formerly communist countries have solved this problem, there is some doubt about Russia. The great danger facing Russia today is that there is so much uncertainty that few agents will undertake investments that would otherwise be profitable and that would promote economic growth. This problem may be pervasive in the economy, and may serve to hamper investments of all sorts.

Weingast (1995) presents a theory of the institutional stability needed to maintain markets. He argues that if enough citizens are fearful of government institutions, then it is possible to devise what he calls a 'market-preserving federalist system'. Without such a system, it is difficult to give government the proper amount of power. Rather government tends to accrue too much power to allow a market to function. While citizens in Russia probably have a proper and well-earned scepticism of government, the institutions needed for a federalist system are clearly lacking. In Weingast's view, this means that government cannot be relied upon to create and maintain proper market-preserving institutions. Thus Weingast's theory offers an explanation for the observed uncertainty and consequent high discount rates in Russia. This theory would imply that many socially valuable market-preserving institutions would be lacking in Russia.

In this work, I consider only one manifestation of this problem: the effect on contractual performance. Efficient enforcement of contracts requires investment by several types of agent. The parties to putative contracts must themselves be willing to invest in reputations and in other types of capital for contracts to work. In addition, government agents must be willing to undertake certain investments to enforce contracts. These investments are of three sorts. First, government must be willing to create efficient contract law, either through a common law process or through a statutory (code) system. Second, it must be willing to use this law actually to enforce contracts. This requires the establishment of a well-functioning court system. Finally, government agents must be willing to honour those contracts and agreements that they themselves enter into.

These conditions seem to be met, at least to some extent, in some of the post-communist economies, but not in all. Again Russia seems to be the case where the conditions are least satisfied. Indeed in the situation of Russia today there is sufficient uncertainty so that even the 'mafia', organized criminal gangs, may find discount rates too high to make investment in contractual enforcement worthwhile.

This monograph is a normative application of law and economics scholarship to the problem of securing an efficient (wealth maximizing) method of enforcing agreements and thus facilitating exchange in the post-communist countries.[1] I do not set forth the detailed tenets of explicit law. Rather I discuss the policies that states can adopt that will allow the law to evolve efficiently. In this scheme, no one need decide *ex ante* what the outcome of the process will be.

THE PROBLEM ADDRESSED

While it is generally agreed that all law needs improvement in post-communist economies, most writing by economists on the 'transition' has dealt with property law. The key issue addressed has been privatization. A major controversy in this literature has been the optimal speed of adjustment: should there be a 'big bang' (rapid immediate privatization) or should the transition proceed at a more modest pace? Relatively little scholarly attention from economists has been devoted to other branches of law.[2]

In this work I deal with the law governing exchange and transactions. These issues are important. For example, Douglass North (1991, 481) indicates that, 'how agreements are enforced is the single most important determinant of economic performance'. North discusses the value of both formal (legal) enforcement of agreements and also the sort of informal mechanisms discussed below.

By 'exchange and transactions', I mean more than what is considered in the legal literature as contract. I include the law dealing with all voluntary agreements. Although this work focuses on contracts for exchange of goods, the principles developed apply more broadly. Securities law, the law of corporate governance, the law of secured property, labour law and bankruptcy are all areas where parties form voluntary agreements and where the arguments advanced here are relevant. Contemporary Western legal systems have erred by interfering excessively with freedom of contract in misguided and largely unsuccessful efforts to generate increased equality. For legal systems of newer economies attempting to grow quickly, it is especially desirable not to commit similar errors.

Contract law is easier to reform than is property law because signing a contract is *ex ante* a positive sum, cooperative game. While negotiating a contract, the interests of the parties are symmetric and both seek the most efficient contract. If a contract is signed in good faith (that is, if neither party plans *ex ante* to break the contract), then parties also have identical *ex ante* interests in methods of settling disputes *ex post*, when the contract has been broken. When the contract is signed, both parties want the most efficient dispute resolution mechanism because this will maximize the *ex ante* surplus to be divided between them. Of course, there may be disputes about the division of the surplus – the price term. Moreover, if there is a breach, then interests diverge. Each party wants the other to bear the costs of the breach. But initially there is agreement on contractual terms.[3]

This commonality of interest is generally much weaker, or even entirely lacking, in other bodies of law. In creating property rights in the post-communist economies, the interests of most players diverge initially. Managers, workers and ordinary citizens all want for themselves ownership rights in existing businesses and, with respect to these rights, the issue of distribution is purely competitive. Therefore, even though there might be substantial gains from creation of property rights, it is difficult to form a coalition in favour of any one scheme. (For a discussion of these difficulties, see Boycko *et al.* (1994).) Moreover, as we see in Chapter 6, in Russia, even after apparent agreement has been reached on allocation of property rights, some actors unilaterally can alter the distribution, creating additional uncertainty.

In accident law the parties are generally strangers before the accident occurs, and so there is no room for *ex ante* agreement. Once the accident occurs, of course, interests are purely in conflict: each party wants the other to bear the costs.

Those interested in law reform can use this symmetry of interests in contract to encourage efficient exchange and to design efficient contract law. There are three related points, the elaboration of which forms the heart of this work. First, in many cases law itself will not be needed. There are many mechanisms available that private parties can use to make agreements self-enforcing. Second, the law can facilitate the use of these mechanisms. For example, the law can agree to enforce arbitration clauses in contracts if parties insert such clauses.[4] This will result in settlement of many disputes without relying on the scarce resources available to the judicial system. Finally, public law can adopt the rules developed privately by arbitrators and others. This will speed up the process of development of the legal system and will ultimately lead to a more efficient system.

Obviously, a system of contract enforcement is more valuable if property rights are clearly defined. Better defined rights facilitate exchange, and the value of exchange increases with the value of the rights. Nonetheless, in designing efficient contract law, it is *not* true that 'everything depends on everything else'. Even with the existing level of property rights definitions, large amounts of exchange take place in the post-communist economies. Individuals are not self-sufficient. More efficient contract law can facilitate this existing exchange and encourage additional transactions, even under current circumstances. As privatization proceeds, more and more transactions will come under the scope of contract principles. If correct mechanisms can be adopted to allow contract law to develop efficiently, then the law can evolve with the economy. At each step in the process, the law can be useful and valuable, and if the law is more efficient it will be more valuable.

As one Russian broker told the *New York Times* (Uchitelle, 1992): 'Russian businessmen have gone ahead of the law, but goods have to move'. This same story indicates that: 'The free market, in effect, is not waiting for a legal system. Deals march on, although the contracts that are bringing the new ventures to life might be difficult to enforce'. If contracts were easier to enforce, deals would march on faster and more deals would be done.

The process described here can proceed independently of the rate of privatization. If the process is rapid, then there will be more transactions to be covered by contract than if the process is slow. However, in either case the principles identified here are applicable. Indeed there are even incentives for dictatorships to design efficient principles for private exchange, so that even if democracy should not survive in some countries the principles discussed here might be relevant for policy-makers. Even communist countries had provided limited incentives for efficient contracting (Kroll 1987).

PLAN OF THE WORK

One alternative to my proposal for gradual evolution of the law is a method of transforming contract law analogous to the 'big bang'. Some have suggested that the post-communist economies should adopt wholesale the commercial code of an existing market economy. Others may attempt to draft such a body of law *de novo*. In Chapter 2, I discuss these proposals and indicate why I do not believe they would be feasible. I indicate that, even if such a proposal were adopted, a process such as the one I describe would be needed to adapt the law efficiently to the countries in transition. I also discuss the major alternative method of legal change, the adoption by legislatures of civil codes. While the countries of interest are generally civil code countries, there are some advantages to a common law process. One option is a use of a common law process until the laws and the underlying political systems have reached some level of equilibrium. If this option is chosen, there are advantages to a private, as opposed to a public, common law process.

In Chapter 3, I discuss the economics of contract law. An important function of this law is to reduce *ex post* opportunism. I provide some evidence that opportunistic behaviour is occurring in the post-communist economies. There are private mechanisms available to individuals to avoid opportunism. These mechanisms are analysed in Chapter 4. In Chapter 5, I discuss in more detail the current legal situations in the Czech Republic, Hungary and Poland. In these three countries, while there are flaws and law is not complete, nonetheless there is a sound body of commercial law in place.

Chapter 6, the longest in the book, discusses Russia. In Russia, in contrast to the other countries, the law is much weaker and much more reform is needed. I provide numerous examples of legal failures. However, many of the problems seem to stem in part from *insufficient* central government power, so that differing levels of government cannot commit to honour agreements.[5] This in turn seems to derive from uncertainty and the associated high discount rates. I also discuss some mechanisms in place that may serve to enforce agreements, and the possibility of organized crime serving an enforcement function. I conclude that it is at this time impossible to tell if Russia will undertake a successful development, although there are reasons for fearing that it will not.

Chapter 7 outlines and analyses government policies that facilitate efficient transactional rules. There are things that governments should do to facilitate exchange. There are also things that governments should refrain from doing that hinder exchange. Both types of policy are discussed.

Chapter 8 relates the informal mechanisms discussed earlier to the process of evolution of efficient rules. It is shown that a combination of formal and informal mechanisms may be the fastest way to achieve efficient rules. For example, drafters of legal codes can incorporate lessons learned about efficient law from the informal mechanisms into their code revisions.

Chapter 9 summarizes the practical implications of the work. There are implications for the behaviour of government, arbitrators, private trade associations, private attorneys and businesses.

Because changes in Russia and in Eastern Europe are continuing, it is important to note the timeliness of this work. I have attempted to make the work up to date to December 1995. There have just been elections in Russia. The results of these elections – significant gains in power for the communists and nationalists – do not seem likely to lead to significant improvements in the behaviour of the country with respect to the matters discussed here.

2. Alternative Methods of Legal Change

In this chapter, I discuss the major alternatives to a common law, evolutionary process for legal change.

A 'BIG BANG' FOR CONTRACT LAW?

There are equivalents in contract law to the 'big bang' proposals for rapid privatization of property. One is the suggestion made by several authorities that the post-communist economies adopt entirely the civil code of some capitalist economy such as Finland or the Netherlands (for example, Leijonhufvud 1993).

Such a code would be difficult to interpret for an economy with no tradition of markets. Indeed even translating the terms from Finnish or Dutch into Russian or Polish would be difficult. The terms are defined only by their use in a market economy and in actual existing transactions and decisions. Leoni (1961) discusses the difficulty of translating legal terms from one language to another because words are rooted in institutions that may be lacking in the second culture. Leoni's discussion is in the context of translating between languages used in relatively free economies; the problems would be exacerbated in trying to translate terms used in market economies to languages spoken in societies that have not had markets and the corresponding institutions for many years. Murrell (1991) makes a similar point by suggesting that a legal code has embedded in it large amounts of practical knowledge, so that a transfer would not be feasible.[6]

Leoni also discusses the problems arising from the fact that it may seem possible to translate words that have different meanings in different legal cultures. We may identify examples of this problem. The Russian 'Arbitration Court' is the general court with business jurisdiction; the term 'arbitration' is not the same as arbitration in English. 'Commercial bank', 'leaseholding property' and 'stockholding' are all used differently in Russian law than in other jurisdictions (Tourevski and Morgan 1993). In Russia, bonds are short-term obligations and bills long term, the opposite of the Western usage, and it requires three sentences to define 'cash flow' (Kranz and Miller 1994). Other such inconsistencies would undoubtedly be found, but if they were found after the adoption of a code substantial problems could be created.

It takes three years for an American college graduate (who has grown up in a market economy) to learn in law school the meaning of US law, and longer until this knowledge is useful in a practical sense. Businessmen must then rely on discussions with trained attorneys in order for the law to affect their behaviour. To expect to circumvent this process simply by adopting an existing code is not realistic.

Similarly, it would not be feasible for authorities to generate an entire body of contract law *de novo*. Difficulties are not a result of incorrect drafting by the legislature, and could not be corrected by better craftsmanship. A body of law such as contract law is in some sense organically grown over a long period of time. It has numerous components that must interact with each other and with other large, complex bodies of law (securities law, corporate law and labour law, to name but a few). As Hayek (1973, 65) says: 'The parts of a legal system are not so much adjusted to each other according to a comprehensive overall view, as gradually adapted to each other by the successive application of general principles to particular problems'. Laws must also be adapted to existing institutions in an economy.

Schmid (1992) points out that contract law may adopt one set of risk-sharing doctrines in a world where market insurance is freely available, but that these institutions may not be desirable if such insurance markets are lacking. For anyone or any group to be able to craft such a body of law is as unlikely as for a single decision-maker to be able to design a complex economy *de novo*. It was of course the impossibility of this latter task (the socialist calculation problem) that caused the current situation in the former Soviet Empire.

When a complex statute (such as the Americans with Disabilities Act, 1990) is adopted in the USA, it commonly takes some years of litigation before its meaning is fully clear. While some blame this on poor drafting by the legislature, it is also true that no one *ex ante* can predict fully the meaning of such a major legal change and its relationship with other law. If American law-makers with large staffs of experienced professional lawyers and input from many others cannot fully predict the implications of only one statute, how could we expect

Russian or Polish law-makers lacking experience in a private law environment to be able to craft an entire code?

All the countries here under consideration have some sort of preexisting contract law. Therefore the choice is not between starting *de novo* or adopting a body of law. Rather the choice is between modifying an existing body of law or adopting some other body of law. However, even if some other country's law were to be adopted, it would require modification to tailor the law to local conditions (where these conditions include the lack of market institutions for many years). Thus in either case, the issue is the most efficient method of modifying some currently maladapted law. The proposals in this work are useful for adapting a body of law to relevant local circumstances, whatever its original source.

COMMON LAW OR CIVIL CODE?

The two major methods of deriving the law governing private relations (property, contracts, tort) are common law and civil codes. Codes are passed by legislatures; common law is judge-made law. Britain and its former colonies (including the USA[7]) use common law; most of the rest of the world, including the post-communist economies (now and before communism), use legislative codes. Nonetheless, I argue here for at least a temporary use of common law principles in these countries.

General arguments in favour of common law in all circumstances have been proposed by Hayek (1973), Posner (1992), Rubin (1977) and Scully (1992). Here I make the more limited argument that, for the conditions in which the post-communist countries now find themselves, a reliance for a time on common law-like processes would be useful. This reliance would not preclude the use of codes, but would be a useful supplement. Indeed a private common law-like process would be even better.

The process of code-drafting generally requires the time of skilled lawyers (often, in advanced countries, academic lawyers) and of legislatures. Generally a commission of attorneys will draft a proposed code that will be submitted to the legislature. The legislature will then request comments from interested and politically relevant parties. This process may go through several iterations. In contrast, common law decisions are by-products of the judicial dispute resolution process.

The argument here is that as a factual matter the relative price of legislators and skilled lawyers is higher in the post-communist countries than elsewhere. Thus whatever the optimal balance between common law and code in more settled countries, the optimal mix is more towards a common law process in the newer economies.

Consider first lawyers. In order to draft a code, what is needed is a lawyer with knowledge of local conditions and laws, but also with knowledge of Western capitalist law. Obviously, law schools in communist regimes did not specialize in training such attorneys, and there are relatively few of them. Their scarcity means that today such attorneys have a high opportunity cost because there is a private market for their services.[8] Code-drafting is not a highly paid occupation; it is commonly performed as part of academic responsibility. Governments in all the countries studied are not likely to pay high wages to attorneys to draft such codes. This does not mean that private attorneys would refuse if asked to serve on code-drafting commissions. Rather they would likely take longer to provide a draft than would otherwise occur. Thus the first input into code-drafting, attorneys' time, seems scarcer in the post-communist economies than would be true at an equilibrium.

Legislator time is also scarce. The relevant countries are in the process of creating new economic, political and social orders. For such efforts, new laws and legislation are necessary. For example, privatization is itself a major change requiring substantial legislative input. In Russia the legislature has been busy with major political decisions, such as determining the role of the various geographic and ethnic components of the country in the new state. Again this means that if a code is proposed to a legislature by a commission, the legislature is likely to take a longer time in responding than otherwise. Legal changes in codes are not high on the political agenda.

Boris Topornin (1993), Director of the Institute of State and Law of the Russian Academy of Sciences, addressed this issue. He indicated that the 'first generation' of Russian laws, adopted in December 1990, were 'insufficiently clear' and 'insufficiently systematic'. Topornin indicated that current (1993) Russian law was inadequate, and that during the transition it would be necessary to change the law rapidly. However, the first generation of laws governed in Russia for some years. The legislature took a long time to pass a 'second generation'. Some of these laws have now been passed but, as outlined below, substantial problems remain and new drafts are needed. Again there have been delays in passing these newer laws. Although Topornin indicates that

Russian law is fundamentally a code system, he also agrees that it might be possible to, 'use the experience of the common law'.

In this context, a major benefit of a common law process is that decisions and legal change occur as a by-product of dispute resolution. Whenever a dispute is settled by an appellate court, then new law is made (if there is a written opinion). Since courts naturally settle disputes, generation of common law is relatively cheap. The only cost is the cost of the judges' time in writing an opinion, as opposed to merely providing a decision. In the post-communist countries, this cost might be higher because judges lack experience.

The trade-off between code and common law systems is in terms of the rate of adaptation of the law to changing conditions. Ideally a code can achieve the optimum set of laws when it is first adopted. In contrast, the common law will never reach optimality. However, as soon as a code is passed it begins to become obsolete, and its maladaptation increases until a new code is adopted. The common law, on the other hand, is always somewhat maladapted, but its lack of adaptation is limited because it is continually changing. In deciding which form of law is most desirable, a country must balance these two types of cost. Since in countries in legal disarray (such as the new economies), adoption of new codes takes relatively longer than in countries in equilibrium, the balance predictably shifts relatively more towards a common law solution.

Moreover, while a shift to a common law-like process would be a change for legal systems that are not accustomed to such a process, the change need not be permanent. Legislatures could announce that rulings by appellate courts would have the force of law until a new codification of the relevant body of law could be passed. These decisions could then be an input into the codification process, but only one input. Such a system would allow some of the benefits of a common law process without eliminating the legal traditions of the relevant countries.

PRIVATE LAW OR PUBLIC LAW?

An even simpler reform would be to rely on a private common law system. Indeed it might be possible to establish such a system with minimal state intervention. The state would need to agree to enforce decisions reached by arbitrators. If it were well known that the state would enforce such decisions, actual enforcement would seldom be required. If such enforcement were available, arbitrators (or associations of arbitrators) themselves could announce that they planned to establish a common law-like system and follow precedent in decision-making.

Once the system of precedents became established, then parties would generally not rely on the arbitrators. Just as most disputes settle out of court, so would we expect most disputes under an arbitration system with a body of common law precedents to settle without a formal hearing. The arbitration association could charge a fee for being named in an agreement as the final arbitrator of potential disputes and refuse to arbitrate any dispute between parties who had not named it. In this way the arbitration association could be compensated for the public good provided when decisions were written (Benson 1990).

Later I discuss some benefits of arbitration. However, many benefits arise because the courts in the relevant countries are themselves in some disarray. In general, a major problem is the lack of skilled personnel – lawyers and judges – for dealing with commercial dispute resolution and contract enforcement. This is due to lack of experience with appropriate law and institutions. While the main principles of contract law in many of the relevant countries are consistent with a market economy, the principles have never been applied directly to contracts between enterprises in free markets. Current judges do not have the required experience, and most countries have not trained many such judges. Moreover, business operators and even lawyers are not familiar with contracts because of the nature of the functioning of the communist system. Since parties will be able to choose arbitrators, there will be selection of those most able to solve the problems associated with particular contracts, whether they be local or Western lawyers, experienced businessmen or professional arbitrators.

As of 1995, Russian courts lack sufficient power. Kornai (1992) indicates that Hungarian courts lack experience with a market economy and lack sufficient resources to adjudicate all disputes that arise in a market economy. Gray and Associates (1993), in their discussions of law in Poland, Hungary and the Czech Republic, indicate in all cases that trained judges are lacking, and that both the legal system and the population at large lack experience in a market economy. Aslund (1992) is even more pessimistic: 'To require the state to do anything means to ask the uninformed and corrupt for assistance...Therefore, the only defensible recommendation is that the role of the state should be limited to a bare minimum in the period of transition to capitalism'.

Thus there are severe difficulties in drafting and enforcing public law for contract enforcement. Moreover, the skilled resources that would be needed for this project might be better employed elsewhere. This is particularly true since it may be possible to go a fair way towards creation of such law through private mechanisms. The proposals set forth here rely much less on a formal judiciary than do proposals for more explicit public law, and may be easier to begin applying.

3. Contracts and Opportunism

The key class of problems facing potential traders in a world with no legal contract enforcement are problems of opportunism (Williamson 1985; Rubin 1990). I first discuss opportunism, and then present evidence that the problem exists in the post-communist countries.

OPPORTUNISM: THEORY

In many transactions, one party will have performed his part of the deal before the other, who will then have an incentive to cheat. One key purpose of the law of contracts is to discourage such opportunism (Muris 1981). Examples of opportunism can be so crude as simply to refuse to make an agreed-upon payment. More sophisticated forms of cheating include offering high quality goods for sale and delivering low quality (Akerlof 1970). A firm may also put a trading partner in a position where the partner is dependent on the firm for some input, and then raise the price, an action called 'hold-up'.

The general form of opportunism is appropriating the 'quasi-rents' associated with some transaction (Klein *et al.* 1978).[9] Such quasi-rents are often created by 'asset specificity', creations of valuable assets that are specialized to one transaction or trading partner. Once these specific assets are created, an opportunistic trading partner can sometimes appropriate their value.

The major cost of opportunism when it cannot effectively be prevented is neither the cost of cheating, nor even the cost of precautions taken to avoid being victimized. Rather it is the lost social value from the otherwise profitable deals that do not transpire. For example, if sellers cannot credibly promise to deliver high quality goods, then consumers will not be willing to pay a higher price for allegedly higher quality and manufacturers will therefore not produce them. Similarly, in economies with no contractual possibilities, transactors often deal with long-term associates or relatives in order to have additional assurances of contractual performance.[10] But this means that many potential transactions will not occur because otherwise suitable parties will not be in appropriate relationships and so cannot guarantee performance, even though such transactions would be value increasing.

There is another cost to the post-communist economies of lack of contractual enforcement mechanisms. As Coase (1937) pointed out, if transaction costs between firms are high, then more activity will occur within the firm and less in markets.[11] But lack of enforcement mechanisms means that firms will be relatively larger because they will internalize more functions. Many authorities have remarked on the inefficiently large size of firms in these economies, and have argued that breaking the firms into smaller parts would be desirable. However, until efficient contract enforcement mechanisms are available, the incentive for such restructuring will be reduced because managers can anticipate difficulties in using contract to achieve coordination that they now achieve by command.

In general, less formal enforcement mechanisms can work better for shorter-term transactions and for transactions involving smaller amounts of money. As the time horizon of a contract becomes longer or the amount at issue becomes larger, the value of formal enforcement increases. Thus an additional cost of lack of enforcement mechanisms is the loss of the long-term investments and the large investments deterred by the lack of enforceability (Clague *et al.* 1995). To the extent that mechanisms can be designed and adopted that reduce or eliminate opportunism, then social wealth can be greatly increased.

OPPORTUNISM: EVIDENCE

Problems of opportunism exist in the post-communist economies. During the communist period, informal small-scale trading networks based on family, ethnicity, friendship, reciprocity, long-term obligations and barter supported trade (Los 1992). Personal relations and trust are still important (Johnson and Kroll 1991). The importance of personal contacts in supporting exchange in Russia is a major theme of Tourevski and Morgan (1993), a book written to provide practical advice to Western businessmen considering investing in Russia. Such contacts are of substantial importance primarily in contexts where there are limited possibilities for more formal governance mechanisms.

Consumers complain about low quality goods. If consumers would be willing to pay higher prices for higher quality, then this indicates a market failure. Goldberg (1992) discusses quality efforts in consumer and other markets. He indicates that several new legislative proposals for increasing quality are being considered. However, none of these involve proper incentives and none create proper reputation effects. A reliance on legislation to achieve goals that markets can better provide is evidence of a carryover in thought processes from the previous economic system.

One major survey found that people in Russia have less confidence about the future and are more likely to believe that institutions are likely to change for the worse than is true of people in capitalist societies (Shiller *et al.* 1992). This would explain in part the unwillingness of owners of firms to invest in brand name capital, and is consistent with other behaviour further discussed below.

Foreign businessmen are cautious in doing business in Eastern Europe. For example, Western firms often take longer to do a job so that less investment is at risk at any point in time. They will also move more slowly in working with partners and subcontractors than would be true in a world with more legal certainty. Many foreign firms are investing in distribution networks in these countries, but not in manufacturing capacity. Part of the reason is the fear of loss of investment. Even so, firms are sometimes victimized by opportunistic Russians. Poe (1993, 158–9) describes episodes in which potential investors have spent time and money in negotiating with individuals who do not have the authority actually to agree to the contract. This problem is associated with the poor definition of property rights in Russia, so that it is difficult to determine ownership.

There is even evidence of the simplest forms of opportunism. Firms in Russia sometimes take money and provide nothing; at other times they accept goods and then do not pay. Enforcement even in these cases is apparently difficult (Buyevich and Zhukov 1992). Uchitelle (1992) indicates that buyers operating on commodity exchanges often renege. In Hungary two-thirds of the 700,000 lawsuits filed in 1991 involved debt collection (Gray and Associates 1993.) Indeed the most significant form of opportunism in the post-communist societies may be simple failure to pay debts. In Hungary, bankruptcy law can be used for debt collection, but such mechanisms are less well developed in other countries.

There is also evidence that the structure of new private firms is due in part to uncertainty about contract enforcement. Many new firms in

Russia are forming holding companies or using vertical integration in order to guarantee needed supplies. Indeed one 'consultant' indicated explicitly that this was the motivation for organizing a large firm containing many otherwise independent firms. Many new firms are associated with existing state firms, again for the purpose of obtaining guarantees of contractual performance (Johnson and Kroll 1991).

In addition to opportunism by firms, there is also a massive problem of government opportunism in Russia. Governments seem to lure investments by making particular promises, and then expropriate the quasi-rents associated with these investments by changing the rules. I discuss this issue in more detail in Chapter 6 when I discuss the problems of Russia.

4. Private Mechanisms

There are several mechanisms that parties could use to facilitate exchange where contracts will not work. Even in developed countries, explicit enforceable (and enforced) contracts are relatively unimportant for much exchange. In the USA 75 per cent of commercial disputes are settled privately through arbitration and mediation (Benson 1990, 2). However, businesses in developed economies have learned (perhaps through trial and error) methods of doing substantial amounts of business without relying on contracts and, of course, the threat of legal enforcement makes private arrangements easier. Businesses in new economies will have less experience with such techniques.

It is helpful to classify private mechanisms that can be used to make agreements credible into three classes, depending on the number of parties involved in generating the enforcement mechanism. All three are based on reputations. These mechanisms are discussed in more detail in Rubin (1993).

UNILATERAL MECHANISMS

The major class of unilateral mechanisms is investments in reputation. Advertising is one form of such investment (Klein and Leffler 1981). Firms can invest in expensive signs or logos that become worthless if the firm cheats. Law firms invest in expensive decor serving the same function.

However, while firms can privately invest in reputation creation, there are some difficulties in the Eastern countries (and in particular in Russia) in this process. Traditionally firms in these countries have valued secrecy, rather than the openness needed for reputations to work: 'Very often Soviet participants take a closed or secretive position and the attempts to hide information can reach ridiculous levels' (Tourevski and Morgan 1993, 245); 'Foreign investors need to be aggressive about getting information, because by inclination and long-standing habit, companies won't divulge it' (Kvint 1993, 79). It is not clear why firms are excessively secretive, but such behaviour can be counterproductive. One possible explanation is that in bargaining, firms have often been concerned with making sure that their partner did not make a profit or surplus, rather than with maximizing any measure of joint surplus. As discussed below, this bargaining strategy may itself be due to short time horizons caused by uncertainty. In addition, fear of organized crime or of excessive government taxation can lead to excess secrecy.

BILATERAL MECHANISMS

Bilateral mechanisms are those involving only two firms, often a buyer and a seller. Three relevant types of bilateral arrangement are: self-enforcing contracts; vertical relationships between dealers and manufacturers; and the use of 'hostages', including collateral. It might appear that contracts including private arbitration clauses would be relevant here, but as we see below, these fit better into the multilateral analysis.

Self-Enforcing Agreements

The most important type of bilateral mechanism is the creation of what has been called a 'self-enforcing agreement' (Telser 1980). This is an agreement between two firms that contains no external enforcement provisions. The agreement operates as long as it is in the interest of both firms to maintain it. For each firm, the value of the agreement is the value of the expected future business from maintaining the relationship. If a firm cheats, then it gains in the short run but loses the value of the future business. If discount rates are high in Russia because of uncertainty about the future, then such agreements would be less likely to work because the present value of the future business would be reduced.

Uchitelle (1992) indicates that exactly this sort of contract is now occurring in Russia: '…two concepts – mutual benefit and trust – have come to play a major role in these early days of Russian capitalism. What these concepts come down to is this: If both parties to an agreement are benefiting from the deal, presumably they will not break the contract'.

Nonetheless, there seems to be a tradition in Russia of hard bargaining: 'Soviet negotiators see business deals as fixed and finite entities.

Only when ensuring that they end up with more and the negotiating partners end up with less do they feel the negotiations are successful' (Tourevski and Morgan 1993, 243); 'One of the chief criteria for evaluating how foreign trade officials do their job is the discount they generate during negotiations, which is supposed to show how persistent and uncompromising they are as businessmen' (Tourevski and Morgan 1993, 243). As long as this sort of bargaining occurs, it will be difficult to establish self-enforcing agreements.

Burandt (1992) discusses the formation of a joint venture for advertising between a Russian organization and the American advertising agency, Young and Rubicam. Young and Rubicam would price its services and pay the media 'fairly' because the goal was to, 'establish ourselves as a reputable and leading company in this business for the long haul'. On the other hand: 'It wasn't atypical in the Soviet Union for organizations to overcharge customers and underpay suppliers'. In other words, Burandt is arguing for prices that would make agreements self-enforcing, and such prices seem to be less common in Russia.

Vertical Controls

An interesting class of bilateral transactions is between manufacturers and retailers of the product. There are various policies that manufacturers with brand name capital might want retailers to carry out. Some are: demonstrating and advertising the product; certification of quality; maintaining freshness; promoting the product to marginal consumers; maintenance of complete inventories; and refraining from 'switching' customers to alternative product lines when consumers respond to manufacturers' advertisements.

There are numerous mechanisms that can achieve these goals. These include: establishment of maximum or minimum prices for the sale of goods (resale price maintenance); territorial restrictions (including exclusive territories); requirements that dealers carry only the brand of the manufacturer (exclusive dealing); and requirements of certain methods of retailing (such as shelf space requirements). Manufacturers may also integrate directly into retailing or may establish franchises for selling their product. It is not my purpose here to discuss the business reasons for these restrictions; such discussions are available elsewhere (Rubin 1990, Chapter 6). These restrictions can be carried out as self-enforcing agreements, with the threat of termination as the only sanction. There is no need for state enforcement of these types of arrangement. However, state hostility (as, for example, through much American antitrust law) can make such agreements non-viable.

Franchising might be particularly useful in the former communist economies. There are many excessively large and excessively centralized enterprises. Splitting some of these entities into separate firms linked through franchise contracts could be a useful way of decentralizing without losing the benefits (if any) of a common brand name. The relationships between components of many large Russian enterprises are already similar to relationships between franchisors and franchisees (Poe 1993). Poland is successfully developing a franchise system, although most of the franchisors are American and European firms (Simpson 1995). One additional important benefit of this method of business development is the training provided by the franchisors.

Hostages

One way for a firm to commit to not cheating is to offer a hostage to its trading partner. A simple hostage is collateral: a cash deposit that will be lost if the firm cheats. Such a hostage requires some outside enforcement, but not by the state. For example, the firms could jointly hire an attorney who would be empowered to decide if cheating had occurred and to award the payment to the victim. Of course, there is a problem in trusting the attorney not to expropriate the hostage. However, firms might exist whose sole value is their reputation capital for enforcing such agreements and who therefore would not have an incentive to cheat in this way as long as their reputations were worth more than any one hostage. Law firms or investment banking firms might be able to perform this function. International firms might be particularly well suited for this role because they have established valuable reputations.

A more natural method is the creation of bilateral hostages. If firm A is dependent on firm B for some input, then firm A would have an incentive to put firm B in a position of being dependent on firm A as well. Moreover, firm B would have an incentive to be put in this position in order to be able to guarantee not to cheat. For example, firms making cardboard boxes commonly trade components with each other across geographic areas, and in this case neither firm can hold up the other without also putting itself at risk.

MULTILATERAL MECHANISMS

These are the most interesting class of adaptations, and the least well studied. A well-defined multilateral arrangement involving a group of member firms can enforce honest dealing both between members of the group and between members and outsiders. The Law Merchant (the medieval body of commercial law) was exactly this sort of multilateral private legal system that enforced honesty by threats of reputation loss (see for example, Berman 1983, Benson 1990 and Milgrom *et al.* 1990). The Law Merchant was then adopted into English common law. Similar institutions survive today in advanced countries. The Better Business Bureau, for example, is a reputation-guaranteeing device with properties similar to those of the Law Merchant. Many trade associations have codes of ethics with many of the properties of the Law Merchant (Hill 1976).

Private contracts requiring arbitration of disputes require similar enforcement mechanisms. Much international commercial law is based on arbitration, with loss of reputation as the major sanction for breach (Benson 1992). I begin with an analysis of private arbitration that demonstrates the need for multilateral enforcement.

Arbitration

The parties to a contract can specify in the contract that, in the event of a dispute, they will settle the issue through arbitration. There will be several benefits to parties from the use of arbitration for dispute settlement.

In a world where judges may not have much experience with business disputes and where legal precedents may be weak, it should be possible to choose arbitrators who will be more likely to reach efficient decisions. Arbitrators will be paid only if hired, and so will have an incentive to reach correct decisions because this will lead to future business. If there are competing 'court' systems, or competing groups of arbitrators, the parties can select the one they desire. Parties to contracts written in good faith will not expect to breach at the time of drafting the agreement. Therefore, *ex ante* the parties will desire to select that forum for dispute resolution in which they expect to obtain the most efficient results, so that *ex ante* competition among arbitrators will favour those with a reputation for providing the most efficient (wealth maximizing) decisions. Moreover, parties can specify the amount to be paid to arbitrators. This means that arbitrators in more important (costly) disputes can be paid more, so that parties will have access to the quality of arbitrator appropriate to the value of the case.

Parties can also choose the body of law or rules that will govern in the event of a dispute. If the formal law in place is inefficient or vague, the parties can indicate that they will have their dispute governed by a different body of law, or by the rules of the arbitration association. This allows more flexibility in choice of law and means that it is more likely that an efficient law will govern. If it turns out that one body of law is generally chosen by parties, then this will be evidence that this law might be the most efficient to be used as public law. Arbitrators can sometimes use industry custom as a method of determining liability. Indeed much common law and most commercial law are ultimately based on custom.

However, in the post-communist societies custom is likely to be less useful as a basis for law than has traditionally been true. Those who write of custom as a basis for law have in mind a situation in which trade is already occurring and a law-maker begins to use the existing customs as a basis for law (Cooter 1994); this is, for example, the approximate way in which the Law Merchant was incorporated into the common law. However, in the post-communist economies, existing custom has evolved largely in circumstances in which trade was illegal and it was necessary to hide or disguise the terms, and even existence, of exchange. Thus existing customs may be less well suited to adoption into formal law than has traditionally been true.

Indeed those who were entrepreneurs under communism may be true criminals today, and existing customs may be more suited to criminal enterprise than to normal business (Kvint 1993, 196–200; Tourevski and Morgan 1993, 210–21). As Handelman (1995, p. 49) says: 'With no clearly defined boundaries between legal and illegal economic behavior, the shrewdest criminal bosses were hard to distinguish from entrepreneurs'. Kranz (1995a) also indicates that, 'the boundary between legality and illegality has never been as blurry'. Thus whether existing customs are efficient or not depends on whether the skill of current businessmen was in engaging in trade and (at that time illegal) market transactions, or in engaging in socially unproductive or counterproductive activities. Moreover, the custom of excess secrecy, mentioned earlier, would be counterproductive in a market economy. Nonetheless, customs developed since the time of liberation onwards should be useful.

There is a limit to purely private arbitration. That limit is that the party which loses in a dispute has an incentive to ignore the decision. In countries with an established body of contract law, the solution is that the courts will often enforce the decree of the arbitrator. In a society where there is no court enforcement of such decrees, the only remedy is a reputation remedy. In small societies where reputation is common knowledge among all parties, then simple publicizing of cheating may work. However, in larger societies, where there are many trading partners, it may be necessary to devise more complex devices for private enforcement of arbitration decrees. This is the topic of the next section.

Multilateral Enforcement Devices

Consider a trade association with the following policies:

1. The association collects dues from all members. These dues are used to subsidize part of the costs of arbitration proceedings in which disputes among members, and between members and customers or suppliers are resolved. Disputants also pay part of the costs.
2. Information is made available to all potential customers and suppliers regarding the list of members, so that it is possible for a potential customer to ascertain at low cost if a potential seller is a member of the trade association.
3. If the decision of the arbitrator goes against a party and the party ignores the decision (for example, refuses to pay damages as ordered by the arbitrator), then the party will be expelled from the association.
4. Therefore, if a party has been expelled, then when a new potential trading partner queries the association, he will learn that the seller is not a member and will accordingly be able to avoid trading with the party, or will trade on different terms.

The structure of this mechanism corresponds to the Law Merchant mechanism. Milgrom *et al.* (1990) provide a game-theoretic analysis of this mechanism and show that the outcome is stable and will lead to efficient trading patterns.

This pattern is also followed by many trade associations that engage in self-policing (see Bernstein (1995), for a partial listing). (The ability to engage in self-regulation in the USA may have been excessively restricted by the application of antitrust laws.) The Code of Ethics and Interpretations of the Public Relations Society of America calls for an investigation of allegations of misconduct, with expulsion and publicity as potential remedies. This code includes interpretations based on actual cases, which form a 'body of law' (Hill 1976, 285). Similarly, the Code of Ethics of the National Association of Realtors has a provision for expulsion of members who do not accept the finding of review boards. This same pattern is followed by diamond 'bourses' (diamond exchange markets) such as the New York Diamond Dealers Club, and by the World Federation of Diamond Bourses (Bernstein, 1992). Better Business Bureaus – private reputation – enforcing groups in the USA – also follow this procedure, although these organizations also provide information about non-member firms. A simple mechanism would be for member firms to display on their doors or in their advertising a logo indicating that they are approved by the Better Business Bureau.

Trade associations and Better Business Bureaus illustrate the types of organization of reputation-guaranteeing associations that might be useful. Trade associations commonly include members of a given business, irrespective of geographic location. Conversely, Better Business Bureaus include businesses in a particular area, irrespective of the nature of the business. The latter type of organization is more likely to be useful to guarantee reputations of those who sell to consumers; the former, of those who sell to businesses.

LIMITS TO PRIVATE MECHANISMS

While private mechanisms can support some exchange, there are limits to the power of these mechanisms. It is useful to assume that a party will behave opportunistically whenever it pays to do so. Explicit enforceable agreements can mean that opportunism will be prohibitively expensive. A court order or an enforceable arbitration decree can remove any profit from opportunistic behaviour. Other mechanisms are less reliable. This means that the amount that can be exchanged without an enforceable agreement will be limited. The most that can be put at risk is the value of the reputation that would be lost if cheating occurs.

In Russia these problems are multiplied. As discussed below, public enforcement is weak. Unfortunately, private mechanisms are also relatively weak in Russia. Most such mechanisms rely on reputations, and in Russia most enterprises are new and lacking in developed reputations. Thus although reputation and contract are substitute methods of enforcing agreements (Klein 1992, 161), the situation in Russia (and to a lesser extent in the other post-communist economies considered here) is that neither mechanism is easily available.

Moreover, there are actual hindrances to the creation of reputations. Fear of extortion creates a positive value for secrecy. Criminals can use information about the reliability and success of firms for purposes of extortion (Black *et al.* 1995; Handelman 1995; Leitzel *et al.* 1995). Pistor (1995) indicates that parties are often unwilling to write complete contracts for this same reason. The same factors make tax collection difficult: firms are unwilling to tell tax collectors about revenues for fear that criminals will use this information for extortion. Frye (1995) indicates that firms are sometimes unwilling to use public contract enforcement mechanisms because of a fear of expropriation by the tax authorities themselves. Thus several factors conspire in the case of Russia to make the creation of reputation capital difficult.

This should not be taken to mean that private mechanisms are valueless. On the contrary, they are common, even in developed economies. However, it is important to realize their limits. Such mechanisms should be supported by formal enforcement devices whenever possible. Clague *et al.* (1996) suggest that a certain amount of trade occurs in all economies, but that developed economies are those that have established formal mechanisms for enforcing long-term agreements.

5. The Czech Republic, Hungary and Poland

It is not correct to view all of the post-communist countries as starting from the same point. Of those countries specifically considered here, the Czech Republic, Hungary and Poland are much more similar to each other than any is to Russia.

Albania, Bulgaria and Romania are probably somewhere in between, although privatization in these countries has not proceeded as far as in Russia. It is likely that the Baltic Republics (Latvia, Estonia and Lithuania) are similar to the first three countries, while the Ukraine and Belorussia may be similar to Russia. Some of the Asiatic republics (Uzbekistan, Turkmenistan, Kirghizstan and Tadjikistan) may be relatively less developed than Russia. The exact ranking is not important: what is relevant is the observation that the countries considered may provide examples for others.

Commerce can function with a relatively small body of contract law. Most terms of contracts are written privately by the parties themselves; as Benson (1990) points out, the parties actually make 'law' by writing a contract. Explicit public law serves two functions in addition to enforcing private terms. First, it fills gaps: it covers situations that the parties did not anticipate. Second, it supplies defaults: if the law provides certain terms or indicates certain results, the parties to a private agreement can save resources by not directly dealing with these issues, or paying lawyers to deal with them. However, the major part of the contract is the result of private agreement. Thus parties can engage in substantial amounts of contractually based commerce with little explicit 'law' on the books.

The civil codes of the countries in the former Soviet Union are based on pre-Soviet European civil codes and, 'many of the principles are not inconsistent with a market economy' (IMF 1991, 247). In many cases, these have been adopted from pre-communist codes. This is also true of the Czech Republic, Poland and Hungary. At the beginning of the transition, these three countries had in place a set of basic contract laws.

Poland's original contract law was a 1933 Western law. A commission was to redraft and update this code. In Hungary, transactions were governed by those parts of the civil code originally written to govern small, non-commercial private transactions. The Czech and Slovak Federal Republic (CSFR) had more of its legal system adapted to communism than most other countries, so that it had less law to build on than others. The CSFR adopted a new civil code and a new commercial code in 1991. Thus in many of the Eastern countries there were indigenous bodies of contract law, but none are fully adapted to contemporary business. Beginning with the existing body of contract law and allowing modifications as discussed below is likely to be the most efficient and most expeditious way to achieve a body of contract law suited to market conditions in the post-communist economies.

Gray and Associates (1993) provides a summary of the situation in Poland soon after the transition that seems to apply more generally:

> Although the legal structure is generally satisfactory in most areas, practice is still uncertain in all areas. The generality of the laws leaves wide discretion for administrators and courts, and there has not yet been time to build up a body of cases and practice to further define the rules of the game. Although the courts are in general honest and are used by the population, they have little experience in economic matters. Judges are not well paid, and the best lawyers have a strong incentive to go into private practice. The wide discretion and general lack of precedent and competence create tremendous legal uncertainty that is sure to hamper private sector development.

All four countries examined enforce arbitration clauses in contracts between domestic and foreign firms. However, as of 1993, only Poland would enforce arbitration agreements between domestic firms. Parties are allowed to specify whose law will govern and who will be the arbitrator in the event of a dispute. The Union of Polish Banks has established an arbitration court for disputes involving banks and their customers. The Polish economy recently performed better than any other formerly communist economy (Perlez 1993). Much of this is due to the productivity of Polish domestic firms, since the country had at that time received relatively little foreign investment. While all the countries studied have efficient rules with respect to arbitration for dealings with foreign investors, Poland has the most efficient system for contract enforcement involving domestic firms. It is interesting that Poland has the most favourable laws of all the countries studied and its economy is outperforming the others, although this observation is of course not proof.

The benefit of efficient laws is continuing. Anecdotal evidence indicates that Poland and the Czech Republic are greatly benefiting from the legal certainty, and Hungary is benefiting to a lesser extent. (Hungary's main problem seems to be a reluctance to privatize, rather than direct contractual uncertainty.) One piece of evidence is negative: the US business press, in writing about these countries, never mentions difficulties with the 'rule of law' or with the legal system. Even in describing cases where Western investments have been unsuccessful in the Czech Republic, Hungary and Poland, the discussion is in terms of business reasons for the failures, rather than contractual or legal difficulties (see, for example, Branegan 1994). As we see in the next chapter, this is totally different from the case of Russia; there, virtually every article discusses legal uncertainty and difficulties with contract enforcement. Moreover, in comparing Eastern Europe with Russia, the point is often made that legal systems are much more advanced in the former countries (see, for example, Pennar *et al.* 1994).

Poland may be the best example. The Polish economy seems to be in good shape. Moreover, there is now substantial foreign investment in Poland. This is both ownership investment in privatized companies and investment in new companies and trading partners. Polish firms are able to raise money on international capital markets as well. Thus the sort of stock watering and managerial shirking observed in Russia (discussed in the next chapter) is not occurring in Poland (Miller *et al.* 1995).

Poland has a sufficiently developed legal system such that franchising as a business method is thriving. Franchisors are both European and American firms (Simpson 1995). There is also foreign investment in the Czech Republic (for example, Toy and Miller 1995). Moreover, foreign companies are finding sufficient certainty in all three countries so that there are substantial business links between Eastern and Western Europe, in the form of acquisitions, partnerships and supplier networks (Miller *et al.* 1994). George Soros, a successful investor in Eastern Europe, is described as 'generally upbeat' about the progress of these countries (Gordon 1995).

Thus the evidence from at least three of the former communist countries indicates that if correct measures are taken, then it is possible to emerge successfully from the desolation created by communism. One part of the required efforts includes creation or re-creation of a rule of law, and these three countries have undertaken the investments needed to do this.

6. Russia

Russia seems to have a less well-adapted body of law than the Czech Republic, Hungary or Poland. This may be because Russia was communist for a longer time than the others, so that existing pre-communist law is older than in the other countries and there are additional generations of people who have had no actual exposure to markets. Moreover, at the time of the Revolution, Russia was less economically advanced than were the other countries when they became communist. Indeed it was not an economy in any real sense of the term.

THE FORMAL LEGAL SYSTEM

The major legal weaknesses do not seem to be only in the area of contract law itself. There is a large body of Russian contract law which was used under the Soviet system to govern transactions between enterprises. This law differs from contract law in market economies. However, it is not as different as we might expect: 'More surprising, perhaps, is the substantial convergence of contractual norms in Soviet and Anglo-American legal systems despite significant differences in the organization of capitalist and socialist economies' (Kroll 1987, 147). Attorneys and businessmen in Russia indicated in private conversations that difficulties in doing business are due more to uncertainty about government actions than contractual weaknesses.

One example of forces leading to legal uncertainty in Russia is what has been called the 'war of laws'. Various levels of government may pass conflicting laws, and there is no mechanism for resolving such conflicts. This makes business planning difficult.

> At the time of this writing, the problem of lack of clarity and uniformity exists at all levels of government and involves uncertainty concerning the location of authority to legislate and implement the laws, the nature and extent of the legislative and executive powers, and the appropriate means and methods for enforcement (IMF 1991, 226).

While the splitting of the Soviet Union into independent countries may have reduced these problems, it has not solved them all, and local laws are continually changing. There are inconsistencies in rules and interpretations of various ministries and departments of Russia. The multiplicity of fora for resolution of commercial disputes is more severe in economies that lack a well-developed body of commercial law because different courts may use different and inconsistent rules and laws.

There are over 800 ministries in Russia, and many of these can stop any given deal (Kvint 1993, 26). Obtaining approval from all relevant parties to undertake a deal has been called 'death by committee' (Poe 1993, 54). Building one property development in Moscow required permits from 130 different committees (Rossant 1994). This leads to possibilities of substantial corruption. Shleifer and Vishny (1993) indicate that the most dangerous form of corruption is that in which several authorities have the power to stop an activity, so that bribes must be paid to many potential enforcers and an actor cannot be certain that he has bribed all the relevant officials; they indicate that this is the case in Russia. Poe (1993, 236-7) describes the same situation. Mauro (1995) provides evidence that societies with more corruption invest less and grow more slowly. Erlanger (1995) also indicates that official corruption is an ongoing problem in Russia, and may be more of a detriment to investment than organized crime. An important theme of Handelman (1995) is that there may be little difference, and that there are close links between criminals and government officials.

The law used in the formal legal system in Russia has been inadequate in many dimensions. The basic commercial law in use until recently was a 1964 law. This was modified by many subsequent decrees and laws, but was nonetheless seriously incomplete. Moreover, there are inconsistencies among the various laws passed or adopted since the fall of communism. Thus the body of law governing commercial relationships is weak and difficult to use.

To quote one example, debt collection has been difficult (Dubik 1994a). Until recently, courts charged 10 per cent of the disputed sum; in October 1994 a decree reduced this amount and applied a sliding scale. Nonetheless, use of the courts is difficult. A legal proceeding can only be filed after a debt is three months overdue, and courts take two months or more to rule on cases. With high inflation, debt collection is problematical with such delays. The inflation rate was over 2500 per cent in 1992, over 800 per cent in 1993 and 200 per cent in 1994. It appears to be lower so far in 1995, but it is still high enough so that delayed debt collection is quite costly. While newer laws sometimes allow inflation adjustments or indexing, this was not always true in the past, and does not seem to be true in all cases even now.

Another example is the difficulty banks have had in seizing certain collateral for loans in default. As a result, loans have tended to be for short time periods, such as 90 days (Filipov 1994). On the other hand, the 29 May 1992 Russian mortgage law does allow for the use of real property as collateral for bank loans. Moreover, this law is quite flexible in allowing parties to choose whatever terms are most congenial (Osakwe 1993, 354–5). However, although there are six private mortgage registers, there is no central register where a lender can establish the priority of his mortgage (Levy 1995). More recently it has been reported that banks' rights to foreclose are still not defined. As a result, mortgages tend to be for short terms (no more than ten years, and often six months to one year with an option to renew). Down payments are high, typically 30–40 per cent. As of September 1995, only about 1000 mortgages have been reported (Banerjee and Teodorescu 1995).

An additional difficulty is that there are three separate court systems (Vlasihin 1993). There is a system of business courts, the arbitration courts (which is not an arbitration court in the Western sense), that hears disputes between businesses. However, if one party to a dispute is a private citizen, another court system is involved. There is yet another system, the Constitutional Court. It is not always clear which court will hear a particular dispute. Moreover, since there are three systems that might hear similar disputes, the rate of development of precedents and predictability of the law will be retarded. While there are potential benefits from competing court systems, this does not seem to be the case in Russia because the parties do not seem able to choose *ex ante* which system will govern their dispute.

Aslund (1995) also discusses difficulties in passing relevant laws. He suggests that the conflicts between the government and the Supreme Soviet, between the government and ministries remaining from the communist era, and between the central government and regional governments created great difficulties.

Even when laws are passed, problems remain. This is because of delays in passing relevant laws and inefficiencies that exist between the passage of laws. Even today, insufficient laws have been passed to enable the economy to function at a high level. As mentioned earlier, this may be a pervasive feature of a legal system based on codes when legal change is difficult and there are lags. I will discuss three major laws.

The 1990 Law 'On Property in Russia'

This law was seriously incomplete. The required subordinate legislation was delayed because of political difficulties, and much is still lacking Moreover: 'There was no clear distribution of state property between the Federation and its member republics, districts, and regions' (Topornin 1993, 17). These problems in allocation of property rights and conflict between governmental units still plague the country today; examples are provided below. It also appears that in Russia, more than in the other countries, there remain people in authority with some hostility towards the adoption of markets, and the number of such people appears to be increasing.

The 1992 Arbitration Procedural Code (APC)[12]

This established a nation-wide system of arbitration courts and provided rules for binding arbitration and enforcement. This law was a major improvement over the previous situation because it did provide more authority for arbitration. However, the APC was a procedural code, and it still depended on the existing body of substantive law. Some of the difficulties addressed by Greif and Kandel (1995) have been remedied by subsequent legislation (the 10 per cent fee for arbitration has been reduced and the legislature has recently passed a new substantive commercial law, as discussed below), but other problems – problems of competence of judges and lack of enforcement – remain. Moreover, the new Commercial Code does not mention arbitration at all.

The official arbitration courts suffer additional problems. For domestic disputes, the major court is the Supreme Arbitration Court.[13] The Arbitration Court is the basic commercial court in Russia. Yakovlev (1994) indicates that his court has difficulty in obtaining enforcement of its orders. He also indicates that the long delays in hearing disputes create severe problems. He blames the 'bloody squabbles' among entrepreneurs on the delays in using the court. Nineteen courts, including the Moscow court, do not have independent physical facilities. The judges in this court are the same as in the Soviet era and, because of low pay, many of the best have left (Black *et al.* 1995). Middle level judges earn only $160 per month and are largely dependent on the goodwill of others in the system for other benefits, such as housing (*Economist* 1995a, at 48).

Pistor (1995) indicates that the enforcement of private arbitration decrees is sometimes possible, particularly if assets are available in banks. However, there are risks, and she indicates that on occasion assets will be 'siphoned off by enforcers'. While the number of cases handled by the Arbitration Court has fallen by almost 30 per cent from 1993 to 1994, the number of debt collection cases has fallen by only 8 per cent, suggesting that users of courts are less unhappy with the courts as debt collectors than with other functions of the courts. She also indicates that the Arbitration Court has in general been willing to enforce awards from private arbitrators, and treats these orders as final and binding. Nonetheless, Pistor indicates that private arbitration courts are used very little. However, more optimistically, Langer and Buyevitch (1995) indicate that the number of cases heard by the International Arbitration Court of the Russian Federation Chamber of Commerce and Industry tripled from 1993 to 1994.

The Russian Arbitration Court attached to the Russian Chamber of Commerce and Industry (discussed in Viechtbauer 1993) handles international disputes. This court is descended from a Soviet court, the Foreign Trade Arbitration Court. However, there are numerous difficulties with this court as well. There is, 'limited availability of persons with the expertise necessary to qualify for the list of arbitrators' (p. 371). The court will not allow the parties to specify the law to govern a dispute; only court rules will be followed (p. 401). Enforcement of awards is difficult and not automatic (p. 420). As a result, relatively few disputes are brought to this court; Western businesses are more likely to name third country (often Swedish) arbitrators. Nonetheless, this court has the most experience in Russia of capitalist economic dealings. It is also beginning to publish its most important decisions, so that disputants may be able to determine in advance the likely outcome of an arbitration. This may also be a step towards a more common law-like process in Russia, as advocated earlier.

The 1995 Commercial Code

A newly adopted Commercial Code came into effect on 1 January 1995 (Russian Federation 1994). This consolidated and updated many laws, so that the law actually in use will be greatly improved. The new code is a definite advance over previous law. One severe problem has been inflation. In the past, with very high inflation rates, the value of settlements decreased substantially as there were delays in collection. Parts of the new code may address this issue. Article 337 says that, 'a pledge shall secure a demand in that amount which it has at the moment of satisfaction, in particular, interest, compensation of losses caused by delay of performance', and this may be interpreted as allowing some inflation adjustment. Payments for 'Maintenance of Citizen' (apparently compensation for lost wages and earnings) will be indexed with the minimum wage ('amount of payment for labour established by law': Article 319). On the other hand, the section on Bankruptcy of an Entrepreneur (Article 25) makes no similar provisions. Since bankruptcy is often used as a method of debt collection, this lack may be costly.[14]

However, the new code is by no means a panacea. Many difficulties remain. First, the judges are the same, and one serious problem with the legal system is the competence and ability of judges. Second, many problems stem from difficulties in enforcing decrees and rulings of the courts, and enforcement problems also remain. Third, while Article 11 indicates that there are three types of court, it does nothing to clarify their relationship. Fourth, there is an insufficient number of lawyers in Russia. Most Soviet era lawyers were criminal lawyers, and there were relatively few of them. Now there are too few lawyers for a large market economy and relatively few of these lawyers are skilled in commercial matters (Siltchenkov 1993). There are only 20,000 independent lawyers in Russia, and 28,000 public prosecutors. Although the USA has too many lawyers, Russia has only one-eighth as many (*Economist* 1995a, at 43).

Finally, the entire code is only 127 pages long and deals with several areas of law, including all of contract law, property law and the law of business associations. This means that there are of necessity large ambiguities in the law, and thus parties will remain uncertain about outcomes of litigation. It is planned that future parts of the code will correct some of these ambiguities, but they have yet to be written or adopted. Unless Russian courts are willing to adopt some sort of common law-type system to codify interpretations of the law, it will be difficult for litigants to predict the outcome of cases. To its credit, the law does indicate that in the event of interpretive uncertainty, the outcome of a dispute, 'shall be determined by the customs of business turnover applicable to the relations of the parties' (Article 419).

Thus while the revision in the Commercial Code is useful and needed, nonetheless, even after this revision, difficulties will remain.[15]

LEGAL FAILURES: EXAMPLES

Even if the law were well developed, the state would be required for enforcement. As indicated above, there is little evidence that the state is providing sufficient enforcement of contracts, even in those cases where there are court rulings. In addition, to establish credibility as an enforcer, it would be necessary for the state to hold itself to its own agreements. There is evidence that willingness to do so is lacking. Part of the problem is that there are several levels of government, and the central government may be lacking sufficient power to compel lower level governments to honour their agreements. A common pattern is for the government to offer terms to a foreign investor to induce specific investments in Russia and then opportunistically to change the terms so as to appropriate some or all of the quasi-rents associated with the investment.

Attorneys and others complain that new laws are passed with no thought to their consistency with existing law. This problem seems to be continuing. However, although numerous inconsistent and inefficient laws are passed, the lack of enforcement and implementation may serve to mitigate some of the problems created (Fogel 1995a). There are no legal provisions for ending joint ventures and allocating their property, so some potential transactors are reluctant to form such ventures. One strategy for dealing with such legal inconsistency is to enter the market on a small scale and observe what happens. Many foreign firms, for example, have small investments in Russia, often involving only the retailing of products. Poe (1993) recommends a similar strategy in determining the reliability of a potential Russian partner. To the extent that quicker or larger investments would occur if there were increased certainty, then the uncertainty is imposing real costs on the Russian economy.

Only 8 per cent of potential joint ventures begin operating (Kvint 1993, 181). Kvint estimates that 10 per cent of the failures of joint ventures are due to legal problems, 28 per cent to an inability to find an appropriate partner and 20 per cent to 'financing'. These difficulties may be exacerbated by legal problems. For example, difficulty in finding financing may be caused by poor property rights definitions or difficulty in foreclosing, making it difficult to use property as collateral. Finding a partner may be made more difficult because of contractual uncertainty. Thus the legal system may be responsible for a greater percentage of failures than is immediately apparent. Sixteen per cent of the failures are due to 'bureaucratic problems' that may also relate to legal uncertainty.

In one (randomly selected) week in May, 1993, the *Moscow Times*, a daily English language newspaper, reported the following examples of market interference and contractual uncertainty:[16]

From 9 April to 25 May, oil prices were controlled at levels well below market prices as a result of a politically motivated decree imposed before the election. As a result, Moscow suffered severe gasoline shortages. Some refineries had refused to sell in Moscow; two refineries had closed down. Even though the price was to rise, the new controlled price was 75 rubles per litre, while mobile tanks were already selling gasoline for 120 to 150 rubles per litre.

A Korean–Russian joint venture had invested $70 million in a timber project in eastern Russia since 1990. An environmental dispute went to the Russian Supreme Court which, 'failed to come to any concrete conclusion, sending the case back to the regional court'. There has also been a 'worsening tax situation'. While it was originally estimated that the venture would earn a profit by the fourth year, 'under current conditions it could take seven to 10 years'. Other potential investors are monitoring this situation closely.

De Beers had signed a five year contract with the Russian diamond marketing agency; now the 'Precious Metals and Stones Committee' is attempting to renegotiate this contract.

The Moscow city government changed the method of taxing land owned by joint ventures. Previously tax was paid at the same rate as that paid by Russians (about $3500 per hectare). Now the rate will range up to $465,000 per hectare, the rate paid by foreigners:

> The new decree is the latest in a series of changes in tax and landownership laws that have made it difficult for foreign and Russian firms to lease property for office space and development in the capital. In recent months, for example, the City Council has annulled leases signed by the mayor's office and passed legislation calling for lease agreements to be renegotiated.

These new tax rates mean that some past investments may not be profitable, and many would not have been undertaken.

Other examples can be cited from Tourevski and Morgan (1993): The Ministry of Foreign Economic Relations is creating an auditing board that will have the right to control or even shut down any independent entity engaged in foreign economic relations, and will be able to question the business decisions of entities subject to its control. Russian customs officials and later the KGB seized automobile batteries produced by an American–Russian joint venture because of a technicality in the joint venture charter. Customs officials refused permission for a Leningrad company to export scrap metal, even though the company had permission from the Russian Federation. A cooperative began to recover and process timber that had sunk during the process of floating it downstream and that otherwise was wasted. Within six months, the government shut down the operation, so that the timber continues to be wasted. A Russian magazine publisher contracted to trade waste paper for computers. However, it was denied a licence to export waste. Galuszka and Chandler (1995) indicate that there are additional problems with joint ventures. However, they also suggest that because of legal changes, joint ventures are no longer being formed as commonly as before, and that foreign companies investing directly in Russia have fewer difficulties.

Western oil companies might spend up to $70 billion annually to develop Russian oil fields were it not for fears of opportunism (Imse 1993). Much of this opportunism is by the government, which seems often to change rules or to increase export taxes in a way designed opportunistically to appropriate past investments. There is private opportunism as well. After one company had invested in machinery for drilling for Russian oil, the firm controlling the pipeline that provided the only route to the sea doubled its rates.

The Raddison Corporation negotiated an agreement with the Kremlin to build a hotel in Moscow. However, once the property was completed, Moscow city council demanded a partnership before allowing the hotel to open. Negotiations delayed the opening for about one year, and the city did get a partnership (Thomas and Sutherland 1992, 147).

Even where investment does occur, investors are aware that contracts are subject to great political uncertainty. Elf Aquitane, the French company, has signed a contract to explore for oil in Russia and Kazakhstan (Salpukas 1993). Other American oil companies have also signed contracts, but Elf's endeavour is the only one that is not part of a joint venture:

> Elf has the first of what is called a production agreement with Russia…but whether the contract will remain in effect as written remains uncertain…It took Elf about a year to get the deal approved by the Russian Parliament, but whether this gives the contract any legal force is still murky, given the struggle between President Boris Yeltsin and some leaders of the Parlia-

ment...A high official in the Tyumen Region, Russia's largest oil area, said there was a continuing tug of war between local officials and the ministers in Moscow over control of new ventures...In such an atmosphere, Elf's straightforward contract could be bent out of shape.[17]

Ikea, the Swedish furniture company, did plan to invest in producing goods as well as selling in Russia. In 1988, Ikea agreed to renovate a dozen Russian furniture factories to produce furniture that it planned to sell in stores it planned to open by 1991. However, the plan failed when the USSR collapsed. Ikea is involved in litigation and in arbitration in Stockholm. Ikea's Chief Executive, Anders Moberg, has been quoted as saying: 'Terrible problems untangling various obligations between the old USSR and the new republics have us much more cautious'. Ikea now plans to invest in Poland, Hungary and the Czech and Slovak Republics, but not in Russia (Moore 1993).

Komineft, a major Russian oil company, diluted its stock by about one-third without telling many stockholders, including foreign investors. However, the secret issue was ultimately reversed and the company agreed to move its shareholder register to Moscow (Banerjee (1995a), *Moscow Times* (1995)). Primorsky Sea Shipping recently doubled its number of shares and sold them to a subsidiary for $90,000, although the value of the firm was $36 million. Two other Russian shipping companies have undertaken similar transactions. So far, such transactions have been held to be legal (Liesman 1995a,b). Lebedinsky Mining Company diluted Rossisky Credit Bank's shares (Galuszka and Kranz 1995). However, one Russian investment fund was successful in replacing the management of Yaroslav Rubber Company (Galuszka and Kranz 1995).

White Nights is a joint venture formed to increase production from existing Russian oil fields (Goldman 1994). After the venture was formed, the Russians increased taxes several times and also required additional investments from the American partners. Goldman (p. 248) indicates that: 'Had they known there would have been such a confiscatory tax, the American partners would probably have negotiated different terms or not signed the contract at all'. Thus this is a classic example of *ex-post* opportunism, as quasi-rent extraction (Rubin 1990).

This seems to be continuing. Chevron is reducing its investment in Kazakhstan and Pennzoil and Gulf Canada resources, Inc. are trying to sell their investments, in part because of 'political chaos and onerous taxes'. One company that set up a joint venture has 'been hit by no fewer than 40 new regulations and taxes' and is almost bankrupt

(Liesman and du Bois 1995). Western investors in oil were originally told they could export the oil, but later were subject to export taxes, quotas and regulations. Export quotas change from month to month. One Western investor says that, 'Russian export and tax laws change with the wind' (Fogel and Reifenberg 1995). Lobbying, however, seems to be effective in muting the costs of some regulations: the oil quotas have been relaxed as a result of lobbying by oil producers (Fogel 1995a). On the other hand, Conoco has successfully developed an oil processing facility and pipeline, and is shipping oil. The return on investment so far is small, but the company views it as a learning mechanism. However, the venture will remain profitable only so long as a tax exemption on the oil export tax remains in effect (Galuszka 1994).

Prime Minister Chernomyrdin promised in the summer of 1994 that laws were in process to exempt foreign business from certain changes in law, but these had not been introduced by April 1995 (Craik 1995). Indeed a law that went into effect on 15 March 1995 removed several tax breaks that foreign investors had previously been promised (Mileusnic 1995a). Many firms planned investment strategies based on a December 1993 presidential decree exempting certain in-kind capital imports from a VAT; the new law may remove that exemption.

On 29 March 1995 the government announced that certain Western offices ('representative' offices, often used as an unprofitable first step to entering the Russian market) would be subject to a 35 per cent additional payroll tax on monthly wages above $25, and that this tax would be retroactive to 1 January 1994. Previously these offices had been exempt from this tax (Fogel 1995b; Galuszka and Dallas 1995). Officials removed a tax exemption on imported construction materials, leading to another large retroactive tax increase. Moreover, taxes often carry retroactive penalties of up to three times the tax itself (Galuszka and Dallas 1995). The capriciousness of the tax system discourages investment and makes planning difficult.

One effect of legal uncertainty is a high cost of doing business. Liesman (1995c) indicates that the rental for office space in Moscow is among the highest in the world, equivalent to rentals in Tokyo or New York. The explanation for such high rates seems to be risk. Much construction seems to be begun and then stopped because of, 'financing questions or problems with the bureaucratic city approval process'. Thus given these risks, rents must be high to compensate builders. These high rents then increase the cost of doing business in Moscow.

Widespread smuggling also creates difficulties (Winestock 1995). Firms that have paid import duties find themselves underpriced by smugglers. Moreover, high officials sometimes grant exemptions to favoured firms, allowing them legally to import with reduced taxes. Yeltsin has granted exemptions from import duties to the National Sports Fund, which now imports 60–80 per cent of all tobacco and alcohol. As a result, firms with no exemptions are less likely to import into the Russian market.

Tourevski and Morgan (1993, 166–7) indicate several areas in which respondents to interviews (Russian and foreign businessmen) have indicated weakness in the law. Indeed this weakness is a major theme of the book. Some problems with law are: vague, contradictory, inconsistent formulations; isolated law-making, divorced from international legislation; conflict between laws which had been centralized and the republics, between the republics themselves, or between the republics and their autonomous territories; and the instability of laws which are unclear and change from day to day.

A formal recent survey of investors has indicated the extent of the problems associated with an ineffective legal system (Craik 1995; Halligan and Teplukin 1995). According to the survey, the 'most important restraints to investment' are, 'fear for shareholder rights and weak contract law'. The story reporting the results of the survey begins: 'Russia's ever-shifting and poorly enforced legal system is by far the biggest single impediment to a much-needed investment boom that could provide the impetus for reform, a survey of domestic and international businesses operating here shows'.

Taxation, which reflects the fear of opportunism, is the second major reason for not investing in Russia. There is also an inability to find suitable business partners, reflecting the amount of uncertainty in the Russian economy and the unwillingness of firms to create valuable reputations. The survey is particularly significant since it indicates that even those businesses that have invested in Russia find the legal system an impediment. Presumably it has been even more of an impediment to those businesses that have considered such investment but decided against it. Indeed the level of investment in Russia is falling.

The survey indicates that the main legal problem is the difficulty of enforcing stock market investments, because of problems with share registers, such as those discussed above with respect to Komineft and Primorsky. The second major concern was contract law, 'which was seen as complex and difficult to implement'. Respondents indicate that the Civil Code has made an improvement but, 'businesses say that in practice, many courts lack the expertise to implement the system'. Apparently, broken promises by the government itself (as discussed in more detail below) are counted as part of the difficulty with contract law.

'Political instability' rated as only the third most serious concern. However, viewed in the framework adopted here, it may be that political instability, by reducing time horizons, has itself created some of the difficulties in establishing the needed certainty for contract law to function well. Fear of a lack of commitment to capitalism on the part of the government is the greatest political fear identified in the survey, and fear of renationalization is second. These fears are a major factor in creating the high discount rates that lead to the other identified problems.

Recently, the Executive Director of the Russian Securities Commission has defended the investment climate in Russia (Vasiliev 1995). However, as of July 1995, the strongest arguments made are that, 'regulations *now being written* will govern all aspects of market activity' and, '*soon*, the Securities Commission will also have formal enforcement mechanisms at its disposal' (emphasis added). Vasiliev does claim that some companies have adequately protected shareholder rights, but the example given (the Red October chocolate factory) is a company needing additional capital. However, the *Economist* (1995a) does indicate that several reforms are being planned or implemented to make the Russian stock market more reliable. Kranz (1995b) indicates that there are institutions that register shares, such as the Moscow Central Depository, and that Chase Manhattan Bank has a cooperative arrangement with this organization. She indicates that certainty and stability in the stock market are increasing (1995a,b). Liesman (1995d) indicates that, as of October 1995, American investors were reluctant to invest in Russia, in part because new securities, tax reform and corporate laws promised by the government had not yet been passed. Articles in the US business press sometimes advise against investing in Russia (for example, Dunkin 1995).

POLITICAL BASES FOR LEGAL UNCERTAINTY

These examples indicate difficulties with the political system of Russia, rather than with the legal system itself. In order for such problems to be corrected, political reform is needed. The sort of remedies proposed in this work are only available in economies where those with political power have the will to impose reforms; they cannot be used where such will is lacking.

Political stability will support legal reform in another way. Part of the difficulty with contract enforcement is caused by uncertainty. Many of the mechanisms discussed here depend on reputations and on other long-term investments (for example, in self-enforcing agreements). If parties believe that legal or property institutions are likely to change in the near future, they will be willing to invest less in such agreements. This may explain the widely noted tendency of Russian negotiators to drive excessively difficult bargains, discussed above. Such bargaining may mean that the Russian participants receive lower long-term returns from the agreement, but if parties have short time horizons this will be less significant.

Short time horizons may also explain some otherwise puzzling behaviour of political authorities. If a political authority radically changes the tax rate faced by businesses, then this can be profitable in the short run because the jurisdiction can appropriate the quasi-rents from the completed investment. However, this policy has long-term costs because other businesses will be less willing to invest in this jurisdiction. But a short time horizon means that the present value of the appropriated investments can outweigh the long-term losses from lost future investments.

Again the problem is uncertainty. If governments breach agreements, they can expect greatly reduced future investment as other potential investors refrain from investing. However, if the relevant officials do not expect the government to last, there is less cost from opportunism and such appropriation becomes more likely. Other potential transactors, observing that the state does not even honour its own agreements, would understandably place relatively little weight on the state as a neutral enforcer of other contracts.[18] Cowley (1995) indicates that this uncertainty has caused the market to place low values on Russian assets. For example, a barrel of oil owned by a Western company is valued at $5.50; by a Russian company, at $0.10. Boettke (1995) indicates that this uncertainty about the stability of government policies and commitment of the government to particular reforms is a continuation of similar uncertainty from the Soviet era. Since such uncertainty and unpredictability have a long history in Russia, it may be difficult to convince the people that any given policy or reform will be stable.

The Coase theorem (Coase 1960) shows that with well-defined property rights and sufficiently low transaction costs, the final use of resources is efficient and invariant with respect to initial rights assignments. Most criticisms of the theorem have focused on the second condition – the magnitude of transaction costs. However, the situation in Russia today is one in which the theorem may not hold because the first condition, the existence of well-defined property rights, is not satisfied. The problem is not anarchy; the situation may be worse than in anarchy. Rather it is the existence of too many governments, with lines of power insufficiently well defined between them. Property rights are not well defined because it is not clear who has the power to define them. The result is that resources will not be used efficiently. It is essential that this problem is solved for any degree of economic progress to be feasible.

For private enforcement mechanisms to function requires investments of exactly the sort that may not be worthwhile given the levels of uncertainty in Russia today. Required investments are of several sorts. The simplest is investment in reputation for honesty. By demonstrating a willingness to refrain from exploiting a situation to its fullest (as, for example, by not offering high quality and supplying low quality goods when detection of quality is impossible before purchase), a firm can establish a reputation for honesty. However, this investment will pay only with sufficiently low discount rates. Otherwise the gains from exploiting the immediate situation will outweigh the gains from greater future profits.

Similarly, self-enforcing agreements work only because the present value of future profits from the expected sequence of exchanges between two parties is greater than the immediate gains from cheating. This again is a form of investment and requires sufficiently low discount rates to make the agreement actually self-enforcing.

It is important to separate multilateral mechanisms that are open to any member from those based on religious or ethnic solidarity (Landa 1981). The traditional pattern of trade in Russia has been based on such ethnic or cultural groups. Greif (1994) indicates that this pattern of trade is associated with 'collectivist' as opposed to 'individualist' culture, and that the latter is more common in developed economies. Here I am concerned with individualist associations, that is, those not based on personal relationships. While groups based on ethnic solidarity are useful for some purposes, such groups enable trade to occur only between members. Valuable transactions with non-members become impossible, and therefore resources are unable to flow to their highest valued use. (Such ethnic solidarity is also often the basis for criminal gangs, in Russia and elsewhere, for the same reason: contract enforcement by courts is unavailable to criminals.)

The argument advanced here has both normative and positive implications for Russia. The normative implication is that agents should form groups based on characteristics other than ethnic solidarity. Businesses should actively seek to generate such organizations, and advisers to businesses should suggest the formation of such associations. Governments should facilitate the formation of groups engaging in multilateral enforcement. Such facilitation should be active, as by passing laws encouraging the formation of multilateral enforcement mechanisms. The most important such law would be to agree to enforce private arbitration decisions where the parties have agreed to voluntary arbitration. Government should provide passive support, as by not overzealously applying antitrust laws to such groups. The new Russian Commercial Code does indicate that: 'The creation of associations of commercial and/or non-commercial organizations in the form of associations (or unions) shall be permitted' (Article 50). This means that there is a possibility for such multilateral enforcement organizations to form.

The positive implication is that we should expect to observe spontaneous formation of associations applying the sort of enforcement mechanisms discussed above. That is, we would expect to observe voluntary formation of trade associations and other groups whose purpose is enforcement of agreements in exactly the ways discussed above. We would expect two types of such organization. First, groups analogous to trade associations would be expected to govern relations between firms in an industry. Members of such groups should be firms in the industry. Second, there should be groups of firms in different industries within a geographic region. These organizations should govern relations between member firms and consumers or suppliers who are not in the same industry. These would be analogous to US Better Business Bureaus, but with more enforcement power with respect to members. I have information on several groups of the second sort – those dealing with several businesses in a given geographic area.

PRIVATE MECHANISMS: EXAMPLES

Self-Regulatory Broker Associations

Regional trading associations of brokers have been established with the encouragement of the recently empowered Russian Federation Commission on Securities and Exchanges and with the assistance of US government-financed resident advisers. These associations will be self-regulating, with a director of enforcement and compliance rules based on US and international standards. So far, four have been established.

These groups have compliance rules and a director of enforcement. It is intended that complaints will be heard by a panel that has the power to issue various sanctions, including publicity, warnings, fines, restitution and suspension or expulsion of the violating member. There is also a possibility of arbitration (called 'the committee to settle disputes' since 'arbitration' has a different meaning in Russian law). However, there appears to be some reluctance to apply the expected sanctions for breach of agreement with respect to the first complaints in the Moscow association. Thus a group exists, as predicted, but so far has been unwilling to apply the expected sanctions for breach of agreements. Mileusnic (1995b) indicates that the Duma has removed the provision allowing self-enforcement from the current draft securities law, perhaps to facilitate bribes to government enforcers. Rulings such as these can do nothing but harm.

Shareholder Rights

Seven large industrial firms and investment funds have recently signed an agreement with respect to shareholder rights (Dubik 1994b). These firms have agreed to provide detailed audited financial information to shareholders and to have independent managers maintain possession and control of shareholder registers so that shareholders can be guaranteed that their holdings will indeed be registered. The agreement bans insider trading and regulates voting by shareholders. The method of enforcement is unclear, but presumably, since the promises of the firms relate to public activities, expulsion from the association would be simple.

Such self-regulatory organizations seem to be having some positive effects. At least three associations (the Association of Broker-Dealers, the League of Investment Funds and the Russian Association of Investment Funds) have been established and undertake some self-policing. For example, when one fund went bankrupt as a result of fraud by management, the League of Investment Funds took it over and has generated some returns for investors. The Association of Broker-Dealers is arbitrating a dispute between two large firms, Troika Dialog and First Voucher Investment Fund (Banerjee 1995b). This is particularly important because the court system has apparently failed to resolve this dispute (Tolkacheva 1995).

On the other hand, significant problems with shareholder rights still exist and investors view these as being highly troublesome, as discussed above. Some firms have refused to list new investors as stockholders, or to allow them to attend meetings. More recently, some firms have unilaterally diluted investments. Managers as lobbyists and members of parliament have succeeded in blocking much legislation that would address this problem (Liesman 1995b). In a survey of 27 Russian privatized firms, Gurkov and Asselbergs (1995, 209) find that managers in all cases have, 'developed several effective mechanisms to ensure their total control over company assets'. The appearance is that determinedly opportunistic firms will be able to devise mechanisms to expropriate investments. This will deter investment. Firms needing capital have refrained from such behaviour, but other firms have not (Liesman 1995b; see also Black *et al.* 1995).

Commodities Exchanges

One class agency that does perform exactly the functions identified above is the 'commodities exchange'. These are trading centres, with many firms as members. Zhurek (1993, 42) indicates that the International Food Exchange offers a variety of services, including, 'arbitration for the rapid settlement of trade disputes'. Volume on this exchange is low, but the Moscow Commodities Exchange did over $500 million in business in May 1991 (Thomas and Sutherland 1992, 136).

There are at least 165 commodities exchanges in Russia and 20 in Moscow (Wegren 1994). Participants understand that methods of dispute resolution between participants are necessary. Moreover, most exchanges require a recommendation from two members and an examination of financial and reputational capital before admitting a new member. However, there does not seem to be a strong system of enforcement of promises. Contracts are often not honoured and payments are often not made. In 1992, approximately 30 per cent of contracts were not fulfilled.

Brokers will sometimes offer their wares on several exchanges and choose the best deal, paying a small fine to the exchanges where promises have been broken. This appears to be because of weaknesses in the exchanges themselves. Buyers and sellers often use the exchange to establish contacts, but conclude deals 'on the side' in order to avoid paying the commission to the exchange and to avoid taxes. Thus while these exchanges would be in a position to enforce agreements if they could govern trade, they seem to be too weak to do so under current conditions. Frye (1995) indicates that members are unwilling to use arbitration courts associated with the exchanges because this would require providing public information about trades that would make taxation of the trades easy.

Additional Mechanisms

Greif and Kandel (1995) report on several related mechanisms. There are several private arbitration courts, including courts set up by commodities exchanges, banking associations and the Bar Association. In 1993 over 100 companies (Russian and foreign) each paid a fee to establish the Moscow Commercial Court, a permanent arbitration committee. The Moscow Arbitration Court will enforce its decisions. Additionally, 'business groups' are associations of businessmen that join together for one-time deals. However, members will engage in several such deals over time. If anyone reneges, they will be prohibited from participating in future deals. These voluntary groups based on multiple interlocking transactions are not cultural or ethnic groups, but they do have common interests and a common code of behaviour.

Cooperatives in Russia have formed two types of association for lobbying purposes (Jones and Moskoff 1991). Some are geographically organized, and include businesses in a particular area. Others are essentially trade associations and include cooperatives in the same business sector. Associations of cooperatives provide services to members, including legal assistance, and pursue a political programme. Two major organizations are the USSR Union of Amalgamated Cooperatives (founded in 1989) and the Union of Leaseholders and Entrepreneurs (1990) (Jones 1992). Representatives of the cooperative movement were involved in decision-making regarding legislation. Again, these structures correspond to the types of potential multilateral organization discussed above, but there is no evidence that these organizations presently perform such functions.

Tourevski and Morgan (1993) indicate that the Soviet Chamber of Commerce has begun performing an information function. This organization publishes a directory regarding foreign trade participants, including information about financial positions and business reputations. Other organizations perform similar functions. Some private organizations also provide such business information. The accounting firm of Ernst & Young has established a joint venture that provides information about various aspects of doing business, including information about 'reliability of the partners' and several other private ventures are providing such information. However, Tourevski and Morgan believe that there is a dearth of useful business information. This has been exacerbated because for a time Soviet private firms were prohibited from performing 'middleman' functions.

Moreover, a fear of organized crime may contribute to the unwillingness of firms to provide public information. The head of one association, the Russian Business Round Table, has recently been poisoned. His associates indicate that the motive may have been the unwillingness of the Association to allow criminal firms to join (Stanley 1995). More generally, any public information useful for establishing a reputation can be used by criminals to target profitable or successful firms for purposes of extortion. This is only one aspect of the danger to the Russian economy from criminal enterprises.

CRIMINALS AS ENFORCERS?

It may be that criminals will act as enforcers for contracts. Leitzel *et al.* (1995) claim that the 'main benefit' of the Mafia is contract enforcement. Similarly, Erlanger (1994) says that, 'the inability to get redress through the courts leads to more crime, as businesses hire muscle to enforce deals otherwise unenforceable'. Black *et al.* (1995, 21–2) indicate that violence is a real option in enforcement of corporate law. Aslund (1995, 169) also suggests that, 'banks take recourse to using gangsters, who force people to pay under threat of physical harm'. Kranz (1995a) indicates that, 'with the judicial system in shambles...Guns, bombs and grenades take the place of arbitration courts'.

On the other hand, Greif and Kandel (1995, 308) indicate that: 'There is no evidence that gangs actively enforced contracts except in those cases that directly concerned their interests'. (Leitzel *et al.* provide no evidence for their claim and neither do Black *et al.*) Greif and Kandel do indicate (p. 316) that with respect to security firms, 'contract enforcement on their part would be natural'. Handelman (1995) discusses the role of criminals as debt collectors at various places in his study of organized crime in Russia (for example, pp. 69, 168). However, whenever he mentions the debt collection function of thugs, he also indicates that they 'stave off unfriendly creditors' and 'intimidate creditors' so that there may be no net effect. Handelman indicates that gangsters have become associated with many firms, and that such associations are a normal and necessary part of doing business in Russia.[19] Such associations would be consistent with the claim of Greif and Kandel, that criminals collect only their own debts. Kranz (1995a) indicates that 40,000 enterprises in Russia may have Mafia connections, and that the Mafia sometimes infiltrates big business by first extending loans and then demanding management control.

Aslund (1995, 169–70) indicates that one-third of bank employees are security guards, indicating that banks either use these guards to fight the Mafia or that banks are 'infested with the Mafia'. Kranz (1995a) indicates that criminals sometimes try to take over companies by taking control of the company's bank, and that, 'as many as 10 of Russia's big banks may also have Mafia connections'.

However, while data are obviously lacking, there are reasons to doubt that the Mafia will actually provide an efficient level of contract enforcement. In particular, the discount rate is again relevant. A criminal gang hired to collect a debt has two options: keep the entire debt or turn over the contractual share to the original creditor. Which strategy is optimal depends on the discount rate. If this is high enough, then the gang may forgo the future gains from additional enforcement contracts and simply keep the money (or even extort additional money). If discount rates are sufficiently high, then creditors, expecting criminals to keep the debt, will not hire them and there will not be contractual enforcement by criminals.

Intriligator (1994) argues that the Mafias have very short time horizons. (He also claims that criminalization is destroying the Russian economy.) Even Leitzel *et al.* (1995), who are more optimistic regarding the role of the Mafia than Intriligator, believe that the mafiosi have short time horizons because of uncertainty. Handelman's suggestion that criminals are equity owners in many firms and Kranz's (1995a) discussion of this issue are consistent with this argument. Aslund (1995) is overall optimistic about the future of Russia, but even he admits

(p. 171) that, 'if no serious action is taken [with respect to crime], the legitimacy of democratic rule will be undermined'.

RUSSIA: SUMMARY

The evidence cited here is largely anecdotal. Data are lacking for a more systematic examination of the issues. However, potential investors in Russia are confronted with the same problem, and the data used here may be similar to the data used by such investors. As indicated above, the problems identified are the same as the problems that investors consider in making decisions about future commitments (Craik 1995; Halligan and Teplukin 1995).

There is insufficient ability to enforce contracts in Russia today. The law is weak, and even when decisions are obtained from courts, enforcement of decisions is often difficult. As a result, parties use private mechanisms for such enforcement. However, the power of such mechanisms is also weak. Firms have not yet established valuable reputations, so that they do not have valuable reputation capital to use to guarantee agreements. There are barriers to creation of such reputations, in the form of fear of expropriation by criminals or by tax collectors, or by corrupt officials. Some multilateral enforcement organizations have been formed, and these are aware of the problems associated with contract enforcement. However, many of them do not seem willing or able actually to take the steps needed to enforce agreements.

What does this mean? Things are bad, but perhaps improving. The question is, will they improve fast enough to enable Russia to become a fully developed economy, or will the economy remain trapped in a low level institutional equilibrium? We know from the examples of the Czech Republic, Hungary and Poland that it is possible for an economy to emerge successfully from the wasteland created by communism. However, since the situation is unique in human history, I cannot at this time predict if Russia will succeed or not. Greif's (1994) argument that collectivist cultures are less likely to be economically developed is one piece of evidence that would lead to pessimism, but it is by no means definitive. The December 1995 elections do not suggest optimism.

The true danger may be that if the legal system cannot function, then the criminal underground may become more and more powerful in both market and non-market activities (Erlanger 1994; Intriligator 1994; Handelman 1995; Kranz 1995a). Jeffrey Sachs (1995), a former adviser to the Russian government, indicates that 'Russia's corruption is singularly deep' and appears pessimistic about the future. George Soros, a well-known successful investor in Eastern Europe, indicates that, although he is investing in Russia because of the potential return, he is 'cautiously pessimistic' about the country. He believes the country is dominated by 'robber capitalism', defined as a 'breakdown of legal and financial controls', and that the economy is characterized as a struggle between rival gangs, including the communists as one such gang (Gordon 1995).[20]

On the other hand, Aslund (1994, 1995) believes that Russia is on the road to a successful transition. Galuszka *et al.* (1994), in a special *Business Week* report, indicate optimism and suggest that Russia has begun to develop and is no longer in danger of collapse. Poe (1993) believes that Russia will prosper, and his book (aimed at potential American investors in Russia) refers in its title to the 'Coming Russian Boom'. But Tourevski and Morgan (1993) and Kvint (1993) in books aimed at the same audience are less optimistic.

As I have stressed throughout, the issue is predictability. If the system becomes sufficiently stable and predictable to make investment in the creation of a rule of law and a set of contract-enforcing institutions worthwhile, then the problems I have discussed will be solved. If this happens, then I believe that the other problems facing the Russian economy will also become manageable. If the system continues to be unpredictable and if agents continue to lack faith in the future, then the problems will persist. At this time I cannot determine which will happen. Agnosticism is appropriate.

The situation in Russia is perhaps typical of what Tainter (1988, 19–20) indicates commonly occurs after the collapse of a complex society:

> With disintegration, central direction is no longer possible. The former political center undergoes a significant loss of prominence and power. It is often ransacked and may ultimately be abandoned. Small, petty states emerge in the formerly unified territory, of which the former capital may be one. Quite often these contend for domination, so that a period of perpetual conflict ensues. The umbrella of law and protection erected over the populace is eliminated. Lawlessness may prevail for a time...but order will ultimately be restored.[21]

Although the collapse of the Soviet Union fulfils many of the conditions discussed by Tainter, one may hope that Russia can avoid the most grim of these ramifications.

7. Government Policy

So far I have discussed private actions to create mechanisms for private enforcement. However, government can facilitate these mechanisms in various ways. Such facilitation can have two beneficial effects. First, by increasing the ability of agents to enter into agreements, the amount of beneficial transactions can increase. Second, by choice of proper policies, government can facilitate the creation of a body of precedent that can ultimately be used to create the beginnings of an efficient body of law.

I have in mind the following rough institutional structure. There is a court system in existence. This system has some rough notion of contract law. It may, for example, believe in 'freedom of contract' and in allowing voluntary private exchanges. However, there is not a complete body of contract law in place, so that decisions of the court system in resolving actual disputes will be somewhat uncertain.

In addition, it is likely that there are delays in reaching the court system. In a world of high inflation, these delays may be particularly costly if court awards are made in nominal currency units, which may be happening in Russia (private comment of Harold Berman). Unindexed contracts and court unwillingness to alter contractual terms were responsible for an epidemic of non-payment in inter-war Germany (Wolf 1993). Thus other mechanisms may be chosen where feasible.

In this section, I deal with two types of policy. Some policies will facilitate the formation of private agreements. However, it is also possible for incorrect government policies to penalize efficient conduct. Judging from past experience in the USA, misuse of antitrust policies is particularly likely to be costly. Even in the USA antitrust has often erred and punished pro-competitive conduct. In post-communist economies, where there may be an excessive fear of 'monopoly capitalism', such misuse may be particularly likely. All relevant antitrust statutes contain provisions that could lead to inefficient rulings (Pittman 1992; Gray and Associates 1993).

Of course, in analysing efficient government policy there is the issue of whether the government actually wants to adopt such policies. Efficient private law policies such as those discussed in this work may be easier to adopt than public law policies, because the role of interest groups is reduced in private law policies. This issue is discussed in more detail in the final chapter. Here I assume that the government wants efficient policies, and discuss their nature.

I analyse policy in the same tripartite framework used for analysing private enforcement mechanisms.

UNILATERAL MECHANISMS

The most important assistance governments can give to private firms for the creation of reputation capital is a willingness to enforce property rights in trademarks. Trademarks allow buyers to determine the quality of purchased goods and therefore enable sellers to invest in provision of high quality. All countries studied seem to have more or less appropriate trademark law on the books, but enforcement is uncertain and penalties may be inadequate.

If counterfeiting and trademark infringement are not sufficiently penalized, then there will be reduced incentives for firms to invest in brand name capital. Given that law enforcement authorities apparently lack adequate resources optimally to enforce laws against counterfeiting, we may identify a second best solution. This is to allow firms whose products are the subject of counterfeiting to enforce rights privately. Such firms would have the right to seize counterfeit goods and sell them on the market (presumably after removing the counterfeit trademark). It can be shown that this policy will not lead to optimal enforcement against counterfeiting, but it is preferable to no or to minimal public enforcement (Higgins and Rubin 1986). Some Western movie companies (including MGM, Warner, Sony and Paramount), have been training and financing full-time, private anti-piracy investigators for enforcement in Hungary. We would want to be sure, however, that such private enforcement was subject to ultimate control by the state, perhaps by allowing an appeal by the target firm.

Beyond this, governments can facilitate other investments in the creation of valuable brand names. Advertising is one prominent method of such investment. Government-owned radio and TV channels (if they cannot feasibly be privatized) should allow advertising. In Russia, as of

1993, 'the three television stations are government owned and run very limited advertising' (Tourevski and Morgan 1993, 105). However, more recently the amount of advertising on Russian TV has increased (Kranz 1994). As a result, many American brand names (Coca Cola, Procter & Gamble, Mars) are becoming well known in Russia. There is a private TV channel in the Czech Republic that sells substantial amounts of advertising (Durcanin 1995).

The Moscow and St Petersburg city governments have passed laws requiring one half of the words on all signs to be in Russian (Cyrillic) script, and that the Russian words must be twice as large as the others (Levine 1993). Such a law is harmful for several reasons. First, it increases the costs of advertising by requiring reconstruction of many signs. Second, it reduces the value of brand names, since companies would have chosen to advertise in whatever way would be most informative to consumers and mandated changes in advertising will therefore provide less information. Finally, by indicating to potential advertisers that they are willing arbitrarily and capriciously to destroy part of the value of past advertising, the government is reducing incentives for future investments in brand names.

In enforcing laws against deception, authorities should be careful not to over-regulate and deter the provision of valuable information (Rubin 1991). Provisions of the various laws regarding deception are sufficiently open-ended so that excess regulation is quite possible. It is particularly important to note that advertising is most likely to appear deceptive in a market that is not in equilibrium. Advertising in this context can be a powerful force for moving markets closer to equilibrium if it is allowed to do so.

In the post-communist economies, all markets may currently be out of equilibrium, and may remain so for some time. Moreover, consumers are likely to have relatively little experience or sophistication in dealing with advertising. Thus in the short run, much advertising might appear deceptive. However, excess regulation will reduce the rate of convergence of markets towards equilibrium, and increase the time it takes for consumers to learn how effectively to deal with advertising. Thus over-regulation is particularly likely and particularly costly in these economies.

Governments should keep in mind that an important incentive for the provision of quality is the higher price a firm can command for higher quality. At times (and particularly until markets have adjusted), those firms providing high quality will earn high profits. These profits will serve as a signal to other potential entrants that the provision of quality is worthwhile. However, authorities must be very careful not to reduce these incentives, for example by regulating (perhaps in the name of antitrust laws) prices charged. As entry occurs prices will naturally fall, but there must be rewards (perhaps very high rewards) for entrepreneurs who first learn the techniques valuable in a market economy.

BILATERAL MECHANISMS

There is relatively little government can do to facilitate bilateral agreements. Self-enforcing agreements, for example, do not need government assistance.

There is, however, substantial danger that improper and excessive use of antitrust policy could hinder the creation of bilateral arrangements. This fear is not based on pure speculation. In the USA improper antitrust policy has greatly hindered the creation of valuable vertical relationships between manufacturers and retailers (Posner 1981; Easterbrook 1984). Any contract between a manufacturer and a retailer should be strictly enforced by whatever enforcement mechanism is specified. The antitrust laws in all countries are sufficiently open-ended so that wealth-reducing over-regulation is at least possible.

Many of these antitrust laws apply only to firms with 'dominant' positions, commonly defined as market shares of 30 per cent or more. However, market shares are difficult to measure without sophisticated methods of defining markets. In US antitrust enforcement, market definition is often the most difficult and contested part of an enforcement action. Thus excessive enforcement is possible if decision-makers define markets too narrowly, as is likely and as has traditionally been true of US antitrust authorities. Aslund (1995, 153) indicates that markets have been narrowly defined in Russia. The Hungarian and CFR laws make it easier for a firm to be defined as a 'dominant' firm than is true in Poland and Russia, although any of the laws could be interpreted as excessively enforcing rules penalizing dominance.

One method of establishing credible commitments for bilateral relationships is the use of hostages. These require reciprocal dealing between firms; the antitrust laws have sometimes penalized this sort of behaviour. The Russian antitrust law forbids, 'imposing on the other party contractual terms that are disadvantageous to him or which are irrelevant to the subject-matter of the contract'. Other countries also forbid such practices. This can be interpreted as forbidding reciprocal transactions and the use of hostages. Again there should be no such restriction. All reciprocal transactions between firms should be legal.

It does not appear at this time that the antitrust laws are being abused. Many businessmen and attorneys indicate that there is a potential for abuse, but there does not seem to be a record of such behaviour. The Czech antitrust agency is located outside Prague, perhaps to weaken the agency and so minimize the danger of excessive enforcement. Similarly, the Polish antitrust agency is in Krakow, not Warsaw. Aslund (1995) indicates that in the past Russian anti-monopoly policy was excessively stringent, but that since 1994 it has been reformed and is likely less harmful.

MULTILATERAL ARRANGEMENTS

Governments have the greatest ability to be helpful with respect to multilateral enforcement mechanisms. Assistance can be provided to enable parties to benefit from such methods of enforcement by agreeing to enforce the decisions of arbitrators. Moreover, if properly done, governments can use the results of multilateral processes to generate efficient law. As of 1993, Poland was the only country studied that would enforce private arbitration agreements between domestic firms.

There are incentives for parties to contracts to choose efficient arbitrators in their agreements. Thus a decision by the courts or a statutory announcement that the courts will honour and enforce arbitration agreements may be the single most powerful method available for achieving efficient short-run decisions and also for generating efficient long-run precedents. (For reasons discussed below, the law may want to announce that it will enforce arbitration agreements only if there is a written opinion from the arbitrator in addition to a decision.)

As with other mechanisms, there is a danger of misuse of antitrust law with respect to trade associations. In particular, it will sometimes be necessary to exclude some firms from the association in order to maintain quality. However, incorrect antitrust law can interpret such exclusion as being an anti-competitive boycott. Moreover, the Russian antitrust law requires that all such associations be approved by the antitrust authorities. This could make the formation of such organizations more difficult. Correct interpretation will be difficult, as such associations can indeed be used for anti-competitive exclusion.

8. Creation of Efficient Rules

The private mechanisms discussed here can be used as the basis for an efficient body of law. I first discuss the mechanisms for such law creation. I then discuss some of the benefits of private law creation. In particular, private law may have some advantages over public law.

MECHANISMS

One advantage of the set of institutions proposed here (and in particular of the multilateral institutions) is that these may actually lead to the evolution of efficient rules. There are mechanisms that might lead a formal legal system to evolve efficient rules, but the power of these mechanisms is limited (Rubin 1977; Landes and Posner 1979). Competing jurisdictions and competition between judges may be the most efficient method of achieving efficient rules quickly. Indeed the common law courts adopted the relatively efficient rules of the private Law Merchant in order to obtain the legal business (and associated fees) of merchants. For such competition to be effective, parties must be able to choose *ex ante* which court will hear their dispute because this will give courts incentives to seek efficient solutions to get more business. In the system in Russia, although there are three separate court systems, they do not seem to compete *ex ante* for business, and parties do not seem able *ex ante* to choose the court that will hear their dispute.

When parties negotiate contracts in good faith (that is, without plans to breach), they will consider methods of enforcement. Generally speaking, breach of a contract will occur only in the event of unanticipated events, so parties cannot know *ex ante* the nature of a breach or the desired remedies. Therefore, the interest of parties *ex ante* is to choose those arbitrators who will maximize the *ex post* joint wealth of the parties – that is, who will choose efficient rules for enforcement. If these arbitrators then establish rules through announcing the reasons for their decisions, the rules will tend to be efficient. If they are not, then disputants in the future will choose different arbitrators. There will be strong pressures for arbitrators who use efficient rules.

Landes and Posner (1979) argue that there is sometimes an inadequate incentive for arbitration to produce rules (as opposed to decisions) because the creation of rules does not benefit the parties who pay for dispute settlement. The rule is a public good whose private value may be less than the cost to the disputants. This has been questioned on factual grounds by Benson (1990), who points out that the Law Merchant did produce rules that were later adopted into the common law. Moreover, Benson suggests that if parties contract in advance with arbitrators, then arbitrators have an incentive to make the rules they will use in the event of a dispute clear in order to facilitate settlement and reduce the number of cases actually arbitrated.

Landes and Posner (1979) agree that there are circumstances in which rules will be created. If the arbitration is performed for an association, then rule creation is feasible because the association can collect dues and use these to pay for rules. The Law Merchant evolved at least in part in connection with trade fairs (one example is the Champagne Fairs), and therefore there was a possibility of creating efficient rules because all participants in the Fairs would have been willing to pay a share for such rule creation and the organizers could have charged a premium to support this outcome (Milgrom *et al.* 1990). As suggested above, a possible method to generate rules would be for the state to agree to enforce arbitration agreements only if the arbitrator agrees to write an opinion.

For private associations, dues could be used to supplement fees paid by disputants and therefore pay for rule creation and promulgation. The rules would benefit all members of the association, not merely those with a dispute at issue, and so members would be willing to pay dues to obtain such rules. Associations depend on members for dues. Firms would be more likely to join associations if the associations credibly promised them efficient rules. Customary rules used in an industry are a likely source of efficient precedents (Epstein 1992; Cooter 1994), and the mechanisms identified here are useful for generation of formal records of such customs. Bernstein (1995) is undertaking a major study of such private associations, and her results should be directly relevant for the issues raised here.

CHARACTERISTICS OF PRIVATE LAW

There will be other advantages of private law. Although it is not possible to describe the details of efficient contract law for each country at each point in time, some broad properties of such law can be described. This is particularly true since American contract law is in some respects inefficient, and it is possible to identify the areas of inefficiency.

In particular, law can err by refusing to enforce voluntarily agreed upon contract terms. In the USA and elsewhere today, courts brand certain types of contract as being 'against public policy'. Such contracts may be considered 'unconscionable'. The courts claim that the parties had 'unequal bargaining power' or that the relevant contracts were 'contracts of adhesion'. Such rulings are particularly common in contracts between individuals and business firms, but sometimes apply to other contracts as well. In these cases, courts will refuse to enforce the contracts.

None of these doctrines is desirable. In all cases, they make the parties to transactions worse off. All of these doctrines have been imposed by courts on parties who have signed contracts with provisions that, *ex post* (after breach, or after an accident) one of the parties has regretted. If there is private enforcement of contracts, then courts will not adopt any such inefficient provisions; courts will enforce contracts as written. Thus private enforcement will lead to a more efficient contract law than would public enforcement, if public enforcement follows the US example.

Of course, there are some contracts that are inefficient. However, these are generally inefficient with respect to third parties. Two examples are contracts to fix prices and contracts to commit a crime. These sorts of agreement can be eliminated by other branches of law: the antitrust laws[22] and criminal laws Moreover, since such contracts are illegal, the parties would want to keep them secret, and thus would not rely on the sort of private mechanisms discussed here, even if these mechanisms could lead to enforcement. Thus with respect to those contracts that are economically efficient and socially desirable, it is likely that there would be some advantages to private enforcement relative to public enforcement. Indeed the best of all worlds might be private determination of liability (as by arbitrators or trade associations) with public enforcement of the private decrees.

Two-party contracts might be inefficient if one party to the contract is incompetent. This might apply to contracts with children or with the mentally incompetent on one side. Contracts will also be inefficient if there is fraud or duress, where duress is defined as involving force, not 'unequal bargaining power' (Posner 1992, 114–17) or 'unconscionability' (Epstein 1976). The medieval Law Merchant, a voluntary body of contract law, would invalidate a contract based on, 'fraud, duress, or other abuses of the will or knowledge of either party' (Benson 1989, 649). Thus private law should be able to handle these problems of inefficient contract formation.

9. Implications

This work provides suggestions for behaviour for governments, arbitrators, private trade associations, private attorneys and businesses in the post-communist economies. I consider each.

Before discussing particular policies, however, a word about Russia is needed. The policy discussion assumes that those in authority desire to develop a market economy and to maximize social wealth, perhaps subject to normal political constraints. This may not be true in Russia. If it is not, then more fundamental change, going beyond the analysis in this work (or beyond the normal suggestions of economists in policy matters) is needed. The nature of the changes was discussed in Chapter 6. Specifically, government must honour its own commitments and enforce promises made by others. If the Russian government can credibly promise to do so, then development is possible. If not, then the country may remain trapped in a low level, crime-ridden equilibrium. Here I deal with policies useful for economies where authorities do want a more efficient market economy. The examples of Poland, Hungary and the Czech Republic indicate that it is possible to succeed in creating institutions to emerge from the wreckage created by communism.

Public choice economists treat government policy as the product of self-interested behaviour by politicians and interest groups. From an extreme public choice viewpoint, policy recommendations may not be useful because existing policies are the product of the set of politically effective pressures that exists in a society at a point in time. There are two points to make with respect to the issues analysed here.

First, it may be possible to use existing interest group pressures to develop more efficient policies. In their discussion of privatization, Boycko *et al.* (1994) explicitly discuss the use of public choice theory in designing privatization schemes that can benefit from the set of interests in place. Since the authors of this article were also instrumental in designing the relatively successful Russian privatization scheme, we must judge this effort as being useful.

Second, this work deals with private law issues, such as contract law. While it is sometimes possible for special interest groups to use private law mechanisms for rent-seeking (Rubin and Bailey 1994) the circumstances under which this is possible are limited. In particular, Rubin and Bailey show that lawyers can sometimes change the law in ways to benefit themselves. However, this possibility is not likely in Russia. First, there are not enough lawyers, and they are not sufficiently powerful. Second, given the small number of lawyers and the underdeveloped state of the legal system, lawyers could probably make more money now by developing more efficient law. Creation of inefficient law for rent-seeking only pays when there is an excessively large number of lawyers in an economy.

However, there are some examples of inefficient Russian law benefiting particular interest groups. Many of the identified inefficiencies are with respect to managers of firms using stock market manipulations of various sorts to disempower investors, discussed at length earlier. While the long-term interests of managers may be in a more open and efficient system of corporate control, the short-term interest of existing managers is in maintaining their position. Moreover, existing managers may not be the best candidates in a market economy, since many of them rose to their positions under the previous regime, so they may fear the loss of their jobs if capital markets begin to work better. Problems of managerial opportunism and shirking are substantial in the USA and other developed economies (for example, Rubin 1990, Chapter 5), and it will be difficult to solve them in Russia. The Czech Republic solved these problems by rapid privatization, so that managers did not have time to organize and delay the process. It is too late for this solution in Russia.

For those parts of the law where such pressures are less strong or do not exist, such as the domain of classical contract law, then there are benefits from more efficient law and few, if any, who would lose. How, then, can we explain the general inefficiency of Russian law? One simple possibility is ignorance: no one in power in Russia may understand the nature of efficient law and its benefits. A second possibility is time: it may simply take more time for efficient law to come into existence than has been available since the collapse of communism. Third, one point emphasized throughout this work is uncertainty: it may not pay for anyone to invest in creating efficient law because of the uncertain pay-off. Since this work has attempted to set forth policies that will enable law to become more efficient more quickly, it may serve to help solve these problems. It is in this spirit that I offer the following explicit policy suggestions.

Governments

Government policy was discussed at length in Chapter 7. Briefly, for governments the major implication is that enforcement of private agreements to arbitrate disputes between domestic firms, as well as between domestic and foreign firms, is useful and desirable. This simple policy would be the most powerful device for quickly adapting the dispute resolution system for a market economy. Governments might want to consider paying a small subsidy to arbitrators if they agree to write opinions, but this is of secondary importance. If arbitrators begin adopting a set of rules and precedents, then governments should consider these in revisions of commercial codes. Governments may also want to make provisions for a common law-type process for the court system during times between revisions of codes.

Other government policies are mainly negative in nature. Governments should refrain from excessive enforcement of antitrust laws, including regulation of vertical relationships, and laws against deception. Western economies established market institutions and developed large economies before such inefficient law enforcement became fashionable, and if new economies unduly burden themselves with such costly policies, growth might be retarded or even precluded. In the case of Russia, a strengthening of the central government is necessary so that it will be possible for government itself credibly to commit to policies facilitating growth. Government should also begin to honour its own agreements so that promises to enforce the commitments of others will be credible.

Arbitrators

If a government will enforce arbitration decrees, then arbitrators can play a major role in the system. The government should pay for some arbitration association to announce that it will establish precedents and decide cases based on these precedents. If this policy is successful and if parties begin using this association, then the association might begin to charge *ex ante* for being named in contracts as the arbitrator of choice. Law firms might find the provision of such arbitration a valuable specialty.

Trade Associations

Private trade associations can begin to play an informational role. Such associations can keep records of behaviour of members of the industry and make this information available to potential transactors. This can be done for a fee paid by those seeking the information. Alternatively, the trade association can charge members for listing. Any firm not listed would then signal to potential partners that it was unwilling to be rated by the association. Trade associations can also establish formal arbitration procedures with enforcement through information and reputation mechanisms. Organizations such as Better Business Bureaus can perform a similar function for businesses (perhaps retail businesses) in a geographic location.

Attorneys

Private attorneys advising firms can make use of information regarding reputations as it becomes generated. Attorneys can also include arbitration clauses in contracts for their clients. Indeed attorneys could now include clauses indicating that arbitration will be used if arbitration decrees should become enforceable in the future. If certain arbitration associations begin to generate precedents, and if these seem useful and efficient, attorneys can name these associations in contracts.

Businesses

Businesses can make use of all the information generated by the processes mentioned above. In addition, certain behaviours of businesses in post-communist economies may be remnants of their past, and are now counterproductive. First, businesses should avoid excessive secrecy. The best way to guarantee performance is to establish a reputation for fair and honest dealing. Creation of reputations is by definition an activity requiring information-sharing, and excessive secrecy can hinder or stop this activity. Second, businesses should become more accommodating in their bargaining strategies. For agreements to be self-enforcing, both parties must value the expected future benefits of continuing the sequence of transacting at more than the one-time benefits of cheating. Businesses with long time horizons should realize this and allow trading partners to make a reasonable return on the stream of transactions.

While the transition from a planned to a market economy and the elimination of the harms caused by communism will take a long time, adoption of the policies suggested here can speed up the process and also increase wealth and thus consumer welfare during the transition period.

Notes

1. I deal specifically with Hungary, Poland, the Czech Republic and especially with Russia, countries I have visited. However, I believe the general principles discussed will be more widely applicable.
2. Some exceptions are IMF (1991), Niskanen (1991), Pittman (1992), Gray and Associates (1993), Greif and Kandel (1995) and Pistor (1995).
3. For a discussion of efficient contract law, see Posner (1992, Chapter 4).
4. 'Probably some combination of private adjudication with ultimate state authority to back up its decisions is the most that a rapidly emerging free-market system can hope for' (Manne 1991, 213). Shavell (1995) agrees that it is efficient to enforce arbitration agreements if the parties voluntarily agree to such agreements *ex ante*.
5. Since I write from a libertarian perspective, a claim that a government has insufficient power is not one I make lightly. However, libertarianism is not anarchism, and libertarians believe that government does have some worthwhile functions and requires sufficient power to undertake these functions. Law enforcement is generally accepted as one such function.
6. It has been suggested at a seminar that a country could import judges and lawyers to operate such a code. This might solve some of the problems, but does not seem a practical alternative. Moreover, language problems would persist.
7. Except for Louisiana.
8. I met with many such attorneys in several countries. Almost all of them were associated with major American law firms, and many who were not seemed able to engage in significant amounts of consulting for foreign businesses. Others were in prestigious positions with important government ministries.
9. A 'quasi-rent' is a return on a fixed investment. Once a fixed investment is made, its return can be expropriated. If it were known in advance that the quasi-rent would be expropriated, then the initial investment would never have been made.
10. Landa (1981). For an interesting formal model of an ethnically based trading network involving the Maghribi, with enforcement mechanisms, see Avner Greif (1993). The Maghribi were 11th century Jewish traders in the Mediterranean.
11. The working out of the effects of this insight on vertical integration was in part due to Klein *et al.* (1978); see also Williamson (1985) and Rubin (1990).
12. Discussed in Greif and Kandel (1995).
13. This information is from Yakovlev (1994). Yakovlev is the Chairman of the Supreme Arbitration Court.
14. There are some other likely difficulties with this law which are important, although not directly relevant to the issues in this paper. The law adopts many of the errors in contemporary American contract law. Article 333 limits contractual damages to an amount which is not, 'clearly incommensurate to the consequences of the violation', equivalent to common law courts' (mistaken) unwillingness to enforce contractually specified damages viewed as 'punitive'. Article 426 allows dissolution of 'contracts of adhesion'. In addition, Article 10 states: 'The use by commercial organizations of civil rights for the purpose of limiting competition, and also abuse by them of their dominant position in the market, shall not be

permitted'. This is an extremely open-ended antitrust law, with great potential for abuse.
15. For example, Viechtbauer (1993), p. 363: 'In addition, the current Russian judicial system, because of deficiencies in staffing, regulation, and infrastructure, cannot reasonably be expected to handle any commercial disputes, let alone international trade cases'.
16. These examples are based on various stories in the *Moscow Times* from 25–29 May 1993.
17. Elf is 50 per cent owned by the French government, so that investment decisions might be made for political reasons. Normally, major stockholders would be expected to monitor such activity, but Elf's, 'management has been making its own decisions for many years – including its journey to the East – with little supervision by the state'.
18. Similar problems may exist in China (see Smith and Brauchli 1995).
19. This book is a very interesting but depressing study of the role of crime in Russia today, with implications well beyond the scope of this work. The theme of the book is that there are close links between government, business and criminals.
20. Soros believes that the most fundamental struggle in Russia is between energy producers and energy users. The former can sell on world markets, and are therefore in favour of reform and open markets. The latter include the large, inefficient industrial and military sector. Unfortunately, Soros believes the latter group is winning.
21. Tainter (1988) is a fascinating study of collapse, and many of the conditions discussed are observed in the former Soviet Union in areas not relevant to the concerns of this paper. One weakness of the book is its prediction that: 'Collapse today is neither an option nor an immediate threat'. Moreover, although writing in 1988, Tainter considered and rejected only the possibility of the collapse of Western civilization; the collapse of the Soviet Union was not contemplated.
22. Although I have discussed inappropriate use of these laws, outlawing of explicit price-fixing agreements is probably within the proper scope of the antitrust laws. Of course, it may be difficult to confine regulators to the appropriate use of these laws.

Bibliography

Akerlof, George A. (1970), 'The market for lemons: qualitative uncertainty and the market mechanism', *Quarterly Journal of Economics*, **84**, 488.

Aslund, Anders (1992), *Post-Communist Economic Revolutions: How Big a Bang?*, Washington: The Center for Strategic and International Studies.

Aslund, Anders (1994), 'Russia's success story', *Foreign Affairs*, September/October, 58–71.

Aslund, Anders (1995), *How Russia Became a Market Economy*, Washington: Brookings Institution.

Banerjee, Neela (1995a), 'Russian oil company tries a stock split in the Soviet style: Komineft didn't tell holders, many of whom didn't get any of the new shares', *Wall Street Journal*, 15 February, p. A14.

Banerjee, Neela (1995b), 'Russian securities trading, a business with a past, bets future on regulation', *Wall Street Journal*, 8 February, p. A11.

Banerjee, Neela and Gabriela Teodorescu (1995), 'Russians become homey with mortgages: pent-up housing demand lends hand to concept', *Wall Street Journal*, 28 September, p. A10.

Benson, Bruce L. (1989), 'The spontaneous evolution of commercial law', *Southern Economic Journal*, **55**, 644–61.

Benson, Bruce L. (1990), *The Enterprise of Law*, San Francisco: Pacific Research Institute.

Benson, Bruce L. (1992), 'Customary law as social contract: international commercial law', *Constitutional Political Economy*, **3**, 1–27.

Berman, Harold J. (1983), *Law and Revolution: The Formation of the Western Legal Tradition*, Cambridge: Harvard University Press.

Bernstein, Lisa (1992), 'Opting out of the legal system: extralegal contractual relations in the diamond industry', *Journal of Legal Studies*, **21**, 115–59.

Bernstein, Lisa (1995), 'Project summary: the newest law merchant: private commercial law in the United States', paper presented at the American Law and Economics Association Meeting, Berkeley.

Black, Bernard S., Reinier H. Kraakman and Jonathan Hay (1995), 'Corporate law from scratch', Columbia University School of Law, Center for Law and Economic Studies, Working Paper, #104, forthcoming in Cheryl Gray, Andrzej Rapaczynski and Roman Frydman (eds), *Corporate Governance in Eastern Europe*, World Bank, in press.

Boettke, Peter J. (1995), 'Credibility, commitment, and Soviet economic reform', in E. Lazear (ed.), *Economic Transition in Eastern Europe and Russia: Realities of Reform*, Stanford, California: Hoover Institution Press.

Boycko, Maxim, Andrei Shleifer and Robert W. Vishny (1994), 'Voucher privatization', *Journal of Financial Economics*, vol. 35, 249–266.

Branegan, Jay (1994), 'White knights need not apply', *Time*, 31 October.

Burandt, Gary (1992), *Moscow Meets Madison Avenue: The Adventures of the First Adman in the USSR*, New York: HarperBusiness.

Buyevich, Alexander J. and Sergey N. Zhukov (1992), 'Dispute resolution in Russia', *Law of the Newly Independent States: The Bottom Line*.

Clague, Christopher, Philip Keefer, Steven Kanck and Mancur Olson (1995), 'Contract Intensive Money: Contract Enforcement, Property Rights, and Economic Performance', University of Maryland.

Coase, Ronald H. (1937), 'The nature of the firm', *Economica*, 386, reprinted in Coase, *The Firm, the Market and the Law*, Chicago: University of Chicago Press, 1988, pp. 33–55.

Coase, Ronald H. (1960), 'The Problem of Social Cost', *Journal of Law and Economics*.

Cooter, Robert D. (1994), 'Structural adjudication and the new Law Merchant: a model of decentralized law', *International Review of Law and Economics*, **14**.

Cowley, Andrew (1995), 'Russia's emerging market', *The Economist*, 8 April.

Craik, Euan (1995), 'Investors rate legal mess as key obstacle', *Moscow Times*, 1 April, p. 1.

Dubik, Mikhail (1994a), 'Of debts and decrees', *Business Central Europe*, November, p. 54.

Dubik, Mikhail (1994b), 'Top firms sign investors bill of rights', *Moscow Times*, 6 October.

Dunkin, Amy (1995), 'After the fire in emerging markets', *Business Week*, 23 January.

Durcanin, Cynthia (1995), 'Whips, chains, car crashes and bingo', *Business Week* (international edition), 20 February.

Easterbrook, Frank H. (1984), 'Vertical arrangements and the rule of reason', *Antitrust Law Journal*, **53**, 135.

Economist (1995a), 'Boris the broker evolves: Russia's primitive stockmarket is at last becoming more sophisticated', 8 July, 69–70.

Economist (1995b), 'Russian law: groping ahead', 2 September, pp. 42–8.

Epstein, Richard A. (1975), 'Unconscionability: a critical reappraisal', *Journal of Law and Economics*, **18**, 292–316.

Epstein, Richard A. (1992), 'The path to the *T.J. Hooper*: the theory and history of custom in the law of tort', *Journal of Legal Studies*, **21**, 1–39.

Erlanger, Steven (1994), 'Russia's new dictatorship of crime', *New York Times*, 15 May.

Erlanger, Steven (1995), 'In Russia, official corruption is worse than organized crime', *New York Times*, 3 July.

Filipov, David (1994), 'Civil code promises to untie red tape', *Moscow Times*, 28 July, p. 3.

Fogel, Marya (1995a), 'Foreigners learn to cope – sort of – with Russia's ever-mutating laws', *Wall Street Journal*, 7 July, p. A6.

Fogel, Marya (1995b), 'Russia expands a tax on payrolls, angering many foreign businesses', *Wall Street Journal*, 5 April, p. A9.

Fogel, Marya and Anne Reifenberg (1995), 'Russia may face an oil rush in reverse: tax laws, export quotas drive western firms away', *Wall Street Journal*, 14 February, p. A19.

Frye, Timothy (1995), 'Contracting in the shadow of the state: private arbitration courts in Russia', prepared for presentation for the John M. Olin Seminar Series, 'The Rule of Law and Economic Reform in Russia', Harvard University.

Galuszka, Peter (1994), 'Only the stubborn strike it rich in Russia', *Business Week* (international edition), 12 September.

Galuszka, Peter and Susan Chandler (1995), 'Russia: a plague of disjointed ventures', *Business Week* (international edition), 1 May.

Galuszka, Peter and Sandra Dallas (1995), 'And you think you've got tax problems', *Business Week*, 29 May.

Galuszka, Peter and Patricia Kranz (1995), 'Look who's making a revolution: shareholders', *Business Week*, 20 February.

Galuszka, Peter, Patricia Kranz and Stanley Reed (1994), 'Russia's new capitalism: it's still chaotic, but private companies are forging a vital economy', *Business Week*, 10 October.

Goldberg, Paul (1992), 'Economic reform and product quality improvement efforts in the Soviet Union', *Soviet Studies*, **44**, 113–22.

Goldman, Marshall I. (1994), *Lost Opportunity: Why Economic Reforms in Russia have not worked*, New York: W.W. Norton.

Gordon, Michael R. (1995), 'Cautiously pessimistic investor eyes Russia', *The New York Times*, 22 December.

Gray, Cheryl W. and Associates (1993), *Evolving Legal Frameworks for Private Sector Development in Central and Eastern Europe*, World Bank Discussion Paper 209, July.

Greif, Avner (1993), 'Contract enforceability and economic institutions in early trade: the Maghribi traders coalition', *American Economic Review*, **83**, 525–44.

Greif, Avner (1994), 'Cultural beliefs and the organization of society: a historical and theoretical reflection on collectivist and individualist societies', *Journal of Political Economy*, **102**, 912–50.

Greif, Avner and Eugene Kandel (1995), 'Contract enforcement institutions: historical perspective and current status in Russia', in E. Lazear (ed.), *Economic Transition in Eastern Europe and Russia: Realities of Reform*, Stanford, California: Hoover Institution Press.

Gurkov, Igor and Gary Asselbergs (1995), 'Ownership and control in Russian privatised companies: evidence from a survey', *Communist Economies & Economic Transformation*, **7**, 195–211.

Halligan, Liam and Pavel Teplukin (1995), 'Investment disincentives in Russia', preliminary draft, mimeo.

Handelman, Stephen (1995), *Comrade Criminal: Russia's New Mafia*, New Haven: Yale University Press.

Hayek, Friedrich A. (1973), *Law, Legislation and Liberty; Volume 1: Rules and Order*, Chicago: University of Chicago Press.

Higgins, Richard S. and Paul H. Rubin (1986), 'Counterfeit goods', *Journal of Law and Economics*, **29**, 211–30.

Hill, Ivan (ed.) (1976), *The Ethical Basis of Economic Freedom*, Chapel Hill, North Carolina: American Viewpoint.

Imse, Ann (1993), 'American know-how and Russian oil', *The New York Times Magazine*, 7 March.

International Monetary Fund (IMF), The World Bank, Organization for Economic Cooperation and Development, and European Bank for Reconstruction and Development (1991), *A Study of the Soviet Economy*, Washington: IMF *et al.*

Intriligator, Michael D. (1994), 'Privatization in Russia has led to criminalization', *The Australian Economic Review*, **4**, 4–14.

Johnson, Simon and Heidi Kroll (1991), 'Managerial strategies for spontaneous privatization', *Soviet Economy*, **7**, 281–316.

Jones, Anthony (1992), 'Issues in state and private sector relations in the Soviet Economy', in Bruno Dallago, Gianmaria Ajani and Bruno Grancelli (eds), *Privatization and Entrepreneurship in Post-Socialist Countries: Economy, Law and Society*, New York: St Martin's Press, 69–88.

Jones, Anthony and William Moskoff (1991), *Ko-ops: The Rebirth of Entrepreneurship in the Soviet Union*, Bloomington: Indiana University Press.

Klein, Benjamin (1992), 'Contracts and incentives: the role of contact terms in assuring performance', in Lars Werin and Hans Wijkander (eds), *Contract Economics*, Cambridge, MA: Blackwell, 149–72.

Klein, Benjamin, Robert Crawford, and Armen Alchian (1978), 'Vertical integration, appropriable rents, and the competitive contracting process', *Journal of Law and Economics*, **21**, 297.

Klein, Benjamin and Keith B. Leffler (1981), 'The role of market forces in assuring contractual performance', *Journal of Political Economy*, **89**, 615.

Kornai, Janos (1992), 'The postsocialist transition and the state: reflections in the light of Hungarian fiscal problems', *American Economic Review*, **82**, 1–21.

Kranz, Patricia (1994), 'In Moscow, the attack of the killer brands', *Business Week*, 10 January.

Kranz, Patricia (1995a), 'Russia's really hostile takeovers', *Business Week*, 14 August.

Kranz, Patricia (1995b), 'Russia isn't Siberia for investors anymore', *Business Week* (international edition), 17 April.

Kranz, Patricia and Karen Lowry Miller (1994), 'Lost in the translations', *Business Week*, 3 October.

Kroll, Heidi (1987), 'Breach of contract in the Soviet economy', *Journal of Legal Studies*, **16**, 119–48.

Kvint, Vladimir (1993), *The Barefoot Shoemaker: Capitalizing on the New Russia*, New York: Arcade Publishing.

Landa, Janet T. (1981), 'A theory of the ethnically homogeneous middleman group: an institutional alternative to contract law', *Journal of Legal Studies*, **10**, 349–62.

Landes, William M. and Richard A. Posner (1979), 'Adjudication as a private good', *Journal of Legal Studies*, **8**, 235–84.

Langer, Robert and Alexander Buyevitch (1995), 'Russia's courts take courage', *Moscow Times*, 18 July, p. 17.

Leijonhufvud, Axel (1993), 'Problems of socialist transition: Kazakhstan 1991', in Laszlo Samogyi (ed.), *The Political Economy of the Transition Process in Eastern Europe*, Aldershot: Edward Elgar, pp. 289–311.

Leitzel, Jim, Clifford Gaddy and Michael Alexeev (1995), 'Mafiosi and Matrioshki: organized crime and Russian reform', *Brookings Review*, 26–29.

Leoni, Bruno (1961; 1991 edition), *Freedom and the Law*, Indianapolis: Liberty Fund.

Levine, Joanne (1993), 'Cyrill rights', *Business Central Europe*, May, p. 32.

Levy, Marcia (1995), 'A look back at '94: progress, promise', *Moscow Times*, 17 January, p. 17.

Liesman, Steve (1995a), 'Russian shipping firm doubles number of shares without consulting investors', *Wall Street Journal*, 4 April, p. A16.

Liesman, Steve (1995b), 'High noon at Russia's annual meetings: directors resent intrusions by "outside" shareholders', *Wall Street Journal*, 21 April, p. A7.

Liesman, Steve (1995c), 'A big buildup: despite long odds, construction work is booming in Moscow: shaky financing and a lack of property laws make office projects risky', *Wall Street Journal*, 28 December.

Liesman, Steve (1995d), 'For US investors, Russia rates caution: enthusiasm fades as Moscow's market fizzles', *Wall Street Journal*, 23 October.

Liesman, Steve and Martin du Bois (1995), 'Russia's "mineral wealth": a dubious buried treasure: investors are deterred by remote and exaggerated reserves, as well as vague laws', *Wall Street Journal*, 22 February, p. A17.

Los, Maria (1992), 'From underground to legitimacy: the normative dilemmas of post-communist marketization', in Bruno Dallago, Gianmaria Ajani and Bruno Grancelli (eds), *Privatization and Entrepreneurship in Post-Socialist Countries: Economy. Law and Society*, New York: St Martin's Press, 111–42.

Manne, Henry (1991), 'Perestroika and the limits of knowledge', *Cato Journal*, **11**, 207–14.

Mauro, Paolo (1995), 'Corruption and growth', *Quarterly Journal of Economics*, **90**, (3), August, 681–712.

Mileusnic, Natasha (1995a), 'New law threatens foreign tax breaks', *Moscow Times*, 28 March.

Mileusnic, Natasha (1995b), 'Securities bill "ruined" by Duma', *Moscow Times*, 29 March.

Milgrom, Paul R., Douglass C. North and Barry W. Weingast (1990), 'The role of institutions in the revival of trade: the law merchant, private judges, and the Champagne Fairs', *Economics and Politics*, **2**, 1–23.

Miller, Karen Lowry, Frank J. Comes and Peggy Simpson (1995), 'Poland: rising star of Europe', *Business Week*, 4 December.

Miller, Karen Lowry, Peggy Simpson and Tim Smart (1994), 'Europe: The Push East', *Business Week*, 7 November.

Moore, Stephen D. (1993), 'Sweden's Ikea forges into Eastern Europe', *Wall Street Journal*, 28 June, p. B6E.

Moscow Times (1995), 'Komineft to annul secret issue', 1 March, p. 14.

Muris, Timothy J. (1981), 'Opportunistic behavior and the law of contracts', *Minnesota Law Review*, **65**, 527.

Murrell, Peter (1991), 'Conservative political philosophy and the strategy of economic transition', IRIS Working Paper No. 7, University of Maryland.

Niskanen, William (1991), 'The soft infrastructure of a market economy', *Cato Journal*, **11**, 233–8.

North, Douglass (1991), 'Institutions, ideology and economic performance', *Cato Journal*, **11**, 477–88.

Osakwe, Christopher (1993), 'Modern Russian law of banking and security transactions: a biopsy of post-Soviet Russian commercial law', *Whittier Law Review*, **V** (14), 301–82.

Pennar, Karen, Peter Galuszka and Karen Lowry Miller (1994), 'Frontier economies: enter if you dare', *Business Week*, 18 November.

Perlez, Jane (1993), 'Poland's new entrepreneurs push the economy ahead', *New York Times*, Sunday 20 June, p. F7.

Pistor, Katharina (1995), 'Supply and demand for contract enforcement in Russia: courts, arbitration, and private enforcement', Prepared for presentation for the John M. Olin Seminar Series, 'The Rule of Law and Economic Reform in Russia', Harvard University.

Pittman, Russell (1992), 'Some critical provisions in the antimonopoly laws of Central and Eastern Europe', *The International Lawyer*, **26**, 485–503.
Poe, Richard (1993), *How to Profit from the Coming Russian Boom: The Insider's Guide to Business Opportunities and Survival on the Frontiers of Capitalism*, New York: McGraw-Hill.
Posner, Richard A. (1981), 'The next step in the antitrust treatment of restricted distribution: per se legality', *University of Chicago Law Review*, **40**, 6.
Posner, Richard A. (1992), *Economic Analysis of Law*, Boston: Little, Brown and Co.
Rossant, Juliette (1994), 'In Moscow, it's location, location, location', *Business Week*, 25 July.
Rubin, Paul H. (1977), 'Why is the common law efficient?', *Journal of Legal Studies*, **6**, 51–63.
Rubin, Paul H. (1990), *Managing Business Transactions: Controlling the Costs of Coordinating, Communicating and Decision Making*, New York: Free Press.
Rubin, Paul H. (1991), 'Economics and the regulation of deception', *Cato Journal*, **11**, 667–90.
Rubin, Paul H. (1993), 'Private mechanisms for creation of efficient institutions for market economies', in Laszlo Samogyi (ed.), *The Political Economy of the Transition Process in Eastern Europe*, Aldershot: Edward Elgar, pp. 158–70.
Rubin, Paul H. and Martin Bailey (1994), 'The role of lawyers in changing the law', *Journal of Legal Studies*, June, 807–31.
Russian Federation (1994), *Civil Code of the Russian Federation, Studies on Russian Law*, London: the Vinogradoff Institute, Faculty of Laws, University College of London.
Sachs, Jeffrey D. (1995), 'Why corruption rules Russia', *The New York Times*, 29 November, p. A19.
Salpukas, Agis (1993), 'In an oil rush to the East, Elf plays pied piper', *The New York Times*, 27 June, p. F7.
Schmid, A. Allan (1992), 'Legal foundations of the market: implications for the formerly socialist countries of Eastern Europe and Africa', *Journal of Economic Issues*, **26**, 707–32.
Scully, Gerald W. (1992), *Constitutional Environments and Economic Growth*, Princeton: Princeton University Press.
Shavell, Steven (1995), 'Alternative dispute resolution: an economic analysis', *Journal of Legal Studies*, **24**, 1–28.

Shiller, Robert J., Maxim Boycko and Vladimir Korobov (1992), 'Hunting for *Homo Sovieticus*: situational versus attitudinal factors in economic behavior', *Brookings Papers on Economic Activity*, **1**, 127–94.

Shleifer, Andrei and Robert W. Vishny (1993), 'Corruption', *Quarterly Journal of Economics*, **108**, 599.

Siltchenkov, Dimitri (1993), 'A stranger in a strange land: practicing law after the breakup of the USSR', *Whittier Law Review*, **V** (14), 503–14.

Simpson, Peggy (1995), 'As Poland embraces the franchise – a master baker cooks up his own', *Business Week* (international edition), 26 June.

Smith, Craig and Marcus Brauchli (1995), 'The long march: to invest successfully in China, foreigners find patience crucial, *Wall Street Journal*, 23 February, p. 1.

Stanley, Alessandra (1995), 'To the business risks in Russia, add poisoning', *New York Times*, 9 August.

Tainter, Joseph A. (1988), *The Collapse of Complex Societies*, New York: Cambridge University Press.

Telser, Lester (1980), 'A theory of self enforcing agreements', *Journal of Business*, **53**, 27.

Thomas, Bill and Charles Sutherland (1992), *Red Tape: Adventure Capitalism in the New Russia*, New York: Dutton.

Tolkacheva, Julie (1995), 'Troika-Dialog JV sues first voucher', *Moscow Times*, 24 January, p. 13.

Topornin, Boris N. (1993), *The Legal Problems of Economic Reform in Russia*, Edinburgh: The David Hume Institute.

Tourevski, Mark and Eileen Morgan (1993), *Cutting the Red Tape: How Western Companies Can Profit in the New Russia*, New York: Free Press.

Toy, Stewart and Karen Lowry Miller (1995), 'An island breeze blows in Prague', *Business Week*, 11 December.

Uchitelle, Lewis (1992), 'The art of a Russian deal: ad-libbing contract law', *New York Times*, 17 January, p. 1.

Vasiliev, Dmitry (1995), 'We Russians can mind our own markets', *Wall Street Journal*, 7 July, p. A10.

Viechtbauer, Volker (1993), 'Arbitration in Russia', *Stanford Journal of International Law*, **V** (29), 355.

Vlasihin, Vasily A. (1993), 'Toward a rule of law and bill of rights for Russia', in Bruce L.R. Smith and Gennady M. Danilenko (eds), *Law and Democracy in the New Russia*, Washington: Brookings Institution.

Wegren, Stephen K. (1994), 'Building market institutions', *Communist and Post-Communist Studies*, **V** (27), 195–224.

Weingast, Barry (1995), 'The economic role of political institutions: market-preserving federalism and economic development', *Journal of Law, Economics and Organization*, **V** (11), April, 1–31.

Williamson, Oliver E. (1985), *The Economic Institutions of Capitalism*, New York: Free Press.

Winestock, Geoff (1995), 'Standoff in smuggler's paradise', *Business Week* (international edition), 25 September.

Wolf, Holger C. (1993), 'Endogenous legal booms', *Journal of Law, Economics, & Organization*, **9**, 181–7.

Yakovlev, Veniamin Fedorovich (1994), 'Interview', *Moscow Rossiyskaya Gazeta*, reprinted in *Federal Broadcast Information Service-USSR*, p. -077, 19 July.

Zhurek, Stephan (1993), 'Commodity exchanges in Russia: success or failure', *Radio Liberty Research Report*, **2**, 41–4.

Index

accident law, 4
adaptation of law, 11
adhesion, contracts of, 61
advertising, 55–6
Akerlof, G.A., 14
Albania, 27
arbitration, 11–12, 28, 46, 65
   government policy and, 58
   multilateral mechanism, 22–4
   and rules, 59–60
arbitration association, 12, 65
arbitration clauses, 4, 28
arbitration courts, 28, 33, 34–5, 49
Arbitration Procedural Code (APC) 1992, 34–5
arbitrators, 59–60, 65
Asiatic republics, 27
Aslund, A., 12, 33, 53, 57, 58
   criminals as enforcers, 50, 51–2
Asselbergs, G., 48
asset specificity, 14
Association of Broker-Dealers, 47, 48
attorneys, 9–10, 36, 66

Bailey, M., 64
Baltic Republics, 27
Banerjee, N., 33, 40, 48
bank loans, 33
bankruptcy, 36
banks, 50, 51
Belorussia, 27
Benson, B.L., 12, 18, 22, 27, 60, 62
Berman, H.J., 22, 54
Bernstein, L., 24, 25, 60
Better Business Bureaus, 22, 25, 46, 66
'big bang' for contract law, 7–9
bilateral mechanisms, 19–21
   government policy and, 57–8
   hostages, 21
   self-enforcing agreements, 19–20
   vertical controls, 20–21
Black, B., 26, 34, 48, 50, 51
body of law: selection in disputes, 23
Boettke, P.J., 44
Boycko, M., 63
brand names, 55–6
Branegan, J., 29
broker associations, 47
Bulgaria, 27
Burandt, G., 20
business courts, 33
business groups, 49
businesses/firms, 66
   firm size, 15
   information for, 50
   structure, 16–17
Buyevich, A., 16, 35

Chandler, S., 39
Chase Manhattan Bank, 43
Chernomyrdin, V., 41
Chevron, 40
civil codes, 5
   adopting an existing code, 7–8
   common law vs, 9–11
   Poland, Hungary and Czech Republic, 27–8
   Russia, 35–6, 43, 46
Clague, C., 15, 26
Coase, R.H., 15, 45
Coase theorem, 45
codes, civil *see* civil codes
collateral, 21, 33
Commercial Code 1995 (Russia), 35–6, 43, 46
committees: permits and, 32

11-81

commodities exchanges, 48–9
common law, 5
  vs civil code, 9–11
  private, 11–13
commonality of interest, 3–4
competing jurisdictions, 59–60
conflicting laws, 31–2
Conoco, 41
Constitutional Court, 33
cooperatives, associations of, 49
Cooter, R.D., 23, 60
corruption, 32
counterfeiting, 55
courts, 2, 54
  lack of experience, 12
  system in Russia, 33
Cowley, A., 44
Craik, E., 41, 42, 52
crime, 23, 26, 50, 52–3
  criminals as enforcers, 2, 50–52
custom, 23, 60
Czech Republic, 5, 27–30, 56, 58, 64

Dallas, S., 41
De Beers, 38
de novo contract law, 8–9
debt collection, 16, 32–3, 35, 51
diamond 'bourses', 25
dilution of investments, 40, 48
dispute resolution, 11
  see also arbitration
du Bois, M., 41
Dubik, M., 32, 47
dues, association, 60
Dunkin, A., 43
Durcanin, C., 56

Easterbrook, F.H., 57
Economist, 34, 36, 43
efficient rules *see* rules
Elf Aquitaine, 39–40
Epstein, R.A., 60, 62
Erlanger, S., 32, 50, 52
Ernst & Young, 50
ethnic solidarity, 45–6
ex ante agreement, 3–4
experience: lack of, 12
extortion, fear of, 26

Filipov, D., 33
firms *see* businesses/firms
First Voucher Investment Fund, 48
Fogel, M., 37, 41
foreign investment, 28–9
  Russia, 16, 37–43
franchising, 20, 21, 29
Frye, T., 26, 49

Galuszka, P., 39, 40, 41, 53
geographic associations, 46, 49
Germany, 54
Goldberg, P., 16
Goldman, M.I., 40
Gordon, M.R., 29, 53
government opportunism, 17, 37, 39, 40–41
government policy, 6, 54–8, 65
  bilateral mechanisms, 57–8
  multilateral arrangements, 58
  unilateral mechanisms, 55–7
Gray, C.W., 12, 16, 28, 54
Greif, A., 34, 45, 49, 50–51, 52
Gulf Canada, 40
Gurkov, I., 48

Halligan, L., 42, 52
Handelman, S., 23, 26, 32, 51, 52
Hayek, F.A., 8, 9
Higgins, R.S., 55
Hill, I., 22
'hold-up', 14
hostages, 21, 57–8
Hungary, 5, 16, 27–30, 55

Ikea, 40
inefficient contract formation, 61–2
inflation, 32–3, 35–6
interest groups, 63–4
International Arbitration Court, 35
International Food Exchange, 48
IMF, 27, 31
Intriligator, M.D., 51, 52

Johnson, S., 15, 17
joint ventures, 37–9, 40–41
Jones, A., 49
judges: competence, 34, 36

jurisdictional competition, 59–60

Kandel, E., 34, 49, 50–51
Klein, B., 14, 18, 26
Komineft, 40
Korean-Russian timber project, 38
Kornai, J., 12
Kranz, P., 8, 23, 40, 43, 56
   criminals as enforcers, 50, 51, 52
Kroll, H., 5, 15, 17, 31
Kvint, V., 18–19, 23, 32, 37, 53

land tax, 38
Landa, J.T., 45
Landes, W.M., 59, 60
Langer, R., 35
Law Merchant, 22, 23, 24, 59, 60, 62
lawyers, 9–10, 36, 66
League of Investment Funds, 47, 48
Lebedinsky Mining Company, 40
Leffler, K.B., 18
legal change, 5, 7–13
   'big bang' for contract law, 7–9
   common law or civil code, 9–11
   private law or public law, 11–13
legislator time, 10
Leijonhufvud, A., 7
Leitzel, J., 26, 50–51
Leoni, B., 7
Levine, J., 56
Levy, M., 33
Liesman, S., 40, 41, 43, 48
Los, M., 15

Mafia, 50–52
'maintenance of citizen' payments, 36
managers: opportunism and shirking, 64
market definition, 57
market-preserving federalist system, 1
Mauro, P., 32
Mileusnic, N., 41, 47
Milgrom, P.R., 22, 24, 60
Miller, K.L., 8, 29
Ministry of Foreign Economic Relations, 38–9

misuse of antitrust law, 54, 57–8
Moberg, A., 40
Moore, S.D., 40
Morgan, E., 8, 15, 23, 53, 56
   business information, 50
   legal failures, 38–9, 42
   negotiation, 20
   secrecy, 18
mortgages, 33
Moscow Arbitration Court, 49
Moscow Central Depository, 43
Moscow Commercial Court, 49
Moscow Commodities Exchange, 48
Moscow Times, 38
Moskoff, W., 49
multilateral mechanisms, 22–5
   arbitration, 22–4
   enforcement devices, 24–5
   government policy and, 58
   Russia, 45–6
Muris, T.J., 14
Murrell, P., 7

National Association of Realtors (US), 25
National Sports Fund (Russia), 42
New York Diamond Dealers Club, 25
North, D., 2–3

oil, 39–41
oil prices, 38
opportunism, 5, 14–17, 39
   evidence, 15–17
   government, 17, 37, 39, 40–41
   theory, 14–15
Osakwe, C., 33

Pennar, K., 29
Pennzoil, 40
Perlez, J., 28
permits/approval, 32
personal contacts, 15
Pistor, K., 26, 35
Pittman, R., 54
Poe, R., 16, 21, 32, 37, 53
Poland, 5, 21, 27–30, 58
policy, government *see* government policy

political system: difficulties, 43–6
Posner, R.A., 9, 57, 59, 60, 62
'Precious Metals and Stones Committee', 38
prices, 56–7
Primorsky Sea Shipping, 40
private law
  characteristics and benefits, 61–2
  vs public law, 11–13
private mechanisms, 4, 5, 18–26
  bilateral, 19–21, 57–8
  and efficient rules, 6, 59–60
  government policy and, 54–8
  limits to, 25–6
  multilateral, 22–5, 45–6, 58
  Russia, 25–6, 45–6, 47–50
  unilateral, 18–19, 55–7
privatization, 2, 4–5, 63
Property Law (Russia) 1990, 34
property rights, 2–3, 4–5, 45, 55
public choice theory, 63
public law, 27
  vs private law, 11–13
Public Relations Society of America, 25

quality, 16, 56–7
quasi-rents, 14

Raddison Corporation, 39
Reifenberg, A., 41
rent-seeking, 64
rents, 41
reputation, 24–6
  investment in, 18–19, 45, 66
retailing, 20–21
Romania, 27
Rossant, J., 32
Rossisky Credit Bank, 40
Rubin, P.H., 9, 14, 18, 20, 40, 59, 64
  government policy, 55, 56
rule of law, 1
rules, efficient, 6, 59–62
  characteristics of private law, 61–2
  mechanisms, 6, 59–60
Russia, 1, 5–6, 31–53, 57, 58, 63
  advertising, 55–6
  criminals as enforcers, 2, 50–52

examples of legal failures, 37–43
formal legal system, 31–6
  Arbitration Procedural Code 1992, 34–5
  Commercial Code 1995, 35–6, 43, 46
  Law on Property 1990, 34
need for strengthened central government, 65
opportunism, 15–17, 37, 39, 40–41
political bases for legal uncertainty, 43–6
private mechanisms, 25–6, 45–6, 47–50
Russian Business Round Table, 50
Russian Federation Commission on Securities and Exchanges, 43, 47

Sachs, J., 52–3
Schmid, A.A., 8
Scully, G.W., 9
Securities Commission, 43, 47
self-enforcing agreements, 19–20, 45
self-regulatory associations, 24–5, 46, 47
  see also Better Business Bureaus; trade associations
shareholder rights, 40, 42, 43, 47–8
Shiller, R.J., 16
Shleifer, A., 32
short time horizons, 44
Siltchenkov, D., 36
Simpson, P., 21
smuggling, 42
Soros, G., 29, 53
Soviet Chamber of Commerce, 50
Stanley, A., 50
Supreme Arbitration Court, 34–5
Sutherland, C. 39, 48

Tainter, J.A., 53
taxation, 38, 40–41, 42
television, 55–6
Telser, L., 19
Teodorescu, G., 33
Teplukin, P., 42, 52
Thomas, B., 39, 48
time horizons, short, 44

Tolkacheva, J., 48
Topornin, B.N., 10–11, 34
Tourevski, M., 7–8, 15, 23, 53, 56
 business information, 50
 legal failures, 38–9, 42
 negotiation, 20
 secrecy, 18
Toy, S., 29
trade associations, 24–5, 46, 47, 58, 60, 66
trade fairs, 60
trademarks, 55
transaction costs, 45
translation of laws, 7–8
Troika Dialog, 48

Uchitelle, L., 4, 16, 19
Ukraine, 27
uncertainty, 31–2, 53
 political bases, 43–6
unconscionable contracts, 61
unequal bargaining power, 61
unilateral mechanisms, 18–19
 government policy and, 55–7
Union of Amalgamated Cooperatives, 49
Union of Leaseholders and Entrepreneurs, 49

Union of Polish Banks, 28
United States (USA), 18, 54, 57, 61
 multilateral enforcement devices, 24–5

Vasiliev, D., 43
vertical controls, 20–21
Viechtbauer, V., 35
Vishny, R.W., 32
Vlasihin, V.A., 33

'war of laws', 31–2
Wegren, S.K., 48
Weingast, B., 1
White Nights, 40
Williamson, O.E., 14
Winestock, G., 42
Wolf, H.C., 54
World Federation of Diamond Bourses, 25

Yakovlev, V.F., 34
Yaroslav Rubber Company, 40
Yeltsin, B., 42
Young and Rubicam, 20

Zhukov, S.N., 16
Zhurek, S., 48

Ethnic Diversity, Liberty and the State

Ethnic Diversity, Liberty and the State

The African Dilemma

Mwangi S. Kimenyi

Associate Professor of Economics, University of Connecticut, USA and Senior Research Associate, African Research Centre for Public Policy and Market Process

THE SHAFTESBURY PAPERS, 12
SERIES EDITOR: CHARLES K. ROWLEY

Edward Elgar
Cheltenham, UK • Northampton, MA, USA

© Mwangi S. Kimenyi 1997

All rights reserved. No part of this publication may be reproduced, stored in a retrieval system or transmitted in any form or by any means, electronic, mechanical or photocopying, recording, or otherwise without the prior permission of the publisher.

Published by
Edward Elgar Publishing Limited
8 Lansdown Place
Cheltenham
Glos GL50 2HU
UK

Edward Elgar Publishing, Inc.
6 Market Street
Northampton
Massachusetts 01060
USA

A catalogue record for this book
is available from the British Library

Library of Congress Cataloguing in Publication Data
Kimenyi, Mwangi S.
    Ethnic diversity, liberty and the state : the African dilemma /
Mwangi S. Kimenyi.
      — (The Shaftesbury papers : 12)
    Includes bibliographical references and index.
      1. Africa, Sub-Saharan—Politics and government—1960–   2. Africa Sub-Saharan—Ethnic relations—Political aspects.   3. Ethnic groups—Africa, Sub-Saharan—Political activity.   4. Civil society—Africa, Sub-Saharan.   I. Title.   II. Series.
JQ1879.A15K54   1998
320.967—dc21   97–38252
                                                                                    CIP

ISBN 1 85898 547 1

Typeset by Manton Typesetters, 5–7 Eastfield Road, Louth, Lincolnshire LN11 7AJ, UK.
Printed and bound in Great Britain by Biddles Ltd, Guildford and King's Lynn

Contents

List of figures vi
List of tables vii
Acknowledgements viii

1 Introduction 1
2 From Tribal Chief to Dictator 10
3 Ethnic Nations and Associations in Africa 21
4 Optimal Ethnic Integration and Separation 32
5 Integration, Centralization and Rent-Seeking 42
6 Integration, Centralization and Ethnic Conflict 53
7 Reducing Ethnic Externalities Through Decentralization 62
8 Maintaining Unity and Diversity: Federalism 73
9 The Demand for Federalism in Africa 83
10 Constitutionalism and Civil Society in Africa 91
11 Protecting Property and Economic Liberties 97
12 Ethnic Representation and Voting Rules 105
13 Political Divorce: Redrawing Africa's Borders 108

Bibliography 110
Index 121

Figures

3.1 A map of Africa   12-23
3.2 Ethnic units in Zaire   12-25
4.1 The market for tribal identity   12-34
5.1 The demand and supply of wealth transfers by tribal
     groups   12-47

Tables

2.1	The political configurations of Africa by 1990	12-19
6.1	Recent ethnic conflicts	12-57
6.2	Refugees and displaced persons, 1992	12-59

Acknowledgements

This study discusses institutional reforms that can better accommodate ethnic diversity in Africa. I consider such reforms to be a necessary condition for the restoration of civil societies in Africa. The project evolved from an earlier study that investigated the viability of federalism in Africa which was conducted while I was visiting the Center for Study of Public Choice. I am grateful to Jennifer Roback for making my visit possible and the Earhart Foundation for supporting that federalism project. This book is again the result of support received from the Earhart Foundation. Over the years, the trustees of the Earhart Foundation have supported my research efforts that have focused on establishing institutions that advance individual liberty. It would not have been possible to complete this study without the support of the Foundation. Needless to say, I am very grateful for this support. I am also extremely grateful to my friends, J.D. and Gretel Von Pischke of Reston, Virginia, who as in many other times in the past, provided me with a home while visiting the Center for Study of Public Choice during the summer of 1995. The final draft has benefited from extensive comments and suggestions from Professor Charles Rowley and I am very grateful. I also thank Professors William F. Shughart II and Tyler Cowen for their helpful comments and suggestions.

1. Introduction

Thomas Hobbes, in his widely read book, *Leviathan*, observed that in the 'state of Nature', implying a state that has no government to regulate the activities of its members, the basic equalities of men's abilities would lead to conflict in the realization of essentially equal goals, with the result that man will live in a constant state of war:

> From this equality of ability arises equality of hope in the attaining of our ends. And therefore if any two men desire the same thing, which nevertheless they cannot both enjoy, they become enemies; and in the way to their end, which is principally their own conservation, and sometimes their delectation only, endeavour to destroy or subdue one another. And from hence it comes to pass that where an invader has no more to fear than another man's single power, if one plant, sow, build, or possess a convenient seat, others may probably be expected to come prepared with forces united to dispossess and deprive him, not only of the fruit of his labour, but also his life or liberty (Hobbes 1958 [1651], 105).

As described by Hobbes, the consequences of a stateless society are grave indeed:

> Whatsoever, therefore, is consequent to a time of war where every man is enemy to every man, the same is consequent to the time wherein men live without other security than what their own strength and their own invention shall furnish them withal. In such condition there is no place for industry, because the fruit thereof is uncertain; and consequently no culture of the earth; no navigation nor use of the commodities that may be imported by sea; no commodious building; no instruments of moving and removing such things as require force; no knowledge of the face of the earth; no account of time; no arts; no letters; no society; and which is worst of all, continual fear and danger of violent death; and the life of man solitary, poor, nasty, brutish, and short (Hobbes 1958 [1651], 107).

The stateless society described by Hobbes lacks social order and provides no incentives for hard work and creativity, ingredients that are essential for increased productivity and technological progress. The stateless society is regressive and provides no protection of individual and civil liberties or property rights of members. In this state of nature, individuals divert their energies away from productive activities to predatory behaviour, seeking to prey on what others have produced. It is therefore a society characterized by economic stagnation, and even the very concept of property rights does not exist. Hobbes suggested that to get out of this 'jungle' men should introduce restraints upon themselves by creation of a common power. Hobbes recognized that, given a chance, individuals would voluntarily transfer authority to the state, even with the full knowledge that in so doing they must necessarily sacrifice some degree of autonomy and therefore limit their liberty. Hobbes considered unlimited government as necessary for the establishment of civil society.

Today, the fact that governments play crucial and legitimate roles in society is universally accepted and rarely provokes debate. However, it has been recognized that the establishment of a common power is not a sufficient condition for the emergence and maintenance of civil societies. Civil society requires that there be clear limits to the scope of government activity. Specifically, the scope of government action in regulating the activities of citizens must be subject to enforceable constraints. That is, government action must be kept within some clearly defined boundaries. These boundaries must be well understood and accepted by the electorate, and there must also be enforceable mechanisms to constrain government within those boundaries.

John Locke [1690 (1988)] was among the early social philosophers who advanced the idea of a limited state as necessary for achieving civil societies. Locke observed that in the state of nature, every man has a right to restrain those who would seek to interfere with his right to his life, liberty and property. To Locke, such interference essentially translates into a 'state of war'. To avoid this state of war, Locke suggested that men should put themselves into society, and thus quit the state of nature. However, Locke's position differs markedly from that advanced by Hobbes. Locke suggested that government is empowered to do what members of society could have done in the state of nature, namely protect their lives, liberties and property. Thus although Locke advocated a common authority as necessary to establish civil society, such was not to be achieved at the expense of sacrificing individual rights to the state. Specifically, Locke conceived of a state authority that was essentially an agent of the members. As stated by Locke, if the government exceeds the authority granted by the members, a state of war emerges:

> The reason why men enter into society is the preservation of their property; and the end why they choose and authorize a legislature is that there may be laws made, and rules set, as guards and fences to the properties of all the members of the society to limit the power and moderate the dominion of every part and member of the society. For since it can never be supposed to be the will of the society that the legislature should have power to destroy that which everyone designs secure by entering into society, and for which the people submitted themselves to legislators of their own making, whenever the legislators endeavour to take away and destroy the property of the people, or to reduce them to slavery under arbitrary power, they put themselves into a state of war with the people, who are thereupon absolved from any further obedience, and are left to the common refuge which God has provided for all men against force and violence (Locke 1988, 412).

While both Hobbes and Locke suggested that government was necessary to avoid the state of war, Locke also considered a limited government essential for civil societies.

Leading contractarians today, led by James Buchanan (1975, 1989), emphasize the importance of rules to constrain the behaviour of the members of society and the exercise of state authority. Buchanan's contractarian view of the state is a logical extension of the theory of exchange. In this model, rules limit each individual's activity relative to others and also define the scope of state authority with the ultimate goal of wealth maximization. Buchanan argues that the primary difference between totalitarian and non-totalitarian societies is that in totalitarian societies, there are no rule-protected spheres within which individuals are guaranteed the exercise of liberty. While state authority yields gains to the members of non-totalitarian societies, there are costs in terms of liberties sacrificed:

> We should never be trapped in the delusion that the enhancement of the state's authority to 'do good things for us collectively' involves no cost to us as free individuals. But recognizing that this cost exists is not the same as saying that it is a cost we shall never pay. The cost in liberty will, over some ranges of state action, be lower than expected benefit from the exercise of state authority within defined limits. We are able to satisfy our preferences, to achieve a higher level of utility, where some of our liberties have been sacrificed and where there does exist a well-defined but limited domain for the exercise of the coercive power of the state (Buchanan 1989, 54).

The fact that once individuals accept state authority they must also pay a price in the form of sacrificed liberties does not preclude the existence of civil societies. The rules regulating state authority guarantee the maintenance of civil society. The contractarian view is also consistent with the development of efficient property rights necessary for economic growth.

The present study is about man and state, focusing on Sub-Saharan Africa. Our concern is with the institutional arrangements that are necessary to restore civil societies in these countries. The primary motivation of the study is the unfortunate state of affairs in Sub-Saharan Africa that reflects a breakdown of civil society. As ironic as it may appear, the state of affairs in Sub-Saharan Africa reminds us of the Hobbesian jungle. In these countries, economic progress has been dismal. The economic well-being of the majority of citizens remains much as it was at the time of independence, and in some countries the well-being of the average citizen has actually declined. Sub-Saharan Africa remains one of the few areas in the world where thousands of people die each year because of hunger. Even in those countries that have not faced extreme famine situations, the proportion of the population living below 'absolute' poverty has either not decreased or has continued to increase. Virtually all of the countries have, at one time or other since independence, experienced a variety of internal conflicts involving different ethnic, religious or linguistic groups. Some of these conflicts have translated into violent military coups, while in other cases they have taken the form of prolonged ethnic and religious rivalries. Many internal conflicts in Africa have been ongoing for extended durations and have involved several regions of the affected countries. Practically all Sub-Saharan African countries are currently experiencing frequent incidences of inter-tribal fighting that have resulted in significant loss of life and property, and the displacement of thousands of people from their homes and land. Like the stateless society described by Hobbes, life for many in Africa is poor, nasty, brutish and short.

To Hobbes, these outcomes occur if there is no common power to harmonize the various interests. In Africa, however, the Hobbesian jungle type of outcomes reflect the activities of the unconstrained state. To a large extent, it is the excessive power of the state that has been responsible for destroying and preventing the emergence of civil societies. In virtually all the countries in the region, governments regularly undertake the violation of individual and group rights and frequently engage in extensive violation of economic liberties. Thus the authoritarian state which Hobbes proposed as the way out of the jungle has actually been largely responsible for keeping the African people 'in a state of war', much like in the original state. It is government power that has been responsible for returning Africans back to the 'jungle'.

The extreme conditions of poverty in African countries are to a large extent the result of excessive government intervention in markets, which creates insecure property rights and thereby destroys production incentives. Violation of property rights takes many forms, ranging from excessive market controls and taxation to outright confiscation of property. In addition to inhibiting economic growth, excessive government intervention leads directly to conflicts among various groups in these countries. This is because most of the interventions that violate property rights benefit members of one group at the expense of other groups. With no effective political mechanisms for solving differences between groups, armed conflict has become the dominant method of expressing grievances and for increasing a group's share of national resources (Kimenyi and Mbaku 1993). The resulting conflicts in turn distort production and resource allocation, and exacerbate violations of rights by governments. Ethnic conflicts in Africa reflect sub-optimal institutional arrangements that make it possible for governments to use discriminatory policies that seek to transfer benefits from one tribal group to another. Ethnic conflicts are probably the clearest indication of the absence, or the breakdown, of civil society in Africa.

Economists are quick to point out that the interventionist policies that violate property rights are largely responsible for poor economic performance in Africa. Reducing government interference in markets is, then, considered central to economic progress. This has been the primary policy reform recommended by international development organizations such as the World Bank and the International Monetary Fund. It is true that extensive government intervention in markets, by violating property rights, has contributed to slow economic growth in Sub-Saharan Africa (Kimenyi 1991). Nevertheless, merely prescribing appropriate market reforms is not sufficient because the success of such policies would largely depend on institutional arrangements. As noted by Rowley (1995, 1) 'a decisive factor determining whether an economy will grow, stagnate, or decline is the quality of its constitution or the set of rules and constraints that serve to regulate the behavior of its political markets'. Recognition of the fact that institutions matter, then, calls for more involved analysis of the nature of African institutions and the various reforms that would constrain government within some limited sphere and thus restore civil society.

In addition to violating property rights, African governments are notorious for violating individual and civil liberties. Human rights abuses are widespread in Africa, though more so in some countries than others.

The tyrannical rule by Idi Amin of Uganda and Bokassa of the Central African Republic are only extreme examples of gross violations of rights that Africans have been subjected to by their leaders. But even where abuses are not currently as extensive, there are clear signs that they will escalate in the near future if radical changes designed to harmonize the interests of various factions and population groups are not made. Even today, many African leaders have taken it upon themselves to infringe grossly on the rights of citizens, restricting political activities, torturing political prisoners and denying the due process of law. In all cases, the extreme violation of individual and group rights in the result of the excessive power of the executive branch. The leaders use their powers arbitrarily to define and limit the rights and freedoms of the people. With weak constitutional frameworks and in the absence of credible mechanisms to limit government activity, leaders frequently interfere with the judicial and legislative branches, thereby hindering any long-term progress towards the achievement of civil societies. As one periodical recently reported, African leaders have too much power and behave as if they are lending institutions of rights and freedoms (*Option* 1995, 10).

As noted, the restoration and maintenance of civil societies require that the state has only limited powers sufficient to secure the people's liberty and to protect their rights to property. It is the protection of such liberties that forms the cornerstone of economic well-being and provides foundations for the evolution of institutions that advance the quality of life in society. Meaningful economic and social development can only be realized if individual and civil liberties are protected adequately, consistently and in a predictable manner. Protection of individual and civil liberties can only be guaranteed if the scope of government activity is clearly defined and limited through the democratic process and by means of enforceable constitutions. Although many African nations have emphasized the need to reform their economies in order to accelerate economic growth, such reforms cannot be sustained, nor can they result in comprehensive development, if they are not accompanied by the adoption of durable and enforceable social contracts that guarantee respect and protection of individual and civil liberties.

Looking at African societies from the perspective of the breakdown of civil society, we realize that ethnicity plays a crucial role. The way different groups in the countries relate to each other in political and economic markets is probably the single most important factor that can help us understand African institutions. Thus in addition to emphasizing that institutions matter, we also emphasize that in Africa it is necessary to take into account the complex ethnic composition of these countries. It is a proper understanding of the ethnic factor that provides for the institutional reforms necessary for restoration of civil societies.

The basic thesis of this study is that economic crises and the extreme violations of civil liberties that characterize the majority of Black African countries are to a large extent the product of institutions that are not suited to dealing with heterogeneous populations. The failure of political institutions to accommodate diverse interests (ethnic, religious and linguistic) has generated conflict situations that adversely affect political and economic outcomes. It is the failure of political institutions to balance the interests of different groups effectively that we consider to be the primary cause of the pathetic conditions in Sub-Saharan African countries. When political institutions adequately harmonize the interests of diverse groups, diversity contributes positively to political stability and to economic growth. On the other hand, the failure of institutions to deal adequately with diverse interests results in political instability, civil strife and economic stagnation.

Over the last few years, democratization movements have spread across many of the Sub-Saharan African countries. These movements have taken the form of opening up political markets to allow opposing political parties, thus replacing the single-party and military dictatorships that have been dominant for the last four decades. There is little doubt that political party competition is likely to make the political leadership more responsive to the electorate. But the problems that characterize African nations are not likely to disappear just because of the introduction of competitive political systems.

In fact the limited experience with political party competition in Africa is not encouraging. Parties have frequently turned out to be no more than tribal factions that have no clear ideology or plan of action other than transferring more benefits to members of their supporting coalitions. Furthermore, the legalization of opposition parties has not really resulted in truly competitive political markets that would otherwise serve as effective vehicles in the design of viable constitutional contracts that guarantee protection of individual and group rights. In virtually all the African countries that have recently entered the era of 'multi-partyism', the structures of government have remained virtually as they were during the single-party era. As a result, African states continue to suffer from the single-party legacy of over-centralization, weakly developed civil societies and a lack of independent institutions that are necessary for proper governance.

Thus the crises in Africa should not be seen as primarily the outcome of single-party dictatorships. In fact it is likely that multi-party political systems under the current political arrangements will degenerate, with similar outcomes as those experienced under single-party dictatorships. We suggest that the various conflicts among groups in Africa cannot be eliminated by political party competition alone. In fact it is conceivable that such conflicts could be intensified by the introduction of political party competition in unitary states. Establishing civil societies in Africa will require not just simple adjustments to the existing systems, but rather calls for the major restructuring of political institutions.

The study suggests that unitary systems of government are not suited to dealing with Africa's diverse populations. On the one hand, the fact that African states have remained very much as they were during independence with regard to the composition of tribal groups may be viewed as a success of the unitary states. On the other hand, the fact that many groups are involved in various sorts of costly conflict reflects the failure of the unitary state to moderate the interests of diverse groups within national boundaries. In fact recent events in Africa suggest that the benefits associated with trying to unify the various groups are more than outweighed by the costs of such unity. Likewise, the concentration of power in unitary states has provided predatory leaders with the opportunity to transfer benefits from one group to another, thereby violating property rights and thus adversely affecting economic growth.

Based on what has transpired in Africa, we are compelled to conclude that the experiment with highly centralized unitary systems of government has been a failure. We contend that such unitary systems of government are largely unnatural to most African settings, and therefore are unlikely to succeed even under the best of circumstances. Instead we provide arguments for decentralized unitary states and also for federal systems of government. Decentralization and federalism would provide broad opportunities for the exercise of civil liberties, more efficient and stable protection of property rights, and more cooperation among the various groups in particular matters. We suggest that federalism in particular would serve to accommodate the self-determination of different groups, and thus may be the most suitable way for African countries to reduce internal conflicts and achieve political stability.

A central theme of this study is that expressions of ethnic preference represent a natural right and thus such expressions are not only desirable but are consistent with the advancement of individual liberty. We therefore advocate the creation of institutions that do not hinder the desire of people and polities to remain separate and preserve their identities. While we acknowledge that there is an ugly side to 'tribalism' or 'ethnic nationalism', we suggest that institutions that seek to suppress ethnic or tribal preference necessarily must involve imposed order and, as a result, must generate conflict. Appropriate institutional arrangements must guarantee the rights of people to maintain their identity while at the same time freely choosing to form political associations with others for the purposes of accomplishing common ends.

2. From Tribal Chief to Dictator

Most Sub-Saharan African countries are either under dictatorial rule or semi-autocratic regimes. In Chapter 1, we noted that some of the main problems in Sub-Saharan Africa have to do with the highly centralized unitary states compounded by heavy government intervention in markets. Highly centralized unitary states provide limited options for expressions of group differences and necessarily limit individual liberty. Heavy government intervention in turn necessarily results in the violation of property rights and acts as a barrier to the efficient functioning of markets, thereby retarding economic growth. We have suggested that, to restore civil society in these countries, radical restructuring of political institutions is necessary to constrain state authority in order to guarantee the protection of individual, civic and economic liberties. These goals cannot be achieved under autocratic rule, and thus a change to participatory democracies must be the first step towards the restoration of civil society.

While it is widely accepted that radical institutional changes are necessary to restore civil society in Africa, views as to what changes are appropriate vary widely. To be sure, reforming the institutions of Sub-Saharan Africa is complex and any changes that are made require time to reach maturity. To appreciate the complexity of reforming the political institutions, it is useful to review the evolution of present-day political institutions. Understanding how Africa's governments evolved will help us to avoid repeating the mistakes that led to institutions that are not consistent with civil society. In this chapter, we trace the evolution of African governments starting with the traditional governments that existed during the pre-colonial era.

Before colonialism in Sub-Saharan Africa, the 'tribe' was the primary unit around which governments were organized. Although in some cases smaller governmental units were organized around clans, frequently such governments had linkages with the larger tribal government. Thus the traditional form of organized authority in Sub-Saharan Africa was what is commonly referred to as 'tribal government'. The ruler of the tribal government was the tribal chief and, in larger and more elaborate governments (kingdoms), the ruler was a king who headed a government that included a council of advisers comprising chiefs. Tribal governments varied widely in size, ranging from those that included only a handful of families to more populous, and often powerful, kingdoms that extended over wide land masses.

The rulers of the traditional governments had several functions, such as presiding in the highest courts, maintaining order in the society and, in some tribes, the chief was also the religious leader. An important function conducted by the rulers was the maintenance of strong and well-organized armies for protection against external threats and also for territorial expansion by conquest. The ruler was therefore the commander-in-chief and was expected to be brave and well organized. Leaders who were not able to organize and command strong armies had relatively short tenure. Rulers were entitled to a wide range of benefits including tributes such as court fines and market levies, and they also benefited from free labour services provided by their subjects. The rulers had claim to produce, particularly that valuable to external trade such as ivory and animal skins. As such, rulers were able to live in greater comfort than their subjects. Chieftainship was therefore a privileged position.

Contrary to the common belief that African governments have always been dictatorial, the truth is that tribal governments had many aspects of representative government (Ayittey 1991). This is not to say that tribal governments were democratic by today's standards. As a matter of fact, there were no direct elections and leadership was hereditary, often reserved for certain lineages. It is also true that the typical African chief (or king) commanded vast powers, and decisions by such rulers were rarely questioned. However, the chiefs and kings typically were not authoritarian, but rather ruled by consultation with respected members of the community who advised them on matters of concern to the general public. No African ruler was ever expected to take decisions in matters affecting his subjects without consulting someone else. Among several Bantu groups, for example, it was customary for the ruler to have as his chief adviser someone who was not of his lineage, 'a commoner who was a mouthpiece of popular dissatisfaction' (Mair 1965). As a matter of fact, in some cases advisers could dispose of a ruler:

> Most traditional rulers are advised by councils, which may consist of kinsmen, or of unrelated officials, or of a mixture of both. In many societies these

councils have the power to reprimand and even fine a ruler; among the Swazi they may even depose him. In most societies, also, a subject who believes himself to have been unfairly treated by a subordinate chief has a right to appeal directly to the paramount ruler (Beattie 1964, 162).

There were other institutional arrangements that acted to check the powers of the rulers. Among these was the decentralization of power and the dependence upon the rule of law. Vaughan (1986, 178), for example, writes:

> It may be suspected that divine kings and such panoply of government might tend to authoritarianism, but several institutions militate against this in African states. In some Kingdoms, such as the Ashanti, village and regional divisions are sufficiently organized so as to decentralize the secular authority of the king. In many instances, the dependence upon the rule of law and a respect for law seems to have inhibited ambitious rulers. Nor should it be forgotten that regicide itself is an ultimate check upon the excess of a king.

We would be overstating the facts if we suggested that traditional governments functioned perfectly well and that rulers never overstepped their authority. Problems often arose and certainly rulers not infrequently sought to extend their authority. However, there were important options for the public that allowed them to avoid despotic rule and thus effectively constrained the exercise of authority by rulers. The most important of these was the 'exit' option that allowed individuals to move to other jurisdictions:

> Within a kingdom an individual could move from one chief's area to another; and on a larger scale, groups could secede, and either make themselves independent or seek the protection of another ruler. The ultimate safeguard against oppressive authority was the desire of rulers and their subordinates alike to keep up the numbers of their following. This is not to say that people in societies which had never heard of democratic freedoms did not put up with a good deal before deciding that they had had enough (Mair 1965, 117).

This exit opportunity, which is analogous to the familiar *'voting with the feet'* (Tiebout 1956), and the fact that there was competition to leaders from outside, must have been crucial in constraining the powers of the rulers, and offers important lessons in reforming today's institutions. Thus by and large the traditional political institutions provided effective constraints on the rulers and, within the given rules, protected the rights of the members. In today's highly centralized unitary states, the exit option is absent and man-made barriers prevent competition for the supply of legislation.

The behaviour of the general public in traditional African societies was also subject to some constraints that ensured that individuals did not infringe on the rights of others. Even in these primitive states, laws regulated the scope of individual activity. In these societies, law existed in the sense that people agreed that certain actions infringed upon the rights of others and that injuries could be made good by some form of stipulated compensation. That is, there was an orderly system by which disputes were settled (Evans-Pritchard 1962). Indigenous African societies, therefore, had accepted codes of behaviour in the form of customs supported by specific sanctions:

> There is so much diversity in the structures and complexities of African political systems that a fundamental underlying principle may be overlooked. Virtually all of these diverse political organizations are based upon the validity of public means of resolving disputes and conflicts, that is, upon the *rule of law*. This is not to say that societies have statutes which in and of themselves regulate behavior. Rarely is there anything so conscious or formal; rather, members of societies accept that there is a moral basis to public order and that publicly sanctioned resolutions of disputes and conflicts are necessary for the continuance of social life beyond the family or clan (Vaughan 1986, 175).

Given the self-interest motive characteristic of all human beings, traditional African societies faced a prisoner's dilemma situation (what Gordon Tullock (1974) appropriately called a 'social dilemma') that confronts members in all societies. The story that emerges from the foregoing discussion is that traditional African societies resolved the dilemma by cooperation as opposed to predation. In essence, traditional African governments represented some sort of implicit contract among the people for the purpose of increasing social value. They were not perfect institutions, but given the circumstances, such arrangements resulted in primitive forms of civil society.

The emergence of modern state governments is largely the result of a number of events that disrupted the traditional African way of life. The most important of these include the African slave trade, the spread of Islam and the imposition of colonial rule. The people of North Africa, for example, readily accepted Islam and governmental institutions introduced by Arabs. Islam also had some influence on people living along the East African coast. The slave trade, on the other hand, provided a lucrative source of wealth to Arabs, Europeans and African kingdoms that were involved in the trade. The trade also created a variety of conflict situations as slave raids spread from the coast to the interior regions of Africa and guns were introduced into African states as payment for slaves. These events disrupted the organization of traditional societies but did not have significant lasting effects on the basic institutions of most of Sub-Saharan Africa.

During the late 1800s, Great Britain, France, Germany, Belgium and, to a lesser extent, Italy and Spain, were heavily engaged in attempts to place under their control parts of the African continent – what is known as the 'scramble for Africa'. Between 1870 and 1880, the European powers rapidly expanded their territorial claims, and as each power acquired more and more of the continent, it became apparent that competition for Africa threatened peace in Europe. In 1884, Chancellor Otto Von Bismarck of Prussia invited European nations to a conference in Berlin with the main goal of regularizing the scramble for Africa. The Berlin Act of 26 February 1885 stipulated how Africa would be partitioned into European colonies. By 1910, the partition of Africa was achieved and, for the next 45 years, only Liberia and Ethiopia (which was occupied briefly by Italy) remained independent nations (Burke 1991).

Colonial rule adversely affected African institutions. Indeed many of the problematic features of current African political institutions are the product of the colonial experience (Mbaku and Kimenyi 1995). First and foremost, in partitioning Africa among themselves across 'spheres of influence' colonial powers rarely took into consideration the issue of ethnic heterogeneity. In some countries, the boundaries were drawn in a manner that separated members of the same ethnic group by placing them in different countries, while at the same time placing other, formerly separate, groups in the same country. Partition was implemented without due regard to ethnicity, culture or even the existing institutions of government.

Second, colonial powers did little to develop democratic institutions in Africa. Colonial powers, for the most part, were interested in maximizing economic gains for themselves and thus were not overly concerned about the overall development of the colonies (Ayittey 1992). There was therefore limited emphasis on training Africans to acquire the capability to govern themselves. Even when Europeans trained or extended favours to some Africans, this was primarily for the benefit of the Europeans in governing the natives.

Finally, Europeans favoured members of certain tribes over others, a policy of divide and rule that weakened the opposition to colonial rule. The ethnic divisions thus created were manifested during the struggles for independence and continue to be important today. Ethnic differences in levels of education and income that exist today are a product, in large part, of the colonial experience.

After independence, African economic and social problems were attributed to the colonial experience. Exploitation of African labour and resources by colonialists was seen as the primary cause of poverty. Colonialists had appropriated most of the fertile land for themselves, leaving the less productive areas to Africans. The colonialists used low-paid African labour to produce cash-crops that were exported to Europe and to other developed countries (Bauer 1934; Curtin *et al.* 1988). Educational opportunities were extended to a limited number of children, often those whose parents were loyal to the colonial government. With limited educational opportunities, the majority of young Africans provided a reliable supply of cheap labour. As a result, at the time of independence, the African countries had a severe shortage of the skilled manpower necessary to transform the economies to modern production.

The colonial powers were also blamed for contributing to poverty as a result of exploitation of primary resources which they exported to their mother countries. Such exploitation, it was contended, led to economic development of the European countries at the expense of African development. Thus founding leaders in Africa often made the case that the economic hardships experienced were not to be attributed to the independent governments' policies because they were the fruits of years of colonial exploitation and of the capitalist system.

Policy-making during the immediate independence period reflected the belief that colonialism and capitalism were the primary causes of poverty in Africa. As such, policies and programmes that emphasized redistribution dominated. There was also increased hostility to market institutions that were considered exploitative. The multinational corporation, for example, was considered to be an extension of colonial exploitation. Unfavourable policies towards foreign investment were therefore implemented. In some countries such as Tanzania, leaders proclaimed socialist ideas as necessary to counter 'Western imperialism'. In a number of countries, there was instituted a mass nationalization of private property and the adoption of various socialist programmes. Even in those countries where socialist planning was not implemented, the role of the government increased tremendously, with large shares of GNP directed to the public sector.

At the time of independence, the new nations had to make crucial decisions concerning the constitutional dimensions of government activities. These dimensions included such characteristics as the number of jurisdictional levels: whether the political system was to be unitary, with power concentrated at one level, or federal, with power distributed between regional governments and a central government. In the case of the federal system, decisions had to be made concerning the number of levels, such as provincial, district, municipal and local, and also the functions that would be performed at each level. Other decisions pertained to procedures and processes of selecting representatives, and the constitutional rules regulating the amendment of the constitution.

In selecting particular constitutional dimensions, the primary objectives included the achievement of economic growth, and of a just and free society that provided freedom from oppression of one group by another. The leaders, at least ostensibly, sought to adopt constitutions that would advance individual liberty while at the same time creating unity among diverse populations.

Because the various tribal, religious and linguistic groups in each of the countries considered themselves different from other groups in various respects, the issue of unity was a primary concern. Specifically, unifying the groups into one national state was considered crucial for political stability. To be sure, Africans had to deal with pressing problems of unity after independence that may have required them to adopt unifying policies. For example, as discussed previously, many tribal communities existed independently. These communities frequently consisted of thousands of members and possessed well-developed cultures, languages and clear tribal consciousness.

However, the existing national boundaries cut across these groups, ignoring the boundaries that defined previously autonomous units. For this reason, leaders advocated the establishment of unitary states with a high concentration of power. It was claimed that centralizing power allowed for the adoption of uniform policies and for the balancing of economic resources, thus uniting diverse populations.

Some leaders argued that single-party political systems were more appropriate for African countries because all groups (tribal, religious and linguistic), regardless of their differences, would be joined together under one party. Thus the single-party system was seen as an important unifying agent of otherwise different groups. The leaders warned that unity would be sacrificed if political party competition were to be introduced (Winchester 1986), because different political parties would be dominated by particular tribal and linguistic groups which in essence would promote tribalism. Thus the common response to diversity was the adoption of policies and institutional arrangements that unified heterogeneous populations by limiting expressions of group differences.

A few years after independence, the high hopes for a better life that Africans had cherished started to fade. It became clear that the policies implemented by the new governments were not yielding the expected results. Socialist planning and redistributive policies were harming large sections of the population by discouraging production and encouraging rent-seeking behaviour. Bloated civil services and heavy government intervention in markets generated widespread corruption. Not only did the economic situation deteriorate, but also internal ethnic divisions rapidly became the norm rather than the exception. As a rate of economic growth slowed down, and even became negative, developed countries responded by providing financial support in the forms of loans and grants. Increasingly, the African countries became dependent on foreign countries.

By the mid 1980s, most of these countries were experiencing serious debt problems. In 1992, Sub-Saharan Africa's debt was US$ 150 billion, in excess of 112 per cent of those countries' GDP. As a result, about 30 per cent of export earnings was devoted to servicing the debt (*Index on Censorship* 1992). Unfortunately, the infusion of foreign aid did not solve the problems facing those nations and, because it fuelled further rent-seeking, it may instead have had a negative effect on growth.

Although the first leaders of the independent African nations rose to power through popular elections and vowed to maintain constitutional government, this was not to be the case for long. For no effective mechanisms existed to constrain the powers of leaders who soon considered themselves to be above the law. Claiming to unite the various ethnic groups, the leaders outlawed opposition politics and thus effectively squashed the development of democratic political systems and blocked any orderly transfer of power.

The African leaders distributed favours – property, government jobs, business licences, and so on – to members of their own tribes, thereby exacerbating the divisions among the different ethnic groups. Senior bureaucrats, following this cue from their leaders, became increasingly corrupt (Mbaku 1994a). As time went on, the leaders became more and more authoritarian, using all means at their disposal to eliminate those who criticized them.

Arbitrary arrests, detention without trial, murder, torture and the confiscation of private property all became common practice for deterring political opposition. Violations of human rights and of property rights escalated, and progressively all hopes for civil society disappeared. Antagonisms between ethnic groups increased as governments continued to discriminate against members of some groups. The single-party rule that was viewed as a unifying factor became a source for instability and political oppression:

> Rather than diminish tribal rivalry and tension, single-party states as often as not establish one 'tribe' or other self-selected elitist group in power with a primary interest in perpetuating that situation. As is the case with centrally planned economies, a small number of people unambiguously benefit, and others are led to believe that they do (or will) as well. Single-party states give rise to political black markets similar to economic black markets. Popular dissident movements, domestic insurgences, and warring factions within the ruling elite inevitably appear, only to be cut down ruthlessly whenever possible (Cohen 1994, 13).

Slowly but surely, Africans were back in a state of war. With limited options for expressing dissatisfaction, violence became the primary method of changing government. Military dictators violently replaced the civilian dictatorships, and the cycle continued through the 1980s with one dictator replacing another. By 1990, virtually all Sub-Saharan Africa was either under military or civilian dictatorship. Even worse, most of these regimes were either brutally repressive or very repressive (Table 2.1).

The collapse of the Soviet Empire, the demise of communism almost world-wide and the abandonment of apartheid in South Africa have opened up a rare opportunity for reform in Africa. During the early 1990s, internal and external pressure for African leaders to relinquish their firm grip on power increased. The result was a wave of democratization movements where opposition parties challenged incumbent dictatorships. Unfortunately, the impact of these movements in transforming political institutions was minimal, because they exacerbated ethnic rivalries.

The foregoing discussion points to what we consider to be the primary feature of the Sub-Saharan African countries that poses the most important barrier to reform, namely the high degree of population heterogeneity. Proposals for reforming Africa's political institutions

Table 2.1 The political configurations of Africa by 1990

1. Military Dictatorships (years of military rule/years of independence)

Brutally Repressive	Very Repressive	Repressive
Benin (27/30)	Burundi (25/8)	Central African
Burkina Faso (20/30)	Congo-Brazzaville (12/30)	Republic (9/30)
Ethiopia (16/–)	Equatorial Guinea (11/22)	Chad (15/30)
Ghana (20/33)	Guinea-Bissau (10/16)	Mali (22/30)
Liberia (10/–)	Guinea (7/32)	Nigeria (20/30)
Mauritania (12/30)	Lesotho (7/24)	Gabon (23/30)
Libya (21/39)	Niger (16/30)	
Somalia (21/30)	Rwanda (17/28)	
Sudan (27/34)	Togoland (27/30)	
Uganda (15/28)	Zaire (25/30)	

2. Civilian Dictatorships (years of one-party rule/years of independence)

Brutally Repressive	Very Repressive	Repressive
Angola (15/15)	Cameroon (30/30)	Algeria (28/28)
Comoros (14/14)	Cape Verde Islands	Cote d' Ivore (30/30)
Malawi (26/26)	(15/15)	Djibouti (13/13)
Mozambique (15/15)	Madagascar (18/30)	Egypt (20/–)
Zimbabwe (10/10)	Kenya (27/27)	Seychelles (13/14)
	Sao Tome & Principal	Sierra Leone (29/29)
	(15/15)	
	Tanzania (29/29)	

3.

Monarchical Rule	Whites-Only Rule*	Indigenously African (Consensual Democracy)
Morocco	Namibia	Botswana
Swaziland	South Africa	Senegal
		Mauritius
		The Gambia

* Both Namibia and South Africa now have majority governments.

Source: (1992, 116)

must therefore focus on dealing with ethnic identity. Reformers must accept that, no matter what means are used to suppress ethnic identification, such identification will continue to dominate political markets in Sub-Saharan African countries. Whether institutional reforms provide for adequate protection of individual, civil and economic liberties will largely depend on how well ethnic identification is accommodated. Reformers must therefore seek to understand and appreciate the role of ethnicity in explaining political outcomes in Sub-Saharan Africa.

3. Ethnic Nations and Associations in Africa

Since independence, African leaders and intellectuals have engaged in highly publicized efforts to denounce tribalism (Nkrumah 1970). Identifying with a particular tribe or behaving in ways that are considered to be influenced by one's tribe while in public service, are viewed as regressive. Tribalism, many claim, has no place in the modernizing nations of Africa. At the national level, identifying with a tribal group and/or other cleavage such as a religious or linguistic group, is considered inconsistent with development. Individuals should identify with the nation and not with a particular tribe. Thus in the design and implementation of government policies and programmes, politicians and civil servants claim to behave in a manner consistent with maximizing the public interest at large and not that of more narrowly defined groups such as their own tribal groups (Smith 1983).

For tribal affiliation not to have any effect on policy outcomes, one would have to assume that the policy-makers are completely 'detribalized'. Thus in all African countries, politicians and bureaucrats make frequent claims to the effect that they are concerned with the well-being of all citizens and not with that of any particular tribe. In fact few policy-makers openly admit that they make policy decisions that reflect preference for their tribe or that they discriminate against other groups. Like the Rawlsian veil of ignorance (Rawls 1971), policy-makers are expected to disassociate themselves completely from any ethnic or tribal attachments that they actually may have.

The truth is, however, that tribal attachment (tribalism, ethnic nationalism) is alive and well in Africa. To be sure, individuals still consider themselves as members of particular groups and are proud to be members of those small groups. While they may consider themselves loyal members of the nation, they also identify with particular groups. There is no question that most Africans are patriotic with respect to their nations. Equally so, however, they are patriotic and loyal to their tribal groups.

Few will deny, when pressed, that even within their own countries, they more often associate with members of their own tribe. A Nigerian Ibo is more likely to associate with other Ibos, to do business with them and to join those groups where most of the members are Ibos. Likewise, a Kenyan Kikuyu is likely to be in business with other Kikuyus and join organizations where there are more Kikuyus, and so on. These forms of voluntary associations are very common in Africa.

Of course, there are clear cases and situations when individuals identify with a particular nation (for example, during times of war with other countries). However, many of the issues that confront persons on a day-to-day basis – schools, labour markets, businesses, and so on – require that individuals identify with a smaller group. In Africa, this group is often the tribe. Thus the institution we refer to as 'tribe' is very important.

THE TRIBAL NATIONS OF BLACK AFRICA

To appreciate the main thrust of this study, it is necessary that the reader understands the complications of ethnic diversity in Africa. For the purpose of this study, we focus on the countries that are often referred to as 'Sub-Saharan Africa' or 'Black Africa'. This excludes Northern African countries such as Egypt, Libya, Morocco and Algeria. These countries have much higher degrees of population homogeneity as compared with other African countries and do not face the types of internal conflict that we focus on in this study.

Figure 3.1 shows the geographical location of the various African countries. As noted earlier, the map of Africa largely reflects boundaries drawn over 100 years ago following the Berlin Act. Although it is well accepted that colonial boundaries did not take into account ethnic or cultural boundaries, the inherited boundaries have remained largely intact. This conforms with the Organization of African Unity's principle of inviolability of colonial frontiers. This principle holds that the political map of Africa should correspond to the map that resulted from the partition of Africa. Although the principle of inviolability has held pretty well, there is nothing special about the boundaries. They still remain as unnatural as they were at the time of partition. For example, the boundary between Kenya and Somalia separates the Somali people, placing some in Kenya while their families are across the border in

Figure 3.1   A map of Africa

Somalia. Likewise, the Masai of Kenya are separated from their families in Tanzania.

While the African national boundaries are well accepted as forming the demarcation between nations, there are other boundaries that separate the various ethnic groups in those countries. Although these boundaries are not as clearly specified, they do nevertheless exist and to a large extent they are respected by the respective groups that live next to each other. Thus the various ethnic groups have what they refer to as their 'territory' and, in many respects, members of other ethnic groups are considered outsiders.

Ethnic units differ in various ways. In most cases, the difference between two groups is language. More often than not, ethnic units will differ in various aspects including their history, language and customs. While groups living close to each other may have several similarities in their ways of life, they also have characteristics that make them distinct. Whether the difference between ethnic groups is large or small, the point to keep in mind is that each ethnic group considers itself different and frequently identifies with a particular region (Knight 1984). Therefore in many respects the ethnic units do form what could be called 'ethnic nations'. If one were to include the boundaries of ethnic nations, the map of Africa would be complicated indeed.

To appreciate the complexity of the ethnic heterogeneity in Black Africa, it helps to look at the ethnic make-up of the continent. In total there are over 2000 distinct tribes or ethnic societies, each of which has its own language or dialect, culture and tradition (Ayittey 1992). These tribes vary in size, with some having as few as 100,000 members and others encompassing millions of people. The degree of ethnic heterogeneity varies widely across the countries. In Rwanda and Burundi, for example, there are only two primary ethnic groups and two languages. In Sudan, on the other hand, there are over 170 distinct languages. In Nigeria there are between 200 and 400 distinct languages.

We provide the example of Zaire to demonstrate the complexity of the ethnic composition of African countries. Zaire, located in Central Africa, is a fairly heterogeneous country much like the majority of other Black African countries. There are actually 250 or so ethnic groups in Zaire. These ethnic groups can be grouped into 23 units that are closely related in terms of culture and language. Figure 3.2 shows these classifications and the regions in which they live. As is evident from Figure 3.2, each ethnic group resides in a particular area and fairly meaningful boundaries separating ethnic territories can be drawn.

Key to ethnic types

1. Mongo
2. Katanga Luba (Luba)
3. Songye
4. Kasai Luba (Lualua)
5. Kongo
6. Lunda (Luimbe + Ndembu)
7. Azandé
8. Manabetu
9. Yaka
10. Pende
11. Téké
12. Sakata
13. Yanzi
14. Kuba
15. Ngbandi
16. Kivu Peoples
17. Hemba (Kunda)
18. Bemba
19. Lala
20. Amba
21. Rega
22. Babwa
23. Alur

Figure 3.2   Ethnic units in Zaire

This feature, that ethnic groups also occupy well-defined regions, has important implications. Cobbah, for example, states:

> In Africa, this ethnic identity is above all other things a territorial identity. Nothing defines the ethnic group better than its 'standing place'. Thus the term geoethnicity has been used to describe the African ethnic phenomenon. Geoethnicity as opposed to non-territorial ethnic identification involves the historic identification of an ethnic group with a given territory, an attachment to a particular place, a sense of place as a symbol of being and identity (Cobbah 1988, 73).

The example of Zaire shows the typical ethnic composition of an African nation. Some countries, such as Nigeria, have a much more complex ethnic map. In addition to ethnicity, it is important to note that other factors such as religion complicate the existing heterogeneity. While religion does perform a unifying factor in some cases, it magnifies existing divisions in others. This is true in those countries where there are two or more dominant religions (Islam and Christianity in Nigeria and Sudan, for example). In these cases, religion cements existing differences. To the extent that each ethnic unit is characterized by distinct cultural values, such as family and social customs, religious affiliation and (frequently) political organization, in many ways they represent separate nations.

Another complicating factor in the organization of African nations – a factor that is related to ethnic diversity – is the size of the nations. Some of the countries are very large in terms of population and area. Nigeria has more than 100 million people; Ethiopia has a population of 54 million and Sudan has a population of 28 million. The geographical size of Sudan is one-third that of the entire United States; Ethiopia is twice the size of Texas; Mozambique is twice the size of California, and Chad, with a population of only 5.2 million, is three times the size of California.

Even those countries that are considered tiny are not that small: Somalia is the size of Texas, while Rwanda is the size of Maryland. Clearly, some of the African countries are excessively large, making it difficult for governments to serve local communities effectively. Frequently, far-flung local communities feel totally isolated from the central government.

ETHNIC ASSOCIATIONS

Identifying with one's tribe is highly valued. As such, resources are devoted to make certain that members of a group continue to identify with that group. In virtually all African communities, children are taught from an early age that they should identify and be proud of their tribe. Thus children learn at early ages that it is honourable to vote for members of their tribe or region, and that members of some tribes are not trustworthy and thus they should not do business with them. In some cases, they are warned against associating with members of particular tribes.

Children in many African countries are taught that loyalty should be to one's region and not the country. In virtually all countries, it would be unacceptable for members of some tribes to marry outside their tribe. It is in fact common for parents to curse their children for marrying outside their tribe. Stereotyping members of other tribes and using derogatory names is fairly common. As stated by Horowitz: 'In general, ethnic identity is strongly felt, behavior based on ethnicity is normatively sanctioned, and ethnicity is often accompanied by hostility toward outgroups' (Horowitz 1985, 7).

Although it is common for leaders to denounce ethnic identification and ethnic associations, examples confirm that Africans have, and do express, a strong preference for associating with members of their own tribe. In many countries, for example, soccer teams are organized along tribal lines. Even in the cities, it is easy to identify entertainment clubs and restaurants that are patronized by members of a particular tribe. The type of food served and the type of entertainment provided by these clubs reflect the tribal composition of the patrons. In other words, individuals are able to 'vote' their tribal preferences by selecting particular clubs.

The point here is that in most areas of everyday life, there are many instances in which individuals identify with members of their own tribe. Thus even in major cities where peoples from different tribes live in close proximity, tribal groupings emerge as individuals freely select with whom to associate. Even today the majority of urban social welfare organizations are organized along tribal lines. Another example of such associations are the land associations that were formed in some countries after independence. Individuals formed groups for the purpose of buying land previously owned by Europeans. Most of the associations were either people from the same tribe, same region or same clan. Rarely were there land-buying associations that included members of different tribes.

Strong tribal preference has been revealed in a variety of studies that seek to measure the social or political 'distance' between ethnic groups. For example, such studies in Zambia showed that:

> ... members of various tribes clustered together on account of their regional and cultural affinities, for instance, western and eastern tribes formed separate clusters due to their particularistic bonds and interests. Those results suggested that ethnic factors played significant roles in the formation of voluntary associations among heterogeneous groups, and voluntary associations normally tend to be specifically organized for the pursuit of special interests, be they economic or political, etc (Breytenbach 1975, 313).

Likewise, Kenneth Little (1957) observed that tribal-oriented associations rated among the most important voluntary associations in West Africa, such as the Ibo State Union which comprised a collection of village and clan groups.

Ethnic identification is reflected in virtually all aspects of life in most African societies. A good example of ethnic identification in wider society concerns participation in political parties. During the pre-independence period, different ethnic groups in Africa had the goal of removing the then common enemy – the colonial powers. However, as the struggle for independence progressed and independence was in sight, self-determination by different groups emerged as each sought more control of the independent government. In other words, individuals started identifying more closely with members of their own tribes. As a result, in many countries the major political parties at independence were dominated by particular ethnic groups. In Nigeria the dominant parties were mainly composed of the Ibo, Yoruba and Hausa. Breytenbach (1975, 315) notes:

> A well-known pioneering example of the secularization of ethnic loyalties was the formation of the Egbe Omo Odudwa movement (Association of the Children of Odudwa) among the Yoruba of Western Nigeria. This movement aimed at the emergence of a modern Yoruba nationalism and as such laid the foundations for the establishment of an almost exclusive Yoruba political party, the Action Group (AG), led by Chief Awolowo. In fact all the political parties in Nigeria had their own distinctive ethnic support bases. Membership of the Northern Peoples Congress (NPC) was predominantly Hausa–Fulani and that of the National Convention of Nigerian Citizens (NCNC) predominantly Ibo.

Likewise, independence movements in other countries were divided across tribal lines. For example, the independence movement in Guinea Bissau was mainly composed of Balante people; in Angola the major liberation organizations, the Front for National Liberation of Angola and the Union for the Total Liberation of Angola, were divided along ethnic lines. The story is the same in Namibia. In Zimbabwe the two main liberation organizations split along ethnic lines: the Ndebele minority and the Shona majority.

Even when coalition parties that included different tribes were formed, they soon came to be dominated by members of one group. Likewise, in cases where the political parties were largely ideological, they soon turned out to be ethnic parties. In Sudan, the Communist Party was dominated by the Ansaris; in Guinea the socialists were Fulani; in Congo the socialists were primarily members of the Mbochi tribe. Examples of non-ethnic political parties being dominated by a particular ethnic group are widespread in all African countries.

Ethnic identification has also been apparent in recent democratization movements. With the recent wave of democratization, many new parties have been launched across the African continent. As it turns out, most of these parties have ethnic bases and frequently lack any ideological foundation. While strategically it makes sense for tribal groups to form coalitions if they are to win elections, such coalitions are often weak. Members of one tribe soon feel that they are dominated by other tribes and thus break away. For example, during the early 1990s the leading opposition party in Kenya, The Forum for the Restoration of Democracy (FORD), was popular across the country and had support across the dominant tribes in Kenya (Kikuyu, Luo and Luhya). A few months before the election the party split into two (FORD-Asili and FORD-Kenya), mostly on ethnic lines.

Probably more telling evidence of the degree of ethnic identification in politics is revealed by the patterns of voting. No matter which country one looks at, it has become clear that people vote very much on ethnic lines, and political ideology in the Western sense rarely plays a significant role.

Trade unions in many African countries reflect ethnic divisions. More often than not, people join unions that are dominated by members of their own tribe. Even where the union initially comprises members of all ethnic groups, soon one group feels that it is being dominated and splits to form a new union. In Kenya, dock workers belonging to the coastal tribes abandoned the Dock Workers' Union that was led by members of the Luo tribe and instead formed into their own union. Likewise in Zimbabwe, the Railway Union comprised branches composed of Ndebele and Shona tribes, but soon the Shona branches broke away to form their own union. In Nigeria, the Miners' Union was initially dominated by the Ibo, but later the Hausa and Birom miners formed their separate unions. A similar pattern of ethnically dominated labour unions has been evident in Zambia's 'copper belt' since the early 1930s.

Probably nowhere is ethnic identification as clear as in the civil service. It is well documented that, in virtually all African countries, employment in government is crucially dependent on one's tribal group. Many studies provide evidence to the effect that senior bureaucrats hire members of their own tribes. In fact 'tribalism' in government is the norm in all African countries. As noted by Horowitz (1994):

> In severely divided societies, ethnic identity provides clear lines to determine who will be included and who will be excluded. Since the lines appear unalterable, being in and being out may quickly come to look permanent. In ethnic politics, inclusion may affect the distribution of important material and nonmaterial goods, including the prestige of the various ethnic groups and the identity of the state as belonging more to one group than another (p. 35).

The foregoing discussion highlights the importance of group identification in Africa. The message here is that when we talk of African nations, it is important to realize that within those nations lie important ethnic divisions that comprise what may be considered separate 'ethnic' nations.

In evaluating the appropriate institutional arrangements for African countries, it is necessary to look beyond the boundaries that divide the individual countries. We should take into account that within each country are micro nations that have many characteristics of autonomous units. Members of different ethnic groups show a preference for associating with members of their respective groups. It is therefore futile to deny the existence of tribalism. Likewise, attempts to homogenize groups that clearly want to retain their identity will be self-defeating. Ake (1992) has made a strong case for recognizing the political relevance of traditional group identities:

> For most of us these social formations and group identities are not externalities but the core of our being; it is by these identities that most of us

define our individuality; its values, its interests and even its developmental possibilities; they are the organic whole of which we are part, but a part which can never be conceptualized in terms of separation, distance and conflict. It is in the oneness with this whole that the self becomes intelligible, enjoys freedom and actualizes its potentialities... I am saying that as long as we denigrate these social formations, these group identities, as long as we deny their legitimacy as vehicles of political expression, we are annihilating the prospects of democracy and freedom, and impoverishing our people spiritually...we must understand that this sensitivity to our culture, to our social experience will, for better or for worse, define the feasibility of democracy in Africa (p. 6).

We suggest that, rather than attempting to suppress tribal identities, political reforms should be geared to using such identities as the basis for political institutions.

4. Optimal Ethnic Integration and Separation

Recognizing that tribal or ethnic units play important roles in the organization of African societies is crucial to the design of appropriate institutions. That individuals voluntarily associate with members of their own tribe suggests that tribal units perform some economically and socially advantageous functions for their members. We suggest that the tribal organizational unit is more efficient in the provision of some collective goods than are national governments of African states. As such, even in unitary states, organizing lower levels of government around the tribe would be expected to economize on organizational costs and impose lower decision costs on members.

It is well known that the most preferred choices are realized when an individual decision-maker has maximum independence. In the real world, however, individuals have to associate with others for particular matters. The more people involved in the decision-making process, the less likely that an individual's most preferred choice will be selected. With more and more heterogeneous preferences, the outcomes differ markedly from each persons' preferred choice. Because tribes are composed of people who, as a result of their past experiences, family ties and aspirations, have preferences that are closely related on a variety of matters, decisions that are made by tribal units are likely to be more representative of individual preferences than would result when many tribes are involved. Thus tribal organizational units are in some respects analogous to voluntary clubs that comprise people whose preferences are fairly similar.

The resulting efficiencies of voluntary organizations such as clubs are well known and have been discussed extensively in the economic literature. James Buchanan (1965) was among the first to explore the efficiency properties of voluntary clubs. The economic model of clubs presented by Buchanan assumes a situation where individuals have identical tastes for both public and private goods. Given these assumptions, optimal club sizes exist at which the marginal benefit club members receive from adding another member equals the additional costs associated with the new member (Buchanan 1965; McGuire 1974).

Other researchers have extended the economic model of clubs to accommodate differences in taste (Sandler and Tschirhart 1984; Cones and Sandler 1986). Central to the efficient results of voluntary clubs are conditions of entry and exit. A member of a club who does not like that particular club's policies is free to exit and to join clubs that better represent his or her preferences. Although such exit involves costs, individuals make decisions by comparing the benefits of exit to the costs. If expected benefits exceed the costs of exit, then the individual exits. It is this mobility property of voluntary organizations that guarantees that an individual's preferences are served even in a group setting. The freedom to select those organizations that best serve one's preferences suggests that voluntary clubs and organizations advance individual liberty.

What about the tribe? Unlike voluntary organizations, entry into a particular tribe, other than the one into which a person is born, is not possible. Likewise, exit from one's tribe is practically impossible. While limits to entry and exit may appear to undermine efficiency, we suggest that 'partial exit' and 'partial entry' are possible and serve the same goals that entry and exit serve in voluntary organizations.

Individuals can select the degree to which they identify with a particular tribe. This opportunity of selective identification allows persons the liberty to associate with members of their tribe on some matters and to disassociate from them on others and instead to associate with members of other tribes. Thus on the one hand, the tribe can be viewed as an involuntary association because of entry and exit barriers. On the other hand, identifying with a tribe is voluntary because one can choose the degree to which one identifies with one's own or any other tribe.

The fact that we observe high degrees of tribal identification should be considered a largely voluntary choice by the individuals concerned. From an economic perspective, the expected benefits of identifying with a tribal group exceed the costs of such identification. When members of a tribe live and organize their activities without interfering with members of other tribes, then the tribal unit is an optimal form of organizing for the purpose of providing some goods and services to its members. In this respect, the tribal unit is analogous to a private club that serves the interests of its members.

Because there are benefits associated with identifying with a particular tribe, the tribal leadership has an interest in investing in tribal identification. Tribal identification is therefore not costless. The interaction of benefits and costs suggests some optimal level of tribal identification. This optimal level of tribal identification determines the degree to which members of a tribe associate with members of other tribes voluntarily. Changes in benefits and costs of tribal identification can then be expected to alter the optimal level of identification and thus the degree of inter-ethnic integration.

Figure 4.1 depicts the demand and supply of tribal identification. The horizontal axis measures the degree to which individuals identify with their tribe. If the value of tribal identification is zero, then the individuals in question do not identify with their tribe at all. They may, for example, give up speaking their mother tongues. For those countries where given names can identify one as a member of a particular tribe, individuals may change their names altogether. In other words, zero tribal identity means that persons are completely 'detribalized'. Higher values of tribal identity mean that individuals have more and more characteristics that are

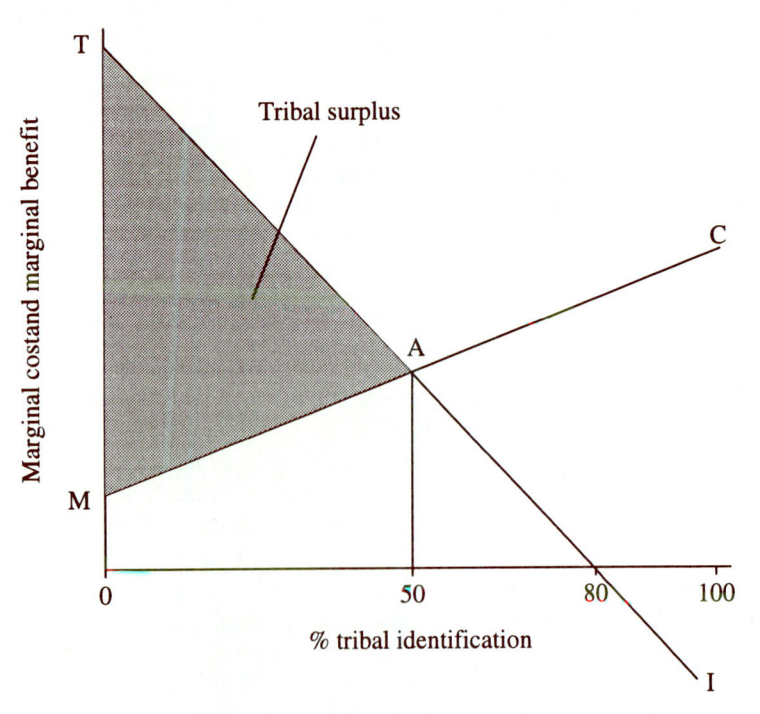

Figure 4.1   The market for tribal identity

specific to a particular tribe. One hundred per cent tribal identification means that entire ways of life, associations, and so on are governed by tribal customs, initiations and rituals. For those persons that are 'detribalized', it does not matter who they associate with in marriage, employment or business. Such persons therefore have no taste for tribal identity. On the other hand, individuals with a 100 per cent level of tribal identity associate entirely with people from their own tribes.

The vertical axis in Figure 4.1 shows the additional benefits and costs associated with levels of tribal identification. As noted above, tribal identification is associated with some investment. In the first place, for one to associate with members of a tribe, one must learn the tribal ways of life such as language and customs. To a large extent, these costs are low since a person born into a tribe must necessarily learn some minimal ways of the life of the group in which he finds himself. Obviously there are opportunity costs in terms of other languages and customs that might otherwise be learned.

However, acquiring minimal tribal ways of life does not necessarily guarantee that individuals will continue identifying with their tribe. Younger generations, for example, may abandon some of the tribal practices that regulate marriages, thereby weakening conformity with a tribe's way of life. Persons may also give up their tribal ways when they move away from their villages or when they acquire education. Thus for the tribe to enforce tribal ways of life across generations, the tribal unit must engage in various costly investments such as initiation ceremonies and rituals. These rituals may be seen as contracts that tie a person to the tribe.

Customs and rituals act as entry and exit barriers. In some tribes, for example, initiation into womanhood and manhood necessarily requires that marriage be restricted to persons who have undergone similar initiation rites. Members of other tribes who do not undergo such initiation rites therefore are excluded as marriage partners. In other cases, initiation rites involve permanent facial marks that identify a person as belonging to a particular tribe. These types of activity make it difficult for a person not to identify with their own tribe, while reducing the probability of marital unions across members of different tribes. At any rate, increased tribal identification is achieved at increasingly higher cost. Costs also increase because of lost opportunities to associate with members of other tribes.

Demand for tribal identification shows the net benefits associated with different levels of tribal identification. Identifying with one's tribe provides various benefits to members in general and, of course, to individual tribe members who choose to identify with the tribe. The tribal ways of life – rules of conduct and norms – regulate behaviour that creates order in that society. This is a public good consumed by all members of the society. Everybody in the community benefits when the tribe enforces good behaviour among its members of society and penalizes those who violate the rights of others. Through tribal sanctions, some acceptable behaviour is enforced for the benefit of society. For example, penalties are prescribed for those who steal from other members or who commit crimes against other persons.

Roback (1991) notes that one of the beneficial tasks performed by ethnic groups is that of assisting the teaching and enforcement of social norms and behaviour. Given the prisoner's dilemma situation that faces individuals in making collective choices, individual members of society have an incentive to cheat because such behaviour is profitable. However, if everybody cheats on every occasion on which they expect to profit, then everybody in society faces the worst possible outcome. Because people have a long-term attachment to their groups (for example, through blood or past memories), they are more likely to have continuous dealings with members of their ethnic group than with members of other ethnic groups. Continuous dealing reduces cheating in prisoner's dilemma situations, and as a result ethnic groups may be more efficient in the provision of public goods than the state:

> Ethnic attachments can provide a significant substitute for contract law. That is, members of ethnic groups that have substantial continuous dealings with each other can develop norms of cooperation, promise-keeping and honesty. Thus ethnic groups can provide alternatives to government in the provision of certain public goods such as the enforcement of social norms, and in the solution of prisoner's dilemma problems. In fact, ethnic groups and other groups smaller than the modern state may actually be more efficient providers of these kinds of goods (Roback 1991, 63).

Benefits to members also arise from the tribal organization of production of goods and services. A tribe may possess its own production technology and its own unique division of labour. Members of the tribe learn different types of production skills and work habits. Thus in addition to the production of valuable social norms, the tribal organizational unit plays a significant part in organizing the production of goods and services. Ethnic groups also provide other services, such as social insurance and entertainment, and act as sources of collegiality and pride (Congleton 1992).

In Figure 4.1, the demand for tribal identification is depicted as the downward sloping line, TI, and the supply is shown by the upward sloping marginal cost curve, MC. Higher degrees of tribal identification are associated with increasing benefits, but only at a decreasing rate. In Figure 4.1, when the tribal identification is 80 per cent, marginal benefit falls to zero. Higher levels of tribal identification are associated with negative marginal benefit. Even if the costs of tribal identification are zero, it will not pay members of the tribe to identify with their tribe beyond the 80 per cent level. Combining the marginal cost and marginal benefit (demand) yields the optimal level of tribal identification. In Figure 4.1, the 50 per cent level of tribal identification is optimal.

The area TAM represents what I refer to as the 'tribal surplus'. The surplus represents rents generated by the tribal unit by its production of goods and services and social norms. The well-being of members of a particular tribal unit depends on the size and distribution of tribal surplus. The tribal unit can increase the well-being of its members, for example, by becoming more efficient in the production of goods and services and in the enforcement of social norms. Such efficiency lowers marginal costs and increases the tribal surplus (TAM). Notice that the tribe is assumed to act like a firm in the provision of particular services to its members. The surplus generated is, however, not open for dissipation to non-members since one has to belong to the tribe to benefit. Thus the rents generated do not lead to inter-ethnic competition for rents. However, such rents may encourage predatory tribal wars.

Tribal surplus can also be increased by engaging in voluntary exchange. Voluntary exchange expands the production possibilities frontier, benefiting all the parties involved in the exchange. We can therefore expect that out of self-interest, different tribal groups will seek to engage in trade with other tribal units. Of course, such trade requires knowledge of the ways of life of other tribes, such as language and customs. History shows that tribal groups in Africa lived in harmony for many years, each tribe – within its own regional boundaries – engaging in various mutually beneficial exchanges. Harold K. Schneider (1977, 200–201) provides a good example of elaborate inter-ethnic exchange in Northern Uganda:

> One of the most interesting examples of such trade early in this century involved the Acholi, Didinga, Dodoth, Kokir, and Tirangori of northeast

Uganda. The basis of this trade system was that each of these societies was trying to obtain a certain balance of grain, livestock, and metal goods, but each was differently successful in producing one or the other. So they traded with each other, directly and indirectly, to balance their wants. Occasionally this required importing some things which were not themselves desired or needed from another society in order to trade these acquired goods to yet another society for more desirable things. For example, the Kokir bought goats from the Tirangori in return for cattle. The Kokir then traded the goats to the Didinga to their south for cattle. The Didinga, in turn shipped grain to their south to get goats. And the Didinga traded goats to the Acholi to their west to get grain and iron goods.... Looked at its entirety, this is an elaborate, interlocked, international system in which goats, cattle, grain, and iron goods are being redistributed to achieve a maximized balance of preferences, and the redistribution is being accomplished by a profit system.

Associations between tribal groups may also involve the provision of collective goods that benefit members of the various communities. Members of various tribes may find that their surplus increases, for example, if they join members of neighbouring tribes to build a bridge, a road or even to counter aggression by distant tribes. Tribal units seeking to improve the well-being of their members may thus engage in voluntary associations with other tribes. In all such cases, the *ex ante* expectation is increased tribal surplus for the groups.

Thus tribal identification does not preclude cooperation with members of other tribes. In fact the tribal unit, by seeking to maximize tribal surplus, will tend to associate with members of other tribes in matters that are mutually beneficial. In this setting, association between tribes involves no coercion. This type of voluntary segregation and voluntary integration is consistent with peaceful coexistence among tribal groups.

It should be clear that organizing along ethnic lines, to the extent that such organization takes the form of voluntary choices of individuals, is consistent with the exercise of liberty. It follows that ethnicity may provide a natural way of constructing appropriate political units. Given the well-established tendency for individuals to associate along ethnic lines, it is evident that political association along such lines is also likely to emerge naturally as individuals seek to advance their own self-interest. Considering the fact that ethnic groups in Africa associate with particular territory, physical political boundaries can coincide with the existing ethnic territories.

We have considered tribal units as analogous to voluntary clubs that are compatible with efficient outcomes. However, even voluntary clubs have problems in enforcing compliance. Mancur Olson (1965) has attacked the orthodox view that voluntary associations are always efficient in the provision of collective goods, and has specifically challenged the view that effective participation in voluntary associations is virtually universal. Because voluntary associations organize around collective goals, it is often not rational for an individual member to pay for such a goal. Instead members may pursue their interests by free-riding on other people's efforts. This problem is worse in large and heterogeneous groups (Olson 1982).

We therefore expect ethnic-based provision of collective goods and services to be undermined by free-riding. As such, members cannot be expected to pay their share voluntarily without some form of organized authority to enforce compliance. Because widespread free-riding lowers the well-being of all members of the ethnic group, everybody benefits when an ethnic government is established. Notice that such a government is analogous to a club management team that enforces payments of fees and dues and ensures that club rules are followed. As observed previously, the free-rider problem is likely to be less prevalent when the group is made up of one ethnic group than when several ethnic groups are involved.

Some ethnic groups may be so large that even an ethnic government may not be efficient in preventing free-riding. In this case the population exceeds the optimal club size. Organizing around such an ethnic group is not efficient, and in such cases it may be necessary for individual members to set up a number of competing governmental units that can monitor free-riding more efficiently. In addition to minimizing free-rider problems, such competing governments open up opportunities for 'voting with the feet' because members have several choices of tribal jurisdiction.

Ethnic tribal units have other limitations that relate to their size. On the one hand, the unit may be too large for organizing some activities. Some goods and services require smaller political units. Such goods and services are likely to be more efficiently organized by the village. Just as, in some cases, individuals organize along tribal lines, at other times they may organize into villages. As a matter of fact, the history of African communities reveals an elaborate division of activities not only along ethnic units, but also along villages and clans.

On the other hand, ethnic units may be too small to organize the provision of some goods and services. For such goods and services, it may be necessary for different ethnic units to form political associations for the purposes of accomplishing these tasks. Notice, however, that such associations take the form of market exchange: they are voluntary and thus benefit ethnic groups that enter into associations. It is also the case that the rules that establish the relationships between such ethnic groups must be reached by agreement. Beneficial political associations will tend to be durable, while those that do not benefit all the groups involved will tend to be unstable. The key, then, is that any form of integration should be by consent.

Voluntary integration is desirable, and should be seen as mutually beneficial political exchange that increases the tribal surplus of all the groups involved. Voluntary separation is also consistent with the maximization of tribal surplus. Both voluntary integration and separation are consistent with the advancement of individual liberty. It is also true that integrating groups on matters that they seek to keep to themselves necessarily involves coercion and must infringe individual liberties.

We have emphasized the need for institutions that nurture voluntary associations and we have suggested that associating along ethnic lines is consistent with advancing individual liberty. The restoration of civil society in Africa, in addition to advancing individual liberty, calls for institutional reforms that are conducive to the advancement of the material well-being of the citizens and that minimize inter-ethnic conflict. Sustaining economic growth requires institutional frameworks that permit individuals to expand their capacity to live, work and cooperate with one another throughout the nation. Such human cooperation is complex and, as Wunsch and Oluwu (1990) have stated, such cooperation is unlikely to occur without a supportive social infrastructure that sustains many diverse organizations. Kinship groups or ethnic groups provide a base around which many such diverse organizations form. Likewise, Robert Nisbet (1975) has argued that kinship or ethnicity can contribute much not only to micro-organization and to development, but can also act as a constraint against the coercive powers of the state.

The discussion in this chapter leads us to a similar conclusion to that reached three decades ago by W. Arthur Lewis (1965), who noted that the new African governments' attempts to suppress tribal loyalties were a futile exercise. Lewis instead suggested the use of such loyalties as a base for establishing institutions that permitted self-expression by all tribes:

> ...any idea that one can make different peoples into a nation by suppressing the religious or tribal or regional or other affiliations to which they them-

selves attach the highest political significance is simply a nonstarter. National loyalty cannot immediately supplant tribal loyalty; it has to be built on top of tribal loyalty by creating a system in which all the tribes feel that there is room for self-expression (p. 68).

The principal message of this chapter is that there are numerous advantages in relying upon the 'tribe' as a basis for organizing governments in Africa. Tribal territories provide natural boundaries that can define stable political jurisdictions. In addition, there are various factors that unite members of a tribe that facilitate solving prisoner's dilemma problems such that cooperative outcomes are achieved. Unlike the common negative view about tribal identification and tribal governments, we suggest that for as long as such identification is not used to seek transfers from other tribes, then an optimal level of identification will emerge consistent with the maximization of each tribe's well-being. Furthermore, associations between tribal units that are by consent can be expected to minimize ethnic conflict.

5. Integration, Centralization and Rent-Seeking

We have observed that during the pre-colonial period, each tribal group in Africa had its peculiar political structure, often headed by a tribal chief. Because each tribal government included members of only one tribe, a tribe's output was maintained by the members and there were no transfers outside the tribe. As such, tribal units maximized the well-being of their members by efficient enforcement of social norms and by organizing the production of goods and services. Tribal units could also increase their surplus by engaging in mutually beneficial market exchanges with other tribes. In addition, members of one tribal unit could associate with members of other tribal units for the production of collective goods that benefited all the units involved. This type of integration was often fairly loose and only meant to accomplish limited goals while leaving tribal units fairly independent on most other matters. By and large, the nature of integration and interaction was the product of consent by the various ethnic groups.

The voluntary principle, whether in market exchange or in political associations, creates harmonious interactions between individuals and polities. Thus any integration between units that is based on the voluntary principle increases the well-being of all involved. We noted in the previous chapter that such voluntary inter-ethnic interactions were commonplace in tribal Africa (Vaughan 1977). There is no doubt that sometimes differences resulted in conflict. For example, there were groups that were involved in warfare in the quest to expand the territory under their control. More often than not, however, tribal groups lived peacefully, and when conflicts arose they would be resolved and agreements reached. In most cases, agreements were respected so that escalation of conflicts rarely extended beyond the tribal boundaries. Thus conflicts were minimized because tribes chose which aspects of life to associate with members of other tribes and which matters to keep to themselves.

The basic conclusion that we arrive at by looking at traditional African institutions is that ethnically based institutions provided a viable base for the evolution of civil societies. These institutions had the necessary ingredients for the development of political arrangements that advance individual and civil liberties. Unfortunately, ethnically based political institutions and associations have been eliminated by modern governments. Current African governments have instead adopted political institutions that hinder the development of civil society.

The demise of civil society in Africa has been a long but steady process that has its roots in colonial rule but which has been accelerated by Africans themselves. Several factors have contributed in the destruction of civil society in Africa. Probably the most important of these are the failure of governments to accommodate the interests and aspirations of different ethnic groups, over-centralization of decision-making authority, and the rise of dictatorial rule. All these factors are related and thus reforms that seek to restore civil society in Africa must take into account all of them simultaneously.

As noted in Chapter 2, colonial rule placed different ethnic groups under the same authority and no adjustments were made to make sense of ethnic differences (Crowder 1968). Thus at independence, the new states included many ethnic nations within one boundary and often divided ethnic national groupings among two or more states. For example, the Ewe were divided between Ghana and Togo; the Maasai between Kenya and Tanzania; the Luo between Kenya and Uganda; the Ibo between Nigeria and Cameroon; the Somali among Ethiopia, Somalia and Kenya; and many others. Also some groups that had traditional rivalries, implying that they would not have chosen to be united under a common government, were placed in the same state (for example, the Ashanti and Brong in Ghana, and the Yoruba and Hausa in Nigeria (Crowder 1968)). Thus by and large, colonialists had no interest in accommodating ethnic interests.

However, the leaders of independent African governments did little to accommodate ethnic interests either. As a matter of fact, even in those countries where the existing institutional arrangements could have been used to harmonize ethnic interests, the new leaders quickly eliminated them because those institutions were considered to be sources of opposition to the central authority. As noted by Wunsch (1990, 61):

> Quick to feel the impatience of independence era leaders were the 'bargaining encumbrances' left behind by colonial authorities as democratic constitutional legacies. Federalism, electoral systems, bicameralism, multipartyism, entrenched protection of the constitutions on such issues as amendments, ethnic representation and the status and authority of regional units of gov-

ernment, were quickly eliminated or neutralized as counter-poses to centralized authority. These were seen by independence era leaders to impose unacceptable costs on decision making and to reflect unacceptable distrust for African governments. Federal clauses were quickly removed from constitutional law in Ghana, Cameroon, Kenya and Uganda. Only in Nigeria, where ethnic competition reinforced federal divisions, were they maintained.

African leaders adopted policies that were therefore geared to increasing centralization and to eliminating institutions that relied on ethnic identity as their organizational base. Such institutions were considered harmful to national unity because they created divisions among the people. Local governments were systematically weakened and all decision-making powers were concentrated in the central government. The new leaders argued that highly centralized unitary states were necessary to balance resource allocation across the regions. Likewise, competitive political systems were outlawed and replaced by single-party systems. Single-party systems were justified on the basis that they had the ability to rise above individualism, regionalism, ethnicity and class-orientation (Wunsch 1990, 43). Thus the leaders chose to concentrate power at the central government, to unify the ethnic groups by outlawing political competition and to use the government to redistribute resources.

Colonialists had also adopted preferential policies that provided opportunities such as education, civil service and military jobs for some tribal groups and not for others. The unequal treatment of tribes resulted in different levels of modernization across tribal groups and thus across regions. As a result, some ethnic groups were able to achieve a much higher level of modernity relative to other groups. The result of such discriminatory practices on the part of the colonialists was to widen ethnic divisions and to create antagonisms among groups that traditionally had enjoyed good relationships (Lemarchand 1983).

The tribal inequalities created by colonial policies meant that those groups that had benefited from colonial rule had a comparative advantage in the competition for control of independent governments. This is because those groups possessed the capital – both financial and human – necessary to organize and manoeuvre the transfer of power from the colonialists. Thus those who were favoured by colonialists continued to occupy relatively more privileged positions than the others. Antagonisms created by colonial rule were therefore inherited and exacerbated by independent governments.

The boundaries drawn by the colonial powers have remained fairly stable and, at first sight, this may seem to indicate optimal political institutions that are able to accommodate the interests of the various tribal groups. In other words, one may interpret the stability of boundaries as evidence of the existence of social contracts that serve to advance the interests of the various ethnic groups. This, however, is misleading. It is important to note that ethnic integration was not the result of consent. Although different units had their own political institutions and structures, those institutions were not utilized to seek consent on the nature of integration between tribal units.

If integration is not voluntary it must be through coercion. Thus the integration of the tribal units into national states was accomplished through coercion. After independence, African leaders did not seek new institutional arrangements that would have defined the relationship between ethnic units. As such, the various constituent units have been held together not by the strong forces that result from mutually beneficial exchange, but by coercion. Thus ethnic 'unification' in Africa does not represent social contracts that advance liberty.

The political institutions adopted by the African leaders have had disastrous effects and have been largely responsible for the demise of civil society. In the first place, the elimination of any form of local autonomy and its replacement by highly centralized unitary governments has created a situation where ethnic competition for resources and power dominates the political landscape. Not only is the decision-making process now far removed from the people, but the leadership has the power to make inter-ethnic transfers. The fact that a lot of resources in centralized states are channelled through the public sector has shifted the scope of ethnic interaction from market exchange and cooperation to competition in political markets. As a result, political office (regardless of how it has been attained) has become extremely valuable.

Under a system where tribal units are largely autonomous, each tribal unit retains its own surplus. Tribes that are more efficient in the production of goods and services and social norms are able relatively to increase their tribal surplus. Likewise, groups that have more efficient systems of property rights will also have higher levels of tribal surplus than those that have more inefficient systems. Thus we can expect wide differences in wealth among tribal groups. Such differences that involve no inter-ethnic transfers are consistent with harmonious coexistence among the groups. In addition, the fact that groups retain their surplus provides the incentive for improved efficiency in production. Furthermore, because each tribal group is likely to specialize in the production of particular goods, we can expect groups to be involved in a variety of comparative advantage-based market exchanges.

Probably the most noticeable negative effect of ethnic integration is the creation of lucrative rent-seeking opportunities. When different ethnic groups are under the same authority, and when the central government is responsible for distributing a large share of the nation's resources, each group can increase its well-being not just by producing goods and services but also by seeking transfers from other groups. In this setting, some groups become net supplies of transfers while others are net recipients. In addition, the transfer process involves real resource costs. In this sense, inter-ethnic transfers must be viewed as the outcome of a negative sum game.

Thus integration altered inter-ethnic interactions so that tribal units must now be viewed as interest groups that seek to maximize the welfare of their members. Instead of investing in productive activities, groups engage in activities to increase their well-being by capturing the surplus generated by other tribes. The most efficient method to effect those transfers is to use the coercive power of the state. Thus different groups will compete intensely to capture the control of government. More frequently than not, such ethnic competition in political markets is associated with disastrous results that undermine civil society.

We can extend the interest group theory of government (Stigler 1971; Peltzman 1976) to explain some of the consequences of ethnic competition in highly centralized African states. The interest group theory of government teaches us that public policy outcomes reflect the interplay between demanders and suppliers of wealth transfers. This competition results in a situation whereby well-organized groups benefit from transfers and other, less well-organized groups, supply those transfers. In this setting, the politicians act as brokers of wealth transfers. Given that members of an ethnic group are interested in maximizing the benefits received by members of their group, we can model ethnic groups as interest groups competing for transfers.

Figure 5.1 (adopted from McCormick and Tollison 1981) shows the demand for, and supply of, wealth transfers. Here we treat the interest groups as different tribal groups. We assume that there is one dollar that is available for transfer and ask each tribal group to indicate how much it would be willing to pay for the right to the transfer. Groups that are well organized will bid a higher amount for the right to the transfer.

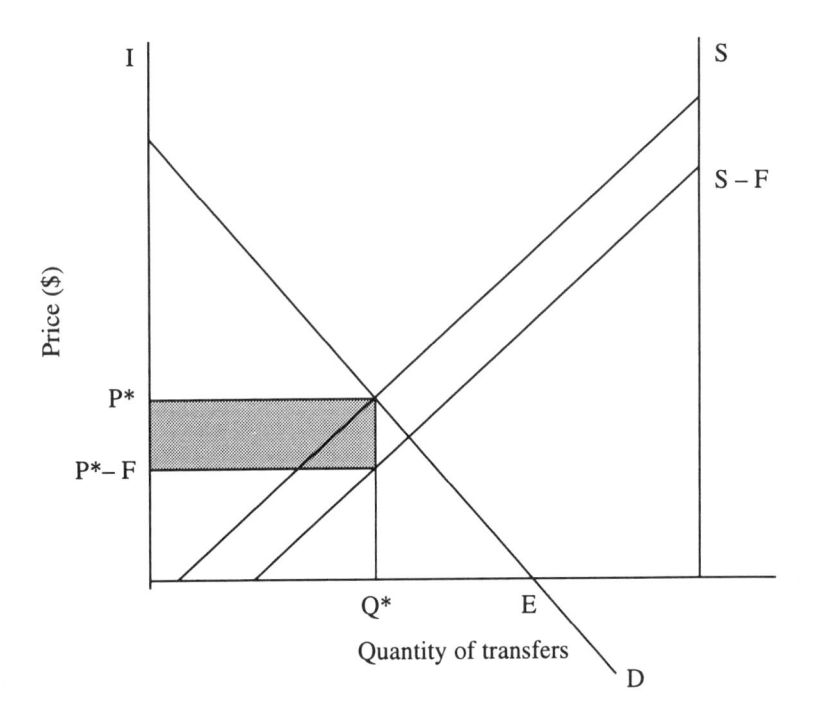

Figure 5.1   The demand and supply of wealth transfers by tribal groups

Each bid reflects the group's netting out from one dollar the costs of organizing. By subtracting each group's costs from one dollar we derive the downward-sloping demand curve. Groups that are located closer to the origin have lower organization costs. The group at point E has organization costs of one dollar and thus its demand price is zero.

S-F is the net supply curve of transfers, which essentially is the mirror image of the demand schedule. Tribal groups that face high costs of organizing demand transfers also have high costs to prevent part of their wealth being transferred to other groups. Each tribal group is asked to indicate how much it is willing to pay to avoid the one dollar transfer. Netting the costs of organizing from one dollar yields the net supply schedule. Thus by ranking groups in terms of their willingness to supply transfers we derive the supply curve. Groups located closer to the origin are those whose costs of organizing are relatively high, and these are the ones from which wealth can be expropriated most cheaply (Shughart 1990).

The role of politicians is to match the demanders and suppliers. This service is performed at a fee equal to $ F which represents the marginal cost of real resources used to effect the transfers. Thus S is the gross supply curve, which is the amount that groups are willing to pay to avoid the transfer plus the fixed brokerage fee. Combining the demand for, and supply of, transfers yields the equilibrium price P*, which equates the quantity demanded to the quantity supplied. The shaded area in Figure 5.1 represents the amount received by the brokers of transfers.

At any particular time, a tribal group is either a net supplier of wealth transfers or a net recipient. Tribal groups that are well organized and that control the instruments of transfer benefit at the expense of other tribal units. Because of the permanent nature of tribal interest groups, some groups are likely to be long-term beneficiaries while others will be long-term losers. Like interest groups in developed countries, ethnic competition for wealth transfers explains a wide array of public policy outcomes.

A limited literature shows that policy-making in Africa is to a large extent the result of the interplay of tribal competition for rents (Brough and Kimenyi 1986; Kimenyi 1987, 1989). Instead of adopting policies that benefit all tribal groups, rulers adopt policies that concentrate benefits to members of one or a few tribes while distributing the costs over many others. Transfers may take the form of taxes, subsidies, regulations, public projects or even government jobs. In virtually all cases, government policy entails a benefit to one group at the expense of others. This capture of the tribal surpluses generated by other tribes is analogous to standard Tullockian rent-seeking (Tullock 1967, 1993).

Robert Bates (1983) points out that ethnic groups in Africa evaluate their relative well-being by comparing their level of modernization with other groups. Because most of the goods and services from the modern sector are distributed by the state, there is intense competition by ethnic groups to control the instruments of transfer. Competition for modernity involves ethnic competition. Ethnic leaders therefore use their capacity to satisfy the demand for the components of modernity to generate political support. Consequently, successful African leaders design effective systems of patronage dispensing jobs, contracts, commercial loans, scholarships, and so on to members of their ethnic groups (Bates 1983). Naomi Chazan (1988) attributes the persistence of strong ethnic identification to the fact that ethnicity has proven to be an effective channel for the extraction of state resources. Likewise, John Lonsdale (1981) suggests that African tribes have become the most economically available constituency for mobilizing pressure to gain state access.

A good indicator of the consequences of centralization and ethnic competition for rents in African states after independence has been the rapid expansion of the bureaucracy. For example, in 1967 the Tanzanian civil service had 67,708 established posts. This figure had increased to 101,183 in 1972, 191,046 in 1976 and 295,352 in 1980. Between 1968 and 1974, civil service employment in Zambia increased by 265 per cent and emoluments increased by 328 per cent (Ayoade 1988). In virtually all Sub-Saharan African countries, civil service employment has increased, even during those times when private sector employment was contracting.

A 1981 World Bank study reported that public employment had reached between 40 and 74 per cent of total recorded paid employment in seven Sub-Saharan African countries for which data were available. Likewise, the study reported that spending on public administration, defence and education had increased far in excess of economic growth in many of those countries. Expenditure on public administration and the military grew at almost twice the annual rate of economic growth of GDP in 21 of the countries in that region (World Bank 1981).

The consequence of such an over-expansion of the public sector has been the reallocation of scarce resources from productive activities to unproductive activities. In Africa this process penalizes some ethnic groups and benefits others. As a result, centralization, in addition to promoting wasteful ethnic rent-seeking that undermines economic growth, also magnifies divisions among tribal groups since some of the groups benefit while others lose. As noted by Donald Rothchild (1985):

> ...the postindepenence state bureaucracy all too often appeared to be captured by politically powerful and well-placed ethnic groups. The Kikuyu in Kenya, the Creoles in Sierra Leone, the Amhara in Ethiopia, the Baganda in Uganda, the Tusti Hima in Rwanda and Burundi, the Malinke in Guinea, the Woloff in Gambia, the Bemba in Zambia, and others gained disproportional influence in the affairs of state bureaucracies. And in Nigeria, according to a 1980 calculation, the five states controlled by Obafemi Awolowo's Western–based Unity Party of Nigeria – Ogum, Ondo, Oyo,

Lagos, and Bendel – have 67 percent of federal civil service posts above grade 14 salary scale. In such cases, state power is not autonomous and separate from the interests of a particular ethnic group (p. 85).

While expansion of the public sector has provided African leaders with opportunities to distribute favours to particular groups, it also means that leaders must design policies to extract rents from other groups. To accomplish this task, rulers must necessarily create inefficient systems of property rights that permit them to extract the resources from some groups and transfer them to others at low cost. North (1981) argues that rulers adopt inefficient property rights because they can raise more revenue from such a structure than with an efficient structure of rights.

In addition, North suggests that rulers can seldom afford efficient property rights since they would offend many constituents and hence would render their leadership insecure. In Sub-Saharan Africa, where most rulers are insecure, creating inefficient property rights is almost always essential for the maintenance of political stability (Kimenyi and Mbaku 1993). Of course, inefficient systems of property rights lead to poor economic performance.

Common policies used by the rulers of Sub-Saharan African countries to extract rents – which create inefficient systems of property rights – include price and interest rate controls, regulation of foreign exchange markets, import licensing schemes, selective subsidization and taxation of industry and agriculture, and so on. All these policies distort market signals and thus hinder the efficient allocation of resources and inhibit economic growth. Nevertheless, these policies are quite useful to the rulers because they provide the resources with which to pay off supporters. Although these policies are used in other countries, they are used more extensively in Sub-Saharan Africa than in other countries (Rowley 1995).

We note that in Sub-Saharan Africa, producer groups are closely linked with particular ethnic groups. This is, of course, due to the territorial nature of the spatial distribution of ethnic groups. As such, taxing a particular product almost always involves placing a burden on a particular ethnic group. Likewise, subsidizing a particular crop or other economic activity concentrates benefits to members of a specific group or groups. Therefore rulers are able to manipulate apparently neutral policies that actually benefit ethnic groups at the expense of others.

Centralization and the associated government intervention in the economy in Sub-Saharan Africa have resulted in widespread corruption. Because government regulations and controls are costly, entrepreneurs find it more profitable to bribe bureaucrats so to bypass such barriers. Even when firms are committed to honouring government controls, they find that, at one stage or another, they must bribe government officials to get tasks accomplished.

Strict licensing schemes, common in these countries, create artificial scarcity and thereby lead to competition to acquire the rights to licences. Bureaucrats are therefore able to extract bribes from those who seek to acquire the rights to licences. Predictably, the extent of such corrupt practices is directly related to the scope of government activity. As Chrisney (1985, 222) has indicated, the demand and supply of corrupt practices is directly related to the existence of government-created rents, and thus corruption is a product of the expansion of state authority.

The expansion of state authority and corruption in Africa should be a major focus on any institutional reform seeking to restore civil society. In some countries, such as Nigeria, Zaire and Kenya, corruption has reached such levels that it is practically institutionalized. Corruption is common not only among bureaucrats, but also among senior politicians including presidents. The majority of African rulers actively engage in a shameless looting of their national treasuries (Ayittey 1992).

The increase in the scope of government that necessarily accompanies centralization raises the value of political office because rulers have more resources and latitude to make transfers to close friends, relatives and members of their own ethnic groups. As a result, centralization creates intense competition to control the institutions of wealth transfer. The desire to control the political machinery motivates members of ethnic groups to undertake such non-democratic means to acquire leadership as military overthrow of existing governments.

Likewise, a leader who comes to power through a democratic electoral process extends his tenure by adopting non-democratic procedures such as outlawing opposition political parties. By doing so, a leader establishes himself as a monopoly supplier of legislation and broker of wealth transfers. Thus the greater the scope of government activity, the more likely that undemocratic means will be used by leaders (Kimenyi 1989). This ethnically based competitive process to control the institutions of transfers has contributed to the rise of dictatorial rule in Africa.

Finally, as the rent-seeking model suggests, in all cases where government is involved in transferring wealth, some groups must lose.

Groups that are net suppliers of rents are likely to engage in rent protection. One method of rent protection is to remove the leadership from power. Disadvantaged groups may rebel against authority and protest at government policies that they consider discriminatory. In some cases, tribal groups may seek exit options so that they can establish their own governments, thereby eliminating the coercion imposed by other groups. Such actions are often met with force. More frequently, however, such ethnic groups face persistent oppression and, because there are no exit options, they remain dominated by privileged groups over prolonged periods of time. Most African governments today are either brutally repressive or very repressive (Ayittey 1992).

6. Integration, Centralization and Ethnic Conflict

As we have observed in the previous chapters, the political integration of various ethnic groups in Africa was not by consent. Given the strong desire for ethnic groups to be independent, at least for certain activities, the current political integration of ethnic groups is not self-sustaining. Coercion is necessary to maintain the different units as one nation. In other words, there are ethnic rivalries that are the result of involuntary integration and that are kept in check only by the use of violence.

Involuntary integration must necessarily involve situations whereby some groups impose costs on others. Groups that end up as losers are likely to engage in activities to prevent authorities from expropriating their wealth, while beneficiaries use force to maintain their advantageous position. Because neither voice nor exit (Hirschman 1970) options are open, the result is the long-term oppression of some groups by others. Over time, however, disadvantaged groups engage in violence and the result is conflict between the government and particular ethnic groups. Because governments serve the interests of particular ethnic groups, any conflict involving an ethnic group and the government is essentially a conflict between ethnic groups.

In Africa, widespread internal conflicts are the norm and these conflicts almost always have a strong ethnic component. The evidence shows that just as ethnic units can be efficient in procuring benefits for their members, so too can they be efficient in organizing violence against other groups. In other words, the unit that can advance the well-being of its members can also undermine the liberty of others (Horowitz 1994; Furley 1995). Thus while we support the idea of individuals expressing their preferences by organizing around tribal lines, we also note that tribes in post-colonial Africa are notorious for imposing costs on non-members (Horowitz 1994).

One of the clearest manifestations of ethnic rivalry in Africa is the military coup. Between 1960 and 1982, for example, almost 90 per cent of the 45 independent Black African countries experienced a military coup, an attempted coup or a plot (McGowan and Johnson 1984). Since 1982, several other coups and attempted coups have taken place in the various African countries (Tordoff 1993). While there are many factors that explain why the military intervenes to change government (Mbaku 1994b), the competition for the control of government by ethnic groups has played a dominant role in contributing to such political instability in Africa. In most cases, coups are organized by members of one ethnic group seeking to remove from power a leadership composed of members of other ethnic groups. As a matter of fact, most armed insurrections are aimed against ethnically based regimes (Horowitz 1994; Furley 1995).

Conclusive evidence of the ethnic orientation of most military coups is revealed by the changes in composition of members of the cabinet and senior civil servants before and after the coup. For example, before the 1966 coup in the Central African Republic that deposed President Dacko (a member of the Baya ethnic group), no member of the Mbaka ethnic group was in the cabinet. After the successful coup led by Jean-Be'del Bokassa of the Mbaka ethnic group, the composition of the cabinet changed so that 23 per cent of its members were Mbaka. Likewise, when Kwame Nkrumah was President of Ghana, 71 per cent of cabinet members were from Nkrumah's Akan ethnic group. Following the coup that deposed Nkrumah, organized by members of the Ga and Ewe ethnic groups, the representation of Akan in the cabinet dropped to 25 per cent, while that of the Ga increased from 7.7 per cent to 25 per cent and the representation of the Ewe increased from 7.7 per cent to 38 per cent (*Black Africa* 1972). In almost all cases, military leaders award top government positions to members of their own ethnic groups (Breytenbach 1976; Kimenyi and Shughart 1989).

While military coups represent conflicts that are of short duration and often localized in urban centres, there are many other ethnic conflicts that involve large parts of the country and last for many years. Since independence, African countries have been involved in several ethnic conflicts. Probably the most significant was the Civil War in Nigeria. The Nigerian Civil War reflected differences between the Ibo people in the eastern region and the other ethnic groups. Fearing domination, the Ibo-dominated region intended to secede and therefore declared itself an independent region (Biafra). The response by the rest of the country was the use of military force that, while costly, prevented the secession.

Sudan is another example of a country where conflicts have been ongoing for decades. The conflict involves the northern peoples against the southerners. Both the northern and southern regions are themselves occupied by heterogeneous ethnic groups. However, the northerners are primarily of Arab descent and are Moslems, while the southerners are black and are primarily Christian. The conflict in Sudan reflects unresolved social tensions that resulted from the British colonial administration's decision to incorporate the south, with its non-Moslem Nilotic and Bantu populations, into a single political entity with an assertive, Islamic north oriented towards the Arab world (Copson 1994).

The southerners have long experienced political domination by the northerners and have attempted to overcome such domination by the use of violence. Northerners in turn have used force to suppress uprisings by the southerners, the result being widespread conflict. The war between north and south Sudan intensified during the 1960s and again during the late 1980s and continues into the 1990s. Such other conflicts between Blacks and Arabs, and Christians and Moslems, have been persistent in Chad and Mauritania.

One of the most intense inter-ethnic conflicts in Africa involves the Tutsi and Hutu tribes of Rwanda and Burundi (Greenland 1976). The Hutu constitute a numerical majority in both countries, but the Tutsi for the most part have dominated post-colonial politics. These two groups have different histories and migrated to Rwanda and Burundi at different times. In both countries, hatred is so intense that each ethnic group has attempted genocide aimed at the entire eradication of the other group. The 1972 holocaust in Burundi in which the Tutsi-controlled government killed between 100,000 and 200,000 Hutus is just one example (Meisler 1976). Likewise, conflicts erupted in Rwanda during the early 1990s, leaving thousands dead. Similar conflicts are continuing in Burundi, though with fewer casualties.

Ethiopia provides yet another case where ethnic rivalry has persisted for hundreds of years. The country is fairly heterogeneous, with over 70 languages. For a long time, the main conflict involved the people of Eritrea, who sought independence from Ethiopia. Eritrea finally achieved self-determination in 1993 after a long and costly struggle. There are also other groups in Ethiopia who have waged nationalist movements. Most notable are the Somalis, who consider themselves as being colonized by the Amhara, who have for years dominated the leadership of that country (Hamilton and Whitcombe 1976). The Ogaden region of Ethiopia, where Somalis live, has on various occasions sought to secede in order to join Somalia (Henze 1985).

THE COSTS OF ETHNIC CONFLICT

Table 6.1 lists some of the more important recent conflicts in Africa and the estimated number of mortalities. All these conflicts were primarily between ethnic or religious groups. Although, in most cases, reported data on the effects of internal conflicts in Africa are largely estimates, it is nevertheless evident that conflicts in Africa have imparted heavy costs in terms of loss of life and displacement of people. Estimates (which by most accounts are on the low side) show that between 1980 and 1992, 2 to 4 million lives were lost as a result of internal conflicts. The war in the Sudan, involving the northern and southern regions, is estimated to have resulted in between 500,000 and 1 million deaths. Similar catastrophes resulted from the wars in Ethiopia and Mozambique.

As would be expected, internal conflicts have resulted in a large number of people with permanent disabilities. In addition to inflicting pain and suffering, such injuries impose a large burden on society in terms of the resources that necessarily have to be devoted to medical care, not to mention the cost in terms of lost production. Of course, the 1960s and 1970s were also marked with various conflicts that involved extensive loss of life. For example, several hundred thousand Ugandans lost their lives as a result of ethnic and political terror during the presidency of Idi Amin (1971–79). The Civil War in Nigeria (1967–70) is another good example of costly ethnic conflict. It is estimated that 1 million deaths resulted from this war (Isaacs 1975). The fact that conflicts continued during the mid 1990s in countries such as Sudan and Rwanda, suggests that the cost of African internal conflict in terms of human suffering during the last three decades is one of the most notable tragedies in human history.

The heavy costs of internal conflict are also evidenced by the millions of refugees and displaced persons (Table 6.2). By the end of 1992, about 5.2 million Africans were refugees, having fled their own countries. In addition, millions of Africans were refugees in their own countries after being displaced from their homes and land. In 1991, 2 million persons in Mozambique were displaced in this manner. In 1994, there were over 5 million persons that had been displaced from their homes in the Sudan.

In Kenya, tribal clashes between the Kalejin ethnic group and the Kikuyu have resulted in hundreds of deaths and thousands of displaced persons. The Human Rights Watch (1994) estimated that by the end of

Table 6.1   Recent ethnic conflicts

Country	Situation/location	Date	Mortality estimates
Angola	Nation-wide, Ethnic	1971–91	300,000–500,000
Burundi	Huto protest Ethnic violence	1988 1993	7000–13,000 Uncertain, probably thousands, surrounding attempted coup by Hutu military elements
Chad	Northern half	1986	7000 +
Djibouti	Armed Afar resistance to Issa-dominated regime	1991	Probably low hundreds
Ethiopia	North	1970–91	450,000–1 million
Kenya	Somali unrest Poaching in the North and East Tribally based cattle rustling	1964 1980s	Few in the 1980s Hundreds
	Political opposition Ethnic clashes in Western Kenya and Rift Valley	1980s and early 1990s	1500 +
Lesotho	Armed opposition along borders, and capital	1970–86	Probably less than 100 during the 1980s
Liberia	North	1989	10,000 +
Malawi	Exiled opposition groups alleged secessionist in north	1981–	Few
Mali, Niger Algeria	Tuareg unrest	1990	Perhaps 100 or more

Table 6.1   continued

Country	Situation/location	Date	Mortality estimates
Mauritania	Black African opposition in the south and capital	1987–	200 or more
Mozambique	Rural areas	1979–92	450,000–1 million
Namibia	North-west	1989–	12,500 +
Niger	Hausa/Peul fighting over cattle-grazing rights	1991–	100
Rwanda	Hutu/Tutsi rivalries	Continuous	Thousands
Senegal	Separatist movement in the south	1982	Low hundreds
	Violence against Mauritians	1989	60
Somalia	North-west	1982	300,000–400,000
Sudan	North/South	Continuous	500,000–1 million
Tunisia	Raids by Libyan-backed opposition at Gafsha	1980	25–30
Uganda	South	1980	100,000–500,000
Western Sahara	Throughout	1976–	16,000
Zaire	Diverse dissident groups in several regions, urban protests	Continuous	Uncertain
Zimbabwe	Ndebele dissidents in south-west	1982–88	2000–2500

Source: Copson (1994) and other sources cited in the text.

Table 6.2 Refugees and displaced persons, 1992

War	Number of Refugees	Number of Displaced Persons
Mozambique	1,725,000	3,500,000
Somalia	864,800	2,000,000
Ethiopia and Eritrea	834,800	600,000
Liberia	599,200	600,000
Angola	404,200	900,000
Sudan	263,000	5,000,000
Rwanda	201,500	350,000
Sierra Leone (destabilized by Liberia conflict)	200,000	200,000
Western Sahara	165,000	–
Chad	24,000	–
Total	5,281,500	13,150,000

Source: Committee for Refugees (1993).

1993, 1500 Kenyans had been killed and 300,000 displaced. The US Committee for Refugees (1993) estimated that in 1992, over 13 million persons had been displaced in Africa. Whether in or out of their countries, African refugees experience hardships that are not easily measurable: hunger, poor sanitation and exposure to disease. The mortality rates for refugees in Africa, especially of children, are shamefully high.

Internal conflicts also propagate the extensive violation of human rights and individual freedom. Many incidents of gross violations of human rights in the form of various atrocities are well documented. These include forced labour, rape, torture, mutilation and the like. In other cases, conflict leads governments to adopt harsh laws that severely curtail freedom of movement and association (Piroute 1995).

Conflicts also have a direct effect on the economic well-being of Africans. Conflicts disrupt production and divert scarce resources from the production of consumer goods and services to the production of military goods and services. As a result, many African countries have experienced an explosion in the size of government, primarily due to spending on military and police forces that put down internal uprisings.

The result has been excessive military spending at the expense of other social services such as health and education.

In a 1990 study, the United Nations Development Programme reported that military spending in Sub-Saharan Africa during the 1980s had greatly undermined investment in human capital. In Angola, Chad, Uganda and Zaire, for example, military spending was two or three times greater than spending on education and health. In Ethiopia and Somalia, there were five times as many soldiers as teachers (United Nations Development Programme 1990).

As would be expected, conflicts often result in violations of property rights and in the breakdown of law and order. All these translate into a misallocation of resources and wealth reduction. In addition, conflicts result in the destruction of valuable infrastructure, such as roads, buildings, factories and bridges, thereby retarding economic activity. The economic stagnation recently experienced in several African countries, to a significant degree, is related to inter-ethnic conflict.

CONSTRAINING ETHNIC ACTIVITY

The evidence presented above shows that tribal units impose costs on other groups. While African conflicts originate from a variety of reasons, including fears of domination, disputes over property rights, and so on, they all have a clear ethnic component. In other words, the conflicts represent the outcome of ethnic group competition for resources and power.

The fact that political institutions do not prevent such conflicts and that, when conflicts occur, peaceful political solutions are often not reached, suggest that current constitutional political arrangements are not suited to dealing with the ethnic diversity characteristic of African countries. Where proper institutional arrangements to resolve disputes do not exist, ethnic competition results in conflict.

Inter-ethnic conflict can be looked at as the outcome of discriminatory practices by different tribes. Economics teaches us that benefits and costs accrue to those who engage in discriminatory behaviour. If the costs of discrimination are low and the benefits high, there will be more discrimination. On the other hand, if discrimination is associated with high costs and low benefits, individuals will engage in less discrimination. Political institutions can increase the degree of inter-ethnic discrimination either because the costs of discrimination are low or because discrimination is well rewarded.

Institutional arrangements in the highly centralized states of Africa increase the benefits associated with ethnic discrimination and reduce the costs to those who discriminate. Given that the taste for discrimination is not easily changed, the ideal way to reduce inter-ethnic conflict is to design institutions that penalize discrimination (raise the costs of discrimination) or that reduce the benefits of discrimination.

By placing different ethnic groups together under one central government that has the power to make inter-ethnic transfers, the unitary states provide ideal conditions for ethnic discrimination. Under a unitary state of government, leaders are able to effect transfers from other tribes to their own tribes. Thus unitary states increase the benefits of discrimination to members of the tribe in leadership. The unlimited powers possessed by the heads of the central governments make it possible to force transfers from one group to another, including the reallocation of rights to favour privileged groups. Such activities are likely to prompt violence as other groups seek to seize control over the instruments of transfers.

Tribes cannot usually live in isolation. Each tribal group requires to associate with other tribes to achieve some ends. Thus although living in isolation eliminates conflicts between groups, limited integration is often necessary. Such integration can be expected to result in a variety of conflicts. The wider the scope for which integration is sought, the higher the likelihood of conflicts. It follows that the way to minimize conflict is for tribal integration to be limited to specific matters. Central to determining the optimal levels of integration must be the application of the voluntary principle. Ethnic groups should integrate only in regard to matters that are mutually beneficial. In other words, to reduce conflict, integration must be limited and by consent.

7. Reducing Ethnic Externalities Through Decentralization

A theme that has been emphasized throughout this study is that ethnicity is important in the organization of African societies. We have observed that the involuntary integration of ethnic groups creates a variety of conflicts. Although African rulers continue to claim that unitary states are best suited to harmonize the interests of different ethnic groups, evidence is to the contrary: ethnic conflicts are the norm in virtually all Black African countries.

Even where violent ethnic conflicts have been averted, this has not been due to groups reaching peaceful agreements over issues of dispute. The appearance of peaceful coexistence is largely the result of governments' use of force to suppress some groups' demands. Thus the unitary states are far from achieving unity among the various ethnic groups.

By and large, the presumed benefits of unitary governments have proved illusionary. The only beneficiaries of the highly centralized states have been the rulers and their appointed bureaucrats and associates, who have been able to enrich themselves by looting national treasuries and by extracting bribes from those seeking government favours. As observed in previous chapters, the post-independence period in Africa has been marked by internal strife, military coups and civil wars. Even where relative political stability has prevailed, there are serious doubts as to whether centralized systems of government are the appropriate institutions for collective action in the ethnically heterogeneous states of Africa. Given the dismal economic performance in many African nations, it is also reasonable to ask whether adopting alternative systems of government might result in better economic performance.

Recent public choice research offers explanations for ethnic conflict, political instability, bureaucratic corruption and the dismal economic performance of African nations. These studies treat ethnic groups as special interest groups that compete for transfers from the central government. Members of a particular tribe consider themselves different from other groups and have an interest in increasing the welfare of their members relative to that of other tribes. Because of the concentration of power in unitary states, the leadership can redistribute resources from some tribes to others. Consequently, tribal groups have incentives to compete for the control of the instruments of transfer since such control ensures them a consistent flow of transfers from other groups.

In the absence of well-functioning democratic institutions, the competition for political control results in tribal conflict, military coups and civil wars. Moreover, non-optimal public policies that seek to benefit some groups lead to poor economic performance because leaders necessarily create inefficient property rights in order to extract rents.

There are many examples of inter-ethnic conflicts in Africa in which members of one group have committed serious atrocities against members of other groups in their attempt to control the central government. In such cases, it is difficult to justify centralized unitary states. Could conflicts be minimized (or even eliminated) if there were more decentralization of political power? Could it be that some ethnic and religious groups are so concerned with preserving some of their ways of life and identities, such that conflicts can only be eliminated by a federal system of government that accommodates such concerns? Or could it be that in some cases the ethnic and cultural divide is so wide that conflicts can only be solved if some regions achieve complete autonomy and thus establish their own independent governments? We suggest that all these options have potential for dealing with the question of ethnicity in the various African countries. It is our contention that decentralization would be good for all Sub-Saharan African countries: federalism for some countries and secession of some regions in a few other countries.

Whether African countries retain unitary systems of government or establish federal systems, there is an urgent need to decentralize decision-making to local levels. Such decentralization allows groups to have a wide latitude in the design and implementation of policy. Decentralization provides local communities with the opportunity to exercise a fair degree of autonomy in determining the scope and nature of interaction with other communities. Decentralization requires minimal changes to the core organizations of the current governments, but can significantly reduce the coercive powers of the state. Decentralization also reduces the points of inter-ethnic contact that result in conflict, and instead increases those contacts that are mutually beneficial. Under such a system, ethnic groups are able to retain their identity.

Most African states have highly centralized systems of government, with political power vested in the central government. Laws and decisions concerning the public sector are enacted and enforced by the central government. Authority is delegated to junior government officials who implement policies within rigid guidelines. Lower levels of government serve administrative roles but do not make laws, collect taxes or make spending decisions. Thus the provincial and district levels of government are under the strict control of central governments and only serve to decentralize administrative responsibilities.

Strictly speaking, political power is centrally concentrated, with the head of state holding the power over all public policies affecting the electorate. Local governments often do make some decisions, primarily those that deal with the provision of local public goods. Nonetheless, the powers of local governments are limited and in all cases the local governments are under the supervision of a government ministry. Thus local governments have limited powers, and their law-making powers are minimal. In fact in many African countries, the central government can dissolve a local government at will. Thus in most of the African countries, no constitutional limitations constrain the central authority from interfering with local government. Apparently, even in countries with ostensibly federal systems (for example, Nigeria and Cameroon), local governments are subordinate to the central government rather than to the people they serve.

That highly centralized systems of government are so common suggests that some important advantages are associated with these systems. For example, the central authority adopts a national development plan that balances resource allocation across the various regions of the country. Because the central government controls tax and spending policies, it can redistribute resources to strike a balance across regions. Many African governments have sought to achieve such a goal through the provision of public services such as education, health care, infrastructure, and so on (Austin 1984).

Some regions, especially those with a relatively low supply of natural resources and whose populations may, on average, have limited capacity to invest in human capital, may lag in economic development in the absence of a unitary government. A unitary state may also be necessary where constituent regional jurisdictions are too small and do not have the resources necessary to operate an autonomous regional government.

Another claimed advantage is that a centralized state fosters national unity. Individuals who otherwise may not associate with each other are organized under a common government and thus direct their loyalty to that government. It is claimed that unitary systems of government reduce the loyalty individuals may have to their tribal groups, and instead all citizens direct their loyalty to the country. Thus unitary systems of government can reduce tribal identity and thus reduce the chances of secession. As such, unitary systems allegedly promote institutional stability.

A unitary state is often the appropriate level of government to provide some public goods due to economies of scale in both production and consumption. Initially, increasing the quantity of the public good or service is associated with declining average cost. That is, as a public good is provided to a larger share of the population, the unit cost of providing the good declines. A unitary system of government can provide public goods and services at a lower cost than regional governments because the regions may not be able fully to exploit economies of scale.

A unitary state has some drawbacks, however, the most important of which stem from the concentration of power. The concentration of power provides authorities in a unitary government with unlimited means to coerce (Breton and Scott 1980). Even where the government is democratic, the concentration of power with the central authority may not translate into ideal outcomes at the local level. In fact local residents may consider many policies as outright dictatorial. Policies enacted by the central government may not reflect what is appropriate for all regions. In other words, policies enacted by unitary governments are not flexible enough to accommodate regional differences in preference.

Although unitary systems may help to forge unity between heterogeneous groups, the system has the potential to oppress some groups. As noted in the previous chapters, with power concentrated at the centre the leadership can adopt discriminatory policies (Jackson and Rosberg 1982). Thus although a country remains unitary by definition, various groups are treated differently, thereby creating anti-government sentiment that may motivate these groups to remove the government from power through undemocratic means. In extreme cases, the failure of the central government to accommodate group differences can lead to civil war or to demands for secession.

Finally, the provision of public goods in unitary states may be inefficient. As large quantities of a public good are provided, eventually unit costs start to increase. These diseconomies of scale reflect the increasing cost of administering activities, bureaucratic inefficiencies, shirking, and so on (Tullock 1965; Downs 1967; Orzechowski 1977). As increasingly more layers of bureaucracy develop, the unit cost of providing the public good increases. Even though some benefits are associated with large jurisdictions, large administrative jurisdictions are probably inefficient. One should keep in mind the fact that the range of economies of scale depends on the particular good in question and the state of production technology. Thus the optimal size of jurisdictions depends on the particular public good or service and also the technology of producing that good or service.

Given that unitary systems have some important advantages, governments can mitigate the problems by decentralizing the decision-making process. Decentralization minimizes the disadvantages of a unitary system while at the same time retaining the advantages. In simple terms, decentralization delegates decision-making power to lower levels of government. If sufficient decision-making authority is delegated, then these lower levels of government do achieve some degree of autonomy. Decentralization provides more direct control by the people who are affected by particular policies. The central government, however, determines how much power is delegated to these lower units of government.

Decentralization may approximate the outcomes that match the 'private' provision of public goods (Davies 1971; Crain and Zardkoohi 1978; Borcherding *et al.* 1982). Numerous studies show that public production is less efficient than private production. Private producers minimize costs since costs have a direct effect on profitability. Owners, therefore, have strong incentives to monitor managers and other employees. Government officials, on the other hand, do not minimize costs as their benefits are not directly linked to their efficiency. This is compounded by the fact that the consumers are not directly linked to their efficiency. This is compounded by the fact that the consumers of public goods and services have little incentive to monitor government officials.

These weak monitoring incentives occur for two main reasons: the free-rider problem and fiscal illusion. The free-rider problem arises because there are so many consumers of the good that efforts by one person to monitor the officials result in gains to all. As a result, no single individual willingly devotes resources to monitoring the officials. Simply put, the beneficiaries are numerous and dispersed and no one has sufficient wealth at stake to make it worth taking an interest in the day-to-day operations of a public bureau or enterprise (Alchian and Demsetz 1972; De Alessi 1982; Shughart and Kimenyi 1991).

Fiscal illusion occurs because consumers do not take into account the full costs of providing public goods and services. For any public good, revenues originate from distant sources while benefits are concentrated in the community. Thus individuals fail to recognize the costs and only see the benefits. As long as some positive benefits occur, they have no concern as to whether the provision is efficient or not. As a result, public provision is often inefficient and is likely to be higher in more centralized states because the relationship between revenue sources and where those revenues are spent is weak.

Decentralization increases the incentives for local communities to monitor officials. If the revenues to provide public goods are generated locally, then costs and benefits are internalized, which eliminates fiscal illusion. In addition, because the public good is provided to a small community, the free-rider problem is tamed. Reducing the fiscal illusion and free-rider problems increases efficiency in production, if not to the extent of private production.

Consider education. The central government can outline a general curriculum for all primary schools in the country in question and also allocate funds to each jurisdiction to meet the goals of the curriculum. The central government, however, allows each community (district, or even another smaller jurisdiction) to operate its own school system, including the allocation of funds to different educational programmes and activities. Thus each jurisdiction adopts its own procedures, such as the selection of teachers, the organizational structure of the schools, student codes of discipline, and so on. This arrangement allows residents more direct control over their schools. For example, they can replace a principal if the school performs poorly in national exams. The community can also refuse to renew teachers' contracts if they are judged incompetent. Note that, depending on the power delegated to the communities, the residents need not navigate complicated bureaucratic processes before their desires are translated into policy.

When local areas directly influence their schools, they adopt the procedures that best meet their needs. Because each community can adopt the most effective local policies and procedures, decentralization provides an environment of competition across jurisdictions. Those jurisdictions that adopt good policies will have better schools. Those that perform poorly can change their policies. In addition to creating competition in the provision of public goods, decentralization allows flexible policy-making and encourages innovation in the delivery of services.

Primary school education is but one example of a variety of publicly provided goods and services that can be provided more efficiently in a decentralized system. Other functions, such as crime protection, are more effectively and efficiently implemented if each community has its own police force. Community police are directly responsible to the residents in the local area.

Decentralization is more successful the less control the central government exerts and the more control local residents have. Decentralization defeats itself if the central government appoints officials to oversee particular functions at the local level. For example, local influence over education is largely undermined if the central authority appoints school principals without the community's participation. Likewise, decentralization fails if the central government sets strict guidelines such that the local residents have little room to express their preferences. In education, for example, although the central government may set some salary guidelines, the local residents should decide the actual pay of teachers. Thus communities could reward some teachers more than others based on performance. This not only permits competition across jurisdictions but also within jurisdictions.

So far we have assumed that all revenue to carry out the functions delegated to communities originates from the central government. That is, the central government holds the taxing power and the local communities do not. While decentralization without the power to tax improves the efficient delivery of public goods and services, a more effective system decentralizes taxing power to local communities. Public goods and services that are financed at the local level are provided at lower cost than when revenues originate from the central government (Couch and Kimenyi 1992).

But, of course, transferring the power to tax reduces the central government's authority even more, and may create problems of inter-jurisdictional differences. Poorer local communities may provide lower quality public goods and services than relatively well-off communities. Central governments, if they can overcome ethnic bias, may minimize this potential problem by transferring resources to poorer regions from those endowed with more resources. However, fiscal equalization must be implemented with care. Efficient outcomes are expected where residents internalize costs and benefits. Resource transfers from one region to another create the fiscal illusion problem that results in inefficient production.

Decentralization is a logical wealth-enhancing policy to adopt in centralized states. As noted, the power delegated is determined by the central government. Thus the delegated authority can be revoked by the central government at will. Therefore, while decentralization has several advantages, a real danger remains that the government may reverse itself frequently, creating confusion and costly reversal of policies. This is because there is no constitutional contract that defines the relationship between the central government and local communities.

One of our primary concerns with regard to political institutions in Africa has to do with the autonomy of ethnic groups. The fact that decentralization provides ethnic groups with more autonomy in meeting preferences means that the potential for conflict is reduced. If decentralization involves giving tax and spending power to lower level political units, accompanied by reduced power of the central government, then naturally the coercive powers of unitary states are reduced. Reducing the coercive powers of the state may often be equivalent to increasing the liberties of individuals in the various groups: cultural, political, ethnic or otherwise.

A primary source of ethnic conflict in unitary states has to do with property rights violations. Leaders in unitary states benefit from inefficient property rights because such a structure provides them with accessible resources. Such violations retard production, investment and market exchange, and ultimately reduce the rate of economic growth. The more centralized unitary states are, the more the power to coerce, and the higher the propensity to violate property rights. Decentralization reduces the power to coerce and thus property rights violations are reduced.

An important advantage of decentralization is that it encourages individuals to participate in all aspects of community life. Where genuine participation takes place in the design and implementation of development efforts, such efforts become self-enforcing and self-sustaining – essentially they become exercises in self-governance (Sawyer 1988). Participation that results from decentralization empowers individuals in the community with the ability to seek out solutions to individual and collective choices (Ostrom 1987). Decentralization also encourages communities to build a complex array of relationships and linkages with other communities in pursuit of mutual interests. Where local institutions of collective choice are organized around ethnic groups, decentralization encourages mutually beneficial inter-ethnic linkages.

Given the many advantages associated with decentralization, one may wonder why such a strategy has not been widely utilized to deal with both economic and political problems in Africa. The truth is that decentralization has been popularized in the African countries for over three decades. However, the results of decentralization efforts have largely been disappointing. Nonetheless, the past failure of decentralization efforts in Africa offers some useful insights as to how to embark on new initiatives (Wunsch and Olowu 1990).

Beginning in the mid 1960s, it became apparent that the highly centralized states that the African leaders had crafted were not effective in serving the people. International development agencies and foreign donors pointed out to the new governments the necessity of decentralizing decision-making powers. As a result, beginning in the mid 1960s, a number of independent Black African countries initiated a variety of decentralization programmes. The alleged goal of these programmes was to bring decision-making processes closer to the people and thus to increase their participation in the development process.

Probably the best known case of decentralization in Africa took place in Tanzania (Hyden 1980). Decentralization was at the core of the 1967 Arusha Declaration that was spearheaded by President Nyerere. The programme involved the establishment of communal farming organized around villages, what is popularly known as *Ujamaa*. Most of the day-to-day decisions were left to the villages, which were headed by local party officials.

Decentralization efforts in the Sudan date back to the early 1960s. The 1960 Local Government Act and the 1971 People's Local Government Act sought to achieve maximum participation by the people at community level by transferring power to local governments. However, these Acts concentrated local government powers at the provincial level under the direction of the provincial administration. The Presidential Orders of 1977 and 1978 transferred more power to local governments. These orders stipulated that the president of the republic was the patron of all local government units (Leonard and Wunsch 1982). Essentially, local government was still under the firm control of the central government.

In Zambia, decentralization measures began with the adoption of the Local Government Act of 1965 that sought to decentralize government activities to local communities. Several other programmes and initiatives, such as the Village Registration and Development Act of 1971 and the Local Administration Act of 1980, aimed at increasing the role of local governments in decision-making (Olowu 1987).

Likewise, the Kenyan government has initiated several decentralization efforts since the late 1960s (Oyugi 1983; Rondinelli 1983). Most of these efforts have involved the creation of Provincial and District Planning and Development Committees. Instead of managing development from the nation's capital, most administrative tasks were transferred to the Provinces and Districts under the supervision of the Provincial and District Commissioners. Similar efforts have been undertaken in other Sub-Saharan African countries (Mawhood 1983, 1987).

Unfortunately, to a large extent decentralization efforts in Africa have not been successful. There are some success stories that can be attributed to decentralization initiatives, but these are few and far between. Several reasons explain the widespread failure of decentralization efforts in Africa. First and foremost, in most decentralization initiatives, decision-making powers have not been transferred to the local communities but to the provincial and district headquarters. In these cases, decentralization has only involved attempts to operate development schemes through committees appointed or supervised by government (Addai 1984; Thoahlane 1984). Thus decentralization has resulted in the concentration of power at the provincial and district levels. In some cases the result has actually been to undermine the role of the local communities. As a matter of fact, decentralization has often resulted in increased bureaucratic involvement in policy design and implementation.

There are other reasons for the failure of decentralization. In Tanzania, for example, although the *Ujamaa* policy was an effective approach to bringing decision-making to the people, the programme was destined to fail since it abolished private ownership and replaced it with communal ownership. Decentralization that does not promote private property ownership is meaningless, a lesson that President Nyerere and the Tanzanian public has painfully learned. In many other countries, decentralization efforts have been periodically interrupted by undemocratic changes of government.

Probably the most important reason why decentralization has failed in Africa is the fact that decentralization policies do not allow groups to express their own preferences in policy design and implementation. In the majority of cases, policy-making and the design of programmes are still the task of the central government. Decentralization has not provided local communities with the authority to design and implement their own programmes. If decentralization is to succeed, it must allow for plurality of interests: ethnic, cultural, economic and political. However, African governments fear that accommodating such plural interests would post a challenge to their regimes. Governments, therefore, have decentralized only to the extent that is consistent with the survival of their regimes.

The failure of decentralization in Africa provides some insights as to how such a strategy might be effectively implemented. First, it is clear that local governments as units of collective choice and action should have a firm constitutional base. For decentralization to succeed, decision-making authority must reside with the local governments and should not be imposed (Olowu 1990). This requires clear constitutional limitations on the power of central governments.

Second, local governments should have significant autonomy in the exercise of their responsibilities. It is such autonomy that permits groups to make the decisions that best serve their own interests.

Third, local government authority should be included in the constitution and protected. As we have observed, in many cases the central government decides how much decision-making authority to delegate and it is free to revoke such authority. Because national leaders benefit from centralized rather than decentralized states, there is a temptation to centralize in order better to serve their own interests.

Fourth, local governments should be responsible to the people they serve and not to the central government. As such, local communities should have the power to design and organize their own institutions of collective choice and their own electoral procedures and rules.

Fifth, decentralization can only succeed if the constitution guarantees the protection of private property rights. Reducing the coercive powers of the government by decentralization is one step in reducing violations of such rights. But this in itself does not guarantee that predatory local government will not violate property rights. Constitutional protection of property rights is therefore essential.

Finally, we suggest that successful decentralization must utilize geoethnicity. Ethnic boundaries define natural territorial divisions where people are already united by many other factors. It is in these communities that people feel that their participation makes a difference in their lives. As Cobbah (1988, 81) has stated, geoethnicity makes a difference in African lives and provides an avenue for popular participation. Furthermore, emphasizing territorial identity would lessen the tension that arises from competition between ethnic groups at the state level.

8. Maintaining Unity and Diversity: Federalism

We have emphasized the fact that different ethnic groups in the unitary states of Africa still consider themselves distinct, and frequently behave as interest groups in their attempt to maximize the well-being of their members at the expense of other ethnic groups. Because competition for transfers and power results in ethnic rivalries, it is clear that an appropriate solution would be to reduce the opportunities for tribal rent-seeking. This calls for smaller units of government, analogous to the indigenous tribal governments.

Today, unlike in the past when societies were organized along completely autonomous tribal units, there are many factors that unite ethnic groups in the same country. Furthermore, the types of public goods and the state of production technology that exist today suggest that those ethnic units may no longer adequately define efficient political units for organizing some activities. Thus although there are many issues that separate tribal groups, suggesting that there are matters that should be left to individual tribal units, there are other matters that demand cooperation among various tribal groups. In essence, then, appropriate political institutions should simultaneously nurture autonomy and unity.

There is no doubt that decentralization of the unitary state will go a long way towards reducing ethnic conflicts and rent-seeking activities, and towards increasing efficiency. Decentralization reduces the concentration of power and thus can be expected to reduce the propensity of governments to violate individual and civil liberties. Thus decentralization should be the first step in reforming the centralized states of Africa.

However, decentralization cannot be relied upon to offer long-term and stable solutions. As noted previously, decentralization is subject to manipulation by the central authority. The powers delegated to lower levels of government through decentralization are often not guaranteed by a constitution. As a result, the central authorities can revoke the powers delegated at will. Although we have suggested constitutional protection for Local Government Acts, that in itself may not be sufficient because predatory governments may seek to change the constitution in a manner that undermines the Acts. Furthermore, central governments may not be willing to transfer substantial powers to local governments. While we believe that decentralization could effectively harmonize the relationships among ethnic groups in some countries, this strategy may not significantly reduce ethnic conflict in other countries. In countries where decentralization may not be effective, the appropriate option may be one that provides for more autonomy of ethnic groups. Such largely autonomous units can then enter into a loose political association with other ethnic groups.

Long-term stable relationships between ethnic groups can only occur if the different groups freely choose to enter into political associations with others. In other words, political associations between different groups should be by consent. Following the voluntary principle, the ideal type of political institution would be one that preserves ethnic integrity while at the same time achieving association of ethnic groups to achieve some common goals. In other words, to solve the many institutional problems in Sub-Saharan Africa, political systems that accommodate both unity and diversity are necessary. Naturally, the appropriate system that accomplishes both of these goals is federalism.

Federal systems of government are fairly common and, to a large extent, function quite smoothly. Examples of federal governments include Australia, Canada, the Federal Republic of Germany, Switzerland and the United States of America. The key characteristic of a federal government is the association of states or regions in which member states or regions retain a large measure of independence. Federal governments adhere to the federal principle: *the method of dividing power so that the general and regional governments are each within a sphere, coordinate and independent* (Wheare 1947; see also Riker 1964; Lemco 1991). Thus federalism balances the unity of groups and preserves their integrity. As noted by Daniel Elazar (1987): 'Federalism has to do with the need for people and polities to unite for common purposes yet remain separate to preserve their respective integrities. It is like wanting to have one's cake and eat it too' (p. 33).

Because both general and regional governments operate directly on the people, a federal government requires a written constitution that stipulates the powers of the general (federal) and regional governments. The stability of a federal government requires division of power in such a way that the powers exercised by the general government are derivative and clearly specified, and that the residual remains with the regional governments or with the people. We note that the powers and responsibilities of federal governments vary. But in general they are clearly specified.

The boundary of what the general government should do must be clearly marked. The distribution of power between regional and general governments is crucial to the smooth functioning of the federal union (Sharma and Choudhry 1967). This is to say that each government in a federal system is limited to its own sphere and within that sphere is independent of the others. The constitution must therefore guarantee that no government – general or regional – can alter the relationship. In a federal system, neither the general government nor the regional government yields fully to the other, thereby abandoning its sovereignty.

Unlike decentralization, where a central government delegates authority, a federal system comprises several independent governments that are free to elect their representatives, to enact tax laws and to decide on spending programmes without the interference of the general government. Just as they are more independent, regional governments also have more responsibility. For example, the financing of education or crime protection could be the responsibility of the regional governments entirely. Individual regions design a tax structure that they deem necessary to finance these programmes. Depending on voter preference and resource availability, wide variations in the tax schemes across regions are expected. One region may decide to tax agricultural produce, another may opt for property taxes, while yet another may rely exclusively on a land tax.

Thus federal polities are non-centralized and power is diffused among many centres. Furthermore, the existence and authority of the centres is not extended by the general government as in the case of decentralization within a unitary system, but rather their existence and authority are guaranteed by the constitution. In fact the powers in a federal system are so diffused that they cannot be legitimately centralized. As Elazar (1987, 34–45) notes: 'In a noncentralized political system, power is so diffused that it cannot be legitimately centralized or concentrated without breaking the structure and spirit of the constitution'. This means that political units in non-centralized political systems are immune from federal interference. Likewise, constituent governments are not a creation of the federal government but derive their authority directly from the people.

The independence of regional governments in fulfilling their functions is crucial. In addition the regions must have the freedom to organize their own government as they wish (Duchacek 1970). For example, regional governments should decide on the election of the representatives to the regional assembly and should determine the term lengths that representatives serve, and so on. Likewise, regional laws must be left to regional courts. This independence must be guaranteed in a written constitution.

The federal government must also have exclusive powers to perform its functions without the interference of regional governments. The defence function belongs with the federal government. Likewise, the federal government should deal with international relations, with immigration and naturalization, with currency, coinage and legal tender, and with all matters relating to inter-regional commerce. Other functions that are frequently assigned to the federal government include the establishment of uniform weights and measures, the establishment and administration of banking and bankruptcy laws, and the administration of railways, air traffic, inter-regional highways, the marine environment, and fisheries, and other natural resources such as forests and wildlife. The effective discharge of federal government duties requires significant resources. Thus the federal government must also be empowered to impose taxes and to use other sources of revenue.

The independence of the general and regional governments, in addition to the fact that each government is independent of the other in conducting affairs within its sphere, also means that the selection of representatives to regional and general governments is independent. In other words, representatives of a federal government should not be selected by the regional legislature. Likewise, representatives of the general (federal) assembly should not have a role in deciding the selection of regional representatives.

An important characteristic of federal governments is that power is so distributed that the rank order of governments is not fixed. That is to say that in some matters the federal government dominates, while in other matters constituent governments dominate. For example, the federal government may be solely responsible for defence, the provincial government for college education, the district government for high school education, and local governments for primary school education. Thus the federal principle is applicable in many settings and also allows for flexibility.

The division of functions between federal and regional governments is crucial since it defines the relationship between the general and regional governments. The division of taxing and spending functions in a federal system, referred to as 'fiscal federalism', requires careful consideration. Specifically, it is necessary to evaluate the most efficient allocation of responsibilities among the levels of government. Fiscal federalism includes not only the functions of the federal and regional governments, but also of local governments.

There are some clear functions that remain with the federal government. These include the provision of public goods and services that are collectively consumed by all regions. For example, only the federal government can perform the defence function. For such a pure public good as defence, citizens in all regions should pay a share of the cost. Likewise, no region can conduct its own stabilization programme, or control inflation or unemployment. Such activities have nation-wide effects and their control must reside with the federal government.

Other functions clearly reside with the regions and local communities. A cattle dip, for example, serves a fairly narrow population group. Nonetheless, because it may be inefficient for individual farmers to have their own cattle dips, collective provision may be justified. This function, however, belongs to the local communities. It is the beneficiaries who should pay the cost. On the other hand, education may be inadequately provided by a small community and should be the responsibility of the regional government.

The cost structure of providing public goods largely determines whether a function should reside with regional or with local governments. For some public goods, the minimum average cost occurs at low levels of output. Such public goods should be provided by small communities. For other public goods, the minimum average cost occurs at large quantities. Here the regional government may be best suited to supply these goods and services.

ADVANTAGES AND PROBLEMS OF A FEDERAL SYSTEM

Before considering whether a federal system would be appropriate for African countries, we discuss the advantages of such a system over a unitary state and also some of the problems that are associated with federal systems. There would be little point in dwelling on the issues of federalism if such a system did not have clear advantages over unitary states. The issue is not only whether the system would result in better political arrangements that reduce conflict, but also whether it would result in better economic outcomes and thus increase the well-being of the population. There are several advantages that are associated with federal systems of government that make such systems viable options for reforming the institutions of the Sub-Saharan African countries. The main advantages of a federal system of government include promoting political development; decentralization of political power; protection of minorities against oppression; ability to accommodate diversity; and the opportunity to experiment with policy options efficiency that results from inter-jurisdictional competition (Breton and Scott 1980). We discuss each of the above in turn.

Political Participation and Development

A federal system brings the government closer to the people. Voters consider issues that affect them directly at the local level. Therefore a close link exists between choices made and the outcomes. Because local communities can influence policy decisions on matters affecting people in those communities, individuals increase their political awareness and are more actively involved in the political process. Voters realize that their choices are important in determining outcomes at the local level and they therefore evaluate the issues and alternatives before them more carefully. This results in increased political development as individuals take on more political responsibility. This grassroots participation develops citizenry.

Decentralization of Power

The most visible advantage of a federal system is that it decentralizes political power to many centres. Neither the general nor the regional governments have absolute power. Because the absolute power of the unitary system is often abused, a federal system reduces the probability of such abuses. Even when abuses occur, their effects are minimized since leaders have only limited powers.

Protection Against Oppression

In a unitary state, the central government is frequently dominated by members of the majority group, race, tribe or religious group. Alternatively, the government may be dominated by a coalition of small groups. In either case, the chances are that in countries where there are heterogeneous groups, some will be excluded from the ruling coalition. Given the unlimited powers of coercion possessed by unitary states, these governments can (and often do) adopt discriminatory policies that oppress groups that are outside the ruling coalition. The organization of a federal government, with the guarantees afforded to regions with regard to their independence and the fact that the federal government has limited powers, offers protection to all groups in the country.

Accommodate Diversity

We have noted that unitary states have the advantage of uniting otherwise heterogeneous populations. Often, however, the policies adopted by unitary governments may not accommodate groups with widely varying differences. By attempting to unify otherwise diverse groups, unitary states may fail to accommodate some groups. Establishment of regional governments allows individual groups to preserve their identity. In fact one of the reasons that groups are motivated to be independent is so that they can preserve their tribal identity.

Policy Experimentation

In a unitary state, identical public policies tend to be implemented uniformly across the entire nation. Frequently these policies are enacted without any prior knowledge or evidence as to their effectiveness. As can be expected, policy failures are frequent, with negative outcomes across the nation. In a federal system, regions adopt their own policies. Some of these policies fail and others succeed. Even where policies fail, they only affect a relatively small area and involve much lower costs. Furthermore, those regions can then change policies and adopt those that have been found to be successful in other regions. Thus in federal systems, different regions are good experimental laboratories for policies.

Consider a case where the government imposes a 10 per cent profit tax on businesses. The result may be that many businesses fail and that the founding rate of new establishments declines across the nation. Such a tax may be expected to result in high unemployment and declining tax revenues. Clearly, such a tax has a high social cost and should be avoided. If regional governments were responsible for setting tax levels to raise revenue, it is likely that some would adopt a profit tax such as the one mentioned above. Other regions might impose income taxes, others property taxes, and so on. Some of the tax structures would have the desired results and others might not. Even where states adopt taxes that have adverse effects, such effects are limited to the regions and the regional governments could adopt those types of tax that have been known to succeed in other areas. It is by allowing this kind of experimentation that a federal system results in the adoption of optimal policies across the nation.

Competition

Jurisdictional competition is probably the most important aspect of a federal system with regard to a nation's economic performance. It is well established that resource allocation is more efficient under competitive conditions as compared to a monopolistic setting. A multilevel system of government provides a competitive environment among constituent jurisdictions, leading to the adoption of efficient policies. This type of competition results in higher levels of economic growth.

Consider, for example, a region where the government adopts high taxes on industry. Such taxes reduce profitability and owners opt to relocate in jurisdictions that have lower taxes. This means that resources will move to areas where they command the highest value. Regions that impose high taxes are unlikely to sit back and watch industries moving to low tax regions. They are instead likely to adopt competitive strategies that attract investment. Investments will therefore be located across all regions, and each region will strive to adopt policies that ensure maximum levels of investment.

Likewise, investors will seek to locate in regions that provide the least impediments to production. For example, areas where local roads are reasonably well maintained, where the regulations are less costly with low bureaucratic corruption, and where schools systems are better will attract more investors. Thus each of the regions, in their attempt to attract employment opportunities, must in essence adopt policies that improve the quality of services and must also enact those policies that make the region attractive for investors. The outcomes of these competitive processes are higher quality provision of services, a better climate for investment and higher levels of economic growth.

Although federal system have clear advantages, some problems are associated with these systems. These include forgone benefits from economies of scale, consumption and production externalities, and the interdependence between persons across jurisdictions (Breton and Scott 1980; Horowitz 1985). We briefly discuss the problems below.

In a federal system, some goods and services are provided at the local level. The more decentralized the system, the larger the proportion of activities provided at the local level to a smaller market as compared with centralized unitary states. This means that in some cases the benefits associated with higher levels of production are sacrificed. Essentially, the provision of some goods and services in decentralized systems may be at a higher cost than when provided by unitary systems. While a more decentralized federal system is desirable in that more powers are distributed to lower levels of government, it is also true that such a fragmented system is associated with higher costs in terms of forgone benefits of economies of scale.

Production and consumption externalities involve spillover benefits in production and consumption from one jurisdiction to another. If, for example, the benefits of providing a service to members of one jurisdiction spill over to members of another jurisdiction, then ideally more of such a service should be provided to take into account the benefits received by members of other communities. In a federal system, however, the government of one jurisdiction does not take into account the benefits that spill over to members of another jurisdiction. As a result, federal systems under-supply those types of service compared with unitary systems of government. The problem of externalities can, however, be resolved through bargaining *à la* Coase (1960).

The other problem of federal systems is due to the interdependence of persons across different jurisdictions. Interdependence may be due to family ties, friendship or any other factor that creates concern for the well-being of people in different jurisdictions. Because of such interdependencies, people in one jurisdiction may want people in another jurisdiction to benefit from some policy (for example, redistribution), but they may not be able to affect such desires in a federal system.

These problems, however, should not be a basis for rejecting the federal system, nor should they mean that the powers of local communities should be significantly reduced by more centralization. By and large, the problems of federal systems discussed above have much to do with establishing the optimal size of jurisdictions and the nature of fiscal federalism. Thus in designing federal structures of government, each country must carefully evaluate the optimal size of the collective units (Buchanan and Tullock 1962) and the nature of fiscal federalism. As noted by Breton and Scott (1980), the problems of federalism can be solved not only by transferring power from one jurisdiction to another, but also through the coordination of policies between the governments involved.

The above problems notwithstanding, federalism provides Africans with rich options to resolve the numerous political, social and economic problems facing their nations. Federalism increases the freedom of individuals and results in more efficient governments and economic systems. We note, however, that the practical implementation of federal principles demands democratic institutions. Unlike unitary systems of government that can exist under both democratic and autocratic systems, true federalism can only exist in democratic institutions. The constitutional contract that defines the powers of regional and general governments must be maintained at all times. This necessarily requires democratic government.

One of our primary interests in advocating federal systems for Sub-Saharan African countries is to provide ethnic groups with more autonomy so as to reduce the inter-ethnic conflict that is common in centralized unitary states. It is conceivable that each tribal group may want to establish its own government. Given the high degree of ethnic heterogeneity in African countries, federalism in those countries may result in a problem of too many sub-optimal jurisdictions in terms of size and resource capabilities. In such cases, some ethnic governments may be too small and others too large; some may be relatively wealthy and others too poor. These potential disparities may create problems for federal systems in some countries.

Clearly, lower level governments should not necessarily be organized on the basis of ethnicity. Instead in some cases ethnic groups should merge to establish common regional governments, while in other cases some groups may form several regional governments. As a result, we can expect that some ethnic groups will end up being permanent minorities in some regions and may face discrimination by majority groups. In Chapter 12, we provide some suggestions for protecting ethnic minorities, both in federal systems and in decentralized unitary states.

9. The Demand for Federalism in Africa

There is no doubt that decentralization, by reducing the concentration of decision-making power at one level and dispersing it to several levels, would result in more efficient governments in Africa. As noted earlier, decentralization of the unitary states of Sub-Saharan Africa is a natural point to start institutional reform in those countries.

The issue of federalism is more complicated. A central question that needs to be addressed is whether federalism would be appropriate for African countries. For federalism to succeed, people in various regions of the particular countries should be prepared to unite with other regions in some matters and to remain separate on other matters. In other words, the success of a federal system would largely depend on whether the people desire such a system. Only then would constituent units enter into the contractual agreements that are at the core of a stable federal system.

Whether federalism is appropriate for African countries largely depends on the desire of different regions to be united and at the same time to be independent. Such desire must be strong and the regions must therefore demonstrate their demand for some degree of independence. Many African leaders suggest that regions have not shown a strong desire for independence in the past and, therefore, that federalism is not appropriate.

The fact that groups have not expressed a desire to be independent should not be used as evidence of the absence of such a desire. Given that, in the past, it would have been almost impossible for any group to express its desires freely without retribution from the authorities, many regions that may have wanted to be independent would have suppressed expressing such desires for fear of retribution. With the recent democratization movements such fear is dissipating. In fact there is now evidence of many grassroots movements that demand more independence. That there are discussions about the establishment of federal systems of government in various countries signals a desire for some degree of independence.

A federal government can be formed by two alternative processes. The first, and by far the more common, is where formerly independent states or regions agree to be united under a common government but still retain a large measure of their independence. The other, less common, process is where different regions in a unitary state desire more independence while still remaining part of one nation. Notice that in both cases it is the preferences of the different regions that initiate the process towards federalism. Specifically, regions must desire to be united under one federal government for some purposes and at the same time they must be willing to establish independent regional governments in other matters. Regions in a federal government, then, *desire to be united but not to be unitary.*

Before we can arrive at judgements concerning the appropriateness of a federal system it is necessary to consider what makes regions or states desire to unite while at the same time retaining a large measure of independence (see Maddox 1941; Wheare 1964; Wildavsky 1967; Earle 1969). Since different regions in the various African countries are already united under one government, the important question for our current purposes is what factors would make different regions desire to secure some measure of independence yet remain part of the countries they are in today (see following discussion). If such factors do not exist, then attempts to establish independent regional governments and a federal system are likely to be futile.

1. *Economic advantage and exploitation*: Regions may want to secure more independence if they have some economic advantage that they do not want to give up. A region that is well endowed with resources and where significantly more economic activities are concentrated may want to retain control of such economic power. Because this may not be possible in a unitary state, residents of such a region may express their desire to be independent.

Economic advantage is one region is neither a sufficient nor necessary condition for that region to desire to be independent. There may be other factors that may increase the desire for such a region to be independent, such as excessive taxation by the central government or the failure of the central government to provide the necessary public goods and services to these areas. If regions that have an economic advantage consider the allocation of resources to be fair, even when relatively higher government revenues are derived from these regions, there is likely to be little incentive for them to desire to be independent. It is when regions consider the central government to be discriminatory in resource allocation that they may desire to be independent.

We have already noted that in Africa, as a result of the rent-seeking behaviour of interest groups, resource allocation is primarily determined by the tribal affiliation of the leadership. Consequently, some ethnic groups are discriminated against in resource allocation. For this reason, such regions would prefer to have more control of their resources and the wealth that they generate. Thus in many countries, especially where minority groups have no opportunity to prevent transfers, there are frequent demands for more autonomy in the control of resources. For so long as tribal identification remains strong, we can expect the continuation of resource distribution from some ethnic tribes to others.

Because tribal groups differ markedly in terms of cultural traits, work habits, economic specialization, land use and system of property rights, there are clear differences in their ability to generate income. Such differences in the ability to use markets create wide differences in the economic well-being of groups. Frequently, groups that are less productive seek to use political institutions to force wealth transfers to themselves. This suggests that there are groups that end up as permanent net suppliers of wealth transfers and others that become permanent net recipients of transfers.

Probably the most persistent source of ethnic conflict in African countries originates from attempts by one group to expropriate transfers to its members. There is no country where this problem does not exist.

2. *Geographical isolation*: Because of geographical isolation, many communities, even in an otherwise homogeneous nation, develop a distinct regional consciousness (Dikshit 1975). Such consciousness makes the communities want to keep to themselves. When different communities in the same country develop such distinct regional awareness, they may all need to secure some degree of independence while uniting for some purposes. Such geographical isolation of communities played an important role in the creation of a federal system in Switzerland. Switzerland has a very rugged topography where mountains and valleys create small, isolated communities that are distinct and that developed some degree of independence (Rappard 1948; Sawer 1969).

When communities are isolated from the rest of the country in a unitary state, they may rightfully feel that the central government is too remote from them. Furthermore, because of the fact that these communities are isolated, the central government may fail to serve them as well as it does the other communities. Those communities may therefore desire more independence and establish a government that is closer to them.

In many African countries, some regions are far removed from the central administration. Given poor communications and the large geographical size of such nations, remote regions have little contact with other regions or with the central government. In some countries, the isolation is magnified by topography and climate. For example, many countries do not have large, navigable rivers that would increase mobility. In other countries, tribal groups are separated by harsh deserts. In Ethiopia, high mountains make contact between groups living on opposite sides of the mountains almost impossible. These factors have kept groups localized within some limited geographical areas isolated from other groups. Because of such isolation, many tribal groups have developed quite distinct consciousnesses. The fact that such consciousnesses are tied to both a particular territory and language increases the desire for independence.

3. *Differences in social institutions*: If different regions have significantly different social institutions, a unitary state government may not be able to accommodate these differences. In such cases, the different regions may desire to be independent in those matters in which they differ while remaining united for most other purposes.

By and large, different regions in each of the countries in Africa have distinct social institutions: marriage laws, burial rites, methods of making decisions, and so on. Uniting the regions under one government and establishing uniform social institutions necessarily means that some groups have to sacrifice their most preferred ways of doing things. National laws that prohibit polygamy are welcome in some regions but are considered oppressive in others. In some cases, groups consider retaining their social institutions to be paramount and oppose attempts to impose new social structures. Such communities are likely to demand independence in the organization of their social matters, but to be united with other regions for economic purposes.

The presence of numerous tribal cultures in Africa suggests that under conditions of freedom, individuals will choose to organize some matters within their tribe and to be largely independent from other groups.

4. *Religious heterogeneity*: In some countries, religious heterogeneity has been one of the factors that has motivated the desire for regions to be independent. A good example is Nigeria, where the Moslem north and the Christian south have clearly expressed their desire to

be separate. The same is true in Sudan. In Ethiopia there are also clear divisions along religious lines.

The demand for separation increases when the government in power attempts to impose religious laws across the whole country. This has been the case in Sudan, where the government imposed Moslem law on its people.

5. *Population heterogeneity*: There is a high degree of tribal and racial attachment among Africans. If individuals are strongly attached to their tribe or race, they may want to be independent in some matters. Given the experience of inter-ethnic conflict in Africa, tribal heterogeneity has the highest probability of creating the desire for independence.

6. *The previous existence of independent regional or community governments*: An important factor that creates desire on the part of regions or communities to be independent is if those regions, at some time in the past, had their own governments. For example, the prior existence of 'tribal' kingdoms or chieftainships may mean that there are already strong ties that hold people in a particular region or community together.

7. *Gains from commerce*: Just as resource endowment motivates groups to be separate, a desire for material gain increases the desire for political units to enter into federal arrangements. The advantages of common trade policies played an important role in the federation of the United States. In Canada, New Brunswick, Nova Scotia and Prince Edward Island joined the dominion of Canada in order to enjoy economic advantages in trade. The unification of many of today's federal regions was motivated at least in part by economics (Dikshit 1975).

While various regions of Sub-Saharan countries may have the desire to be independent, complete autonomy may be detrimental economically. There are already many economic linkages that benefit all regions in each of the countries, and thus regions are better off maintaining ties with other regions. Thus although secession may be an option for some regions in a few countries, by and large those regions can not afford to secede. This then presents ideal conditions for federal systems.

8. *Defence*: Autonomous units may seek to be united in a federal system for security reasons. The fear of invasion by hostile foreign powers may accentuate demand for federal union among otherwise unitary states. The unification of the Swiss cantons was to an extent motivated by concerns for defence. In Africa, many of the regions that desire to become independent would not have the capacity to defend

themselves from aggression. Thus while they seek more independence, they still need to remain united with other regions.

There are many examples of countries where groups have sought more independence from the central government. Ethiopia is a good example, where the Ethiopian Somalis want the incorporation of the Ogaden region into a 'Greater Somalia'. Likewise, the people of southern Sudan have for years been involved in bitter civil wars with the central government as they seek more autonomy because they consider the government of Sudan to be oppressive and illegitimate. In Uganda, the former kingdoms have been seeking to re-establish their prior autonomy. In Senegal, the people of the Casamance region have been involved in secession movements, claiming economic and social marginalization by the central government.

In Nigeria, some ethnic minorities in the oil-producing regions have waged secessionist movements because of what they consider unfair distribution of resources by the federal government. Although most of the government revenues are derived from oil, the oil-producing regions in the south have not benefited a lot because most oil revenues are spent in the northern part of the country. This is mainly occupied by the Hausas, who have dominated Nigerian politics over the last three decades (Osaghae 1995). Likewise, in Angola, the oil-rich Cabindan enclave has on occasion attempted to secede from the rest of the country (Banks 1993).

The various inter-ethnic conflicts in Africa reflect the desire of different groups to overcome domination by others. In Rwanda and Burundi, for example, it is clear that neither the Hutu nor the Tutsi accept governments dominated by members of other groups. In many African countries, ethnic groups have been willing to pay a high price to achieve autonomy. The case of the Ibo of Nigeria, who declared themselves independent and suffered the subsequent civil war, is a good example.

The other key indicator of whether federalism is appropriate is that the regions must have the capacity to operate such a system. Regardless of how intensely regions desire a federal system, such a system cannot be appropriate if they do not have the capacity to operate it. Capacity is used to imply the possession of both the financial and human resources necessary for regional governments to perform the functions assigned to them, while at the same time financing the federal government.

Just because some regions may not have the capacity to operate a federal system at the present time does not imply that over time these communities will not achieve that capacity. In fact my own judgement that many regions do not have the capacity necessary to operate a federal government at the present time may be because I have accepted certain arbitrarily drawn boundaries that mark the regions and which may not coincide with the actual boundaries (Kimenyi 1995).

While federal systems promise many benefits, we warn that the creation of federal systems by *existing governments* is likely to be detrimental. The existing government will be tempted to create regional government boundaries with the primary goal of ensuring that the regions so created will have the necessary capacity to contribute to the federal system. By so doing, however, the government may force tribes to associate with long-term enemies. At the same time, such boundaries may separate groups that would have preferred to be together. In such cases, the regional governments so created will not have a strong desire to be independent.

This means that attempts by a central government of a unitary state to establish a federal government may result in chaos and confusion, and almost certainly in failure of the federal system. If a federal government is established by a government of a unitary state, it would almost certainly involve coercion and oppression. As Krauthammer (1990) notes: 'Federalism affords economies of scale and nurtures democracy. It also allows groups to both keep and transcend their national identities. Federation only works, however, if the people choose it freely; otherwise, it is really colonialism'. Thus while there are many benefits of establishing a federal system of government, such a system cannot be forced on the public. It must be by consent.

Based on the discussion presented above regarding the situation in Sub-Saharan Africa, one can conclude that, by and large, the main conditions that make federalism appropriate already exist. In some countries the desire for regions to establish independent governments is quite strong, while in others such desire is just emerging. Although it is difficult to pass judgement on the capacity of the regions to operate within a federal system, the fact that regions are increasingly demanding more independence suggests that federalism is appropriate.

While in the past democracy in Africa was seen merely in terms of replacing single-party regimes with competitive political systems, it has now become clear that radical institutional reform is necessary. In particular, it is now becoming increasingly accepted that ethnicity is an important aspect of African states and that political reform should seek to accommodate ethnic interests (Ottaway 1995). African rulers must come to terms with the idea that democracy may not only involve allowing regions a large measure of independence but, in some cases, complete autonomy may be necessary. Federalizing may therefore serve to avert the costly civil wars that often accompany secessionist movements.

The recent constitutional proposal in Ethiopia that divides political boundaries along the main ethnic and linguistic groups and also provides more autonomy to the respective regions, promises to go a long way to reducing the ethnic rivalries that have characterized that country for decades (*Washington Post* 1995). It is our belief that such reform, that accepts the importance of ethnicity in organizing institutions, is a step in the right direction and should be seriously considered by other countries in Sub-Saharan Africa.

10. Constitutionalism and Civil Society in Africa

Constitutionalism, which basically means the legal limitations placed upon the power of government in its relationship to citizens, is crucial to the restoration of civil society. For nations emerging from communist rule and those that have had non-democratic traditions, the restoration of civil society must involve the establishment of constitutional democracies in which the rule of law replaces the personal rule of man. This essentially requires the adoption of democratic constitutions that stipulate the fundamental rights and obligations of citizens and that define the appropriate scope of government activity.

Constitutionalism as an essential feature of civil society has a long tradition that can be traced back to classical political philosophers such as John Locke (1632–1704), David Hume (1611–76), Baron de Montesquieu (1689–1755), Jean Jacques Rousseau (1712–78), and Immanuel Kant (1724–1804). Although these social philosophers emphasized different aspects of what a society's constitution should include, they all discussed the need for clear rules that constrain government and protect the rights and freedoms of the people (Montesquieu 1977; Rousseau 1984; Hume 1985; Locke 1988).

It is worthwhile mentioning the basic thrust of Locke's constitutionalism, as it embodies key elements that have been responsible for sustaining civil society in several countries including the United States (McGrath and McDaniel 1987). Locke's constitutionalism can be summarized by some of the rules that he considered essential to 'guarantee peaceful political life and tolerable public authority' (Armour 1988). According to Locke, constitutional rules should: place clear limits on the powers of government; provide for a legal system to arbitrate disputes; incorporate majority voting rule; provide for separation of executive and legislative powers; guarantee natural rights; and protect freedoms of religion and other fundamental freedoms. These rules have proved to be essential in the maintenance of civil society and should be used as a guide in drafting constitutions for Sub-Saharan African countries.

The current chaos in Sub-Saharan Africa reflects the lack of appropriate and enforceable constitutional rules. There is little doubt that the constitutions of these countries are deficient in a variety of matters. Most important, the constitutions have failed to constrain the powers of government. Whether the countries retain unitary (but decentralized) states or adopt federal arrangements, as suggested in the previous chapters, they must rewrite their constitutions to ensure that the powers of the government are effectively constrained. This chapter focuses on some of the basic elements that should be contained in the new constitutions. We do not focus on the process of achieving the constitution (such as the ratification process) which is itself an important issue. We instead focus on only the primary contents of constitutions.

In writing constitutions for countries emerging from dictatorial rule, such as the majority of countries in Sub-Saharan Africa, a basic guiding principle should always be that the constitutions should not limit the rights of the people but instead should serve to constrain the powers of government. It is well known that unconstrained government will infringe on the rights of the people. A constitution should therefore serve to limit the power of the government while at the same time preserving people's liberties.

Thus a good constitution, one that is consistent with civil society, should ensure that the government has sufficient power to protect the rights and liberties of the people but should be constrained from oppression. As suggested by Locke, the government should only have the power that is necessary to secure people's lives, liberty and property. To restore civil society in Africa, the task of constraining government power is crucial, and thus there is an urgent need to write and adopt new constitutions that effectively control the power of governments.

Probably the most effective constitutional mechanism for constraining government power is the provision for separation of powers (Siegan 1994). The need to separate the powers of the branches of government has much to do with the realization that, because of human nature, individuals in leadership positions are likely to manipulate laws to their advantage. Combining the powers of the executive and legislature increases the probability that laws will be used to serve special interests. In addition, where branches of government are united, rulers have unlimited opportunities to oppress particular groups and thus undermine civil liberties.

Montesquieu (1977) was probably the first to demonstrate the vital connection between civil liberty and the separation of powers. Although Montesquieu may have taken an extreme position by requiring complete segregation of the various branches of government, the fears he expressed concerning the consequences of uniting various branches of government are worth noting:

> The political liberty of the subject is a tranquility of mind, arising from the opinion each person has of his safety. In order to have this liberty, it is requisite the government be so constituted as one man need not be afraid of another.
> When the legislature and executive powers are united in the same person, or in the same body of magistracy, there can be then no liberty; because apprehensions may arise, lest the same monarch or senate should enact tyrannical laws, to execute them in a tyrannical manner.
> Again there is no liberty, if power of judging be not separated from the legislative and executive powers. Were it joined with the legislative, the life and liberty of the subject would be exposed to arbitrary control; for the judge would be then the legislator. Were it joined to the executive power, the judge might behave with all the violence of an oppressor (p. 202).

Today most African governments have unicameral parliamentary systems with powers highly concentrated in the executive branch. In addition, there is no real separation between the judiciary, executive and legislative branches. As a result, the executive branch frequently influences the outcomes of judicial and legislative decisions. As such, rulers have a wide latitude in policy-making and in determining legislative and judicial outcomes. In many Sub-Saharan African countries, the president appoints members of the judiciary, including those serving in the highest courts. No confirmation of presidential appointees by the legislature is required and therefore rulers face no constraints in the selection of judges. This means that the executive branch is not constrained in its influence on the judiciary and can often interfere directly in influencing court decisions. Thus in most countries, the judicial branch is an extension of the executive branch and serves the wishes of the president. As a matter of fact, presidents have the power to manipulate resignation of judges whose decisions do not serve the interests of the regime.

Likewise, the president appoints his cabinet and senior civil servants and requires no approval from the legislature. In countries that have single-party political systems, individuals have to be cleared by the ruling party before they can stand for election in their constituencies. The legislatures of these countries are therefore dominated by individuals who cannot effectively oppose policies proposed by the government, and it is not uncommon for rulers to suspend from the party members of parliament who are critical of the government. Of course, suspension from the party in single-party states means an automatic loss of a parliamentary seat. Even where there is significant freedom for opposition political parties, the legislature has no powers to constrain the executive branch.

Under the current arrangements in Sub-Saharan African countries, the president has excessive powers and faces few, if any, constraints from other branches of government. As a result, there is no effective system of checks and balances essential to limit the government. While it is true that systems where there is no separation of powers allow for less costly policy-making processes, it is also true that such systems often provide many opportunities for predatory governments to violate the rights of the people (Samuelson 1992; Kaus 1993).

Thus an essential feature of the constitutions that African countries must adopt is the separation of powers. The American system is probably the best example of how separation of powers between executive, judiciary and legislature constrains the potential excesses of government. Each of the branches of government functions separately and each has powers to restrain the others (Hamilton 1937; Siegan 1989).

Separation of powers in ethnically heterogeneous countries would help minimize the probability that one ethnic group would dominate policy outcomes. Thus even though one group may dominate the legislature and may pass laws that are favourable to members of a particular group, such legislation is likely to be overridden by another branch of government. As such, separation of powers is crucial for protecting individual and group rights.

In a system where there is separation of powers, the powers of each branch of government are clearly defined. In addition, each branch should be restricted from undertaking any activities that infringe on the rights of individuals or grant some individuals or groups special privileges or preferences. Such restrictions are particularly necessary to constrain the influence of special interest groups.

The executive branch should have powers sufficient to constrain the legislature to some degree. The presidential veto is an important tool in a government where there is separation of powers. The power to veto legislative measures provides the executive branch some significant authority to protect minority groups. In ethnically diverse African countries, the presidential veto may serve to protect minorities from adverse outcomes of majoritarianism. Therefore the power of the president to veto some legislative measures may encourage members of the legislature belonging to various ethnic groups to engage in compromises in the legislative process. For a presidential veto to be effective, there ought to be a mechanism by which such a veto can be overridden by the legislature, though requiring a higher percentage of the vote than initially required to pass the measure. Again, the American model is a good example of the working of a presidential veto.

Even though it is essential that a president should have a wide range of powers and responsibilities, such as the power to pardon wrong-doers, to exercise emergency measures and to appoint cabinet members and judges, there must also be clear constraints on some matters. In Africa it would be critical that all presidential nominations to the cabinet, senior civil service and judiciary be subject to confirmation by the legislature. Under the current systems, presidents have the power to appoint individuals to these positions and there are not requirements for confirmation by the legislature. African rulers have therefore been able to create branches of government that are not in the least responsive to the wishes of the general public and which instead serve the interests of the rulers.

To restore civil society in Africa, it is necessary that the judicial branch be independent. The judiciary should be immune from manipulation by the executive branch or the legislative branches. An independent judiciary is critical to the enforcement and interpretation of the constitution and the protection of the rights of the people. If the judiciary is not completely independent of the other branches of government, then the constitution may be used to serve the interests of the leadership and there would be no effective means of ensuring that the rights of the people were protected. As a matter of fact, if the judiciary is not completely independent, then the constitution becomes ineffective no matter what guarantees are stipulated in that constitution.

In addition to the separation of powers among the branches of government, the constitution should contain a bill of rights. These rights should include civil and political, social and economic rights. Civil and political rights include freedom of expression, speech and equality in political participation, among others. Social rights include freedom of association and rights to work, security, and so on. Economic rights include the freedom to engage in exchange and rights to property. While it is not possible to enumerate all rights, it is necessary that constitutions broadly stipulate the general rights that are protected. They should protect the liberties of the people whether or not enumerated in the constitution (Siegan 1994).

An issue of concern for African countries has to do with ethnic discrimination. It is critical that the constitutions provide safeguards against the oppression of one group by another. A workable constitution for African countries should guarantee the rights of all ethnic groups, including their rights to self-determination.

Whether Africans choose to decentralize the unitary states or to adopt federal systems of government, there is a need that the machinery of government be based on constitutional arrangements. Thus the constitution should define the relationship between local government and central government in unitary states. Specifically, the powers and limitations of each should be well stipulated. In federal systems, the relationship between the regional and federal systems should also be well defined to safeguard the autonomy of each.

Finally, constitutions should include specifics as to how they can be amended. It is necessary that rules for amending the constitution be stringent, such that it would be quite difficult to change the constitution without the consensus of a large number of people.

11. Protecting Property and Economic Liberties

An important goal of civil society is to establish conditions that facilitate increases in material well-being. Thus in reforming the institutions of Sub-Saharan Africa, a primary objective must be the creation of conditions that promote economic growth. Given the poor economic performance of Sub-Saharan African countries, reforms that seek to restore civil society must focus on the factors that have been responsible for constraining growth in these countries.

The material well-being that people of a particular country enjoy largely depends on the degree to which individuals are able to engage freely in market exchange in pursuit of self-interest. Simply put, material progress is greatest if individuals pursue their affairs without hindrance from the state. The economic theory of *laissez-faire* advanced by Adam Smith (1937) [1776] has proved to be far superior in promoting economic development than approaches that rely on government planning and control. It is well established that individuals in countries where property rights are well defined and government intervention in markets is minimal achieve much higher standards of living than those in countries that are characterized by heavy government intervention and poorly defined property rights. Simply put, economic growth is highest in countries characterized by well-defined property rights that guarantee economic liberties.

One source of poorly defined property rights is what is referred to as the 'common pool problem'. This is the case where resources are overused because many individuals have rights to use them (North 1981; Ostrom 1990). Hart and Moore (1990) rightfully consider the common pool problem as an example of the non-existence of property rights. A good example of the common pool problem in Africa relates to communal ownership of land. While many countries have made significant progress in establishing privately held land, communal ownership remains an important feature in these countries.

Another aspect of poorly defined property rights is so-called 'control rights'. In developing countries, a primary source of inefficiency in resource allocation is that politicians and bureaucrats have excessive control rights over the economy (Shleifer 1995). Political control of the economy in Africa is manifested in various ways, including numerous regulations and controls of the private economy. An important indicator of political control rights also has to do with government ownership. African governments have established numerous public enterprises that, in addition to being inefficient in production, are a drain on the economy. Finally, political control is manifested by governments' use of arbitrary reasons to confiscate private property and businesses or deny individuals the right to start businesses. Thus establishing property rights in these countries means reforming institutions so that the political control of the economy is reduced.

By and large, African economies have property rights structures that are not conducive to economic growth. In some cases, no property rights exist, such as the case of communal grazing lands or other cases where the land is owned by a clan or tribe. In those types of arrangement, although individuals may have the right to farm a certain portion of the land, they do not have the right to sell that land. In other cases the property rights are insecure because ownership can be revoked by the government. In Sub-Saharan Africa, governments have almost unlimited control of the economy. As such, they enact regulations, controls and taxes that reduce the value of investments. The lack of property rights, insecure property rights and excessive political control of the economy that characterize the economies of Sub-Saharan African countries are probably the most important reasons for the dismal economic performance of those countries.

Empirical evidence shows that property rights and economic liberties are important determinants of economic growth. Several studies have investigated the role of institutions on economic growth by focusing on factors such as the protection of property rights, and civil and economic liberties (Scully 1988, Gwartney *et al.* 1982, Kamm 1993, Singer 1993). These studies generally show that institutions that advance individual freedom in the market-place and which protect civil liberties are associated with higher rates of economic growth. Gerald Scully (1988) investigates the effects of institutions on economic growth, focusing on political openness, individual rights, and civil and economic liberties. His results show that countries that have open political institutions and that protect individual and economic liberties have significantly higher rates of economic growth compared with countries that are politically closed and do not protect property and economic liberties. Scully concludes that the, 'institutional framework is not only a statistically significant explanation of inter country variation in the growth rate of real per capita gross domestic product but also a phenomenon of considerable magnitude' (p. 658).

Other studies have used measures of economic freedom to investigate the role of economic liberties on economic growth. These studies show that countries that score high on measures of economic freedom, such as Hong Kong and Singapore, also record much higher rates of economic growth than countries that score lower on measures of economic liberties (Gwartney *et al.* 1992). The importance of economic freedom on economic growth is also evidenced by looking at reforms that minimize government intervention in developing countries. For example, reports show that economic liberalization, such as the elimination of subsidies and price controls, privatization and deregulation, in Peru have had a significant effect in accelerating economic growth in that country (Kamm 1993; Singer 1993). Similar results of liberalization efforts have been reported in Ghana, Kenya and other African countries.

The link between free markets and economic growth is straightforward: under conditions of unregulated markets resources flow to areas of their most valuable use, as directed by market signals. Such a flow of resources is consistent with economic growth. Economic well-being is therefore directly related to the degree of freedom that individuals have in market exchange. Such exchange requires a system of well-defined and secure property rights and only minimally necessary government intervention. Such minimal intervention is necessary to correct for market failure, for the definition and protection of property rights, for the enforcement of contracts, and for the maintenance of law and order.

In general, such roles of government facilitate market transactions by lowering the costs of exchange. However, when a government intervenes by adopting numerous regulations and controls, it increases transaction costs (thereby leading to inefficient markets) and thus reduces the rate of economic growth. Because of the costs associated with meeting regulations and controls, entrepreneurs avoid the legal framework and conduct business outside the formal sector. The result is the emergence of dual markets: a formal sector and an informal sector.

Heavy intervention in markets prevents the development of markets and thus hinders economic growth. An important factor that leads to economic growth is the division of labour. As the division of labour in society increases, producers become more specialized and are therefore more productive. Economists have long realized that the growth of market exchanges is determined by the extent of the division of labour, which is in turn determined by the size of the market. Heavy government intervention hinders the development of markets and therefore inhibits the division of labour.

Heavy government intervention also increases the cost of doing business legally. As a result of the high costs of transacting legally, the number of firms in the formal sector is fewer than would be the case in the absence of heavy government intervention. Consequently the degree of competition is reduced, with further increases in inefficiency in production. Thus in general, excessive government intervention reduces competition and provides those firms that operate in the formal sector secure opportunities for earning economic rents. Even in what would otherwise have been a competitive market, heavy government intervention acts as a barrier to entry.

As noted, heavy government intervention in developing countries has had the effect of creating a large informal sector. The formal and the informal sectors operate under different institutional constraints. The formal sector enjoys legal protection, has access to formal credit markets, and contracts agreed upon in this sector are enforced by the government. The informal sector, on the other hand, is quasi-illegal and receives no protection from the government; nor are contracts legally enforced. Thus heavy government intervention creates a privileged sector and an unprivileged sector, with the informal sector being characterized by a system of insecure property rights such as the lack of government protection, no legal mechanism for enforcing contracts, and frequent harassment by law enforcement officials. The result is that the costs of doing business in the informal sector are high. Although operations in the informal sector avoid government regulations, costs are incurred in various ways, such as the avoidance of authorities and insecurity in entering into contracts. All these factors hinder profitable market exchange and inhibit economic growth.

In recent years, the informal sectors of developing countries have expanded at a much faster rate than the formal sectors. The emergence of an informal sector is evidence that government involvement in the economy has exceeded the level consistent with optimal economic growth. Litan *et al.* (1986) observe that desertion of a substantial portion of population from the legal business system (from the formal sector to the informal sector) is a sure sign that a nation's institutional structure is restraining economic progress.

Complex regulation structures are commonplace in developing countries. For example, a November 1994 CNN news report indicated that Jordan had such complex import-clearing procedures that an importer requires as many as 40 signatures before goods can go through customs. Similar procedures are required in many of the Sub-Saharan countries, both in international and domestic exchange.

The high cost of doing business in Sub-Saharan Africa due to government regulations is well documented (Kimenyi 1991). One such interventionist policy involves exchange rate controls and quantity restrictions on imports. The presence of exchange rate controls creates a shortage of foreign exchange and results in an illegal market (the black market) for foreign currency. The discrepancy between the controlled rate and the one that would exist if the rate were determined by market forces creates opportunities for gains in dealing with currencies outside the legal structure. The discrepancy between the official rate and the black market rate shows the degree of government intervention in the market. The larger the discrepancy between the rates, the more strict the government regulations, that is, the official rate is set far above the would-be market-clearing price. Second, the larger the discrepancy between the rates, the higher the number of transactions taking place illegally. This provides evidence to the effect that the cost of doing business legally is high and, because of such government-imposed costs, transactions take place illegally. Finally, a large discrepancy between the official rate and the black market rate shows that, because of the risk involved in operating illegally, there are real resource costs involved in undertaking such transactions (Bhaqwati 1974).

A good example of the result of excessive government intervention in Africa is revealed by the volume of illegal transactions and the differences between the official and black market exchange rates. Between 1977 and 1980 in Uganda, for example, the black market exchange rate was over ten times the official rate. Likewise, between 1979 and 1988, the black market exchange rate in Ghana was between 5 and 40 times the official rate (International Monetary Fund 1980–1991). During the same periods, a large portion of these countries' external trade involved illegal transactions. For example, between 1970 and 1980, 25–50 per cent of the total volume of cocoa produced in Ghana was smuggled out of the country (May 1981).

There are many other costs that result from heavy government intervention. When restrictions are imposed, for example, on the number of business licences, the expected gains to those who hold such licences increase. When a government imposes entry restrictions into the market for some activities, the consequence is the creation of artificial scarcity. For example, if the government limits the number of import licences, the value of the licences increases because only a few have been issued and a large number of people are seeking the rights to those licences. As a result, entrepreneurs spend resources seeking favours from government officials for the rights to the few licences, what is referred to as rent-seeking. Such competitive rent-seeking involves a destruction of value rather than the creation of value.

There are a number of ways through which rent-seeking affects economic growth. Rent-seeking leads to a redistribution of resources, not necessarily to the most efficient producers but to the most efficient rent-seekers. Political allocation replaces market allocation, so that inefficient producers are able to remain in the market not because of their efficiency in meeting consumer demand, but because they receive political protection from competition. Rent-seeking also involves real resource costs that do not contribute to the creation of value. Finally, when political allocation replaces market allocation, there is a tendency for people to specialize in rent-seeking instead of market production. Thus the margin of competition that leads to efficient markets is replaced by rent-seeking. The result is a situation where markets operate inefficiently and resources are wasted. Consequently, rent-seeking retards economic growth (Blomqvist and Mohammand 1986).

Another cost of government intervention in markets is the extraction of bribes by the authorities. In the formal sector, bribes may be required by the officials enforcing the rules, either to perform some business-related function or to exempt businessmen from adherence to regulations. In the informal sector, bribes are extracted as a substitute for legal prosecution for undertaking illegal activities. In other cases, bribes are required by law enforcement officials to avoid the arbitrary harassment that is frequent in a system characterized by insecure property rights. The extent of bribery is dependent on both the level of government intervention and the nature of the institutions (Johnson 1975).

A final aspect of political control of the economy has to do with government ownership. In Sub-Saharan Africa, governments are involved in the production of various goods and services that would be more efficiently provided by the private sector. For example, public enterprises are involved in transportation, agricultural marketing, banking, book and newspaper publishing, and so on. These enterprises are overstaffed, make losses year after year and have to be supported by resources extracted from the private sector. The fact that public enterprises are associated with misallocation of resources is well documented (Vernon and Aharoni 1981). Such public enterprises have an even more detrimental effect on economic growth in developing countries where rulers face few constraints in hiring the managers of those enterprises (Kimenyi 1985).

Most of the institutional reforms suggested in previous chapters have focused on ways of reducing the power of governments. Thus these reforms would help to increase the protection of property rights and economic liberties. Any reform that reduces the power of the government, at least to the level of the minimal state, will necessarily advance property rights and economic liberties.

Nonetheless, property and economic liberties should be protected by the constitution. It is important that legislators be constrained from adopting laws that interfere with property and economic liberties. The constitution should clearly stipulate that regulations and controls that undermine economic liberties cannot be passed by the legislature. In addition, the constitution should provide for economic due process (Siegan 1980).

Limiting the overall scope of government is crucial to maintaining economic liberties, and constitutional provisions are an effective way of accomplishing such a task. Siegan (1994) proposes constitutional provisions specifying maximum annual taxes on real property, limits on the share of GNP that goes to taxes, and restrictions on the size of government debt. Such provisions would serve to constrain the power of government and thus increase people's liberties. In addition, constraining government growth necessarily limits rent-seeking and corruption.

It should be clear that the task of establishing property rights cannot be left to predatory governments. The current African dictators and their governments cannot be expected to oversee the reforms necessary to guarantee property rights and economic liberties. This task requires constitutional democracies with powers limited by a system of checks and balances. Such a government more credibly can promise not to grab assets for itself (Shleifer 1995; see also Brennan and Buchanan 1980; North and Weingast 1989).

We also note that adequate protection of property rights and economic liberties would enhance the peaceful coexistence of ethnic groups. Reducing the political control of rights reduces the value of political leadership and thus reduces ethnic competition for control of government. In addition, the power of leaders would be reduced so that those in leadership positions would have limited ability to discriminate against members of other ethnic groups. Thus protection of property rights and economic liberties would shift competition away from political markets to economic markets. Competition in economic markets results in a betterment of society materially and can be expected to reduce ethnic conflict.

12. Ethnic Representation and Voting Rules

In reforming the institutions of Sub-Saharan Africa, a primary concern is whether the various ethnic groups would support the reforms. For reforms to have the desired results, it is crucial that they be supported by a sizeable majority of all the groups in each of the countries. A key determinant as to whether particular ethnic groups support the reforms is what they perceive to be their ability to influence public outcomes. This chapter briefly outlines some strategies that may be necessary to ensure that all ethnic groups have a role in the policy process and that they can block legislation that is detrimental to them.

The most important barrier to the reforms suggested in the previous chapters is that some ethnic groups may fear that they would not be adequately represented because of their relatively small numbers. Specifically, minority ethnic groups may fear discrimination by majorities. Although the suggested reforms (decentralization, federal systems and constitutional provisions) would certainly reduce ethnic discrimination, some additional guarantees may be necessary. Such guarantees, in addition to protecting minorities from oppression by majorities, would increase the probability of consent among ethnic groups in reforming the African states.

As an example, consider the case of Ethiopia, which has over 80 ethnic groups. These groups, however, can be gathered into eight main categories in terms of similarities such as language, geoethnicity and other factors that unite them. As in other African countries, the relative size of ethnic groups in Ethiopia varies widely: the Oromo group forms 40 per cent of the population, the Amhara 20 per cent, the Tigrayan 12 per cent, the Sidamo 9 per cent, the Somali 6 per cent, the Beni Shangu and other similar groups 6 per cent, the Afar 4 per cent and the Gurage 2 per cent, and other groups make up about 1 per cent of the population. Given the long-standing rivalries among the various ethnic groups in that country, the small ethnic groups have a lot to fear, as even a democratic government based on majority rule can effectively exclude some of them. This problem typifies a common concern of many ethnic groups across Sub-Saharan Africa.

It is clear that, under majority rule, a few groups could form a coalition that excludes the other ethnic groups. For example, in Ethiopia the Oromo and Tigrayan ethnic groups make up 52 per cent of the population, and thus under majority rule these two groups could pass legislation that benefited them disproportionately. Even with democratic reforms, there are no guarantees that coalitions of ethnic groups would not exclude others. Clearly, majority rule would not provide guarantees to most of the ethnic groups. Even a super-majority voting scheme would not offer the necessary protection to the smallest groups. For example, requiring two-thirds of the members of the legislature to support bills before they could become law would still not ensure that the interests of the smaller ethnic groups were protected.

Some ethnic groups can be able to establish stable ruling coalitions that effectively exclude others. As has been the case in the past, those groups that are excluded from the ruling coalition are likely to resort to violence. Thus merely prescribing some super-majority rules without taking into account ethnic representation may not solve the long-standing conflicts that have been going on in the African countries.

In a unicameral parliamentary system, the protection of minority ethnic groups could be minimized by requiring that before legislative bills become law, at least 51 per cent of the representatives should support the measure, including at least a certain percentage of members of each ethnic group. This additional requirement would place a binding constraint on the larger ethnic groups, so that they would continually negotiate with minority ethnic groups. The fact that each ethnic group has an input in the legislative process would necessitate political bargaining that encourages ethnic cooperation.

Establishing bicameral legislatures would probably be an effective way of ensuring that minority interests are protected. In such systems, members of one of the legislative houses could reflect the composition of the population such that large ethnic groups would have more representatives. Members of the other legislative house would be elected, distributed equally among the ethnic groupings. For example, each ethnic group could elect two or three representatives. Such representation increases the power of minority ethnic groups. Further protection of minority groups could be ensured by adopting super-majority voting rules in one or both of the legislative houses.

One approach that can be effective in ensuring that minority ethnic groups have significant input in the policy-making process is to require that for an individual to win the presidency, not only should he or she have a plurality of votes, but they should also receive a certain minimum number of votes from each region. Again this requirement would force national leaders to take into account the interests of all groups. In addition, such requirements would encourage the formation of multi-ethnic political parties.

Another strategy that could be used to protect minority groups would be to institute a rotating presidency. Under this scheme, a country would be divided into a number of regions, each encompassing closely related ethnic groups. Each region would have a chance to produce a national president for a specified term. After the expiration of the term, the presidency would go to another region. Such a strategy has recently been proposed for Nigeria. There are, of course, a number of shortcomings with such a strategy, but in severely divided societies it may be the only way to ensure the protection of minority groups.

13. Political Divorce: Redrawing Africa's Borders

The unification of ethnic groups in Africa was not by consent. Thus the formation of those countries can be compared with arranged marriages where individuals have no choice of their partners. Although it is true that some arranged marriages work well, ethnic unification in Africa represents many cases of unhappy marriages. In most countries, some ethnic groups have been unwilling partners and have only remained part of those countries through coercion. The result has been persistent domestic violence.

We have suggested that the main cause of such domestic violence is that some ethnic groups have been able to use the powers of the state to oppress and transfer resources from others. In previous chapters, we have provided suggestions to improve the relationships between the various groups. Specifically, we have sought to rescue ethnic unions by distributing power among the various groups. We believe that when groups organize more of their activities as they wish and only interact with other groups on matters that are mutually beneficial, better relationships will develop. In addition, by constraining the power of governments, the opportunities for one group to oppress another are diminished. Thus although the marriages were arranged, the relationships can be improved if all partners have an input in determining the nature of their relationship. Thus the proposed reforms should lead to happier marriages.

However, we must also accept that some marriages simply will not work. There are countries where the ethnic divide is so wide that the reforms suggested previously are not sufficient to unite the groups. Therefore, we must be prepared to accept that in some countries, ethnic conflicts can only be resolved if groups have the option to secede and establish autonomous nations. It is our opinion that attempts to prevent such secession will create even more ethnic conflict. Thus a viable solution is to permit those groups that want to separate to do so.

Some ethnic groups may not seek to be autonomous nations but instead may look for another suitor. It is likely that many ethnic groups would prefer to be joined to other groups in other countries. But before they can be joined to another partner, they must first separate from their current partners. Again, we suggest that this process should not be blocked.

A careful look at ethnic relationships in Africa reveals that some groups will end up as autonomous nations or will join other countries. It therefore serves no useful purpose to reject the existence of major ethnic divisions in some of the countries that can only be accommodated by allowing groups to separate. For example, for all practical purposes, northern and southern Sudan are really two countries. Unless a federal system that allows a large measure of autonomy to the regions is established, it is difficult to imagine Sudan remaining as one country. Likewise, the Ogaden region of Ethiopia is unlikely to remain part of that country much longer.

The stability of Nigeria very much depends on the maintenance of the federal principle. Even then, the long-term stability of this country's borders is uncertain. The mere size of the country and its complex ethnic composition suggests that it is unlikely that it will remain intact. Ethnic demands in this country point to strong secessionist movements in the future. As a matter of fact, the possibility of successful secession by several regions in Africa is very real. We suggest that such movements be allowed to proceed without hindrance. Secession is clearly consistent with the advancement of liberty.

Although the Organization of African Unity continues to insist on the maintenance of the principle of non-inviolability of colonial frontiers, we believe that such a principle is not consistent with liberty and will not stop the break up of the African countries. There are many indications that the map of Africa will change dramatically in the next two decades or so. Probably the issue we should be concerned with is what the map of Africa will look like 10 or 20 years from now and what the implications of such changes are likely to be. This issue itself demands a separate book.

Bibliography

Addai, G.K. (1984), 'People's participation in development at grassroot Level: a case study of Malawi', in A.C. Mondjanagni (ed.), *People's Participation in Development in Black Africa*, Doula: Pan African Institute for Development, pp. 203–18.

Ake, C. (1992), *The Feasibility of Democracy in Africa*, Centre for Research, Documentation and University Exchange, Institute of African Studies, University of Ibadan, Nigeria.

Alchian, A.A. and H. Demsetz (1972), 'Production, information costs, and economic organization', *American Economic Review*, **62**, 777–95.

Armour, L. (1988), 'John Locke and American constitutionalism', in A.S. Rosenbaum (ed.), *Constitutionalism: The Philosophical Dimension*, New York: Greenwood Press, pp. 9–30.

Austin, D. (1984), *Politics in Africa*, Hanover: University Press of New England.

Ayittey, G.B.N. (1991), *Indigenous African Institutions*, Dobbs Ferry, NY: Transnational Publishers.

Ayittey, G.B.N. (1992), *Africa Betrayed*, New York: St Martin's Press.

Ayoade, J.A.A. (1988), 'States without citizens: an emerging African phenomenon', in D. Rothchild and N. Chazan (eds), *The Precarious Balance: State and Society in Africa*, Boulder: Westview Press, pp. 100–18.

Banks, A.S. (1993), *Political Handbook of the World 1993*, Binghamton: CSA Publications.

Bates, R.H. (1983), 'Modernization, ethnic competition, and the rationality of politics in contemporary Africa', in D. Rothchild and V.A. Olorunsola (eds), *State Versus Ethnic Claims: Africa Policy Dilemmas*, Boulder: Westview Press, pp. 152–71.

Bauer, L. (1934), *Leopold the Unloved*, London: European Books.

Beattie, J. (1964), *Other Cultures*, London: Routledge and Kegan Paul.

Bhaqwati, J.N. (1974), *Illegal Transactions in International Trade: Theory and Measurement*, Amsterdam: North-Holland Publishing Company.

Black Africa: A Comparative Handbook, 1972, New York, Free Press.

Blomqvist, A. and S. Mohammand (1986), 'Controls, corruption, and competitive rent-seeking', *Journal of Development Economics*, **21**, 161–80.

Borcherding, T.E., W.W. Pommerehne and F. Schneider (1982), 'Comparing the efficiency of private and public production: the evidence from five countries', *Zeitschrift für Nationalökonomie*, **89**, 127–56.

Brennan, G. and J.M. Buchanan (1980), *The Power to Tax: Analytical Foundations of a Fiscal Constitution*, Cambridge: Cambridge University Press.

Breton, A. and A. Scott (1980), *The Design of Federations*, Montreal: Institute for Research on Public Policy.

Breytenbach, W.J. (1975), 'Inter-ethnic conflict in Africa', in W.A. Veenhoven (ed.), *Case Studies on Human Rights and Fundamental Freedoms*, The Hague: Martinus Nijhoff, pp. 311–31.

Brough, W.T. and M.S. Kimenyi (1986), 'On the inefficient extraction of rents by dictators', *Public Choice*, **48**, 37–48.

Buchanan, J.M. (1965), 'An economic theory of clubs', *Economica*, **32**, 1–14.

Buchanan, J.M. (1975), *The Limits of Liberty: Between Anarchy and Leviathan*, Chicago: University of Chicago Press.

Buchanan, J.M. (1989), *Explorations into Constitutional Economics*, College Station: Texas A&M University Press.

Buchanan, J.M. and G. Tullock (1962), *The Calculus of Consent: Logical Foundations of Constitutional Democracy*, Ann Arbor: University of Michigan Press.

Burke, F. (1991), *Africa*, Boston: Houghton Mifflin Co.

Chazan, N. (1988), 'Patterns of state–society incorporation and disengagement in Africa', in D. Rothchild and N. Chazan (eds), *The Precarious Balance: State and Society in Africa*, Boulder: Westview Press, pp. 121–48.

Chrisney, M.D. (1985), 'A century of corruption: corruption as rent-seeking in nineteenth century America', unpublished Manuscript, World Bank, Washington, DC.

Coase, R. (1960), 'The problem of social cost', *Journal of Law and Economics*, **3**, October, 1–44.

Cobbah, J.A.M. (1988), 'Toward a geography of peace in Africa: redefining sub-state self-determination rights', in R.J. Johnson, D.B. Knight and E. Kofman (eds), *Nationalism, Self-Determination, and Political Geography*, London: Croom Helm.

Cohen, H.J. (1994), 'Free markets: economics and politics', *Maoni ya America*, May, pp. 11–14.

Congleton, R.D. (1992), 'Ethnic clubs, ethnic conflict and the rise of ethnic nationalism', unpublished Manuscript, Center for Study of Public Choice, George Mason University.

Copson, R.W. (1994), *Africa's Wars and Prospects for Peace*, Armonk, NY: M.E. Sharp.

Cornes, R. and T. Sandler (1986), *The Theory of Externalities, Public Goods and Club Goods*, Cambridge: Cambridge University Press.

Couch, J.F. and M. Kimenyi (1992), 'Fiscal illusion in public school finance in the United States', *The Southern Business and Economic Journal*, **5**, 246–61.

Crain, W.M. and A. Zardkoohi (1978), 'A test of the property-rights theory of the firm: water utilities in the United States', *Journal of Law and Economics*, **21**, 395–408.

Crowder, M. (1968), *West Africa Under Colonial Rule*, London: Hutchinson.

Curtin, P., S. Feierman, L. Thompson and J. Vansina (1988), *African History*, New York: Longman.

Davies, D.G. (1971), 'The efficiency of public versus private firms: the case of Australia's two airlines', *Journal of Law and Economics*, **14**, 149–65.

De Alessi, L.D. (1982), 'On the nature and consequences of public and private enterprises', *Minnesota Law Review*, **67**, 191–209.

De Soto, H. (1989), *The Other Path*, New York: Harper and Row.

Dikshit, R.D. (1975), *Political Geography of Federalism*, New York: John Wiley & Sons.

Downs, A. (1967), *Inside Bureaucracy*, Boston: Little Brown.

Duchacek, I.D. (1970), *Comparative Federalism: Territorial Dimension of Politics*, New York: Holt, Rinehart, and Winston, Inc.

Duchacek, I.D. (1977), 'Antagonistic cooperation: territorial and ethnic communities', *Publius*, **7**, 3–29.

Earle, V. (ed.) (1969), *Federalism: Infinite Variety in Theory and Practice*, Itasca, Ill: F.E. Peacock.

Elazar, D.J. (1987), *Exploring Federalism*, Tuscaloosa: University of Alabama Press.

Evans-Pritchard, E.E. (1962), *Essays in Social Anthropology*, New York: Free Press.

Furley, O. (ed.) (1995), *Conflict in Africa*, London: I.B. Tauris Publishers.

Greenland, J. (1976), 'Ethnic discrimination in Rwanda and Burundi', in W.A. Veenhoven (ed.), *Case Studies on Human Rights and Fundamental Freedoms, Vol. IV*, The Hague: Martinus Nijhoff, pp. 97–133.

Gwartney, J., W. Block and R. Lawson (1992), 'Measuring economic freedom', in S.T. Easton and M. Walker (eds), *Rating Global Economic Freedom*, Vancouver: Fraser Institute.

Hamilton, A. (1937), *The Federalist*, New York: Modern Library.

Hamilton, D. and M. Whitcombe (1976), 'Discrimination in Ethiopia', in W.A. Veenhoven (ed.), *Case Studies on Human Rights and Fundamental Freedoms*, Vol. III, The Hague: Martinus Nijhoff, pp. 277–302.

Hart, O.D. and J. Moore (1990), 'Property rights and the nature of the firm', *Journal of Political Economy*, **98**, 1119–58.

Henze, P. (1985), 'Rebels and separatists in Ethiopia: regional resistance to a Marxist regime', report prepared for the Office of the Under Secretary of Defense for Policy, Santa Monica: Rand Corporation.

Hirschman, A.O. (1970), *Exit, Voice and Loyalty*, Cambridge, MA: Harvard University Press.

Hobbes, T. (1988), *Leviathan*, Indianapolis: The Bobbs-Merrill Company, Inc.

Horowitz, D. (1984), 'Democracy in divided societies', in L. Diamond and M.F. Plattner (eds), *Nationalism, Ethnic Conflict and Democracy*, Baltimore: The Johns Hopkins University Press.

Horowitz, D. (1985), *Ethnic Groups in Conflict*, Berkeley: University of California Press.

Horowitz, D. (1994), 'Democracy in divided societies', in L. Diamond and M.F. Plattner (eds), *Nationalism, Ethnic Conflict and Democracy*, Baltimore: The Johns Hopkins University Press.

Human Rights Watch World Report 1994, New York: Human Rights Watch.

Hume, D. (1985), *Essays: Moral, Political, and Literacy*, edited by F. Miller, Indianapolis: Liberty Classics.

Hyden, G. (1980), *Beyond Ujamaa in Tanzania: Underdevelopment and an Uncaptured Peasantry*, Berkeley: University of California Press.

Index on Censorship (1992), 'What chance for democracy?', pp. 7–8.

International Monetary Fund, *Currency Yearbook*, May 1981.

Isaacs, H.R. (1975), *Idols of the Tribe: Group Identity and Political Change*, New York: Harper and Row.

Jackson, R.H. and C.G. Rosberg (1982), *Personal Rule in Black Africa*, Berkeley: University of California Press.

Johnson, O.E.G. (1975), 'An economic analysis of corrupt government, with special application to less developed countries', *Kyklos*, **28** Fasc 1, 47–61.

Kamm, T. (1993), 'Chile's economy roars as exports take off in post-Pinochet era', *Wall Street Journal*, 25 January, p. 1.

Kaus, M. (1993), 'The Madison curse', *The New Republic*, Vol. 208, p. 4, 31 May.

Kimenyi, M.S. (1985), 'Political party competition and managerial behavior: an issue analysis of parastatal management', *East African Economic Review*, **1**, 39–46.

Kimenyi, M.S. (1987), 'Bureaucratic rents and political institutions', *Journal of Public Finance and Public Choice*, **3**, 189–99.

Kimenyi, M.S. (1989), 'Interest groups, transfer seeking and democratization: African political stability', *The American Journal of Economics and Sociology*, **48**, 339–49.

Kimenyi, M.S. (1991), 'Barriers to the efficient functioning of markets in developing countries', *Konjunkturpolitik*, **37**, 199–227.

Kimenyi, M.S. (1995), 'Is federalism viable in Kenya?', *The Independent Review*, Proceedings of a Conference on Economic and Political Reforms, December 1994, Nairobi, Kenya.

Kimenyi, M.S. and J.M. Mbaku (1993), 'Rent-seeking and institutional stability in developing countries', *Public Choice*, **77**, 385–405.

Kimenyi, M.S. and W.F. Shughart (1989), 'Political successions and the growth of government', *Public Choice*, **62**, 173–9.

Knight, D.B. (1984), 'Geographical perspectives on self-determination', in P.J. Taylor and J.W. House (eds), *Political Geography: Recent Advances and Future Directions*, London: Croom Helm.

Krauthammer, K.C. (1990), 'Blest the ties that bind', *Time*, August, p. 76.

Lemarchand, R. (1983), 'The state and society in Africa: ethnic stratification and restratification in historical and comparative perspective', in D. Rothchild and V.A. Olorunsola (eds), *State Versus Ethnic Claims: Africa Policy Dilemmas*, Boulder: Westview Press, pp. 44–66.

Lemco, J. (1991), *Political Stability in Federal Governments*, New York: Praeger.

Leonard, D. and J. Wunsch (1982), *Recent Decentralization Initiatives in the Sudan: A Preliminary Assessment of Their Implications*, Berkeley: California Institute of International Studies.

Lewis, W.A. (1965), *Politics in West Africa*, New York: Oxford University Press.
Lijphart, A. (1977), *Democracy in Plural Societies*, New Haven: Yale University Press.
Litan, R., L. Morales-Bayro and J. Fernandez-Bala (1986), 'Internal reforms in Peru: a promising road out of the debt crisis', Working Paper, Institute for Liberty and Democracy, Peru.
Little, K. (1957), 'The role of voluntary associations in West African urbanization', in P.L. Van den Berghe (ed.), *Africa: Social Problems of Change and Conflict*, San Francisco: Chandler.
Locke, J. (1988), *Two Treatises of Government*, edited by Peter Laslett, New York: Cambridge University Press.
Lonsdale, J. (1981), 'State and social processes in Africa: a historiographical survey', *African Studies Review*, **24**, 201.
Maddox, W.P. (1941), 'The political basis of federation', *American Political Science Review*, **35**, 1120–27.
Mair, L. (1965), *An Introduction to Social Anthropology*, Oxford: Clarendon Press.
Mawhood, P. (ed.) (1983), *Local government for Development: The Experience of Tropical Africa*, Chichester: John Wiley.
Mawhood, P. (1987), 'Decentralization and the Third World in the 1980s', *Planning and Administration*, **14**, 10–22.
May, E. (1983), 'Exchange controls and parallel market economy in sub-Saharan Africa: focus on Ghana', World Bank Staff Working Paper No. 711.
Mbaku, J.M. (1994a), 'Bureaucratic corruption and policy reform in Africa', *Journal of Social, Political and Economic Studies*, **19**, 149–75.
Mbaku, J.M. (1994b), 'Military coups as rent-seeking behavior', *Journal of Political and Military Sociology*, **22**, 241–84.
Mbaku, J.M. and M.S. Kimenyi (1995), 'Democratization in Africa: the continuing struggle', *Coexistence*, **32**, 119–36.
McCormick, R.E. and R.D. Tollison (1981), *Politicians, Legislation, and the Economy*, Boston: Martinus Nijhoff.
McGarth, P. and A. McDaniel (1987), 'In order to form a more perfect union', *Newsweek*, Vol. 109, 50–52; 25 May.
McGowan, P. and J. Johnson (1984), 'Military coup d'etat and underdevelopment: a quantitative analysis', *Journal of Modern Africa Studies*, **22**, 633–66.

McGuire, M. (1974), 'Group segregation and optimal jurisdictions', *Journal of Political Economy*, **82**, 112–32.

Meisler, S. (1976), 'Holocaust in Burundi, 1972', in W.A. Veenhoven (ed.), *Case Studies on Human Rights and Fundamental Freedoms*, Vol. V, The Hague: Martinus Nijhoff, pp. 227–38.

Montesquieu, Baron de (1977), *The Spirit of the Laws*, Berkeley: University of California Press.

Nisbet, R. (1975), *The Twilight of Authority*, New York: Oxford University Press.

Nkrumah, K. (1970), *Class Struggle in Africa*, New York: International Publishers.

North, D. (1981), *Structure and Change in Economic History*, New York: W.W. Norton and Company.

North, D. and B. Weingast (1989), 'Constitutions and commitment: the evolution of institutions governing public choice in 17th century England', *Journal of Economic History*, **49**, 803–32.

Olowu, D. (1987), 'The study of African local government since 1960', *Planning and Administration*, **14**, 48–59.

Olowu, D. (1990), 'The failure of current decentralization programs', in J.S. Wunsch and D. Olowu (eds), *The Failure of the Centralized State*, Boulder: Westview Press, pp. 74–99.

Olson, M. (1965), *The Logic of Collective Action*, Cambridge: Harvard University Press.

Olson, M. (1982), *The Rise and Decline of Nations: Economic Growth, Stagflation, and Social Rigidities*, New Haven: Yale University Press.

Option (1995), 'Constitution, constitution everywhere', July, 10–11.

Orzechowski, W. (1977), 'Economic models of bureaucracy: survey, extensions, and evidence', in T.E. Borcherding (ed.), *Budgets and Bureaucrats: The Sources of Government Growth*, Durham: Duke University Press.

Osaghae, E.E. (1995), 'The Ogoni uprising: oil politics, minority agitation and the future of the Nigeria state', *African Affairs*, **94**, 325–44.

Ostrom, E. (1990), *Governing the Commons*, Cambridge: Cambridge University Press.

Ostrom, V. (1987), *The Political Theory of a Compound Republic: Designing the American Experiment*, Lincoln: University of Nebraska Press.

Ottaway, M. (1995), 'Democracy and the challenge of ethnicity', *Africa Demos*, March, 22–4.

Oyugi, W.O. (1983), 'Local government in Kenya: a case of institutional decline', in P. Mawhood (ed.), *Local Government in the Third World*, Chichester: John Wiley, pp. 107–40.

Peltzam, S. (1976), 'Toward a more general theory of regulation', *Journal of Law and Economics*, **19**, August, 211–48.

Pirouet, M.L. (1995), 'The effects of conflict, I: human rights and refugees', in O. Furley (ed.), *Conflict in Africa*, London: I.B. Tauris Publishers, pp. 275–94.

Rappard, W.E. (1948), *Collective Security in Swiss Experience, 1295–1948*, London: George Allen & Unwin.

Rawls, J.A. (1971), *A Theory of Justice*, Cambridge: Harvard University Press.

Riker, W.H. (1964), *Federalism: Origin, Operation, Significance*, Boston: Little Brown.

Roback, J. (1991), 'Plural but equal: group identity and voluntary integration', *Social Philosophy and Policy*, **8**, (2), 60–80.

Rondinelli, D. (1983), *Development Projects as Policy Experiments*, London: Methuen.

Rothchild, D. (1985), 'State–ethnic relations in Middle Africa', in G.M. Carter and P. O'Meara (eds), *African Independence: The First Twenty-Five Years*, Bloomington: Indiana University Press.

Rousseau, J.J. (1984), *Of the Social Contract*, translation by C.M. Sherover, New York: Harper and Row.

Rowley, C.K. (1995), 'Institutional choice and public choice: lessons for the Third World', unpublished manuscript, George Mason University.

Samuelson, R.J. (1992), 'The virtues of "gridlock"', *Newsweek*, Vol. 120, 50, 14 September.

Sandler, T. and J.T. Tschirhart (1984), 'Mixed clubs: further observations', *Journal of Public Economics*, **23**, 381–9.

Sawer, G. (1969), *Modern Federalism*, London: C.A. Watts & Company.

Sawyer, A. (1988), 'The Putu Development Association: a missed opportunity', in V. Ostrom, D. Feeny and H. Picht (eds), *Rethinking Institutional Analysis and Development*, San Francisco: International Center for Economic Growth, pp. 247–78.

Schneider, H.K. (1977), 'Economic man in Africa', in P. Martin and P. O'Meara (eds), *Africa*, Bloomington: Indiana University Press.

Scully, G.W. (1988), 'The institutional framework and economic development', *Journal of Political Economy*, **96**, 652–62.

Sharma, B.M. and L.P. Choudhry (1967), *Federal Polity*, New York: Asia Publishing House.

Shleifer, A. (1995), 'Establishing property rights', *Proceedings of the World Bank Annual Conference on Development Economics 1994*, Washington, D.C.: The World Bank.

Shughart, W.F. (1990), *Antitrust Policy and Interest-Group Politics*, New York: Quorum Books.

Shughart, W.F. and M.S. Kimenyi (1991), 'A public choice analysis of transit operating subsidies', *Research in Law and Economics*, **14**, 251–76.

Siegan, B.H. (1980), *Economic Liberties and the Constitution*, Chicago: University of Chicago Press.

Siegan, B.H. (1989), 'Separation of powers and other divisions of authority under the constitution', *Suffolk University Law Review*, **23**, 1–14, Spring 1989.

Siegan, B.H. (1994), *Drafting a Constitution for a Nation or Republic Emerging into Freedom*, Fairfax: Institute for Humane Studies.

Singer, C. (1993), 'Why Chile's economy roared while the world's slumbered', *Wall Street Journal*, 22 January, p. A15.

Smith, A. (1937), *An Inquiry into the Nature and Causes of The Wealth of Nations*, New York: The Modern Library.

Smith, A. (1983), *State and Nation in the Third World*, New York: St Martin's Press.

Stigler, G. (1971), 'The theory of economic regulation', *Bell Journal of Economics*, **2**, Spring, 3–21.

Thoahlane, T. (1984), *A Study of Village Development Committees: The Case of Lesotho*, Roma, Lesotho: Institute of Southern African Studies.

Tiebout, C.M. (1956), 'A pure theory of local expenditures', *Journal of Political Economy*, **64**, 416–24.

Tordoff, W. (1993), *Government and Politics in Africa*, Bloomington: Indiana University Press.

Tullock, G. (1965), *The Politics of Bureaucracy*, Washington, D.C.: Public Affairs Press.

Tullock, G. (1967), 'The welfare costs of tariffs, monopolies and theft', *Western Economic Journal*, **5**, 227–32.

Tullock, G. (1974), *The Social Dilemma: The Economics of War and Revolution*, Fairfax: Center for Study of Public Choice.

Tullock, G. (1993), *Rent Seeking*, Aldershot: Edward Elgar Publishing.

United Nations Development Programme (1990), *Human Development Report 1990*, Oxford: Oxford University Press.

United States Committee for Refugees (1993), *World Refugee Survey 1993*, Washington, D.C.: US Committee for Refugees.

Vaughan, J.H. (1977), 'Social and political organization in traditional societies', in P.M. Martin and P. O'Meara (eds), *Africa*, Bloomington: Indiana University Press, pp. 169–88.

Vaughan, J.H. (1986), 'Population and social organization', in P. Martin and P. O'Meara (eds), *Africa*, Bloomington: Indiana University Press.

Vernon, R. and Y. Aharoni (eds) (1981), *State-Owned Enterprises in Western Economies*, London: Croom Helm.

Washington Post (1995), 'Ethiopia takes new ethnic tack: deliberately divisive', 18 June, A2.

Wheare, K.C. (1947), *Federal Government*, New York: Oxford University Press.

Wildavsky, A. (ed.) (1967), *American Federalism in Perspective*, Boston: Little Brown.

Winchester, N.B. (1986), 'Africa politics since independence', in P. Martin and P. O'Meara (eds), *Africa*, Bloomington: Indiana University Press.

World Bank (1981), *Accelerated Development in Sub-Saharan Africa: An Agenda for Action*, Washington, DC: World Bank.

Wunsch, J.S. (1990), 'Centralization and development in post-independence Africa', in J.S. Wunsch and D. Olowu (eds), *The Failure of the Centralized State*, Boulder: Westview Press, pp. 43–73.

Wunsch, J.S. and Olowu, D. (1990), *The Failure of the Centralized State: Institutions and Self-Governance in Africa*, Boulder: Westview Press.

Index

Addai, G.K., 71
advisers, 11–12
Aharoni, Y., 103
Akan ethnic group, 54
Ake, C., 30–31
Alchian, A.A., 67
Amhara ethnic group, 55
Amin, Idi, 6, 56
Angola, 29, 88
armies, 11
Armour, L., 91
Arusha Declaration 1967, 70
associations
   ethnic, 22, 27–31
   voluntary clubs/associations, 32–3, 38–9
Austin, D., 64
autonomy
   ethnic groups, 69, 82
   regional, 63, 72, 74, 75–6, 90
Ayittey, G.B.N., 11, 14, 24, 51, 52

Banks, A.S., 88
Bates, R.H., 48–9
Bauer, L., 15
Beattie, J., 11–12
Berlin Act 1885, 14, 22
Bhaqwati, J.N., 101
Biafra, 54
bicameral legislatures, 106
bill of rights, 95–6
Bismarck, O. von, 14
Black Africa, 54
black market exchange rate, 101
Blomqvist, A., 102
Bokassa, J.-B., 6, 54
Borcherding, T.E., 66
borders/boundaries, 22–4, 45
   redrawing, 108–9

Brennan, G., 103
Breton, A., 65, 81, 82
Breytenbach, W.J., 28, 54
bribery, 102
   see also corruption
Brough, W.T., 48
Buchanan, J.M., 3, 32–3, 82, 103
bureaucracy, 30, 49–50, 51
Burke, F., 14
Burundi, 24, 55, 88

cabinet: composition of, 54
Canada, 87
capitalism, 15
Central African Republic, 54
centralization
   integration, ethnic conflict and, 53–61
   integration, rent-seeking and, 42–52
Chad, 26
Chazan, N., 49
chiefs, tribal, 11–12
   see also leaders/rulers
Choudhry, L.P., 75
Chrisney, M.D., 51
civil rights, 5–6, 95
civil service, 30, 49–50, 51
civil society, 2, 3–4, 43
   constitutionalism and, 91–6
civilian dictatorships, 18, 19
clubs, voluntary, 32–3, 38–9
Cobbah, J.A.M., 26, 72
coercion, 45
Cohen, H.J., 18
colonial rule, 14–15, 43–5
commerce, 37–8, 87
common pool problem, 97
concentration of power, 65

conflict, ethnic, 42, 62–3, 88, 103–4
  costs of, 56–60
  integration, centralization and, 53–61
Congleton, R.D., 37
Congo, 29
consent, 38–9, 40, 42, 61, 74, 89
constitution, 72, 103
  constitutionalism and civil society, 91–6
  federalism, 74–6
  at independence, 16
consumption externalities, 81
contractarianism, 3–4
control rights, 97–8, 99–103
Copson, R.W., 55, 58
Cornes, R., 33
corruption, 17, 50–51, 102
costs of ethnic conflict, 56–60
Couch, J.F., 68
councils, 11–12
countries: size, 26
coups, military, 53–4
Crain, W.M., 66
Crowder, M., 43
Curtin, P., 15
customs, 35

Davies, D.G., 66
De Alessi, L.D., 67
debt, external, 17
decentralization, 8, 12–13, 73, 78
  reducing ethnic externalities, 62–72
  see also federalism
decision-making, 63, 66, 70
defence, 77, 87–8
demand for federalism, 83–90
demand and supply
  tribal identification, 34–7
  wealth transfers, 46–8
democracy, 82
democratization movements, 7, 18, 29
Demsetz, H., 67
dictatorship, 17–18, 19
Dikshit, R.D., 85, 87
discrimination, ethnic, 60–61, 65, 78–9, 96

displaced persons, 56–9
District Planning/Development Committees, 71
diversity, accommodation of, 74, 79
division of labour, 99–100
Downs, A., 66
dual markets, 99
Duchacek, I.D., 76

Earle, V., 84
economic advantage, 84–5
economic growth, 97, 98–9
economic rights, 95, 97–104
economies of scale, 65–6, 81
education, 67–8, 77
Elazar, D., 74, 75
entry and exit, 33, 35
Eritrea, 55
Ethiopia, 14, 26, 55, 88, 109
  constitutional reform, 90
  ethnic composition, 105–6
ethnic conflict *see* conflict
ethnic integration *see* integration
ethnic nations, 22–6
Evans-Pritchard, E.E., 13
Ewe ethnic group, 54
exchange rates, 101
executive: legislature, judiciary and, 92–5
exit, 12–13, 33, 35, 52
experimentation, policy, 79–80
exploitation, colonial, 15
externalities
  production and consumption, 81
  reducing ethnic externalities through decentralization, 62–72

famine, 4
federalism, 8, 63, 73–82
  advantages and problems, 77–82
  demand for, 83–90
fiscal equalization, 68–9
fiscal federalism, 76–7, 81–2
fiscal illusion, 66–7
foreign aid, 17
Forum for the Restoration of Democracy (FORD), 29

free-rider problem, 39, 66–7
Furley, O., 54

Ga ethnic group, 54
geoethnicity, 26, 72
geographical isolation, 85–6
Ghana, 54, 101
government
　constraint of power by constitution, 92–6
　and delegated authority, 69
　excessive intervention, 4–5, 99–103
　functions of a federal government, 76–7
　impact of expanded authority, 51
　local, 63–4, 72, 73–4, 96
　need for the state, 1–4
Guinea, 29
Guinea Bissau, 29
Gwartney, J., 98, 99

Hamilton, A., 94
Hamilton, D., 55
Hart, O.D., 97
Hausa people, 28, 88
Henze, P., 55
heterogeneity, 86–7
Hirschman, A.O., 53
Hobbes, T., 1–2
Hong Kong, 99
Horowitz, D., 27, 30, 53, 54, 81
human rights violations, 5–6, 18, 59
Human Rights Watch, 56
Hume, D., 91
Hutu tribe, 55, 88
Hyden, G., 70

Ibo people, 28, 54, 88
Ibo State Union, 28
identification, tribal, 27–31, 33–8
illegal transactions, 101
implicit contract, 13
independence, 15–16, 43–4
independence movements, 28–9
Index on Censorship, 17
informal sector, 99, 100
initiation ceremonies, 35

institutions
　democratic and federalism, 82
　and economic growth, 98–9
　political *see* political institutions
　social, 86
integration, ethnic
　centralization, conflict and, 53–61
　centralization, rent-seeking and, 42–52
　optimal, 32–41
interdependence of persons across jurisdictions, 81
interest groups, 46
inter-ethnic linkages, 38, 69–70, 74
inter-ethnic transfers, 45–8
International Monetary Fund (IMF), 5, 101
investment, 80
inviolability, principle of, 22, 109
Isaacs, H.R., 56
Islam, 13
isolation, geographical, 85–6

Jackson, R.H., 65
Johnson, J., 54
Johnson, O.E.G., 102
Jordan, 101
judiciary: executive, legislature and, 92–5
jurisdictional competition, 67–8, 80

Kamm, T., 98, 99
Kant, I., 91
Kaus, M., 94
Kenya, 22–4, 51, 71
　conflict, 56–9
　ethnic associations, 29, 29–30
Kimenyi, M.S., 67, 68, 101, 103
　capacity for federal government, 89
　colonial rule, 14
　political leaders, 51, 54
　property rights, 5
　tribal competition for rents, 48
Knight, D.B., 24
Krauthammer, K.C., 89

laissez-faire, 97

land associations, 27–8
language, 35
law, rule of, 12–13
leaders/rulers
   ethnic competition for rents, 48–51, 61
   separation of powers, 93–5
   tribal chiefs, 11–12
   see also presidency
legislation, 106
legislature: executive, judiciary and, 92–5
Lemarchand, R., 44
Lemco, J., 74
Leonard, D., 70
Lewis, W.A., 40–41
liberalization, economic, 99
Liberia, 14
limited state, 2–3
Litan, R., 100
Little, K., 28
Local Administration Act 1980 (Zambia), 71
local government, 63–4, 72, 73–4, 96
   see also decentralization; federalism
Local Government Act 1960 (Sudan), 70
Local Government Act 1965 (Zambia), 70–71
Locke, J., 2–3, 91
Lonsdale, J., 49

Maddox, W.P., 84
Mair, L., 11, 12
majority rule, 106
marriage, 35
Masai people, 24
Mawhood, P., 71
May, E., 101
Mbaka ethnic group, 54
Mbaku, J.M., 5, 14, 17, 54
McCormick, R.E., 46
McDaniel, A., 91
McGowan, P., 54
McGrath, P., 91
McGuire, M., 33
Meisler, S., 55

military coups, 53–4
military dictatorships, 18, 19
military expenditure, 59–60
modernization, 44, 48–9
Mohammand, S., 102
monitoring incentives, 66–7
Montesquieu, Baron de, 91, 92–3
Moore, J., 97
mortality estimates, 56, 57–8
Mozambique, 26, 56

national unity, 64–5
Nigeria, 24, 26, 51, 86–7, 107, 109
   Civil War, 54, 56
   ethnic associations, 28, 30
   secessionist movements, 88
Nisbet, R., 40
Nkrumah, K., 21, 54
norms, social, 13, 36
North, D., 50, 97, 103
Nyerere, J., 70, 71

Olowu, D., 40, 70, 71, 72
Olson, M., 39
oppression, 52, 53
   protection against, 78–9
Option, 6
order, social, 13, 36
Organization of African Unity (OAU), 22, 109
Orzechowski, W., 66
Osaghae, E.E., 88
Ostrom, E., 97
Ostrom, V., 69
Ottaway, M., 90
Oyugi, W.O., 71

participation, political, 69–70, 78
partition of Africa, 14
Peltzman, S., 46
People's Local Government Act 1971 (Sudan), 70
Peru, 99
Piroute, M.L., 59
police, 68
policy experimentation, 79–80
political associations, 39–40
political development, 78

political institutions, 7, 98–9
  evolution, 10–20
  reduction of ethnic discrimination, 60–61
political parties, 7–8, 28–9, 93–4
  see also single-party systems
political rights, 95
population heterogeneity, 87
poverty, 4, 15
power
  concentration, 65
  decentralization, 78
presidency, 93–5
  rotating, 107
prisoner's dilemma, 13, 36
production externalities, 81
production of goods and services, 36–7
property rights, 72
  inefficient, 50
  protecting, 97–104
  violations, 5, 18, 69, 71
Provincial Planning/Development Committees, 71
public expenditure, 49, 59–60
public goods and services, 36, 65–9, 76–7
public sector, 102–3
  expansion, 49–50, 51

Rappard, W.E., 85
Rawls, J., 21
redistribution, 15–16, 17, 64
refugees, 56–9
regional autonomy, 63, 72, 74, 75–6, 90
regulation, 101
religion, 26
  heterogeneity, 86–7
rent protection, 52
rent-seeking, 42–52, 102
representation, 76
  ethnic and voting rules, 105–7
repression, 18, 19, 52, 59
resource allocation 64, 84–5
  rent-seeking, 44–50, 102
rights
  bill of, 95–6

civil, 5–6, 95
economic, 95, 97–104
human rights violations, 5–6, 18, 59
political, 95
property *see* property rights
social, 95
Riker, W.H., 74
rituals, 35
Roback, J., 36
Rondinelli, D., 71
Rosberg, C.G., 65
rotating presidency, 107
Rothchild, D., 49–50
Rousseau, J.-J., 91
Rowley, C.K., 5, 50
rule of law, 12–13
Rwanda, 24, 26, 55, 88

Samuelson, R.J., 94
Sandler, T., 33
Sawer, G., 85
Sawyer, A., 69
Schneider, H.K., 37–8
Scott, A., 65, 81, 82
'scramble for Africa', 14
Scully, G.W., 98–9
secession, 63, 88, 108, 109
self-interest, 97
Senegal, 88
separation, ethnic, 32–41
separation of powers, 92–5
Sharman, B.M., 75
Shleifer, A., 98, 103
Shughart, W.F., 48, 54, 67
Siegan, B.H., 92, 94, 95, 103
Singapore, 99
Singer, C., 98, 99
single-party systems, 7–8, 16–17, 18, 44
slave trade, 13–14
Smith, A., 21, 97
social institutions, 86
social norms, 13, 36
social rights, 95
socialist policies, 15–16, 17
Somalia, 22, 26
Somalis, 22, 55, 88
state *see* government

state of nature, 1–2
Stigler, G., 46
Sudan, 24, 26, 29, 88, 109
    conflict, 54–5, 56
    decentralization, 70
supply and demand *see* demand and supply
surplus, tribal, 37, 45
Switzerland, 85, 87

Tanzania, 49, 70, 71
taxation, 68–9, 75, 79–80
Thoahlane, T., 71
Tiebout, C.M., 12
Tollison, R.D., 46
Tordoff, W., 54
trade, 37–8, 87
trade unions, 29–30
tribal government, 10–13, 87
tribal identification, 27–31, 33–8
tribal surplus, 37, 45
Tschirhart, J.T., 33
Tullock, G., 13, 48, 66, 82
Tutsi tribe, 55, 88

Uganda, 37–8, 56, 88, 101
Ujamaa policy, 70, 71
unitary states, 8, 16, 44, 61, 62
    see also centralization
United Nations Development Programme, 60
United States, 94, 95
United States Committee for Refugees, 59

unity, 74
    national, 64–5
urban social welfare organizations, 27

Vaughan, J.H., 12, 42
Vernon, R., 103
Village Registration and Development Act 1971 (Zambia), 71
villages, 39, 70
voluntary clubs/associations, 32–3, 38–9
voluntary exchange, 37–8
voluntary principle, 38–9, 40, 42, 61, 74, 89
voting patterns, 29
voting rules, 105–7

war, state of, 1, 2–3
Washington Post, 90
Weingast, B., 103
Wheare, K.C., 74, 84
Whitcombe, M., 55
Wildavsky, A., 84
Winchester, N.B., 17
World Bank, 5, 49
Wunsch, J.S., 40, 43–4, 70

Yoruba people, 28

Zaire, 24–6, 51
Zambia, 30, 49, 70–71
Zardkoohi, A., 66
Zimbabwe, 29, 30